DREAMS OF GERMANY

SPEKTRUM: *Publications of the German Studies Association*
Series editor: David M. Luebke, University of Oregon

Published under the auspices of the German Studies Association, *Spektrum* offers current perspectives on culture, society, and political life in the German-speaking lands of central Europe—Austria, Switzerland, and the Federal Republic—from the late Middle Ages to the present day. Its titles and themes reflect the composition of the GSA and the work of its members within and across the disciplines to which they belong—literary criticism, history, cultural studies, political science, and anthropology.

Volume 1
The Holy Roman Empire, Reconsidered
Edited by Jason Philip Coy, Benjamin Marschke, and David Warren Sabean

Volume 2
Weimar Publics/Weimar Subjects
Rethinking the Political Culture of Germany in the 1920s
Edited by Kathleen Canning, Kerstin Barndt, and Kristin McGuire

Volume 3
Conversion and the Politics of Religion in Early Modern Germany
Edited by David M. Luebke, Jared Poley, Daniel C. Ryan, and David Warren Sabean

Volume 4
Walls, Borders, Boundaries
Spatial and Cultural Practices in Europe
Edited by Marc Silberman, Karen E. Till, and Janet Ward

Volume 5
After The History of Sexuality
German Genealogies with and beyond Foucault
Edited by Scott Spector, Helmut Puff, and Dagmar Herzog

Volume 6
Becoming East German
Socialist Structures and Sensibilities after Hitler
Edited by Mary Fulbrook and Andrew I. Port

Volume 7
Beyond Alterity
German Encounters with Modern East Asia
Edited by Qinna Shen and Martin Rosenstock

Volume 8
Mixed Matches
Transgressive Unions in Germany from the Reformation to the Enlightenment
Edited by David M. Luebke and Mary Lindemann

Volume 9
Kinship, Community, and Self
Essays in Honor of David Warren Sabean
Edited by Jason Coy, Benjamin Marschke, Jared Poley, and Claudia Verhoeven

Volume 10
The Emperor's Old Clothes
Constitutional History and the Symbolic Language of the Holy Roman Empire
Barbara Stollberg-Rilinger
Translated by Thomas Dunlap

Volume 11
The Devil's Riches
A Modern History of Greed
Jared Poley

Volume 12
The Total Work of Art
Foundations, Articulations, Inspirations
Edited by David Imhoof, Margaret Eleanor Menninger, and Anthony J. Steinhoff

Volume 13
Migrations in the German Lands, 1500–2000
Edited by Jason Coy, Jared Poley, and Alexander Schunka

Volume 14
Reluctant Skeptic
Siegfried Kracauer and the Crises of Weimar Culture
Harry T. Craver

Volume 15
Ruptures in the Everyday
Views of Modern Germany from the Ground
Andrew Bergerson, Leonard Schmieding, et al.

Volume 16
Archaeologies of Confession
Writing the German Reformation, 1517–2017
Edited by Carina L. Johnson, David M. Luebke, Marjorie E. Plummer, and Jesse Spohnholz

Volume 17
Money in the German-Speaking Lands
Edited by Mary Lindemann and Jared Poley

Volume 18
Dreams of Germany
Musical Imaginaries from the Concert Hall to the Dance Floor
Edited by Neil Gregor and Thomas Irvine

Dreams of Germany

Musical Imaginaries from the Concert Hall to the Dance Floor

Edited by Neil Gregor and Thomas Irvine

berghahn
NEW YORK · OXFORD
www.berghahnbooks.com

First published in 2019 by
Berghahn Books
www.berghahnbooks.com

© 2019, 2020 Neil Gregor and Thomas Irvine
First paperback edition published in 2020

All rights reserved. Except for the quotation of short passages
for the purposes of criticism and review, no part of this book
may be reproduced in any form or by any means, electronic or
mechanical, including photocopying, recording, or any information
storage and retrieval system now known or to be invented,
without written permission of the publisher.

Library of Congress Cataloging-in-Publication Data
Names: Gregor, Neil, 1969- editor. | Irvine, Thomas, editor.
Title: Dreams of Germany : musical imaginaries from the concert hall
  to the dance floor / edited by Neil Gregor and Thomas Irvine.
Description: New York : Berghahn Books, 2019. | Series: Spektrum :
  publications of the German studies association ; 18 | Includes
  bibliographical references and index.
Identifiers: LCCN 2018026908 (print) | LCCN 2018051469 (ebook) | ISBN
  9781789200331 (ebook) | ISBN 9781789200324 (hardback : alk. paper)
Subjects: LCSH: Music--Social aspects--Germany--History--20th century. |
  Music--Germany--20th century--History and criticism. | National
  characteristics, German. | Music--German influences.
Classification: LCC ML3917.G3 (ebook) | LCC ML3917.G3 D74 2019 (print) | DDC
  780.943/0904--dc23
LC record available at https://lccn.loc.gov/2018026908

British Library Cataloguing in Publication Data
A catalogue record for this book is available from the British Library

ISBN 978-1-78920-032-4 hardback
ISBN 978-1-78920-826-9 paperback
ISBN 978-1-78920-033-1 ebook

In memory of the United Kingdom's membership
of the European Union, 1973–2020

Dank der krankhaften Entfremdung, welche der Nationalitäts-Wahnsinn zwischen die Völker Europas gelegt hat und noch legt, Dank ebenfalls den Politikern des kurzen Blicks und der raschen Hand, die heute mit seiner Hülfe obenauf sind und gar nicht ahnen, wie sehr die auseinanderlösende Politik, welche sie treiben, nothwendig nur Zwischenakts-Politik sein kann,—Dank Alledem und manchem heute ganz Unaussprechbaren werden jetzt die unzweideutigsten Anzeichen übersehn oder willkürlich und lügenhaft umgedeutet, in denen sich ausspricht, dass EUROPA EINS WERDEN WILL.

Owing to the morbid estrangement which the nationality-craze has induced and still induces among the nations of Europe, owing also to the short-sighted and hasty-handed politicians, who with the help of this craze, are at present in power, and do not suspect to what extent the disintegrating policy they pursue must necessarily be only an interlude policy—owing to all this and much else that is altogether unmentionable at present, the most unmistakable signs that EUROPE WISHES TO BE ONE, are now overlooked, or arbitrarily and falsely misinterpreted.
　　　　　　　—Friedrich Nietzsche, *Beyond Good and Evil*

~: CONTENTS :~

List of Figures and Tables ... ix

Acknowledgments ... xi

Introduction ... 1
    Neil Gregor and Thomas Irvine

Part I. Spaces and Moments of Affect

Chapter 1. "The German in the Concert Hall": Concertgoing and National Belonging in the Early Twentieth Century ... 33
    Hansjakob Ziemer

Chapter 2. "Music Made in Hamburg": How One City's Music Scene Helped Make Rock and Roll the Lingua Franca of Youth ... 54
    Julia Sneeringer

Chapter 3. "With Every Inconceivable Finesse, Excess, and Good Music": Sex, Affect, and Techno at Snax Club in Berlin ... 73
    Luis-Manuel Garcia

Part II. The Local, the Regional, the National

Chapter 4. Bruckner, Munich, and the Longue Durée of Musical Listening between the Imperial and Postwar Eras ... 97
    Neil Gregor

Chapter 5. Female Musicians and "Jewish" Music in the Jewish Kulturbund in Bavaria, 1934–38 ... 123
    Dana Smith

Chapter 6. Pride of Place: The 1963 Rebuilding of the Munich Nationaltheater ... 145
    Emily Richmond Pollock

Part III. Globalizing Musical Germanness

Chapter 7. Was ist Japanisch? Wagnerism and Dreams of Nationhood in Modern Japan   169
Brooke McCorkle Okazaki

Chapter 8. Hubert Parry, Germany, and the "North"   194
Thomas Irvine

Part IV. Fantasies, Reminiscences, Dreams, Nightmares

Chapter 9. Between Musicology and Mythology at the *Stunde Null*: Austria's 950th "Birthday" and the 50th Anniversary of Bruckner's Death   221
Lap-Kwan Kam

Chapter 10. Hearing the Nazi Past in the German Democratic Republic: Antifascist Fantasies, Acoustic Realities, and Haunted Memories in Georg Katzer's *Aide –Mémoire* (1983)   247
Martha Sprigge

Chapter 11. Sprockets + Autobahn: Kraftwerk Parodies, German Electronic Music, and Retro Dreams in Amerika   272
Sean Nye

Index   296

FIGURES AND TABLES

Figures

Figure 6.1. Full-page call for support for the Nationaltheater.   154

Figure 6.2. Transcribed festival concert program from the opening of the rebuilt Nationaltheater.   160

Figure 8.1. Incidental Music to *The Acharnians of Aristophanes as Written for Performance by the Oxford University Dramatic Society* (1914). 1. Prelude: "War and Peace," mm. 54–59.   204

Figures 10.1. and 10.2. Hanns Eisler and Rudi Goguel, "Die Moorsoldaten," published in *Das Lied im Kampf geboren*.   251

Figure 10.3. Outline of the fifth nightmare of Katzer's *Aide – Mémoire* (resistance movements).   257

Figure 11.1. Dieter is introduced in the "Sprockets" title sequence.   280

Figure 11.2. Technopop Germanness on display. Dieter meets Karl-Heinz (Kyle MacLachlan) to discuss "Germany's Most Disturbing Home Videos."   281

Figure 11.3. The Sprockets Dance—with full set viewable in the style of *The Man-Machine*.   282

Figure 11.4. The Dude discovers Autobahn's *Nagelbett* album.   287

Figures 11.5. and 11.6. The Dude, discussing the "complicated case" while holding Autobahn's technopop album.   288

Figure 11.7. Desert Storm in Los Angeles. (Right to left) The Dude, Walter Sobchak, and Donny in the parking lot.   289

Figure 11.8. Desert Storm in Los Angeles. Autobahn in the parking lot—Uli Kunkel in the center.   290

Figure 11.9. Eurofashion terrorists invade Los Angeles in *Die Hard* (1988).   291

Tables

Table 6.1. Timeline of the "Opening Festival for the Rebuilt National Theater," Munich, 1963. 161

Table 8.1. Hubert Parry's Writings on Music History. 200

Table 10.1. Nightmares of *Aide –Mémoire* (1983). 256

Table 10.2. Excerpts from the *Manifesto of the National Committee for a Free Germany* used in *Aide –Mémoire*. 259

~: ACKNOWLEDGMENTS :~

This book is the product of many conversations. It emerged out of an informal back and forth over a number of years between the two of us—a historian and a musicologist—about things German, musical, historical, and cultural, which has ranged from activities as simple as talking about pieces of music during a concert interval to shared teaching to reading and discussing each other's work. We eventually decided that it was time to turn some of our common interests into a project.

That this personal conversation has evolved with such ease reflects the fact that it sits inside of a wider one between our disciplines that has indisputably gained momentum in recent years. Those who are given to proclaiming "turns" might note the very long archaeology of this conversation. But it seems reasonable to observe that there has been a pronounced thickening of it in the last ten years or so. This volume reflects that and aims to take our interdisciplinary conversation further.

Somewhere in between these sits a third conversation—the discussion many of us started having in the wake of Celia Applegate and Pamela Potter's 2002 collection *Music and German National Identity*. If a single volume can claim to have acted as the catalyst for the coalescence of the intellectual space in which the present volume moves, then it is surely this. Indeed, one of us remembers well the sheer excitement of the collection's arrival when he was still a graduate student in musicology; it felt to him like there was finally "history" in "music history." For the other, it was instrumental in showing that historians did not need a full arsenal of analytical training in music to engage with the field. So we want to acknowledge the inspiration that Applegate and Potter have provided over the years. Fifteen years on, much has changed. We think it an appropriate tribute to the original intervention to take the temperature of the field as it now stands and to observe the impact of some new ways of thinking that have emerged across the humanities in the meantime.

We thank Celia Applegate, Nicholas Attfield, Tobias Becker, Annika Forkert, Andreas Gestrich, Jeff Hayton, Berthold Hoeckner, Carolin Krahn, J. Brooks Kuykendall, Felipe Ledesma-Núñez, Ryan Minor, Daniel Morat, Kirsten Paige, Martin Rempe, and Laura Tunbridge, as well as Mark Everist, Florian Scheding, and Maiken Umbach, for helping us to shape the ideas that this volume represents. In particular, we also wish to express our enormous gratitude to both the German Historical Institute London and the German

History Society for the generous financial support that made possible the preparation of this volume.

Thanks are due as well to Berghahn Books, who have provided a more than appropriate home for a book that sits between musicology, history, and German studies. Our editors there—Chris Chappell, Amanda Horn, Caroline Kuhtz, and Soyolmaa Lkhagvadorj—have been models of support and patience. We are especially grateful to Alison Jacques for her careful and sensitive copyediting. We likewise thank David Luebke, the editor of *Spektrum: Publications of the German Studies Association*, for extending the flattering invitation to join the series, not least because the wonderfully interdisciplinary spirit of the German Studies Association has been precisely what has animated our efforts here. Berghahn also facilitated a smooth and productive process of peer review. The input of two anonymous reviewers has shaped this book profoundly, and for the better.

Finally, our gratitude must go to our partners and (between us) five school-age children, who were not asked if we should take on this project, and who have shared some of its burdens with good humor.

Neil Gregor
Tom Irvine
Southampton, May 2018

INTRODUCTION

NEIL GREGOR AND THOMAS IRVINE

In 2002 Celia Applegate and Pamela Potter's groundbreaking edited collection, *Music and German National Identity*, mapped the historical terrain on which the notion of Germans as the "people of music" was constituted and an intellectual terrain on which that trope might be fruitfully historicized.[1] Its opening essay registered clearly the constructed notion of the proposition that Germans were, and always have been, inherently musical, or musically superior.[2] Applegate and Potter proposed that "Germanness in music" was an idea that had been called forth by writers, critics, pedagogues, and philosophers; inscribed in literary genres such as journals, catalogs, and critical editions; institutionalized in concert associations, conservatoires, and university departments; and monumentalized in statues and commemorative culture. At the same time, they acknowledged its longevity, its rhetorical power, and its capacity to transcend the specific politics of time and place. Animated by a critical spirit that drew on the thought of Benedict Anderson, they placed music at the center of an ongoing process of imagining national community throughout the nineteenth and twentieth centuries. German national identity, they argued, had been talked, written, and printed into existence, and with it the notion of Germans as the "people of music."[3]

Applegate and Potter simultaneously acknowledged the effects that this "invented tradition" had on the wider culture of which it was part and cautioned gently against overemphasizing its historical significance in retrospect.[4] The book was instrumental in encouraging historians to engage with a field of human activity that many had hitherto regarded as the recondite preserve of others; it also played a key role in helping musicologists, then grappling with the implications of the predominantly Anglophone "new musicology," to think productively about how they might historicize musical works, musical practice, and the discourse of musicality that cleaved, and still cleaves, so firmly to discussions of what it may mean to be German.[5]

In the intervening decade, inspired by the questions Applegate and Potter raised, historians and musicologists have explored further how to think about musical cultures in Germany within a national frame. At the same time, a number of wider shifts in focus across the humanities have underscored the importance of the skeptical note that unmistakably underpinned Applegate and Potter's intervention. The master categories with which Applegate and Potter worked—"Music," "German," "Nation," and "Identity"—have all undergone sustained critique for the manner in which they transport stable, essentialized, and often reified understandings of what they seek to describe. Scholars have realized that each category is loaded with normative understandings that, we would argue, still structure—in ways unspoken, unacknowledged, and often simply unrecognized—habits of thought that we find intellectually, politically, and ethically constraining.

For example, one long-lasting legacy of the historical culture that Applegate and Potter sought to dissect has been the survival of intellectually conservative criteria regarding the definition of "music"—or, at least, music worth making the object of sustained scholarly inquiry. These criteria both reflect and sustain conventional notions of heritage, canon, and aesthetic value and have ensured that until recently the overwhelming focus of musicology as a discipline was on "art music." It is also surely no accident that, when seeking to juxtapose "art music" with materials and insights drawn from other repertoires, commentators have so often been drawn to the field of folk music, a genre and tradition that scholars of German music have long validated and sanctioned for academic study because of its capacity to draw on discourses of permanence and authenticity tied to a vague idea of being specifically "German."[6]

In the last two decades the cultural power of such aesthetic hierarchies has eroded significantly. At the same time, musicologists (and, increasingly, historians with interests in music) have widened the scope of their enquiries. New fields such as popular music studies and the interdisciplinary field of sound studies—with its even more trenchant questioning of hitherto stable notions of what music is—have engaged with a much wider spectrum of musical activities.[7] Such processes invite reconsideration of the questions Applegate and Potter raised from vantage points that were not available at the time. They also allow the posing of other questions that, a generation ago, scholars simply did not ask.

Similarly, the national frames of conventional historiography, and master narratives of German history in particular, are not what they once were. German studies now attends with greater urgency to the question of how the national may be related to other spatial markers of identity, be they supranational ("central Europe") or subnational ("Thuringia," "Hamburg"). At the same time, due to shifts in scholarly sensibility engendered by the dynamics of globalization, mobility, and migration, histories of modern (and indeed premodern) Germany have become more transnational and global in scope.[8] As a result, the "national" in German history has acquired far more texture, even if more skepticism is called for concerning its explanatory potential (or at least its claims to explanatory hegemony). In previous narratives of national history, local and regional cultures appeared, implicitly, as prenational residues to be bulldozed over by the homogenizing march of national integration. Now not only are civic, local, and regional cultures permanently present in modern German history; they emerge as the sites on which various iterations of "national" identity were constituted.[9]

Notions of "identity" are perhaps the biggest challenge to using the "national" to frame a coherent object of study. It has become a commonplace that any given subject position embodies a range of different identities and that these exist both independently and in relation to one another in malleable and fluid dispositions. It is equally common to note that they are formed in highly specific and historically situated ways. Beyond this, the emergence of other subdisciplinary or interdisciplinary fields such as memory studies, the history of emotions, gender studies, and postcolonial studies have opened up compelling perspectives on more visceral aspects and moments of human experience. These too encourage us to revisit the questions Applegate and Potter posed and to ask them afresh.

The evolving approaches that have inspired our book are governed by shifts in intellectual culture that are not the preserve of scholars working in one or two disciplines (in our cases, history and musicology). Yet it also bears pointing out that there has been a pronounced rapprochement between our two disciplines in the last decade or so. Indeed the "cultural history of music" has largely naturalized itself as a domain of study located somewhere at the interstices of the two.[10] Such labels can themselves too easily imply the existence of a coherent, stable field of scholarly practice informed by a shared set of clear assumptions about what the object of study is and what theoretical and methodological approaches should be brought to bear on it, assumptions that belie the varied, open, messy, and still fundamentally incoherent nature of the field they seek to describe. A cursory glance at the multitude of different approaches that sail under the banner of the "cultural history of music" should suffice to make that immediately clear.[11]

If there is one move that has made this interdisciplinary conversation easier, however, it is the shared willingness of increasing numbers of musicologists and historians to acknowledge the methods, insights, and commitments that govern a cognate discipline, anthropology (or, as it is more readily recognized in this area, ethnomusicology). This willingness includes a commitment to thinking not just about the discourse that *surrounds* music—the writing *about* music that was so central to Applegate and Potter's approach—but also about music's own "generative role," i.e., its capacity to call forth sentiment, affect, and also behavior through its own material in performance, albeit almost always (and this is perhaps precisely the point) temporarily.[12] Secondly, and relatedly, we might point to Thomas Turino's definition of culture as the "habits of thought and practice that are shared among individuals," highlighting here his emphasis not just on "thought," which would take us back again to the discursive construction of music, but also on "practice."[13] For it is precisely where historians and musicologists have successfully dislodged the erratic block embodied in aesthetically conservative understandings of what "music" is to explore the myriad social practices that center on it in all its varied forms—domestic music-making, concertgoing, attendance at festivals, commercial broadcasting and radio listening, dance-floor chanting, and so on—that the potential for a conversation has hitherto been greatest.[14]

Mindful particularly of the need to absorb more fully a notion of practice into our understanding of the identities that Applegate and Potter sought to foreground, we have sought to organize the notions of Germanness in music represented in this volume around the concept of the social imaginary. The political philosopher Charles Taylor proposes that the concept of the social imaginary represents the unspoken principles that govern a social order and the commonsense regimes of knowledge that shape behaviors under it.[15] We share his sense that students of culture need to find ways of considering the forms of "wordless knowledge" that constitute identity—knowledge that is not always detectable in written discourse.[16] In reaching for notions of the imaginary we are just as interested in capturing something of the simultaneously fluid, mobile, and unstable—and yet long-lasting, persistent, and resistant—qualities of the visions we are discussing across long durations as we are in their allegedly governing capacities.

We seek to capture visions of Germany that were present, whether temporarily or persistently, in a variety of different communities; to emphasize that they did and do not map easily onto conventional markers of political space, least of all onto an analytically overprivileged national one; to stress that they simultaneously moved across and through temporal boundaries, weaving in and out of political moments, taking on those political inflections but not becoming reduced to them and that, in a German context, their visceral dreaminess has taken on aspects of both fantasy and nightmare. Like Taylor we start from the assumption that social imaginaries "are never just ideology" and that "like all forms of human imagination, the social imaginary can be full of self-serving fiction and suppression, but it is also an essential constituent of the real."[17]

Dislodging the aesthetic hierarchies that governed the intellectual preferences of an older generation in the academy does not render it any less valid to consider "classical music" as a set of historical social practices too. A lot of people used to listen to it, after all. It would not be too far from the truth to see it as having been one of a number of forms of middle-class popular music for much of the late nineteenth and twentieth centuries. The historical presence of the Austro-German canon is acknowledged in this volume, accordingly, in two essays on that most "monumental" of composers, Anton Bruckner; the cultures of listening that cohered around that canon are reflected in an essay on symphony concert hall life in the early twentieth century.

And yet we have long reached a point where the habitual privileging of this canon in the stories that we tell surely obscures as much as it reveals, and conventional habits of narrating the history of German musicking now work to reinscribe inherited assumptions in ways that are simply constraining rather than to promote exciting new lines of inquiry. One of the central contentions of this volume, demonstrated by our juxtaposition of symphony concert attendance, rock and roll, and queer-scene electronic dance music in our opening section, is that many of the most interesting themes that this field presents become far more visible, and far more open to fruitful analysis, if those distinctions between different genres, and those conventional habits of chronological narrative, are simply dissolved. In what follows, we seek to trace some of the avenues of thought that our individual essays suggest when read against one another. We close with some reflections on the ethical implications for future scholarship.

Spaces and Moments of Affect

For all of its innovation and diversity, the new cultural history of music, at least in a modern European context, has been governed—as are so many histories—by an unacknowledged and yet unmistakable sense of telos. Scholars have traced the transition from aristocratic to bourgeois cultures of musicking; the replacement of courtly with civic and commercial modes of organization; the emergence of modern musical professionalism and the concomitant marginalization of the amateur; the regulation of musical entertainment; the gradual domestication of the "spontaneous"; and the establishment of the musical "work" as the main object of music history.[18] One particularly seductive telos is the emergence of the "listening subject."[19] As the rich vein of literature on the choral singing practices of nineteenth- and twentieth-century Europe underlines, the producing and listening subject could still, in fact, be one and the same, and active participation in the production of sound could thus remain the key generative agent in the production of "community."[20] In other fields of musical activity, the nineteenth century did witness, in tendency at least, the emergence of the distinct listening subject who sat, at first sight, in a relationship of distance to that which was being produced insofar as he or she was the consumer and the consumer *only*. Somewhere near the center of such stories usually sits a new listener defined by his or her distance and difference to the body producing the musical sound. The locus classicus of this listening subject was the symphony concert hall.[21]

The age of the concert hall is our starting point. Hansjakob Ziemer explores issues of ideology, affect, bodily comportment, and community as they were experienced in the concert halls of Germany during and after World War I. This was the moment, it is so often assumed, when a particular ideal of the listener was most firmly and clearly sutured to a corresponding vision of the ideal nation. Even here, however, this is an ambiguous story. It is indeed true that an emerging consensus about *Bildung* drew on Enlightenment ideas of the autonomous knowing subject capable of forming his or her own judgment according to the correct moral and aesthetic criteria. On the other hand, he or she was simultaneously recognized as part of a public governed by shared codes, practices, and sensibilities. But as Ziemer demonstrates, all of this was constantly the stuff of argument and dispute rather than a matter of settled opinion: the discourse was open and plural, the arguments trenchant but the visions correspondingly tentative.

Some took a more Romantic view and foregrounded music's alleged capacity to engender emotion and to overwhelm the autonomous listener by subsuming him or her within something broader and more powerful.[22] Such associations between music and power, music and the irrational, music and the mysterious became the stuff of belletristic cliché. That should not stop us asking how, in the modern era, both the nature of the musical object and the conditions of its performance continued to call forth a sense of shared affect that approximated the phenomenon the cultural anthropologist Victor Turner once termed "communitas"—a liminal state in which the conventional rules of a polity temporarily dissolve, if only (and precisely) for the purpose of reinscribing their otherwise permanent presence.[23]

To approach the establishment of musical community this way is to foreground the momentariness, fleetingness, and situatedness of the individual musical event and the sense that at least one of its key characteristics lies in its being "in the moment" that it is performed, listened to, or experienced. Ziemer has emphasized elsewhere that the cultural dynamics of German concert hall life around the time of World War I cannot simply be inserted into an unfolding telos of bourgeois social practice, but instead reflected the highly specific and situated context of the hypernationalist climate of World War I.[24] Concertgoing, then, was not merely a continuation of the bourgeois social routine of the pre-1914 period, but a site on which patriotic sentiment was publicly displayed, reconstituted, and fortified. As he argues here, defeat and chaos after 1918 generated a different dynamic again.

It is some distance—physically, temporally, culturally, metaphorically—from the concert halls of World War I Frankfurt to the rock and roll dance floors of 1960s Hamburg. Yet many of the issues raised by Ziemer appear in Julia Sneeringer's study of the emergence of rock and roll in Germany's main port city. The spaces in which such musical events took place could hardly have been more different. If those attending symphony concerts rose on gilt stairwells to enter the auditorium, undergoing a moment of elevation that was simultaneously physical, symbolic, and auratic, then working-class youth descended into the basements of the Hamburg pleasure zone, moving literally and figuratively into an underground space.

Space, in other words, worked very differently, but space was always at work. It co-constituted a liminal moment, in which social rules were at once suspended and reinscribed. It was the site of a performance—the act of "musicking" in the narrower sense—a background against which new and ideal social relationships were imagined. But it was also the site of multiple performances, in which a variety of behavioral scripts were acted out. In Ziemer's example it was those of the bourgeois and/or national subject; in Sneeringer's those of the young, the "cool," the liberal and emancipated. If, in the concert halls of Frankfurt in World War I and the 1920s, concertgoers and critics were working out what it meant to be German, young club-goers in Hamburg were working out how to get away from it—or at least how to get away from a certain kind of imagined, and now highly suspicious, Germanness that they saw in the politically compromised generation of their parents. They were doing so, moreover, through encounters with young British musicians and other travelers for whom this musical scene signified a very different dream—a dream, ironically, of excitement and emancipation from what they experienced as the drab, dull culture of everyday postwar life at home. Different ideals, motives, and interests drew locals and visitors into this scene, and out of this transnational encounter a new musical culture was constituted.

Music's multivalent capacities to generate affective community are highlighted by Luis-Manuel Garcia's account of queer club culture in contemporary Berlin. Here the dynamics of erasure of boundaries between performers and audiences that Sneeringer discerns in Hamburg are yet more visible. Here, too, the transnational qualities of the musical encounters—between DJs, bar staff, international visitors, and local dance club frequenters—are at the center of the story. Garcia's ethnography engages with visitors to the "Snax" gay club night at Berghain, where listening, dancing, and sexual encounter become so inextricably linked that all participants, "producers" and "consumers" alike, simultaneously figure as performers, listeners, and observers. During Snax the experience of music is only intelligible as an integral part, firstly, of a wider act of consumption—in this case, travel and tourism—and, secondly, as part of a wider, multisensory experience (the lights, the sounds, the smells, the touch of the dance floor, and the sex booths) that is itself embedded in the fuller set of corporeal experiences that constitute dancing or, indeed, having sex (or watching others do so).

It is an even longer way from Germany's interwar concert halls to Snax. But many striking similarities of both substance and methodology emerge. Space, Garcia shows, is highly constitutive of affect. Affect is temporary and is allied strongly to a sense of the liminal; it is located, and available for analysis, within a wider set of corporeal dispositions and experiences. In Ziemer's case, the rules of the space insist that the correct corporeal disposition is one of stillness; in Sneeringer's and Garcia's, musicking means movement. Yet whether in the auratic space of the symphony concert hall, the sweat-drenched and smoky dance floor of the basement nightclub, or the *mise-en-scène* of the Berlin gay sex party, space, sound, and bodies interact to produce a momentary sense of communal participation. This participation may, or may not, be filled with national meaning.

We do not claim that the three moments that Ziemer, Sneeringer, and Garcia examine are analogous or interchangeable. Indeed, the differences in their essays point to a key issue: the impossibility of essentializing accounts of "how music works" to call forth shared affect in any given context. Of course each author cautions against taking the rhetoric of community at face value and allowing the language of community to become naturalized. "Public," "audience," and "community" are all words from the sources (*Quellenbegriffe*) and thus concepts that should be the objects of analysis rather than its tools. There were many alternative and countervailing subjectivities in each story that were hardly overcome by whatever momentary sense of shared affect music was able to generate. German cities contained strong strands of opinion opposed to World War I. Encounters between British and German teenagers, sailors, and sex workers also sometimes ended in fisticuffs aggravated by a sense of national difference. The terms "queer" and "straight" do not do justice to the gradations of self-identity that are found in the Snax audience; it is unlikely that the music fully dissolves those competing sexual identities in a haze of communal affect.[25] Perhaps above all, as far as complicating notions of musical "Germanness" is concerned, all three accounts make clear that the object of analysis in these essays is as much a culture anchored in a particular city as it is one that reflects the presence of something generically national. Postwar pleasure-seekers were being drawn to Hamburg as much as to Germany, as are queer dance-scene tourists to Berlin in the contemporary world, so that any sense of "Germanness" that animates the encounter is refracted through very specific experiences of particular urban cultures. Even in the era of high nationalism, the early twentieth century, articulations of "Germanness" were inseparable from musical practices anchored in a profound sense of the civic.

The Civic, the Regional, and the National

German national identity has never been a unitary phenomenon. German national feeling has evolved across the vicissitudes of Germany's emergence, making, unmaking, and remaking as a nation-state, with all the attendant moments of crisis and rupture.[26] It has also presented itself in a wide variety of local and regional manifestations. The word *Heimat*, and the landscapes that go with it—physical, cultural, emotional—is not just an atavistic residue of a prenational era, a site of resistance to the unfolding project of the modern nation-state, but rather *the* site, and the endless set of sites, on which that nation was imagined and forged. In what follows, we take Bavaria as a space in which to explore in more detail how local, regional, and national stories were entwined. Focusing more directly on the place of National Socialism within the broader narratives of Germany's musical histories, the three essays in this section demonstrate how, both at the moment of hypernationalism's temporary triumph and in its immediate aftermath, regional and civic identities remained central to the story.

The local and the regional were also far more, however, than a variety of places in which a larger set of narratives unfolded with particular inflections. As the essays in this section underline, musical imaginaries emerged not only in space but also through and across time. Accordingly, historically meaningful spaces such as Bavaria or Munich were not just political or territorial containers. They were also sites of memory, repositories of experiences and stories that gave cultural imaginaries much of their visceral quality. The reopening of the Bavarian State Opera house in Munich in 1963 ostensibly marked a moment of reconstruction, an important symbolic point in the transition between the rubble years of the late 1940s and 1950s (the years of shortage, of introspection, of cultural "restoration") and the more vibrant 1960s (years of plenty, of liberalization, of the "second Enlightenment" of the Federal Republic). Yet Munich in that era—as both city and state capital—was also a site of multiple memories reaching back to the turn of the century. Elderly music-lovers would have remembered Bruno Walter conducting during World War I, or even Gustav Mahler directing the premiere of his own fourth symphony in 1901. Indeed Richard Strauss, whose own family recollections included those of his father having played in the state (at the time royal) opera's orchestra at the premieres of Wagner music dramas, had died in Garmisch-Partenkirchen only a decade previously. His late works echoed with nostalgia for the hautebourgeois musicking that centered on institutions such as the Bavarian State Opera and were heard as such by contemporaries.[27]

Such mentalities cut across the conventional divides of local political cultures. Today's hyperaffluent Bavaria seems shaped by the culturally conservative legacy of Franz Josef Strauss's Christian Social Union. But in the 1950s it was one of West Germany's poorer regions. At state level, where issues of cultural policy such as the rebuilding of theaters were determined, until the latter part of the decade its politics were strongly codetermined by the Social Democratic Party.[28] The city itself, meanwhile, was a citadel of moderate Social Democratic politics; the tone for its political classes was set by the comparatively liberal *Süddeutsche Zeitung*. As Emily Richmond Pollock's account of the campaign to rebuild the state opera house and the opening gala festival shows, there were strong civic and regional cultural memories and identities in operation in the choice of works performed. Wagner, Strauss, Egk, Orff, and Hartmann were all composers strongly associated with the city. The very different experiences during the Third Reich of the latter three composers suggest, however, that in the micropolitics of Munich's postwar musical scene tensions anchored in conflicting memory were never far from the surface, just as they were in the politics of German cities after 1945 more generally.[29]

Mention of Walter, or the many other Jewish musicians who passed through Munich, and of Strauss, the founding president of the National Socialist Reich Music Chamber, reminds us that the city played host to the full range of horrifying stories that unfolded in Germany from World War I to the end of World War II. Radical nationalism left its traces in musical life in the inflection of performance and reception histories of "monumental" composers such as Bruckner, as Neil Gregor traces. But contrary to what is often assumed to be the case, Nazi Germany exerted a considerably less homogenizing influence on music reception than one might expect. Rather, a wide variety of cultural imaginaries that centered on Bruckner echoed through the period and through each other, mingling, coagulating, occasionally contesting but as often as not simply coexisting. All gained easy traction within the contained ideological pluralism of the Third Reich.[30] Postwar tropes that appeared to carry specifically National Socialist residues and reflect mental continuities from that era reveal themselves to have had a longer archaeology. If anything, the success of National Socialism in naturalizing itself in German society reflected its own ability to insert itself into those deeper cultural continuities.

At the same time, Bavaria, like all areas of the Reich, witnessed the vicious, and ultimately murderous, processes of marginalization, exclusion, expulsion, and genocide of the Jews between 1933 and 1945, leaving a memory that haunted the local landscapes as a largely unspoken, but palpably present knowledge. The towns of Bavaria—above all, Munich—hosted not just a variety of conservative, nationalist, and racist musical cultures but also a beleaguered minority that sought to assert its own identity musically as the persecution intensified. Dana Smith explores these themes in her account of the Bavarian branch of the Jewish Kulturbund. Her essay offers a valuable counterpoint not just to histories of the dominant gentile culture of exclusion, but also to stories of the *Kulturbund* that have hitherto been told from a strongly Berlin-centered perspective. Crucially, she brings gender to bear on her analysis. In her focus on the female musicians who played such a central role in the Bavarian *Kulturbund* she demonstrates the importance of recognizing that musical—and, by extension, other—imaginaries have a strongly gendered aspect that much scholarship conventionally ignores. The end of this story is well known: Bavaria's Jews were driven into exile, incarcerated and murdered en masse; very few survived in Germany at the end of the war, haunting the postwar landscape.

Local and regional spaces were not, then, simply variants of a national story. To examine them is to discover archaeological layers of often troubling emotional experience and memory, each overlayering the previous one yet inflected with its echoes. Such echoes had and have the potential to rupture the surface of any given moment. They were a substantial part of what gave events such as the reopening of the Bavarian State Opera their complex power. The presence of memories of extreme violence that haunted local communities in such moments demonstrates how histories of "musical Germanness" need telling inside of, and as part of, histories of colonialism, massive violence, and war, but without reducing histories of either military aggression or cultural activity to simple cause or effect of the other.

Globalizing Musical Germanness

The history of musical Germanness, and German "musicality," is not the same as the history of Germany. This book also asks how the story of musical Germanness unfolds in larger contexts. Marx and Engels theorized the "global turn" in class terms more than 150 years ago: "The bourgeoisie ... [compels] all nations, on pain of extinction, to adopt the bourgeois mode of production; it compels them to introduce what it calls civilization into their midst, i.e., to become bourgeois themselves. In one word, it creates a world after its own image."[31] The dissemination of German musical values in the nineteenth and twentieth centuries, from ringing declarations of the "universal" value of German music to the first performances of Wagner in Japan to the persistence of German-derived values of "process" and "depth" in Hubert Parry's conception of musical evolution, remade, or attempted to remake, musical worlds—sometimes on pain of extinction—in the image of a certain kind of German *Bürger*, in tension of course with the local conditions of Japan or Britain around 1900.

Our quotation from the *Communist Manifesto* does not necessarily signal an explicit political or theoretical position. We wish to emphasize, rather, Marx and Engels's own global outlook and to point out the unparalleled success of

German art music as an export product, a success that surely had something to do with the concomitant worldwide adaptation of "the bourgeois mode of production." The contemporary "global turn" in historical scholarship, one of the most important sites of disciplinary innovation in the years since the publication of Applegate and Potter's *Music and German National Identity*, has yet to make a substantial impact on the cultural history of music. Our book seeks to place German national feeling experienced in music in a global frame. This global frame need not in any way erase the national. Far from it: following Sebastian Conrad, we would like to suggest ways in which the growth of global structures of trade, migration, and imperial power are "not only ... the necessary context, but also ... the necessary precondition for the emergence of particular forms of nationalism."[32]

How far back in time one should go in seeking a peculiarly German story regarding the nation's relations to its internal and external others is a question that has, *nolens volens*, governed the writing of German history for decades. Over the last thirty years, scholars have beat a comprehensive retreat from the notion that German history traveled along a Special Path (*Sonderweg*) marked by a native authoritarianism and a structurally determined, continuous expansionism.[33] Whatever catastrophes Germany visited upon Europe and the world in the first half of the twentieth century, the longue durée of its history was considerably less "peculiar" than many scholars of the 1960s and 1970s once argued. Yet, at least as a heuristic tool, the idea that there is something "special" about German music has lost none of its seductive explanatory power. Indeed, we would hardly be writing these words were this not the case.

One way to overcome this is to acknowledge consistently the agency of the non-European "others" who became musical Germany's interlocutors from the early modern period onwards. Just as, for example, Germans were constantly traveling, encountering, interpreting, and imagining the East, making sense of it in frameworks learned at home, so were Eastern counterparts engaged in complementary, and mutually implicated, processes. The need to draw attention to the equal agency of German and non-German actors in the making of any global cultural history of music underlies our juxtaposition of Thomas Irvine's text with Brooke McCorkle Okazaki's study of the reception of Wagner in Meiji Restoration Japan.

McCorkle Okazaki explores the ways in which Wagner became known in Japan before he was heard there. Literary scholars discussed the composer's political, social, and aesthetic ideals; conservatoire students performed extracts of Wagnerian dramas; poets adapted libretti to the forms of Japanese epic poetry; and abridged versions of Wagnerian stories circulated in forms suited to Japan's literary and cultural marketplace. Much as many Germans first experienced jazz during the Weimar Republic visually rather than sonically, Wagner's work first made its way through Japanese society in written rather than aural—let alone fully staged—form.³⁴ McCorkle shows that this was not simply a process of cultural transfer in which Western musical texts traveled through non-Western contexts to be embraced by Japanese and other non-European Germanophiles. Rather, Wagner was translated in a double sense. The text did not simply move: it was transformed into genres and forms that made sense in Japanese traditions.

Ideas and assumptions about musical "Germanness" sometimes functioned as an unspoken governing presence in contexts that were always highly specific rather than interchangeable. This, indeed, underscores the importance of the recent turn from the "transnational" to the "global." Transnational histories (and related ideas of "culture transfer") assume that nations and the discourses that accompany them are immutable and that their cultures can transfer from one national "envelope" to another. Global histories, by contrast, follow networks that transcend simple spatial markers. Irvine's account of composer Hubert Parry's engagement with musical "Germanness" is no less global for the fact that it played out in the micro frame of reference represented by the educational and pedagogical institutions of London's South Kensington, from the Great Exhibition of 1851 to the South Kensington (later Victoria and Albert) Museum to Parry's own Royal College of Music to the Royal College of Science (later Imperial College of Science and Technology) next door. Indeed, networks of colonialist thought at work in and across those institutions provided precisely the setting in which Parry's Germanocentric and white-supremacist account of global musical history could be worked out.³⁵

Parry, Irvine argues, reconfigured musical "Germanness" by subtly altering the frame of world music history. Founders of modern music history writing in German from the mid eighteenth century onward had positioned Germany as the right geographical place for a supposedly special "mixed" taste of (superior) music to form. As the nineteenth century unfolded, (mostly) German writers embellished this narrative to include ever more personal and historical traits supposedly specific to German people: industriousness, spiritual profundity, ties to soil and history, transcendent idealism. By 1914 in some quarters musicality itself became a special property that marks Germans as German. Thomas Mann even argued after 1914 that Germany's deep, "irrational" musicality (as opposed to her enemies' "civilized" liberalism) made war inevitable.³⁶ Into this discourse strode Hubert Parry, director of the Royal College and Heather Professor at Oxford, a leading composer, and author of numerous widely read texts on music history. Parry, who spoke fluent German and had met Wagner personally, was by his own admission a "pro-Teuton." Yet in his history, the backbone of which is provided by Bach, Handel, Haydn, Mozart, Beethoven, Schubert, Schumann, Wagner, and Brahms, the guiding principle is not Germanness but (white) "Northernness," as opposed to (brown and black) "Southernness." Parry's "South," it must be said, started at the Danube.

He once wrote that his beloved student Samuel Coleridge-Taylor, a Londoner with an African father, found his compositional voice when he discovered Dvořák, "between whom and himself there was some racial analogy." The elision of German and North in Parry's writing, Irvine shows, allows for a vision of music history in which British composers can share German profundity and the networks of the British Empire (centered in South Kensington) can transport "great" music on a global scale. Today one might argue that such "great" music *is* everywhere. The two essays in this section suggest that this "everywhere" has a history.

Fantasies, Reminiscences, Dreams, Nightmares

To parse conventional notions of musical canon, to consider discourse alongside practice, to examine the relationship between different layers of political space, to globalize the stories that we tell, and to interrogate them for the emotional landscapes they reveal are all approaches that may be applied to other national spaces and national historiographies. Yet as our consideration of the complex emotional resonances echoing through the reopening in the 1960s of an opera house destroyed by wartime bombing has already shown, modern German history—both its experience and its telling—has been shaped by a distinctive set of histories of extreme mass violence. The character and qualities of this violence demand that we listen for its echoes in musical life. Fantasies of conquest, and nightmares of multiple histories of appalling suffering visited upon others and experienced oneself, are central to any account of modern German history. At the same time, today sensibilities regarding the Holocaust and its immediate aftermath are taking on a palpably different tone. This is the product of the slow but inexorable historicization of the National Socialist era. With this historicization other forms of reverie that flourished alongside the Nazi dictatorship and in the years after its defeat are also coming into view. Nostalgia for the Habsburg era in post-1918 Austria, for the habitus of Wilhelmine *Bürgerlichkeit* in 1950s West Germany, or for the various lost lands of former eastern Germany among the many different refugee and expellee communities after World War II are but some of the most obvious.

A generation ago scholars of memory were given to explaining the formation of memory cultures primarily in terms of political utility. In the case of the post–World War II era the framing context of the Cold War, Western integration, and political "restoration," or, conversely, the establishment of a new ideological dictatorship under the Socialist Unity Party of Germany (SED), facilitated the creation of a set of usable pasts that distanced the present from the National Socialist era and quarantined its ethical and political challenges.[37] We have now come to understand that the visceral legacies of the pre-1945 era and their capacities to erupt into the present in challenging, unpredictable ways cannot be reduced to politics in this way.[38] This is not to say that pragmatism and political utility did not play a role. Lap-Kwan Kam demonstrates that a conscious act of self-distancing was in operation in the attempts of Austrian cultural arbiters to define a non-Nazi version of the Austro-German canon and to re-annex it for a distinctly Austrian cultural patrimony after 1945. In the course of reimagining Austrian history, cultural commentators transformed their country from defeated rump state to a vessel of timeless culture; from an integral element of "Austro-Germanness" to the guardian of a specifically Austrian musical inheritance that was superior to its (tainted) German counterpart; and from actor in a story of heroism to passive victim of the forces of history. Kam reminds us that, for all the continuities stressed by Gregor, it mattered who was in power. Nonetheless, the lost legacies of the "Greater German" vision of 1848 echoed through nostalgic laments for Austria's cultural heritage on the occasion of its 950th anniversary commemorations in 1946. The profound resurgence of this vision in the postwar era was a complex phenomenon, not least because elements of National Socialism's own nationalist, colonialist, and racist fantasies had drawn on the same rhetorical traditions. Their resonances demonstrated the presence of set of attachments, orientations, experiences, and memories that had clearly not simply been expelled from German national history in 1866. Short-term political exigencies and long-term cultural processes remained as entangled as ever.[39]

The capacity of histories of violence and their aftereffects to rupture the surfaces of formal political and ideological frames forms a central element of Martha Sprigge's account of Georg Katzer's 1983 sound collage *Aide – Mémoire* in the context of wider compositional tradition in the German Democratic Republic (GDR). As with other recent studies that have sought to texture the musical life of East Germany and take it beyond clichéd, reductionist accounts of culture, propaganda, and totalitarianism, she explores how the culture of antifascism was both an imposed expressive constraint and the site of memory work vested with a considerably greater anchoring in authentic experiences and commitments than some critiques would allow.[40] As much as the SED sought to impose an official narrative of recent German history and to celebrate the agency of working-class resistance in the creation of the GDR, more troubling memories of racist violence and murder in which ordinary Germans (now the citizens of the GDR) had figured as perpetrators could never be entirely domesticated. The outcome, again, is a sense of cultural life that, even under conditions of single-party domination, cannot be reduced to a simple set of political narratives, but rather needs to be analyzed for the ways in which it transported something considerably more multivalent, open, ambiguous, and complex.

The presence of multiple layers of historical memory and their capacity to echo in many musical media is underlined, finally, by Sean Nye. His essay is surely the first long-form scholarly engagement with several iconic moments in US popular culture toward the end of the millennium: the films *Die Hard* (1989) and *The Big Lebowski* (1998) and, between them, Mike Myers's dancing German creation, Dieter, for *Saturday Night Live*. All three involve Germans acting as pseudo-intellectual German "others" (in the films as villains) to Americans of all stripes, and all three invoke techno as a specifically German music. Nye demonstrates, again, the importance of examining the constitution of national imaginaries across, and in spite of, national borders. On first sight, the representations of Germans in the North American film and commercial television he dissects simply embody an easy, ahistorical set of stereotypes: efficiency, ruthlessness, and humorlessness. The reinscription of such stories is as tiresome as it is superficial. Yet something far more interesting is at work here. In particular, the trope of the (Berlin noir) designer suit–wearing Euroterrorist both moves beyond the insistent foregrounding of the Nazis and Holocaust in global popular cultural evocations of "bad Germans" and simultaneously reanimates something older. It is not, after all, difficult to see in the austere, obedient figure of the German Euroterrorist popularized in films such as *Die Hard* the descendant of the cold, disciplined Prussian of the late nineteenth-century European imagination, at once provoking admiration, hostility, and fear. Here, again, we are reminded of the capacity of such tropes to weave in and out of the political frames for which we conventionally reach when telling the history of Germany, constantly evolving, yet persistently returning and repeating, resisting their domestication by conventional narrative as they do.

German Musicking, "Culture," and Eurocentrism

Ironically, national identity arrived as a compelling context for interrogating inherited histories of Germany's musical cultures just as the events of 1989 and the wave of euphoria about globalization that followed swept national frameworks from the conceptual repertoires of many historians. Today we live in an age of global history, in which national envelopes (in Sebastian Conrad's words, "regimes of territoriality")—and in the case of German music the Eurocentrism that unavoidably goes with them—are rightly viewed with suspicion.[41] The essays in this book, by interrogating and complicating the special status of the idea of "Germanness" in music, reassess the ways in which national ideas can shape musical practices in light of the "global turn." The inadequacy of the category of the national, beholden as it still is to processes of nineteenth-century nation building, as a simple frame for historical analysis should be clear. Global approaches can open historical studies to new and far more nuanced ways of assessing what Conrad calls "positionality."[42] As the authors in this book argue, musical "Germanness" can appear in unexpected places, such as 1890s Japan or *Saturday Night Live*. It can appear between cultural geographies and can help to make new ones where it does.

After the Brexit referendum and the election of Donald Trump as president of the United States, uninterrogated celebrations of global, transnational, cosmopolitan, and other such "open" methods appear in another light. The essays here engage with borders: those between Germany and its national others, but also those between "high" and "low" art, nation and region, men and women, rich and poor, queer and straight, the remembered and the forgotten, and, crucially, Europe and the rest of the world.[43] Recently Europe's borders, including Germany's, have been the subject of passionate political debate and the site of violence and an appalling loss of life. They are once again materially real. The mass migration of refugees to Europe fleeing war and inequality around the Mediterranean and farther afield—and the concomitant rise of "identity"-based ultrarightist movements in Europe, Britain, and the United States—has sparked a resurgence of what Conrad calls "culture talk": the insistence, which never really went away, on a specifically European or Western civilization whose "values" need defending from—as former British Prime Minister David Cameron, a politician with a reputation for liberal "cosmopolitanism," put it—a "swarm" of people heading our way who might not share them.[44]

The resurgence of "Western culture" as *Leitkategorie*, especially in the years since 9/11, has also found echoes elsewhere. In China and Japan, for instance, one reaction to the long processes of decolonization and deimperialization has been recourse to talk of Chinese, Japanese, or "Confucian" civilization, even when this serves as cover for a renewed imperial gaze toward neighbors or increasing repression within.[45] The same could be said of the rise of Hindu nationalist parties in India and the allures of an imaginary "global" (read: Sunni) caliphate on the borders of Syria and Iraq. And even the global perspective, as Conrad reminds us, can slip too easily into a transcendental, all-knowing subject position that is itself a hallmark of Western thinking determined and legitimated by centuries of (as it happens, often German) philosophical world-making.[46] Conceptual "centrisms" are harder to shake off than we think.

What could a study of German music history free of "conceptual Germanocentrism" look like? The idea might sound absurd at first: Can there be *any* kind of German history that dispenses with "Germanness"? We would argue that there could be. The first step in the direction of such a history would be to build on the successes of the methodological tools of reception history and culture transfer by opening ourselves up to larger and less stable frames. Cultural historians of music have used both tools, with great and lasting effect, to interrogate stale national categories.[47] Particularly in the realm of culture transfer, the best work is open, as Annagret Fauser and Mark Everist write, to "the idea that identity and difference are not contradictory but complementary."[48] Yet as Walter Mignolo argues, the idea of culture itself is not neutral: lying somewhere "between 'nature' and 'civilization' it has helped Western thinkers classify (and divide up) the world from the eighteenth century onwards."[49]

Those who proclaim a "new cultural history of music" would be advised to take account of this blind spot. Mignolo's discussion of the terms "acculturation" and "transculturation" illuminates this issue. Acculturation, applied to the case studies in this book, would mean that non-Germans—or indeed those who are not the classic white, male, heterosexual, bourgeois subjects of German music history—exposed to German musical culture would take it on and make it their own: Germans act, others react. On a broader scale, reliance on overdetermined structures has (inadvertently) hobbled postcolonialist thought as well.[50] Unlike postcolonialism, acculturation theories often look past the violence (conceptual and real) that might have accompanied such exposure. "Transculturation" offers a less hegemonizing alternative, but still depends on static models of cultural practices in motion "across" arbitrary borders.

An alternative term would be what Mignolo calls "cultural semiosis," the precondition of "border thinking." Border thinking, Mignolo claims, happens in the moment when those living in the modern, globalized world—with its claim to be united by one history of progress leading to the present—realize that they really live *on the border* between the claims of this history and a different local reality. In this moment the way one interprets the world ("cultural semiosis") can change. The result, Mignolo argues, is a kind of decolonizing move, one that reveals "that the system of knowledge, beliefs, expectations, dreams, and fantasies upon which the modern/colonial world was built is showing, and will continue to show, its unviability."[51] This is a near corollary of what Conrad calls "the emergence of the world as a social category," a process in which "historians express their views on connections and exchange, and their visions of the totality ... of which they feel a part." The result could be "plural" historical worlds, in which "each version reflects the position from which it was conceived."[52] In some of these worlds Germany might be constituted in the absence of any Germans at all. It might also be constituted outside of the real. Indeed, one of Mignolo's most insightful (and, for some perhaps, troubling) claims is that "Western civilization" itself "may be a dream: the dream of actors and institutions that managed and built the modern/colonial world in the name of the universality of Western values."[53] In this sense the much heralded "special" history of German music, with all of its similar claims of universal value, might be just another dream of Germany.

Transcending conceptual Germanocentrism in music(al) history also means overcoming, once and for all, the dead weight of received narrative structures. Thinking of the history of German musical cultures as a kaleidoscopic array of overlapping "made" worlds might empower us to resist the attraction of teleological metanarratives. Historians of German music tend toward two of these. The first is the Romantic story of progress, often expressed in Hegelian terms of overcoming contradictions. In these a (German) musical genius such as Beethoven, Wagner, or Schoenberg arrives just in time at the end of Act Three to save the day and propel the story of German music history forward. In others, the narrative is tragic, but a narrative all the same. In this story all the glories of German musical art are not enough to save German civilization from German barbarity.[54] The *Sonderweg* idea—which in music-historical terms can lead, for instance, to reductive accounts of musical life under National Socialism in which totalitarian ideology is always the determining factor—is as seductive in its way as the story of German musical heroism. It preserves a notion of German difference that resonates unmistakably throughout the manifold discourses of German music history. But it is a dead end as a historical method, because it robs historical actors of their agency and removes that agency from the contexts in which it was deployed, depriving it in the process of much of whatever meaning it may have had.

Embracing border thinking and world-making as models alongside reception and transfer, and rejecting the seductions of Special Paths, can turn histories of German music into histories of German musicking and return agency to those who really made this history in all of its complexity and contradictions. The essays in this book attempt to do justice to these actors. But they are only a beginning. Approaches like the one we attempt here depend on the linkage of microhistories—of audience behavior, repertoire choice, historical imagination, memorial practices, and club-going—with larger processes such as the emergence of mass media, rapid changes in travel and communication, mass migration, and, of course, war and destruction. There are many microhistories left to write. The writing of these will continue to change as our understanding of the larger processes in which they are embedded does.

The project of stripping the ingrained Eurocentric conceits from our conceptions of what constitutes German music history needs to be pursued not only by identifying such ideologies and holding them to account in texts such as those in this volume, but also in the sites where we, as scholars, have voice and agency to change the world. In the winter of 2015–16, both musicology and history were shaken by separate but related controversies connected to debates around the decolonization of our disciplines. While historians at Cape Town, Missouri, Yale, Harvard, and Oxford debated the issues raised by the legacies of slavery and colonialism, musicologists, further from the public eye, found themselves no less bitterly divided over claims made in a scholar's blog post about the allegedly improving capacities of Mozart's *Don Giovanni* when played to inmates in an American prison.[55] The implicit, but uninterrogated, Eurocentrism of the blog post unleashed a storm of protest, but also vigorous defenses of the underlying act of public engagement. The protests centered on, among other things, the ideology behind the author's assumption of the universal values the opera supposedly embodied—ones that we would identify as contingently German—and their ability to improve the minds and lives of prisoners who, given the demography of the US prison population, may have preferred to celebrate any number of alternative cultural heritages. As the debate continued it became clear that some of its interlocutors, many of whom identified themselves as belonging to or sympathizing with minorities of age, gender, race, disability, or sexual orientation underrepresented in professional musicology, felt compelled for fear of career reprisal to make their contributions under the cover of anonymity.[56]

Such disputes are not isolated cases. Rather, they reflect and help to shape a wider contemporary unease about the implication of university humanities curricula—and the conceits of Western humanities in general—in cultures of power that exclude, coerce, and oppress, both in the polities in which they are at work and in relation to global others. Reforms to the music curriculum at Harvard University and deliberations on the decolonization of the *American Historical Review* are more recent examples of how such concerns have gradually gained traction in sections of our own disciplines; pressure to reform the English curriculum at the University of Cambridge in a similar spirit shows something of the reach of such arguments in cognate intellectual communities. Yet just as striking is the entrenched "common sense" opposition that such critiques continue to provoke. To us this underscores the urgency of the critique we attempt here. We share Samuel Moyn and Andrew Sartori's call for a more "pluralized" historiography in line with such a critique. With them, in light of recent events in our academic environments, we would like to stress the importance of taking this plurality further, "to the level of the profession itself, in which the inequitable distribution of institutional power and authority stands as the biggest obstacle to overcoming Eurocentrism."[57] We hope that the voices represented in this book can contribute constructively to a necessary critique, and dismantling, of such inequalities.

Neil Gregor is professor of modern European history at the University of Southampton, UK. He has published widely on the economic, social, and cultural history of twentieth-century Germany, including *Daimler-Benz in the Third Reich* (Yale University Press, 1998) and *Haunted City: Nuremberg and the Nazi Past* (Yale University Press, 2008), both of which won the Fraenkel

Prize for Contemporary History. He is currently writing a book on the symphony concert in Nazi Germany.

Thomas Irvine is associate professor in music at the University of Southampton, UK. His recent research explores the intellectual history of music and musical practices in transnational and global frames. In 2015–16 he was a Mid-Career Fellow of the British Academy. His book *Listening to China: Sound and the Sino-Western Encounter, 1770–1839* is published by University of Chicago Press.

Notes

1. Celia Applegate and Pamela Potter, eds., *Music and German National Identity* (Chicago, 2002).
2. Celia Applegate and Pamela Potter, "Germans as the 'People of Music': Genealogy of an Identity," in Applegate and Potter, *Music and German National Identity*, 1–35.
3. Benedict Anderson, *Imagined Communities: Reflections on the Origins and Spread of Nationalism* (London, 1983).
4. On "invented traditions," see the classic Eric Hobsbawm and Terence Ranger, eds., *The Invention of Tradition* (Cambridge, 1983).
5. For the "new musicology," see Joseph Kerman, *Contemplating Music: Challenges to Musicology* (Cambridge, MA, 1985); Susan McClary and Richard Leppert, eds., *Music and Society: The Politics of Composition, Performance and Reception* (Cambridge, 1987); Ruth A. Solie, ed., *Musicology and Difference: Gender and Sexuality in Music Scholarship* (Berkeley, 1993); Richard Leppert, *The Sight of Sound: Music, Representation, and the History of the Body* (Berkeley, 1993); and Nicholas Cook and Mark Everist, eds., *Rethinking Music* (Oxford, 1999). For a (skeptical) reaction in German, see Laurenz Lütteken, ed., *Musikwissenschaft: Eine Positionsbestimmung* (Kassel, 2007). A more positive response is Michele Calella and Nikolaus Urbanek, eds., *Musikwissenschaft: Grundlagen und Perspektiven* (Stuttgart, 2013).
6. See the survey in Philip V. Bohlman, *Music, Nationalism and the Making of a New Europe* (London, 2004), which makes clear that many of the processes of musical "nationalization" sustain the argument that German music history is similar to, rather than fundamentally different from, its European counterparts. For comparative arguments that undermine the sense of German singularity in the sphere of art music, see Sven Oliver Müller, *Das Publikum macht die Musik: Musikleben in Berlin, London und Wien im 19. Jahrhundert* (Göttingen, 2014); on popular theater and music hall, see the excellent Tobias Becker, *Inszenierte Moderne: Populäres Theater in Berlin und London, 1880–1930* (London, 2014); and Tobias Becker, Len Platt, and David Linton, eds., *Popular Musical Theatre in London and Berlin, 1890–1939* (Cambridge, 2014).
7. Trevor Pinch and Karin Bijsterfeld, eds., *The Oxford Handbook of Sound Studies* (Oxford, 2012).
8. "Forum: Globalising Early Modern Germany," *German History* 31, no. 3 (2013): 366–82.

9. Emblematic of this move is Celia Applegate, *A Nation of Provincials: The German Idea of Heimat* (Berkeley, 1990); more recently, Martina Steber, *Ethnische Gewissheiten: Die Ordnung des Regionalen im bayerischen Schwaben vom Kaiserreich bis zum NS-Regime* (Göttingen, 2010); the formation of national identities in civic musical life is explored in Rüdiger Ritter, *Wem gehört Musik? Warschau und Wilna im Widerstreit nationaler und städtischer Musikkulturen vor 1939* (Stuttgart, 2004); for an exploration of such civic cultures across the longue durée of German history, see Christian Thorau, Andreas Odenkirchen, and Peter Ackermann, eds., *Musik—Bürger—Stadt: Konzertleben und musikalisches Hören im historischen Wandel* (Regensburg, 2011).
10. For thoughtful reflections, see Celia Applegate, "Music among the Historians," *German History* 30, no. 3 (2012): 329–49.
11. See Jane Fulcher, ed., *The Oxford Handbook of the New Cultural History of Music* (New York, 2011).
12. Kay Kaufman Shelemay, "Musical Communities: Rethinking the Collective in Music," *Journal of the American Musicological Society* 64, no. 2 (2011): 349–90. See also Gary Tomlinson, "Musicology, Anthropology, History," *Il Saggiatore Musicale: Rivista Semestrale di Musicologia* 8, no. 1 (2001): 21–37; Nicholas Cook, "We Are All (Ethno)musicologists Now," in *The New (Ethno)musicologies*, ed. Henry Sobart (New York, 2008), 48–70; and Georgina Born, "For a Relational Musicology: Music and Interdisciplinarity, beyond the Practice Turn," *Journal of the Royal Musical Association* 135, no. 2 (2010): 205–43. For the perspective of younger historians writing in German, see Sven Oliver Müller and Martin Rempe, "Vergemeinschaftung, Pluralisierung, Fragmentierung: Kommunikationsprozesse im Musikleben des 20. Jahrhunderts," in *Kommunikation im Musikleben: Harmonien und Dissonanzen im 20. Jahrhundert*, ed. Sven Oliver Müller, Jürgen Osterhammel, and Martin Rempe (Göttingen, 2015), 9–26.
13. Thomas Turino, *Music as Social Life: The Politics of Participation* (Chicago, 2008), 95.
14. Christopher Small, *Musicking: The Meanings of Performing and Listening* (Hanover, NH, 1998).
15. Charles Taylor, *Modern Social Imaginaries* (Durham, NC, 2004).
16. We take the concept of "wordless knowledge" from Antonio Damasio, *The Feeling of What Happens: Body, Emotion and the Making of Consciousness* (London, 1999), 26.
17. Taylor, *Modern Social Imaginaries*, 183.
18. See William Weber, *The Rise of Musical Classics in Eighteenth-Century England: A Study in Canon, Ritual, and Ideology* (Oxford, 1996); William Weber, *The Musician as Entrepreneur, 1700–1914: Managers, Charlatans, and Idealists* (Bloomington, 2004); William Weber, *The Great Transformation of Musical Taste: Concert Programming from Haydn to Brahms* (Cambridge, 2008); Rebecca Grotjahn, *Die Sinfonie im deutschen Kulturgebiet 1850–1875: Ein Beitrag zur Gattungs- und Institutionengeschichte* (Sinzig, 1998); David Gramit, *Cultivating Music: The Aspirations, Interests, and Limits of German Musical Culture, 1770–1848* (Berkeley, 2002); Anselm Gerhard, *London und der Klassizismus in der Musik: Die Idee der "absoluten Musik" und Muzio Clementis Klavierwerke* (Stuttgart, 2012); and Müller, *Das Publikum macht die Musik*. On the emergence of the category of the "work," see Lydia Goehr, *The Imaginary Museum of Musical Works: An Essay in the Philosophy of Music*, 2nd ed. (New York, 2007).
19. James Johnson, *Listening in Paris: A Cultural History* (Berkeley, 1995); Matthew Riley, *Musical Listening in the German Enlightenment: Attention, Wonder and Astonishment*

(Aldershot, 2004); Mark Evan Bonds, *Music as Thought: Listening to the Symphony in the Age of Beethoven* (Princeton, 2006); Michael P. Steinberg, *Listening to Reason: Culture, Subjectivity, and Nineteenth-Century Music* (Princeton, 2006); and Melanie Lowe, *Pleasure and Meaning in the Classical Symphony* (Bloomington, 2007). All of these respond to the impetus of Carl Dahlhaus's widely received *Nineteenth-Century Music*, trans. J. Bradford Robinson (Berkeley, 1989), originally published as *Die Musik des 19. Jahrhunderts* (Laaber, 1980).

20. James Garratt, *Music, Culture and Social Reform in the Age of Wagner* (Cambridge, 2010); Ryan Minor, *Choral Fantasies: Music, Festivity and Nationhood in Nineteenth-Century Germany* (Cambridge, 2012).
21. See the overview of recent research in Sven Oliver Müller, "Die Politik des Schweigens: Veränderungen im Publikumsverhalten in der Mitte des 19. Jahrhunderts," *Geschichte und Gesellschaft* 38, no. 1 (2012): 48–85.
22. Nicholas Mathew, "Beethoven's Political Music, the Handelian Sublime, and the Aesthetics of Prostration," *19th-Century Music* 33, no. 2 (2009): 110–50.
23. Victor Turner, *The Ritual Process: Structure and Anti-Structure* (Ithaca, 1969).
24. Hansjakob Ziemer, "Listening on the Home Front: Music and the Production of Social Meaning in German Concert Halls during World War I," in *Sounds of Modern History. Auditory Cultures in 19th- and 20th-Century Europe*, ed. Daniel Morat (Oxford, 2014), 201–24; more generally, Hansjakob Ziemer, *Die Moderne Hören: Das Konzert als urbanes Forum 1890–1940* (Frankfurt, 2008).
25. See the reflections in Jennifer V. Evans, "Introduction: Queering German History," *German History* 34, no. 3 (2016): 371–84.
26. See the thoughtful comments in Geoff Eley, "How and Where Is German History Centered?," in *German History from the Margins*, ed. Neil Gregor, Nils Roemer, and Mark Roseman (Bloomington, 2006), 268–86.
27. Neil Gregor, "Music, Memory, Emotion: Richard Strauss and the Legacies of War," in *Music & Letters* 96, no. 1 (2015): 55–76.
28. Maximilian Lanzinner, *Zwischen Sternenbanner und Bundesadler: Bayern im Wiederaufbau 1945–1958* (Regensburg, 1996), 309–89.
29. Neil Gregor, *Haunted City: Nuremberg and the Nazi Past* (New Haven, 2008).
30. We borrow the term "contained plurality" from Martina Steber, "Regions and National Socialist Ideology: Reflections on Contained Plurality" in *Heimat, Region and Empire: Spatial Identities under National Socialism*, ed. Claus-Christian W. Szejnmann and Maiken Umbach (Basingstoke, 2012), 25–42.
31. Karl Marx and Friedrich Engels, *The Communist Manifesto*, trans. Samuel Moore (New York, 1964), 64–65.
32. Sebastian Conrad, *What Is Global History?* (Princeton, 2016), 87–88. A first attempt at mapping music onto the field is Jürgen Osterhammel, "Globale Horizonte europäischer Kunstmusik, 1860–1930," *Geschichte und Gesellschaft* 38, no. 1 (2012): 86–132. Reinhard Strohm's three-year Balzan Prize research project promises to add substantial literature to the field: see "Towards a Global History of Music: A Research Programme in Musicology – 2013–2017," retrieved 13 May 2016 from http://www.music.ox.ac.uk/research/projects/balzan-research-project/.
33. The locus classicus of the *Sonderweg Thesis* is Hans-Ulrich Wehler, *Das Deutsche Kaiserreich 1871–1918* (Göttingen, 1973); the classic critique is David Blackbourn and Geoff Eley, *The Peculiarities of German History: Bourgeois Society and Politics*

in Nineteenth-Century Germany (Oxford, 1984). More recently, Helmut Walser Smith, *The Continuities of German History: Nation, Religion, and Race across the Long Nineteenth Century* (Cambridge, 2008).
34. Michael J. Schmidt, "Visual Music: Jazz, Synaesthesia and the History of the Senses in the Weimar Republic," *German History* 32, no. 2 (2014): 201–23.
35. For a discussion of the compatibility of "micro" approaches to global methodologies see Conrad, *What Is Global History?*, 129–32.
36. Hans Rudolf Vaget, "National and Universal: Thomas Mann and the Paradox of 'German' Music," in Applegate and Potter, *Music and German National Identity*, 155–77.
37. See, for example, Ulrich Brochhagen, *Nach Nürnberg: Vergangenheitsbewältigung und Westintegration in der Ära Adenauer* (Berlin, 1994); Jeffrey Herf, *Divided Memory: The Nazi Past in the Two Germanies* (Cambridge, MA, 1997); and Robert G. Moeller, *War Stories: The Search for a Usable Past in the Federal Republic of Germany* (Berkeley, 2001).
38. Malte Thiessen, *Eingebrannt ins Gedächtnis: Hamburgs Gedenken an Luftkrieg und Kriegsende 1943 bis 2005* (Munich, 2007); Svenja Goltermann, *Die Gesellschaft der Überlebenden: Deutsche Kriegsheimkehrer und ihre Gewalterfahrungen im Zweiten Weltkrieg* (Munich, 2009); Jörg Arnold, *The Allied Air War and Urban Memory: The Legacy of Strategic Bombing in Germany* (Cambridge, 2011).
39. See, in a similar vein, Zoë Alexis Lang, *The Legacy of Johann Strauss: Political Influence and Twentieth-Century Identity* (Cambridge, 2014).
40. More generally, see Elaine Kelly, *Composing the Canon in the German Democratic Republic: Narratives of Nineteenth-Century Music* (Oxford, 2014); for comparison, see the similar argument of Pauline Fairclough, *Classics for the Masses: Shaping Soviet Musical Identity under Lenin and Stalin* (New Haven, 2016).
41. For a broad summary introduction to the "global turn," see Conrad, *What Is Global History?* (here: 123).
42. Ibid., 162–84.
43. On the prospects of a "musicology beyond borders," see the eerily prescient essays in Tamara Levitz, convenor, "Colloquy: Musicology beyond Borders?," *Journal of the American Musicological Society* 65, no. 3 (2012): 821–61.
44. "David Cameron: 'Swarm' of Migrants Crossing Mediterranean," *BBC News*, 30 July 2015.
45. See Kuan-Hsing Chen, *Asia as Method: Toward Deimperialization* (Durham, NC, 2010).
46. On the rise of alternative conceptual "centrisms," see Conrad, *What Is Global History?*, 174–84.
47. See Mark Everist, "Reception Theories, Canonic Discourses, and Musical Value," in Cook and Everist, *Rethinking Music*, 378–402; and Annegret Fauser and Mark Everist, ed., *Music, Theater, and Cultural Transfer: Paris, 1830–1914* (Chicago, 2009).
48. Annegret Fauser and Mark Everist, "Introduction," in Fauser and Everist, *Music, Theater, and Cultural Transfer*, 6. For a more recent critical discussion of difference in music historiography, see the essays in Olivia Bloechl, Melanie Lowe, and Jeffrey Kallberg, eds., *Rethinking Difference in Music Scholarship* (Cambridge, 2015).
49. Walter D. Mignolo, *Local Histories/Global Designs: Coloniality, Subaltern Knowledges, and Border Thinking*, 2nd ed. (Princeton, 2012), 15.

50. Daniel Carey and Lynn Festa, "Introduction: Some Answers to the Question: 'What Is Postcolonial Enlightenment?,'" in *The Postcolonial Enlightenment: Eighteenth-Century Colonialisms and Postcolonial Theory*, ed. Daniel Carey and Lynn Festa (Oxford, 2009), 5–6. See also Chen, *Asia as Method*, 65–113.
51. Mignolo, *Local Histories/Global Designs*, ix.
52. Conrad, *What Is Global History?*, 187–88.
53. Mignolo, *Local Histories/Global Designs*, x.
54. Thomas Irvine, "Normality and Emplotment: Walter Leigh's 'Midsummer Night's Dream' in the Third Reich and Britain," *Music and Letters* 94, no. 2 (2013): 295–323.
55. Pierpaolo Polzonetti, "Don Giovanni Goes to Prison," *Musicology Now* (blog), American Musicological Society, 16 February 2016. Responses included William Cheng, "Musicology, Freedom and the Uses of Anger" and Bonnie Gordon, "The Perils of Public Musicology," *Musicology Now* (blog), American Musicological Society, 21 February 2016.
56. brownamsavenger, "#AMSSOWHITE: For the Public Record," 18 February 2016, retrieved 11 May 2016 from http://brownamsavenger.livejournal.com/612.html.
57. Samuel Moyn and Andrew Sartori, "Approaches to Global Intellectual History," in Samuel Moyn and Andrew Sartori, eds., *Global Intellectual History* (New York, 2013), 18.

Bibliography

Anderson, Benedict. *Imagined Communities: Reflections on the Origins and Spread of Nationalism*. London: Verso, 1983.
Applegate, Celia. *A Nation of Provincials: The German Idea of Heimat*. Berkeley: University of California Press, 1990.
———. "Music among the Historians." *German History* 30, no. 3 (2012): 329–49.
——— and Pamela Potter, eds. *Music and German National Identity*. Chicago: University of Chicago Press, 2002.
Arnold, Jörg. *The Allied Air War and Urban Memory: The Legacy of Strategic Bombing in Germany*. Cambridge: Cambridge University Press, 2011.
Becker, Tobias. *Inszenierte Moderne: Populäres Theater in Berlin und London, 1880–1930*. London: De Gruyter Oldenbourg, 2014.
Becker, Tobias, Len Platt, and David Linton, eds. *Popular Musical Theatre in London and Berlin, 1890–1939*. Cambridge: Cambridge University Press, 2014.
Blackbourn, David, and Geoff Eley. *The Peculiarities of German History: Bourgeois Society and Politics in Nineteenth-Century Germany*. Oxford: Oxford University Press, 1984.
Bloechl, Olivia, Melanie Lowe, and Jeffrey Kallberg, eds. *Rethinking Difference in Music Scholarship*. Cambridge: Cambridge University Press, 2015.
Bohlman, Philip V. *Music, Nationalism and the Making of a New Europe*. London: Routledge, 2004.
Bonds, Mark Evan. *Music as Thought: Listening to the Symphony in the Age of Beethoven*. Princeton, NJ: Princeton University Press, 2006.

Born, Georgina. "For a Relational Musicology: Music and Interdisciplinarity, beyond the Practice Turn," *Journal of the Royal Musical Association* 135, no. 2 (2010): 205–43.
Brochhagen, Ulrich. *Nach Nürnberg: Vergangenheitsbewältigung und Westintegration in der Ära Adenauer*. Berlin: Propyläen, 1994.
Calella, Michele, and Nikolaus Urbanek, eds. *Musikwissenschaft: Grundlagen und Perspektiven*. Stuttgart: J. B. Metzler, 2013.
Carey, Daniel, and Lynn Festa. "Introduction: Some Answers to the Question: What is Postcolonial Enlightenment." In *The Postcolonial Enlightenment: Eighteenth-Century Colonialisms and Postcolonial Theory*, ed. Daniel Carey and Lynn Festa, 1–38. Oxford: Oxford University Press, 2009.
Chen, Kuan-Hsing. *Asia as Method: Toward Deimperialization*. Durham, NC: Duke University Press, 2010.
Cheng, William. "Musicology, Freedom and the Uses of Anger." *Musicology Now* (blog). American Musicological Society, 21 February 2016. Retrieved 11 May 2016 from http://musicologynow.ams-net.org/2016/02/musicology-freedom-and-uses-of-anger.html.
Conrad, Sebastian. *What Is Global History?* Princeton, NJ: Princeton University Press, 2016.
Cook, Nicholas. "We Are All (Ethno)musicologists Now." In *The New (Ethno)musicologies*, edited by Henry Stobart, 48–70. New York: Scarecrow Press, 2008.
——— and Mark Everist, eds. *Rethinking Music*. Oxford: Oxford University Press, 1999.
Dahlhaus, Carl. *Nineteenth-Century Music*. Translated by J. Bradford Robinson. Berkeley: University of California Press, 1989. Originally published as *Die Musik des 19. Jahrhunderts* (Laaber: Laaber-Verlag, 1980).
Damasio, Antonio. *The Feeling of What Happens: Body, Emotion and the Making of Consciousness*. London: Houghton Mifflin Harcourt, 1999.
"David Cameron: 'Swarm' of Migrants Crossing Mediterranean." *BBC News*, 30 July 2015. Retrieved 9 May 2016 from http://www.bbc.co.uk/news/uk-politics-33714282.
Eley, Geoff. "How and Where Is German History Centered?" In *German History from the Margins*, edited by Neil Gregor, Nils Roemer, and Mark Roseman, 268–86. Bloomington: Indiana University Press, 2006.
Evans, Jennifer V. "Introduction: Queering German History," *German History* 34, no. 3 (2016): 371–84.
Everist, Mark. "Reception Theories, Canonic Discourses, and Musical Value," In *Rethinking Music*, edited by Nicholas Cook and Mark Everist, 378–402. Oxford: Oxford University Press, 1999.
Fairclough, Pauline. *Classics for the Masses: Shaping Soviet Musical Identity under Lenin and Stalin*. New Haven, CT: Yale University Press, 2016.
Fauser, Annegret, and Mark Everist, eds. *Music, Theater, and Cultural Transfer: Paris, 1830–1914*. Chicago: Chicago University Press, 2009.

"Forum: Globalising Early Modern Germany." *German History* 31 no. 3 (2013): 366–82.
Fulcher, Jane, ed. *The Oxford Handbook of the New Cultural History of Music*. New York: Oxford University Press, 2011.
Garratt, James. *Music, Culture and Social Reform in the Age of Wagner*. Cambridge: Cambridge University Press, 2010.
Gerhard, Anselm. *London und der Klassizismus in der Musik: Die Idee der "absoluten Musik" und Muzio Clementis Klavierwerke*. Stuttgart: J. B. Metzler, 2002.
Goehr, Lydia. *The Imaginary Museum of Musical Works: An Essay in the Philosophy of Music*. 2nd ed. Oxford: Oxford University Press, 2007.
Goltermann, Svenja. *Die Gesellschaft der Überlebenden: Deutsche Kriegsheimkehrer und ihre Gewalterfahrungen im Zweiten Weltkrieg*. Munich: DVA, 2009.
Gordon, Bonnie. "The Perils of Public Musicology." *Musicology Now* (blog). American Musicological Society, 22 February 2016. Retrieved 11 May 2016 from http://musicologynow.ams-net.org/2016/02/the-perils-of-public-musicology.html.
Gramit, David. *Cultivating Music: The Aspirations, Interests, and Limits of German Musical Culture, 1770–1848*. Berkeley: University of California Press, 2002.
Gregor, Neil. *Haunted City: Nuremberg and the Nazi Past*. New Haven, CT: Yale University Press, 2008.
———. "Music, Memory, Emotion: Richard Strauss and the Legacies of War." *Music and Letters* 96, no. 1 (2015): 55–76.
Grotjahn, Rebecca. *Die Sinfonie im deutschen Kulturgebiet 1850–1875: Ein Beitrag zur Gattungs- und Institutionengeschichte*. Sinzig: Studiopunkt, 1998.
Herf, Jeffrey. *Divided Memory: The Nazi Past in the Two Germanies*. Cambridge, MA: Harvard University Press, 1997.
Hobsbawm, Eric, and Terence Ranger, eds. *The Invention of Tradition*. Cambridge: Cambridge University Press, 1983.
Irvine, Thomas. "Normality and Emplotment: Walter Leigh's 'Midsummer Night's Dream' in the Third Reich and Britain." *Music and Letters* 94, no. 2 (2013): 295–323.
Johnson, James. *Listening in Paris: A Cultural History*. Berkeley: University of California Press, 1995.
Kelly, Elaine. *Composing the Canon in the German Democratic Republic: Narratives of Nineteenth-Century Music*. Oxford: Oxford University Press, 2014.
Kerman, Joseph. *Contemplating Music: Challenges to Musicology*. Cambridge, MA: Harvard University Press, 1985.
Lang, Zoë Alexis. *The Legacy of Johann Strauss: Political Influence and Twentieth-Century Identity*. Cambridge: Cambridge University Press, 2014.
Lanzinner, Maximilian. *Zwischen Sternenbanner und Bundesadler: Bayern im Wiederaufbau 1945–1958*. Regensburg: Pustet, 1996.
Leppert, Richard. *The Sight of Sound: Music, Representation, and the History of the Body*. Berkeley: University of California Press, 1993.

Levitz, Tamara, convenor. "Colloquy: Musicology beyond Borders?" *Journal of the American Musicological Society* 65, no. 3 (2012): 821–61.

Lowe, Melanie. *Pleasure and Meaning in the Classical Symphony*. Bloomington: Indiana University Press, 2007.

Lütteken, Laurenz, ed. *Musikwissenschaft: Eine Positionsbestimmung*. Kassel: Bärenreiter, 2007.

Marx, Karl, and Friedrich Engels. *The Communist Manifesto*. Translated by Samuel Moore. New York: Pocket Books, 1964.

Mathew, Nicholas. "Beethoven's Political Music, the Handelian Sublime, and the Aesthetics of Prostration." *19th-Century Music* 33, no. 2 (2009): 110–50.

McClary, Susan, and Richard Leppert, eds. *Music and Society: The Politics of Composition, Performance and Reception*. Cambridge: Cambridge University Press, 1987.

Mignolo, Walter D. *Local Histories/Global Designs: Coloniality, Subaltern Knowledges, and Border Thinking*. 2nd ed. Princeton, NJ: Princeton University Press, 2012.

Minor, Ryan. *Choral Fantasies: Music, Festivity and Nationhood in Nineteenth-Century Germany*. Cambridge: Cambridge University Press, 2012.

Moeller, Robert G. *War Stories: The Search for a Usable Past in the Federal Republic of Germany*. Berkeley: University of California Press, 2001.

Moyn, Samuel, and Andrew Sartori. "Approaches to Global Intellectual History" In *Global Intellectual History*, edited by Samuel Moyn and Andrew Sartori, 3–32. New York: Columbia University Press, 2013.

Müller, Sven Oliver. "Die Politik des Schweigens: Veränderungen im Publikumsverhalten in der Mitte des 19. Jahrhunderts." *Geschichte und Gesellschaft* 38 no. 1 (2012): 48–85.

———. *Das Publikum macht die Musik: Musikleben in Berlin, London und Wien im 19. Jahrhundert*. Göttingen: V & R, 2014.

Müller, Sven Oliver, and Martin Rempe. "Vergemeinschaftung, Pluralisierung, Fragmentierung: Kommunikationsprozesse im Musikleben des 20. Jahrhunderts." In *Kommunikation im Musikleben: Harmonien und Dissonanzen im 20. Jahrhundert*, edited by Sven Oliver Müller, Jürgen Osterhammel and Martin Rempe, 9–26. Göttingen: V & R, 2015.

Osterhammel, Jürgen. "Globale Horizonte europäischer Kunstmusik, 1860-1930." *Geschichte und Gesellschaft* 38, no.1 (2012): 86–132.

Pinch, Trevor, and Karin Bijsterfeld, eds. *The Oxford Handbook of Sound Studies*. Oxford: Oxford University Press, 2012.

Polzonetti, Pierpaolo. "Don Giovanni Goes to Prison." *Musicology Now* (blog). American Musicological Society, 16 February 2016. Retrieved 11 May 2016 from http://musicologynow.ams-net.org/2016/02/don-giovanni-goes-to-prison-teaching_16.htm.

Riley, Matthew. *Musical Listening in the German Enlightenment: Attention, Wonder and Astonishment*. Aldershot: Ashgate, 2004.

Ritter, Rüdiger. *Wem gehört Musik? Warschau und Wilna im Widerstreit nationaler und städtischer Musikkulturen vor 1939*. Stuttgart: Franz Steiner Verlag, 2004.

Schmidt, Michael J. "Visual Music: Jazz, Synaesthesia and the History of the Senses in the Weimar Republic." *German History* 32, no. 2 (2014): 201–23.
Shelemay, Kay Kaufman. "Musical Communities: Rethinking the Collective in Music." *Journal of the American Musicological Society* 64, no. 2 (2011): 349–90.
Small, Christopher. *Musicking: The Meanings of Performing and Listening*. Hanover, NH: Wesleyan University Press, 1998.
Smith, Helmut Walser. *The Continuities of German History: Nation, Religion, and Race across the Long Nineteenth Century*. Cambridge: Cambridge University Press, 2008.
Solie, Ruth A., ed. *Musicology and Difference: Gender and Sexuality in Music Scholarship*. Berkeley: University of California Press, 1993.
Steber, Martina. *Ethnische Gewissheiten: Die Ordnung des Regionalen im bayerischen Schwaben vom Kaiserreich bis zum NS-Regime*. Göttingen: V & R, 2010.
———. "Regions and National Socialist Ideology: Reflections on Contained Plurality." In *Heimat, Region and Empire: Spatial Identities under National Socialism*, edited by Claus-Christian W. Szejnmann and Maiken Umbach, 25–42. Basingstoke: Palgrave, 2012.
Steinberg, Michael P. *Listening to Reason: Culture, Subjectivity, and Nineteenth-Century Music*. Princeton, NJ: Princeton University Press, 2006.
Taylor, Charles. *Modern Social Imaginaries*. Durham, NC: Duke University Press, 2004.
Thiessen, Malte. *Eingebrannt ins Gedächtnis: Hamburgs Gedenken an Luftkrieg und Kriegsende 1943 bis 2005*. Munich: Dölling und Galitz, 2007.
Thorau, Christian, Andreas Odenkirchen, and Peter Ackermann, eds. *Musik—Bürger—Stadt: Konzertleben und musikalisches Hören im historischen Wandel*. Regensburg: ConBrio, 2011.
Tomlinson, Gary. "Musicology, Anthropology, History." *Il Saggiatore Musicale: Rivista Semestrale di Musicologia* 8, no. 1 (2001): 21–37.
Turino, Thomas. *Music as Social Life: The Politics of Participation*. Chicago: University of Chicago Press, 2008.
Turner, Victor. *The Ritual Process: Structure and Anti-Structure*. Ithaca, NY: Cornell University Press, 1969.
Weber, William. *The Rise of Musical Classics in Eighteenth-Century England: A Study in Canon, Ritual, and Ideology*. Oxford: Oxford University Press, 1996.
———. *The Musician as Entrepreneur, 1700–1914: Managers, Charlatans, and Idealists*. Bloomington: Indiana University Press, 2004.
———. *The Great Transformation of Musical Taste: Concert Programming from Haydn to Brahms*. Cambridge: Cambridge University Press, 2008.
Wehler, Hans-Ulrich. *Das Deutsche Kaiserreich 1871–1918*. Göttingen: V & R, 1973.
Ziemer, Hansjakob. *Die Moderne Hören: Das Konzert als urbanes Forum 1890–1940*. Frankfurt: Campus, 2008.
———. "Listening on the Home Front: Music and the Production of Social Meaning in German Concert Halls during World War I." In *Sounds of Modern History: Auditory Cultures in 19th- and 20th-Century Europe*, edited by Daniel Morat, 201–24. Oxford: Oxford University Press, 2014.

PART I

Spaces and Moments of Affect

CHAPTER 1

"The German in the Concert Hall"
Concertgoing and National Belonging in the Early Twentieth Century

HANSJAKOB ZIEMER

For many early twentieth-century observers of musical life, it seemed a truism that music had the power to build social and national communities. Karl Storck, a German music journalist, author, and commentator, noted in 1906 that music offered the "strongest powers for the creation of a feeling of togetherness, and in general for the creation and formulation of a shared sensation."[1] According to Storck, visiting the symphony hall fostered in the audience an image of itself as a national community, one that closely connected listeners with fellow listeners, with musicians, and with composers. Performances in the concert hall created social meaning by allowing listeners to assume the similarity of their experiences to others'. These ideals attained great significance in the social and political context of World War I, when music was ascribed an active role in the construction of a German *Heimatfront*. A few weeks into the war, Storck reiterated his belief in the community-building power of music when he wrote that the concert hall was the place "where effectively the one and only thinking, the same yearning, the same anxiety, and the same joy fill all hearts."[2] In Storck's view, the symphony hall created an audience that could symbolize and actualize the nation in a joint experience.

For contemporaries, the concert hall was a site where the abstract idea of the nation became tangible in a sensory way. The experience inside the concert hall seemed to allow the nation to be heard, felt, and visualized very much in the sense set out by historian Michael Geyer, who has defined the function of culture in wartime as an "enactment of the identity of the nation."[3] But although historians have often readily accepted the assumed community-building function of concert and opera halls and the accompanying national connotations, few have analyzed how these social relationships were constructed and the national imaginary appropriated in specific historical settings. If concert halls indeed function as "islands of community among the great sea of impersonal relations of the modern city," as Christopher Small has argued, we need to ask how such communities were in fact constructed as national, and how they embodied social ideals.[4] I use these two verbs here to emphasize the distinction between them: communities were *constructed*, not naturally given; and they *embodied* ideals of social imaginaries that existed prior to the concert-hall visit. But what was the precise role of the national in this process, given that it was in competition with other social imaginaries circulating at the time? What did the references to the body during performances and the assumptions of similarity of experience mean, and how and to what ends was the national used in listening experiences? This chapter addresses the everyday culture of concert-going and its role in the emergence of contemporary reflections on community, body, and nation. It shows how images of the national were constructed and deconstructed in the concert hall during and after World War I, and how they symbolized certain supposedly German characteristics. If there was a "German in the concert hall," as the well-known journalist Hans Heinz Stuckenschmidt claimed in 1927, that figure was contested by contemporaries, who used the concert hall as a model of perfection and imperfection at the same time.[5] From the historian's point of view, the ephemerality of both the performance and the audience can shed light on the ephemerality of the nation as well.

This approach builds on insights from recent scholarship on the imagining of German national identity in relation to music. Rather than focusing on composers as nationalist icons, intellectuals as agents of nationalist ideologies, or musicians as bearers of German superiority, scholars have emphasized how conceptions of identity and recognition can articulate themselves in the concrete act of music-making within a certain community and thus "take the presence of that community as a more or less stable entity, with dominant values and beliefs, for given," engendering "a shared sense of nation, confession, class, gender, occupation or something quite different again."[6] One could easily add to this list a sense of the regional, the local, or the international. The fundamental point is the move away from essentialist definitions of what music can potentially reveal or represent as national traits and toward the practices of music-making and listening—in short, of concertgoing. It is in these acts that, as Celia Applegate has pointed out, "music-making and nation-making converged in many places and times."[7] Such an approach is possible when ideologies of music as an "absolute art" and the "most abstract art" are no longer the starting point for historians. Instead of its supposedly objective qualities, I emphasize the sensory quality of music, the "most concrete art and least mediated of all artistic activities": the audience members are immersed in a world of sounds that are interpreted.[8] To this extent, an audience can indeed be described as an "imagined community" in Benedict Anderson's sense—not just as a fantasy, a simple escape or mere contemplation. Arjun Appadurai reminds us that imagination always entails concrete acts and that "imagination has become an organized field of social practices, a form of work and form of negotiation between agencies."⁹ In what follows, this interaction between imagination and practice is analyzed in order to show the precariousness of nationalized communities in the Weimar Republic.

The chapter begins with the radicalized national imagination during World War I and focuses on writing about and practices of concertgoing before and after the defeat of 1918. It examines these practices on three different levels: the level of ideas, where the ideal of achieving homogeneity was critically discussed; the level of behavior, where pathologies of the body were observed and reforms to concertgoing were proposed in bodily terms; and the level of listening experiences, where projections of race and nature were used to describe music in a practice of national othering. Concertgoing practices around 1920 were expressions of larger conflicts of the time, and concertgoers felt they were at a historical crossroads. In a piece on changes in music listening published in 1928, for example, the young music critic Kurt Westphal remarked that "we do not yet master the nineteenth century; for the greatest part it still masters us."¹⁰ This applied not just to challenges within the concert hall, but also to challenges within society at large.

Imagining Communities during World War I

Dreams of national unity seemed closest to realization in reports about the convergence of nationalist imaginaries and nationalist practices in symphony concerts during World War I.¹¹ The journalist Karl Storck, mentioned above, was just one example of a larger group of music intellectuals who promoted national unity through shared musical experience and saw the concert hall as an ideal location in which to experience such unity in reality. In a society entirely dominated by war, journalists, conductors, musicians, and composers relied upon prewar practices of concertgoing and on Romantic visions of the power of music as they established a consensus about how to encourage "Germanness." They nationalized repertoires, dedicated particular concerts to nationalist purposes ("patriotic concerts"), excluded foreigners from the program, and interpreted musical experience solely as an emotional expression of the present. Rudolf Cahn-Speyer, a conductor, composer, and journalist, pointed out that the concert hall was not there for abstract intellectual pleasure, but served to "heighten the feelings we are aware of at this moment."¹² Wartime concerts were credited with the power to overcome the internal fragmentation of the audience and the dominance of individual experience:

> All our current striving is directed at emphasizing what is shared by all; we are ready to subordinate the individual to the grand general goals and needs. ... As interesting as it is in normal times to get to know things alien to us—we now

want to enjoy what everybody can enjoy. ... Everybody strives to feel together with others as a great unity, and that is why the audience wants to listen to the works of older masters.[13]

Seen as a microcosm of society, the concert hall seemed to offer an experience of emotional community. Conductors, critics, and musicians concluded that concertgoing could function as a model for how society in general should be experienced.

This model of unity was appropriated for other features of the nationalist imagination. Faced with the loss of lives and a growing uncertainty as to the outcome of the war, the themes of mourning, death, transfiguration, and consolation acquired special attraction for listeners in search of coping mechanisms. The concert-hall experiences offered a space for identification with war victims. With the help of the hermeneutic approach still in fashion among journalists at the time, observers could portray the concert performance as an embodiment of mourning and a translation of the battlegrounds in France and Russia to the home front. Thus, a concert report written after listening to Franz Liszt's *Heldenklage* interpreted the musical performance as a ceremony "for all the heroes who have already sacrificed their lives for the German way of life and the German land."[14] The performance was visualized as a funeral procession marching through the concert hall, the woodwinds representing the "weeping and sobbing of the crowd" as it mourned the hero.[15] Visual images such as these, and the widely used interpretive tools of musical hermeneutics, helped to create a heroic moment and drew the music into the service of nationalism.

Although such images of mourning and heroism did not disappear after the war, questions of how to achieve social cohesion in the face of national defeat now became the chief concern among observers of concert life. The general belief in the nationalizing function of the concert-hall experience began to crumble. However, the fiction of a unified audience did not completely lose traction. Prewar ideas of the concert hall as an urban gathering place were already being revived by reformers of the concert hall toward the end of the war. In 1916, from the trenches of Verdun, the *Frankfurter Zeitung* journalist Paul Bekker wrote a monograph on perception in the concert hall in which he attempted to establish "musical form" as an outcome of the work of social relationships in society. For Bekker, music was the product of relationships between composer and listener engendered through their embeddedness in a specific environment and their sharing of a particular context. "The sound image is an image of society realized as acoustic material, not an aesthetic but a sociological sound property."[16] Since the listeners filled the perception space together, they created a "collective being."[17] For Bekker, the concert hall replaced the earlier functions of church and religion and became a site where the "people," or *Volk*, could be defined: "Resting on the broad basis of a *Volk* community without religious or social distinctions—that is our concert hall."[18] In Bekker's vision, music complemented what the state had already created in pursuit of a unified society, and his ideal of a classless, emancipatory gathering resembled the views of other authors, such as Ferruccio Busoni, who had believed before the war that a unified audience could only be imagined in the context of a classless society.[19] For Bekker, the main socializing agents were within his own profession, the journalists. Their reporting would counter social decay by translating the aesthetic unity of the concert hall into a broader social unity.[20]

Bekker regarded this transfer from aesthetic to social concerns as the primary function of concertgoing. But the nation was by no means absent from his social utopia, even though it did not take on a prominent role. Indeed, the nation was present everywhere in Bekker's work; he believed that "musical form is the form of national culture"[21] and located the nation alongside the aesthetic and the social as a third expression of community:

> A national culture can only be won from the conscious interaction of two forms: the socio-aesthetic and the state-political, which must both give to each other and take from each other, of which neither must dominate the other and neither disregard the other if they are not to descend into mere formula, if they are to affirm the unity of national culture, the truth of its underlying will to community.[22]

Bekker found evidence for the conjunction of music and society in history, especially in church practices and the reception of Beethoven's symphonies. In other writings, such as his book on the international standing of German music, *Die Weltgeltung der deutschen Musik*, Bekker fostered a notion of musical nationalism very much in the cosmopolitan tradition of the eighteenth century, in which national consciousness was paired with the belief in transnational communication through music.[23] He combined this conviction with a firm belief in the social power of the experience of sound during a concert performance.

Contested Conceptions of Audience in the Postwar Period

The wide reception of Bekker's social ideas in the next decade not only showed that he voiced widespread hopes and beliefs but also proved that the search for social cohesion was a fiercely contested field in the early years of the Weimar Republic. Bekker's strongest opponent was Hans Pfitzner, who became established shortly after the war as the voice of radical nationalist ideas and put forward a very different audience ideal. Whereas Bekker hoped for a holistic unity that echoed Busoni's ideals of a free and emancipatory society, Pfitzner preferred a hierarchical and nostalgic model. For Pfitzner, the audience was an aesthetic elite, not the whole of society. Listeners had to be musically educated in order to participate, and that meant being silent, passive, and well trained. German masters were superior to other composers, but they were not accessible to all—only to the happy few:

> That does not matter, for of course we know from Herr Becker [sic!] that the "society-building force," as the "highest property of a work of art," is external to the artwork, in other words that the music can be however it wants. This is the program of the society-building amusement that will take the place of our splendid art. Not being accepted into such a League of Nations is something to be heartily grateful for.[24]

Pfitzner's antagonism toward Bekker rested on their incompatible aesthetic positions. The main divide was set out by his interpretation of Bekker's alleged battle against the "musical idea" (*Einfall*) as an attack on German art in general. It was not just one particular kind of music that was at stake here, argued Pfitzner. One did not need the slightest musical talent to fulfill the requirements of such an aesthetic, because "if there is no more use for music in and of itself, but only for the 'poetic idea,' for the 'program,' the 'society-building forces,' then composing is an easy matter."[25] Such a view offered a different perspective on the concert hall, for Pfitzner's definition of music also entailed a particular concept of listening: as natural, organic, mystical. "The man who does not understand that a Beethovenian theme, for example, must be enjoyed directly, as a world unto itself, as indivisible, untranslatable; who feels the need to dissect it, describe it, cut it up into its components as a child dismembers a doll or a butterfly—that man does not know what music is."[26] This concept of listening, located at the core of Pfitzner's conception of the audience, clearly privileged a particular, well-educated group.

In both Pfitzner's and Bekker's concepts we can observe inconsistencies that reveal the contextual nature of their thinking. Pfitzner promoted anti-intellectual traditions and ideals of spontaneous and direct experiences while at the same time still believing in the predominance of German *Bildung* (education) as a precondition for listening in the concert hall. Bekker's vision of a unified society was undercut by his own denigration of bourgeois concertgoing practices, especially in the period between 1918 and 1920, which illustrated the utopian nature of his approach. But beyond the inner inconsistencies of these pamphlets, which obviously reflect the journalistic context in which they were published, both concepts contradicted each other. The politically charged vocabulary deployed by Pfitzner and Bekker and their dichotomous viewpoints certainly influenced the discussion of musical culture during the Weimar Republic.[27] Yet those debates were also informed by wider social issues of belonging and citizenship, especially concerns about identity.[28] For Pfitzner, the main question was: Who actually belonged to the community that the concert seemed to epitomize? "Clear distinctions! Who is still a German now? What is still German? Who is meant when someone in Germany says 'we'?," he asked.[29] The issue at stake here was that of with whom the music should be shared. If the concert hall was indeed, as Christopher Small argues, a place where strangers met and stayed strangers, the question was how the "underlying kinship" was sensed and how middle-class people could "feel safe together."[30] In the aftermath of war and inflation, this feeling of safety had been cast into doubt, as part of what Gerald Feldman has called the "misappropriation of spiritual values and a soiling of what the *Bürgertum*—above all the *Bildungsbürgertum*—held to be holy."[31] In the context of such fundamental feelings of uncertainty, the process of rethinking concepts of the audience was influenced by different discourses on musical genres and music aesthetics.[32] I will now, however, turn to the question of how issues of identity figured in the concert hall when these issues were translated into bodily behavior.

The National Body in the Concert Hall: Observation and Behavior

For contemporaries, social ideologies such as nationalism could be conveyed in the concert hall through references to the body. The body played a crucial role during the performance. From Small's ethnomusicological perspective, "the gestural dialogue" of musical situations probably has "more to tell us about the actual relationships between the conversers—and thus, quite possibly, about the real meaning of the encounter—than do the words that are being uttered."[33] Small describes the gestures, posture, movement, facial expressions, and physical encounters during the act of "musicking" as a "paralanguage" that helps to articulate and express social relationships, especially through training and repetition.[34] It has proved very difficult for historians to capture these kinds of gestures, and only recently, in the work of scholars such as Richard Leppert, has the history of such acts been written.

For a long time, historians painted a uniform portrait of events in the concert hall from the beginning of the nineteenth century on, in which the listeners appeared as silent and focused on the music on stage.[35] In newer work, however, more attention has been paid to deviating behaviors that pluralized the listening process and showed how musical performances could function in different ways for listeners.[36] The discourse on reinforcing rules such as being on time, keeping quiet, leaving the auditorium only after the end of the performance, not wearing hats, and so on remained a common feature of program notes throughout the 1920s. A veritable "aesthetic police"—a term that goes back to Eduard Hanslick and has recently been investigated by historian Martin Thrun—attempted to eliminate whistling, shouting, and booing from the concert hall and to formalize the rules for applause.[37] Although it is hard to generalize about practices in the concert hall, especially given regional differences, the first decades of the twentieth century—particularly the period immediately after World War I—were a period of continuing discussion of what constituted right and wrong behavior. This was fueled partly by disturbances during performances and by attempts at reforming bodily practices in order to enhance the social and aesthetic nature of the experience, but also by the usage of the concert hall as a battleground for the playing out of political scandals toward the end of the Weimar Republic.

A short example of the body politics at work in the concert hall may help to illuminate the context in which the national body could be portrayed. Among the reformist endeavors was the redefinition of the visual-aural nexus in the concert hall and, especially, the denigration of the visual in favor of the aural. For reformers such as journalists, a profoundly visual experience had to be changed in order to free music from the superficialities of fashion. Bekker, for example, saw the elimination of the visual as a precondition for his utopian ideals to be put into practice. Having attended a *Volkskonzert* (People's Concert) at the Frankfurt Opera House in 1918, he used his observation of a new style of staging to legitimize his goal of a social gathering unified through music. Bekker depicted the crucial change as a redefinition of the visual and the aural once the concert managers moved the orchestra to the pit and dimmed the lights:

> A fancy toilette, lorgnette, opera glasses are superfluous, for there is nothing to see. The auditorium is dark, each person's individuality is submerged in the collective, the senses concentrate on what is audible, and even the distraction that the figure of the conductor otherwise offers the eager eye is reduced to a minimum, because the orchestra and conductor are not on the stage but in the orchestra pit, and thus only partially accessible to the audience's view.[38]

For Bekker, this concert seemed to be an ideal experience, in which the aural and the visual entered into a new combination. He observed a break with prewar practices that had found the social purpose of the concert primarily in the display of fashion and introducing bourgeois young ladies into middle-class culture. Now these superficial traits were gone; instead, there was a general "rejection of the character of social class." Bekker went on to define the concert as the perfect place to experience the "people" without class differences:

> The "people" of these concerts will be not a lower social stratum, not a stratum at all in the sense of the old society, but precisely "the" people, which we all aspire to be, and which art—with its constituting, unifying, equalizing, and elevating effect—will help us become.[39]

Bekker placed his hopes for achieving social unity in the demotion of the visual and the elevation of the aural. Other listeners, however, were somewhat less enthusiastic about these changes in the staging of the concert. Paul Hirsch, one of Frankfurt's most influential musical philanthropists, a music collector, and a liberal music-lover, complained to Bekker that he had been unable to hear the music from his seat: the sounds of the two parts of the orchestra did not merge and he could not hear much more than the second violins. Even more importantly, he was disappointed by his experience of the *Eroica* because of a lack of shared emotion: "A performance of the *Eroica* ... was always a special occasion for me. Today, that festive atmosphere simply refused to materialize. I—and several others—missed the 'certain something,' the feeling of a common bond between the orchestra and 'society.'"[40] Hirsch especially felt the absence of the performance's visual aspect, finding the dark hall, without sight of the orchestra, "prison-like."[41] The dispute between Hirsch and Bekker continued despite Hirsch's agreement with many of Bekker's views on how to improve concert life. For Hirsch, concertgoing remained a crucial element of his own identity, and the intrusion of politics into the experience of art disappointed him: "As for myself, ... I remain what I always was: a 'bourgeois.'"[42] Bekker, in contrast, established himself as an advocate of an ideal audience and increasingly lost interest in the empirical audience that had to come to terms with these experiments.[43] As noted earlier, Bekker's position was not without its inconsistencies, and his descriptions of concert-hall experiences revealed ideals of silence and direct attention that brought him much closer to the normative discourse of the nineteenth century than they did to the reform movement of the twentieth century to which he wanted to adhere and contribute.

What emerges from these very different observations of seeing, hearing, posture, and so on is that the "semiotic contradiction," as Leppert calls it, between the physical activity of sound-making and the abstract nature of the music itself has traditionally been resolved through "the agency of human sight."[44] "When people hear a musical performance, they see it as an embodied activity," Leppert writes; he underlines that in musical performance it is the eye that connects the listeners to one another and to the performance—by observing how the performers look and behave, what they are wearing, and how they interact. The frequent reports of disturbances or protests against the dimming of the lights and other practices only emphasize how, despite the calls for reform, in the 1920s special importance was attached to the social character of visiting the concert hall. Audiences both nationally minded and bourgeois perceived it as a socialized activity.

Let us now turn to more explicit references to bodily behavior in the concert hall and to its supposed ability to express national traits. Hans Heinz Stuckenschmidt, the very well-known music critic of the *Berliner Zeitung am Mittag* in the 1920s, was determined to detect Germanness in the concert hall by observing bodily behavior. In an article titled "The German in the Concert Hall," he claimed that Germans could nowhere be better described than in the concert hall: "This is the place where the middle-class German soul is unmasked most forcefully and with a brazenness born of being unobserved."[45] Every time he visited a concert hall in Germany, Stuckenschmidt wrote, he was shocked to see how concertgoers behaved and the ways they approached the music. Like many journalists toward the end of the 1920s, his intention was to critique conditions and practices in the concert hall. But what is striking in his description of the listening situation is his use of the listener's body and of visual metaphors to describe a pathological state of the nation:

> I have the impression of a hospital, and one day I knew with certainty that this people would perish by its music, which robs it of the last remnants of self-control, reason, and masculinity, like a vampire, like a dangerous epidemic. That is because the average German's relationship with music is a hopeless sexual dependency.

Stuckenschmidt describes this decay, the loss of control and reason exemplified in the bodily behavior of the individual listener, using the language of pathology:

> The eyes close involuntarily, the spine seems no longer able to support the weight of the skull, so that the hand has to serve as a prop, the posture becomes slack and sickly, the whole body descends into a state of progressive lethargy; it is as if this being had been drained of everything invigorating, everything cohesive, of brain, marrow, and musculature. The worst thing, however, is that this effect is manifested as a contagious mass psychosis that few can elude. Not even the strongest men are spared, and whole generations of music-loving youngsters ruin themselves by the daily exercise of this enervating psychological onanism.[46]

Stuckenschmidt observes the effects of music on the body and describes the listening postures that, for him, expressed what German listening could look like. This correlation between the listener's body and Germanness went back to a certain revived definition of music as an expression of Germanness that must ultimately lead to "German listening." Although Stuckenschmidt criticized the various forms of bodily expressions, and used "the German" as a negative projection surface, he nevertheless remained convinced that the Germans had a special relationship with music, or, as he put it, "It is true that the Germans are an unusually music-loving people."[47] Such essentialist definitions formed the basis for the power that Stuckenschmidt attributed to music in general. As he wrote in another piece, which focused more specifically on music's social effects, music had special powers over the body: "One may, then ..., surely be permitted to think that every human being is, to a certain degree, subjugated to the emotionally releasing power of music." Based on this definition of music's power, he concluded that music was "capable more than any other art of inspiring the listener with enthusiasm for a sensation, thus indirectly also for an idea."[48] Stuckenschmidt even went so far as to claim that the low quality of contemporary German music was the reason for Germany's misery in general and to advise excluding German music from concert programs for one entire year.

For Stuckenschmidt, the concert hall was the site where Germanness was embodied, where it could be heard, felt, and seen. It was his role to observe it and describe it to his readers. Stuckenschmidt did not explicitly articulate thoughts on the sociability of the events that he described as "German," but he assumed a similarity of experience that allowed him to generalize about the audience. In his view, the pathological body was shared by all Germans.

Othering in the Concert Hall: Unity and Difference in Listening

Stuckenschmidt, Bekker, and many other observers of musical life shared an underlying assumption that to go to the concert hall was to find out who one was. But, like other concertgoers, they struggled to bring together ideals of unity and experiences of difference at once. The problem of differences had already become apparent in the utopian conceptions of audiences, but they also became tangible when listening to performances of music from other countries that used musical languages different to those of the German Romantic canon, which had triumphed during World War I, or from a historical epoch not previously represented.[49] Indeed, the journalistic observations of these experiences reveal a certain "self-as-other ethnography," to use a phrase coined by political scientists Susanne and Lloyd Rudolph: "as a participant, an observer, an informant, a narrator, and an author" of such ethnography, the native "constitutes an ethnographic other in constituting an ethnographic self."[50] The observation and analysis of the "other" in the concert hall was pinned down through a combination of the visual and aural experiences that were constructed at the moment of performance. The music these journalists heard, and the audience that they described, was rendered "other" in order to make sense of the changes that were occurring in the concert hall. It offered tools to formulate ideas about belonging, and the journalists' ethnographic self emerged in their reflections on musical experiences in the concert hall with a new urgency during the Weimar Republic.[51]

The issue of audience unity had been called into question for some time, but in the 1920s, especially under the impact of the economic crisis brought on by inflation, there was increasing awareness of a change in its composition. This was illustrated by a number of articles with titles such as "Das neue Publikum" (The new audience), "Reaktivierung des Publikums" (Reactivating the audience), and "Musik und Publikum" (Music and audience). These audience descriptions were usually concerned with the integration of new social groups, the survival of bourgeois traditions, or the effects of music on community building. The Dresden music critic F. A. Geissler feared for the concert season in 1923, worrying that the middle class was underrepresented and would show signs only of poverty, whereas the "foreigners"—the "hard-currency people"— would dominate audiences.[52] Rudolf Kastner of the *Berliner Morgenpost*, who traveled through western German cities in 1920 and saw an internationalization of concert-hall audiences, described the outward changes:

> But German musical life continues nonetheless—indeed, the British, French, and Belgians take part in it with the greatest enthusiasm. In the concert halls and opera houses one sees not only our German women, who always predominate, but also many khaki and red-and-blue uniforms. Under the auspices of Beethoven, Schubert, or Mahler, Wilson's League of Nations, doomed for now to be a utopia, has already become a peaceable reality.[53]

From such a perspective, the "other" could be discerned in the sight of fellow listeners, and the experience of otherness could easily be intensified by the sounds of new compositions entering the newly cosmopolitan concert hall.

The years after the nationalist outbursts of World War I saw a heightened awareness of such visual and aural differences within performances. The reopening of concert programs to composers from other nations after 1918 brought with it a need to contextualize the listening experiences for concertgoers, and this search coincided with the "quest for the origins of music," as Alexander Rehding has termed it, that had been conducted by music ethnologists since the early 1900s.[54] They used biologists' findings on race to explain the superiority of Western musical models. They also identified characteristics of Western music—such as the harmonic system—with the culture of the European continent and as reliant on education, which appeared to be especially widespread in Germany. The language used in these discussions was not restricted to academia but entered the public domain, for example, at the monumental 1927 Frankfurt exhibition *Musik im Leben der Völker* (Music in the life of the peoples), which claimed to be the first world-music exhibition. While this large-scale project aimed to give an overview of musical practices on many different continents and to show the universal role of music, the result was an identification of differences between the civilized and uncivilized nations (*Kulturland* and *Naturvolk*) that was also to be found in the discourse on the experience of contemporary music in the concert halls.

The contemporary music production offered a projection space to connect boundary-drawing and listening to music. The emergence of jazz, vaudeville, folk tunes, church hymns, street noises, and other sound innovations during the regular symphony concert invited commentary and provoked cultural and social explanations. When, for example, American compositions by Aaron Copland or Henry Gilbert that insinuated American folk tunes were performed, the reactions used stereotypes of the wilderness to explain jazz. Journalists complained that these compositions were attempting to cut lose any ties with "European traditions," leading to a music reminiscent of operettas and garden music that would not fulfill the standards of art music.[55] Such a music was an "impossibility for the concert hall," and critics reported laughter in the audience as a way to distance themselves from a performance that was "remarkably different" from the usual.[56]

The construction of cultural, national, and social differences can also be traced to the debate about Arnold Schoenberg and Igor Stravinsky, who were considered the leaders of the musical world in the 1920s. It is worth mentioning this debate in the context of a history of boundary-drawing as the experiences of their music and the images of the composers as public figures were used as vessels to be filled with issues from the social to the religious, from the national to the biological, which were then polarized and grouped around one or the other of these emblematic figures.[57] It becomes evident from most reactions of the early 1920s, for example, that Stravinsky's and Schoenberg's music were often associated with a nature/culture divide, in which Stravinsky was positioned as representing "nature," as opposed to Schoenberg's "culture." For many listeners, it was especially their "naturalness" of expression that stamped all Stravinsky's pieces as masterpieces and made them so enthralling for audiences.[58] Listeners opined that the Russian background to Stravinsky's music explained his attachment to nature and had remained untouched by the periods that he spent in Paris.

Stravinsky's association with nature was substantiated not only by the references to primitives that littered concert reports, but also by attempts to locate the racial origins of his music, primarily through the use of the available ethnic stereotypes. Despite Stravinsky's popularity in the concert halls in the 1920s, he remained a stranger, an outsider, especially as a foil to Schoenberg: "One cannot understand Stravinsky if one looks at him from the angle of German musical culture. ... Arnold Schoenberg draws the boldest and most radical conclusions from German musical culture, but although Stravinsky is not opposed to him as an enemy, even so he is felt to be an antithesis to Stravinsky."[59] Explanations such as these also drew direct connections between the supposedly national connotation and the possibility of listening to their music and illustrate how the nature/culture divide came to be a signifier in the boundary-drawing exercises that allowed community building in the concert hall.

It is important to note how flexible and moldable these imaginations were—and how far removed from what musicologists today believe to be the essence of the works performed. Reflecting on what they had just heard, music journalists used their experiences to establish differences and apply these to ideas of belonging. They added layers of imagination that illustrated their preoccupations, such that imaginations of nature inspired by *Le Sacre* could live on throughout at least the 1920s even though by that time Stravinsky had established a neoclassical style very different from the musical language of that piece. While some layers survived, others could be eliminated, substituted, or added. Stravinsky's allegedly false return to history in his composition could be viewed as another piece of evidence for his complex and heterogeneous identity that was in flux and not fixed by history. His affiliation with Paris could be seen as particularly urban and an expression of civilization or, negatively, as an expression of disruption and distortion. One dominant motif identified Schoenberg as the heir of the German masters and Stravinsky as Russian. The foreign seemed to represent what had gone missing from German concert halls and needed to be recreated. "Stravinsky is a Russian, we are not," Karl Holl stated in 1925.[60] These examples show how ideas about belonging and citizenship, about origin and place, about the need to secure tradition and the uncertainty of the future helped to shape musical experiences and how, in turn, musical experiences helped contemporaries to shape their own views on social issues such as relationships with particular ethnic groups.

Conclusion

The national dimension imbued concert halls in the 1920s at different levels and in different forms. It informed conceptions of audiences, it helped to explain patterns of listening behavior, and it functioned as a cognitive tool to create social meaning. But the specific feature of the 1920s was the competition of the national with other social ideologies: the socialist idea of unifying the audience as a people, the persistence of bourgeois listening styles, or biological and racial modes of differentiation were other tools used to attach meaning to music and legitimize its practice in times of profound crisis. Contemporaries were very aware of the ephemerality of the audience and its fragile nature, but they did not extrapolate from this fragility an ephemerality of the nation. Instead, hopes were expressed that the audience (its composition and its behavioral styles) might be improved precisely in order to stabilize that nation.

Such hopes for reform were soon disappointed. But despite a growing frustration with the lack of success of the reforms, the essentialized view of music as expressing specific national traits—and indeed a German superiority in matters musical—remained largely intact. This was the basis on which the rhetoric of national community in the concert hall was revived and radicalized in new ways in the 1930s. In 1935, music historian Eberhard Preußner claimed that the concert was a "German form" that accommodated the "German nature":

> The concert as a form was very amenable to the German nature. It is no exaggeration to say that the concert, even if it originated outside Germany, only attained its true form in Germany. ... If England chiefly shaped the economic form, France the social side of the concert, it was Germany that made of the concert a form of community.[61]

This analogy between community, music, and Germanness could easily be exploited to foster ideas of the concert hall as an ideal site for the realization of the National Socialist concept of a *Volksgemeinschaft*—an ideal audience that was based on well-established rhetoric and used the imagination to change practices.

In the early twentieth century, the concert hall served as a place to materialize the nation and embody it. A concert experience was a way to answer the questions of what the nation sounded like, how it could be visualized, and how it felt. The concert hall provided a space in which to translate abstract ideas into practice and sensations, and the nation could be experienced there concretely in an array of sometimes contradictory terms. As far as "dreams of Germany" are concerned, a point made by Clifford Geertz seems appropriate here: the concert hall was a place for rituals where the "lived-in order" could "merge with the dreamed-in order," even if this acquired a nightmarish quality for those excluded from such visions.[62]

Hansjakob Ziemer is senior research scholar and head of cooperation and communication at the Max Planck Institute for the History of Science, Berlin. He is the author of Die Moderne hören: Das Konzert als urbanes Forum, 1890–1940 (Frankfurt: Campus, 2008), coeditor (with Daniel Morat) of the Handbuch Sound: Geschichte—Begriffe—Ansätze (Metzler, 2018), and coeditor (with Christian Thorau) of the Oxford Handbook of Music Listening in the 19th and 20th Centuries (Oxford University Press, 2019). He has published widely on the cultural history of emotions, concert life, listening, and journalism.

Notes

1. Karl Storck, *Die kulturelle Bedeutung der Musik: Die Musik als Kulturmacht des seelischen und geistigen Lebens* (Stuttgart, 1906), 33. Here and throughout, all translations are my own unless otherwise attributed.
2. K. Storck, "Krieg und Musikpflege," *Allgemeine Musik-Zeitung* 37, no. 81 (1914): 1127.
3. Michael Geyer, "The Stigma of Violence: Nationalism and War in Twentieth-Century Germany," *German Studies Review* 15 (Winter 1992): 86.
4. Christopher Small, *Musicking: The Meanings of Performing and Listening* (Hanover, NH, 1998), 41. For an enlightening reconsideration of the concept of community,

see Kay Kaufman Shelemay, "Musical Communities: Rethinking the Collective in Music," *Journal of the American Musicological Society* 64, no. 2 (2011): 349–90.
5. Hans Heinz Stuckenschmidt, "Der Deutsche im Konzertsaal," *Weltbühne* 23 (1927): 631–33.
6. Neil Gregor, "Why Does Music Matter?," *German History* 34, no. 1 (2016): 123. On other new approaches to the relationship of nation, nationalism, and music, see, for example, Anthony J. Steinhoff, "Embracing the Grail: Parsifal, Richard Wagner and the German Nation," *German History* 30, no. 3 (2012): 372–94; and Beat Föllmi, ed., *Music and the Construction of National Identities in the 19th Century* (Baden-Baden, 2010).
7. Celia Applegate, "Music among the Historians," *German History* 30, no. 3 (2012): 334.
8. Small, *Musicking*, 143.
9. Arjun Appadurai, *Modernity at Large: Cultural Dimensions of Globalization* (Minneapolis, 1996), 31. On recent use and critique of this concept, see also Carolyn Birdsall, *Nazi Soundscapes: Sound, Technology and Urban Space in Germany, 1933–1945* (Amsterdam, 2012), 105–7.
10. Kurt Westphal, "Das neue Hören," *Melos* 7, no. 7 (1928): 354 (*"wir beherrschen das 19. Jahrhundert noch nicht; es beherrscht zum großen Teil uns."*).
11. For more detail, see Hansjakob Ziemer, "Listening on the Home Front: Music and the Production of Social Meaning in German Concert Halls during World War I," in *Sounds of Modern History: Auditory Cultures in 19th- and 20th-Century Europe*, ed. Daniel Morat (New York, 2014), 201–227.
12. Rudolf Cahn-Speyer, "Der Krieg und die Konzertprogramme," *Allgemeine Musikzeitung* 43, no. 18 (1916): 250.
13. Ibid., 251.
14. Hans Pohl, "*Heldenklage* von Franz Liszt. Zum 2. Freitagskonzert im Museum," *Frankfurter Nachrichten*, 14 November 1914.
15. Ibid.
16. Paul Bekker, *Das deutsche Musikleben* (Berlin, 1916), 8. On the intellectual history of Bekker's thoughts and context, see special issue on "Paul Bekker," *Musik und Ästhetik* 20, no. 77/1 (2016).
17. Bekker, *Das deutsche Musikleben*, 7.
18. Ibid., 66.
19. Marc Weiner, *Undertones of Insurrection: Music, Politics, and the Social Sphere in the Modern German Narrative* (Lincoln, 1993), 50.
20. Bekker, *Das deutsche Musikleben*, 137 and 274.
21. Paul Bekker, *Die Sinfonie von Beethoven bis Mahler* (Berlin, 1918), 35.
22. Bekker, *Das deutsche Musikleben*, 53.
23. Paul Bekker, *Die Weltgeltung der deutschen Musik* (Berlin, 1920). See also Michael P. Steinberg, *The Meaning of the Salzburg Festival: Austria as Theater and Ideology, 1890—1938* (Ithaca, 1990).
24. Hans Pfitzner, *Die neue Ästhetik der musikalischen Impotenz. Ein Verwesungssymptom?* (Munich, 1920), 131.
25. Ibid., 29.
26. Ibid.
27. Peter Franklin, "Audiences, Critics and the Depurification of Music: Reflections on a 1920s Controversy," *Journal of the Royal Musical Association* 114, no. 1 (1989): 80–92.

28. Weiner, *Undertones of Insurrection*, 70. See also, especially, the introduction and chapter 1 for the wider social and political significance of such constructions of meaning.
29. Pfitzner, *Die neue Ästhetik*, 126.
30. Small, *Musicking*, 40. It would be fruitful to compare Bekker's and Pfitzner's concepts with Small's theoretical outline of the audience, but this is beyond the scope of this chapter, which uses Small for theoretical purposes. For a contextualization of Bekker in his sociological thinking, see also Hansjakob Ziemer, "Klang der Gesellschaft: zur Soziologisierung des Klangs im Konzert, 1900–1933," in *Auditive Medienkulturen: Techniken des Hörens und Praktiken der Klanggestaltung*, ed. Axel Volmar and Jens Schröter (Bielefeld, 2013), 145–63.
31. Gerald Feldman, *The Great Disorder: Politics, Economics, and Society in the German Inflation, 1914–1924* (New York, 1993), 858.
32. For recent reinterpretation of the intellectual debates in the Weimar Republic, see Matthew Pritchard, "Who Killed the Concert? Heinrich Besseler and the Inter-War Politics of Gebrauchsmusik," *Twentieth-Century Music* 8 no. 1 (2011): 29–48.
33. Small, *Musicking*, 62.
34. Ibid., 61.
35. See, for example, Peter Gay, *The Naked Heart* (New York, 1995).
36. See Katharine Ellis, "Who Cares if You Listen? Researching Audience Behavior(s) in Nineteenth-Century Paris," in *The Oxford Handbook of Music Listening in the 19th and 20th Centuries*, ed. Christian Thorau and Hansjakob Ziemer (New York, 2019): 37–54.
37. Martin Thrun, "Der Sturz ins Jetzt des Augenblicks: Macht und Ohnmacht 'ästhetischer Polizei' im Konzert nach 1900," in *Kommunikation im Musikleben: Harmonien und Dissonanzen im 20. Jahrhundert*, ed. Sven Oliver Müller, Jürgen Osterhammel, and Martin Rempe (Göttingen, 2015), 42–68.
38. Paul Bekker, "Volkskonzert im Frankfurter Opernhaus," *Frankfurter Zeitung*, 1 March 1919.
39. Ibid.
40. Paul Hirsch to Paul Bekker, 28 February 1919, Paul Bekker Collection, MSS 50, Irving S. Gilmore Music Library, Yale University, New Haven (hereafter, Bekker Collection).
41. Ibid.
42. Paul Hirsch to Paul Bekker, 28 May 1919, Bekker Collection.
43. Andreas Eichhorn, *Paul Bekker: Facetten eines kritischen Geistes* (Hildesheim, 2002), 360.
44. Richard Leppert, "The Social Discipline of Listening," in *Le concert et son public: Mutations de la vie musicale en Europe de 1780 à 1914 (France, Allemagne, Angleterre)*, ed. Hans Erich Bödeker, Patrice Veit, and Michael Werner (Paris, 2002), 466.
45. Stuckenschmidt, "Der Deutsche im Konzertsaal," 631.
46. Ibid.
47. Ibid., 633.
48. Hans Heinz Stuckenschmidt, "Musik und Publikum," *Europäische Revue* 5 (1929), 187.
49. For an informative discussion of the complexities of national identity in programming, see William Weber, "Cosmopolitan, National, and Regional Identities in Eighteenth-Century European Musical Life," in *The Oxford Handbook of the New Cultural History of Music*, ed. Jane Fulcher (Oxford, 2011), 209–28. For a recent overview of the

relationship of the universal and the national in Weimar Germany, see Daniel Laqua, "Exhibiting, Encountering and Studying Music in Interwar Europe: Between National and International Community," *European Studies*, no. 32 (2014): 207–23.
50. Susanne Hoeber Rudolph and Lloyd I. Rudolph, eds., *Reversing the Gaze: Amar Singh's Diary, A Colonial Subject's Narrative of Imperial India* (New Delhi, 2000), 38.
51. See also Wolfgang Kaschuba, *Einführung in die Europäische Ethnologie* (Munich, 1999), 107.
52. F. A. Geissler, "Das neue Publikum," *Die Musik* 15, no. 2 (1923): 873–76.
53. Rudolf Kastner, "Westdeutsche Musikstädte," *Anbruch* 2, no. 11–12 (1920), 430–31.
54. Alexander Rehding, "The Quest for the Origins of Music in Germany circa 1900," *Journal of the American Musicological Society* 53, no. 2 (2000): 345–85.
55. F. Müller-Rehrmann, "Fünftes Musikfest," *Königsberger Hartungsche Zeitung*, 19 July 1927.
56. Ibid.
57. For a detailed elaboration of this example, see Hansjakob Ziemer, "Opferstiere und Barbaren im Konzert: Zu einer historischen Anthropologie des Musikhörens der 1920er Jahre," in *Geschichte und Gegenwart des musikalischen Hörens: Diskurse—Geschichte(n)—Poetiken*, ed. Klaus Aringer, Franz Karl Praßl, Peter Revers, and Christian Utz (Freiburg, 2017), esp. 264–68.
58. Hans Walter Draber, "Igor Strawinsky," *Neue Zürcher Zeitung*, 9 November 1925.
59. Adolf Weißmann, "Strawinsky," *Musikblätter des Anbruch* 6, no. 6 (1924): 230.
60. Karl Holl, "Strawinsky: Zusammenhänge und Eindrücke," *Frankfurter Zeitung*, 29 November 1925 ("*Stravinsky ist Russe, wir sind es nicht.*").
61. Eberhard Preußner, *Die bürgerliche Musikkultur: Ein Beitrag zur deutschen Musikgeschichte des 18. Jahrhunderts* (Kassel, 1935), 30.
62. Quoted in Small, *Musicking*, 95.

Bibliography

Appadurai, Arjun. *Modernity at Large: Cultural Dimensions of Globalization*. Minneapolis: University of Minnesota Press, 1996.
Applegate, Cecilia. "Music among the Historians." *German History* 30, no. 3 (2012): 329–49.
Bekker, Paul. *Das deutsche Musikleben*. Berlin: Schuster & Loeffler, 1916.
———. *Die Sinfonie von Beethoven bis Mahler*. Berlin: Schuster & Loeffler, 1918.
———. "Volkskonzert im Frankfurter Opernhaus." *Frankfurter Zeitung*, 1 March 1919.
———. *Die Weltgeltung der deutschen Musik*. Berlin: Schuster & Loeffler, 1920.
Birdsall, Carolyn. *Nazi Soundscapes: Sound, Technology and Urban Space in Germany, 1933–1945*. Amsterdam: Amsterdam University Press, 2012.
Cahn-Speyer, Rudolf. "Der Krieg und die Konzertprogramme." *Allgemeine Musikzeitung* 43, no. 18 (1916): 249–51.
Draber, Hans Walter. "Igor Strawinsky." *Neue Zürcher Zeitung*, 9 November 1925.

Ehrenreich, Nathan. "Strawinsky-Nachklänge." *Volksstimme* (Frankfurt), 5 February 1926.
Eichhorn, Andreas. *Paul Bekker: Facetten eines kritischen Geistes.* Hildesheim: Georg Olms Verlag, 2002.
Eksteins, Modris. *Rites of Spring: The Great War and the Birth of the Modern Age.* Boston, MA: Houghton Mifflin, 1989.
Ellis, Katharine. "Who Cares if You Listen? Researching Audience Behavior(s) in Nineteenth-Century Paris." In *The Oxford Handbook of Music Listening in the 19th and 20th Centuries,* edited by Christian Thorau and Hansjakob Ziemer, 37–54. New York: Oxford University Press, 2019.
Feldman, Gerald. *The Great Disorder: Politics, Economics, and Society in the German Inflation, 1914–1924.* New York: Oxford University Press, 1993.
Föllmi, Beat, ed. *Music and the Construction of National Identities in the 19th Century.* Baden-Baden: Koerner, 2010.
Franklin, Peter. "Audiences, Critics and the Depurification of Music: Reflections on a 1920s Controversy." *Journal of the Royal Musical Association* 114, no. 1 (1989): 80–92.
Gay, Peter. *The Naked Heart.* New York: Norton, 1995.
Geissler, F. A. "Das neue Publikum." *Die Musik* 15, no. 2 (1923): 873–76.
Geyer, Michael. "The Stigma of Violence: Nationalism and War in Twentieth-Century Germany." *German Studies Review* 15 (Winter 1992): 75–110.
Gregor, Neil. "Why Does Music Matter?" *German History* 34, no. 1 (2016): 113–30.
Holl, Karl. "Strawinsky: Zusammenhänge und Eindrücke." *Frankfurter Zeitung,* 29 November 1925.
Kaschuba, Wolfgang. *Einführung in die Europäische Ethnologie.* Munich: C. H. Beck, 1999.
Kastner, Rudolf. "Westdeutsche Musikstädte." *Anbruch* 2, no. 11–12 (1920): 430–33.
"Konzerte." *Neue Zürcher Zeitung,* 13 November 1925.
Laqua, Daniel. "Exhibiting, Encountering and Studying Music in Interwar Europe: Between National and International Community." *European Studies,* no. 32 (2014): 207–23.
Leppert, Richard. "The Social Discipline of Listening." In *Le concert et son public: Mutations de la vie musicale en Europe de 1780 à 1914 (France, Allemagne, Angleterre),* edited by Hans Erich Bödeker, Patrice Veit, and Michael Werner, 459–85. Paris: Éd. de la Maison des Sciences de l'Homme, 2002.
Meisterbernd, Max. "Das Frankfurter Strawinsky-Fest." *Frankfurter Nachrichten,* 27 November 1925.
Pfitzner, Hans. *Die neue Ästhetik der musikalischen Impotenz. Ein Verwesungssymptom?* Munich: Verlag der Süddeutschen Monatshefte, 1920.
Pisling, Siegmund. "Konzertchronik: Neue Musik." *Berliner Börsen-Zeitung,* 24 November 1922.
Pohl, Hans. "Heldenklage von Franz Liszt. Zum 2. Freitagskonzert im Museum." *Frankfurter Nachrichten,* 14 November 1914.

Preußner, Eberhard. *Die bürgerliche Musikkultur: Ein Beitrag zur deutschen Musikgeschichte des 18. Jahrhunderts.* Kassel: Hanseatische Verlagsanstalt, 1935.
Pringsheim, Hermann. "Die deutsche Musik der Gegenwart." *Berliner Tageblatt*, 3 December 1925.
Pritchard, Matthew. "Who Killed the Concert? Heinrich Besseler and the Inter-War Politics of *Gebrauchsmusik*." *Twentieth-Century Music* 8, no. 1 (2011): 29–48.
Rehding, Alexander. "The Quest for the Origins of Music in Germany circa 1900." *Journal of the American Musicological Society* 53, no. 2 (2000): 345–85.
Rudolph, Susanne Hoeber, and Lloyd I. Rudolph, eds. *Reversing the Gaze: Amar Singh's Diary, A Colonial Subject's Narrative of Imperial India.* New Delhi: Oxford University Press, 2000.
Shelemay, Kay Kaufman. "Musical Communities: Rethinking the Collective in Music." *Journal of the American Musicological Society* 64, no. 2 (2011): 349–90.
Small, Christopher. *Musicking: The Meanings of Performing and Listening.* Hanover, NH: Wesleyan University Press, 1998.
Steinberg, Michael P. *The Meaning of the Salzburg Festival: Austria as Theater and Ideology, 1890–1938.* Ithaca, NY: Cornell University Press, 1990.
Steinhoff, Anthony J. "Embracing the Grail: Parsifal, Richard Wagner and the German Nation." *German History* 30, no. 3 (2012): 372–94.
Storck, Karl. *Die kulturelle Bedeutung der Musik: Die Musik als Kulturmacht des seelischen und geistigen Lebens.* Stuttgart: Greiner & Pfeiffer, 1906.
———. "Krieg und Musikpflege." *Allgemeine Musik-Zeitung* 37, no. 81 (1914): 1127–29.
Stuckenschmidt, Hans Heinz. "Der Deutsche im Konzertsaal." *Weltbühne* 23 (1927): 631–33.
———. "Musik und Publikum." *Europäische Revue* 5 (1929): 186–97.
Thrun, Martin. "Der Sturz ins Jetzt des Augenblicks: Macht und Ohnmacht 'ästhetischer Polizei' im Konzert nach 1900." In *Kommunikation im Musikleben: Harmonien und Dissonanzen im 20. Jahrhundert*, edited by Sven Oliver Müller, Jürgen Osterhammel, and Martin Rempe, 42–68. Göttingen: Vandenhoeck & Ruprecht, 2015.
Weber, William. "Cosmopolitan, National, and Regional Identities in Eighteenth-Century European Musical Life." In *The Oxford Handbook of the New Cultural History of Music*, edited by Jane Fulcher, 209–28. Oxford: Oxford University Press, 2011.
Weiner, Marc. *Undertones of Insurrection: Music, Politics, and the Social Sphere in the Modern German Narrative.* Lincoln: University of Nebraska Press, 1993.
Weißmann, Adolf. "Strawinsky." *Musikblätter des Anbruch* 6, no. 6 (1924): 228–34.
———. "Igor Strawinsky." *Blätter der Staatsoper* 5, no. 8 (1925): 2–7.
Westphal, Kurt. "Das neue Hören." *Melos* 7, no. 7 (1928): 352–54.
Ziemer, Hansjakob. "Homo Europaeus Musicus: Musikwissenschaftler, Musik und kulturelle Identität im ersten Drittel des 20. Jahrhunderts." In *Der Europäer—ein*

Konstrukt: Wissensbestände, Diskurse, Praktiken, edited by Kiran Klaus Patel and Veronika Lipphardt, 33–57. Göttingen: Wallstein, 2009.

———. "Klang der Gesellschaft: zur Soziologisierung des Klangs im Konzert, 1900–1933." In *Auditive Medienkulturen: Techniken des Hörens und Praktiken der Klanggestaltung*, edited by Axel Volmar and Jens Schröter, 145–63. Bielefeld: transcript, 2013.

———. "Listening on the Home Front: Music and the Production of Social Meaning in German Concert Halls during World War I." In *Sounds of Modern History: Auditory Cultures in 19th- and 20th-Century Europe*, edited by Daniel Morat, 201–27. New York: Berghahn, 2014.

———. "Opferstiere und Barbaren im Konzert: Zu einer historischen Anthropologie des Musikhörens der 1920er Jahre." In *Geschichte und Gegenwart des musikalischen Hörens: Diskurse—Geschichte(n)—Poetiken*, edited by Klaus Aringer, Franz Karl Praßl, Peter Revers, and Christian Utz, 257–75. Freiburg: Rombach, 2017.

CHAPTER 2

"Music Made in Hamburg"
How One City's Music Scene Helped Make Rock and Roll the Lingua Franca of Youth

JULIA SNEERINGER

When one speaks of the Germans as "the people of music," rock and roll is generally not the genre that springs to mind. Indeed, critics have typically described German contributions to the genre as minimal at best and derivative at worst, even casting rock and roll as a marker of West Germany's "quasi-colonial" relationship to the United States.[1] Yet one German place did make a critical contribution to rock's evolution: Hamburg. Starting in 1960 in its portside district, St Pauli, young bands from Britain—including the Beatles—were hired by local nightclubs to entertain tourists. Intrepid young Germans soon joined in to experience the thrill of rock and roll at a time when this "jungle music" had been driven underground. By 1962, with the opening of the Star Club, the scene drew thousands each weekend. In 1964, the year of Beatlemania, Hamburg garnered worldwide attention as the "cradle of the Beatles." St Pauli brought musicians and fans together who used rock and roll to live out their dreams—dreams of stardom, of physical liberation, of relief from an oppressive national identity. Hamburg's innovative role consisted not of the production of a new German music, but of the incubation of a new style that fused rock's sneer with art-school adventurousness and modernist aesthetics. This synthesis of Anglo-American music and German visual style, which traveled the world through the "pop explosion" of Beatlemania, helped rock and roll transcend its proletarian origins and evolve into an artistically ambitious cross-class, transnational *lingua franca* of youth in the 1960s.[2]

Affirming Sven Oliver Müller's call for historians of music to move away from debates over aesthetics toward investigation of the experiences and practices of participants,[3] this chapter explores the activities of British Beat (as rock and roll was rechristened) musicians and their German fans in early 1960s Hamburg.[4] It is inspired by Christopher Small's concept of "musicking": the idea that the meanings of music lie "in action, what people do."[5] This is particularly useful for thinking about the social history of rock and roll, a music whose meanings only fully come alive through performance. This essay treats music-making as a communal activity and system of communication between performers and audiences, using participants' memories and archival sources to explore the meanings of music in the "Hamburg scene."[6]

This scene incubated in the sweaty, smoky spaces of St Pauli's Beat clubs, which erased the distance between performer and audience. These spaces forged an affective community built around a shared love of an American music. But what they created went beyond mere imitation: participants added their own impulses, acting as cultural producers in their own right.[7] Unlike the use of music (particularly forms now called "classical") by earlier generations of Germans to forge a national identity, in the postwar context rock and Beat music offered an idea of community that *transcended* nation for a generation born to a world nearly destroyed by German nationalism. Participants pursued liberation through encounters with the Other and the body, not *Bildung*. This foreshadowed the counterculture's flight from Germanness through rock, even if participants would deny any intention to upend existing political or economic relations.[8] Indeed, their use of commodities to fashion identities put them in the vanguard of consumer capitalism. Yet their use of spaces free of parental supervision helped erode the era's sexual conservatism and social conformity, with effects that reverberated into the late 1960s and beyond.[9] Their counter-world harnessed the international impulses that flowed through the port city of Hamburg, creating moments of utopia that celebrated the joys of amplified sound and physical connection in a place where the pleasures of the body were the coin of the realm.

Dreams of Fun in the "Anchorage of Joy"

Postwar Hamburg makes a rich site for exploring the theme of this volume—dreams of Germany expressed through musical cultures. After 1949, with Berlin isolated and divided, Hamburg became the Federal Republic's largest city. Its port was a key engine of German economic recovery. As West Germany's media capital, Hamburg served (and marketed itself) as the exemplar of a new German identity rooted in liberalism, commerce, and cosmopolitanism. Yet Hamburg, known as much for St Pauli's hedonism as for merchant capitalism, was simultaneously *unlike* any other German place. It had always been outward looking, with strong ties to England in particular.[10] St Pauli had centuries-long traditions of popular entertainment and sexual commerce only briefly disrupted by Nazi rule and Allied bombing.[11] The 1950s saw the popularity of its main mile, the Reeperbahn, soar as postwar privations receded and record numbers of tourists flocked to this "anchorage of joy" (*Ankerplatz der Freude*). If the official tenor of the Adenauer era (1949–63) emphasized hard work and a return to respectability for the disgraced nation, St Pauli contributed to recovery by serving as the nation's id. Punters went there to manage feelings of loss or stress by drinking themselves silly in faux-Bavarian beer halls or gawking at mud-wrestling amazons and "lingerie shows." They came to partake in the kind of revelry they saw in movies starring local son Hans Albers, such as the postwar hits *Grosse Freiheit Nr. 7* and *Auf der Reeperbahn nachts um halb eins*. Striptease and open prostitution attracted curiosity-seekers—male and female, gay and straight, black and white.[12]

Live music had long provided the soundtrack to this bacchanalia, so when rock and roll emerged around 1956, it seemed logical that it would join the local entertainment roster. But this music's path into Germany was rocky. While Elvis Presley enthralled some youths, he provoked hostility in the press and the pulpit. Between 1956 and 1958, violence at Bill Haley's concerts or showings of films like *Rock around the Clock* led this "degenerate music" to be effectively banished from German airwaves.[13] Resourceful fans could sometimes catch snatches of it on American or British Forces radio or on Radio Luxembourg, Europe's first commercial pop station. In Hamburg, social divisions consigned rock and roll—coded as lascivious, proletarian, and racially Other—to jukeboxes in working-class bars or the carnival midway. Records were scarce: one fan was told by a retailer, "No, ... there [are] no Chuck Berry records in Germany because the gentleman [is] in prison in the US."[14] Labels put their weight instead behind German-language remakes and *Schlager*—popular songs (without syncopated rhythms) that conveyed wholesome, nostalgic themes, sung in German. *Schlager* dominated the charts well into the 1960s, while American-made rock and roll became a niche taste primarily among working-class young men.[15]

Before 1960, West Germany's few rock and roll venues were clustered around US military installations.[16] Hamburg, in contrast, was a bastion of jazz, particularly Dixieland or "trad" jazz, which functioned well as the soundtrack to a night out and carried a sexually charged exoticism that fit into both St Pauli's traditions of racialized display and its modern adult entertainment landscape.[17] Jazz also provided openings into rock and roll (indeed, Germans initially used the terms interchangeably). Both offered licensed deviancy from the norm. Both represented decades-long engagement with African-American musical forms, which German fans invested with dreams of cultural reinvigoration.[18] Both were seen by acolytes as "authentic" music played with "real feeling," unlike kitschy, mass-produced *Schlager*.[19] While rock fans had few places in which to consume their music publicly in the late fifties, jazz became increasingly respectable and accessible, appealing particularly to middle-class intellectuals and students.[20] The latter's presence in Hamburg jazz clubs attracted notice as the harbinger of a new market force: youth.[21]

While youths shared in the prosperity generated by the Economic Miracle, few nightclub owners initially saw their potential as consumers.[22] One who did was Bruno Koschmider, an ex-circus performer who landed after the war in St Pauli. There he ran the down-market Indra strip club and a grindhouse cinema called the Bambi Kino. Koschmider also dealt in jukeboxes, which exposed him to youths' musical tastes. In late 1959 he opened a "dance palace for youth" called the Kaiserkeller in the Grosse Freiheit, just off the Reeperbahn. This street's name referred to the freedom of trade and religion granted there in the seventeenth century; by 1960 it was *the* address for St Pauli's most risqué entertainments, particularly transvestite revues and striptease. At number 36, while couples whirled to dance orchestras upstairs at the Lido ballroom, Koschmider experimented in the basement. Live shows of trad jazz and *Schlager* found few takers, so Koschmider tried rock and roll—fitting music for a subterranean venue in a disreputable street. He installed a jukebox stocked with American 45s. He booked Dutch-Indonesian show bands that played frenetic rock instrumentals laced with Hawaiian and *Krontjong* elements.[23] These "Indorockers" with their flashy suits and acrobatic moves went over well, but they did not come cheap, so Koschmider kept searching for cheaper ways to stand out from the competition.

He found one in England, whose skiffle craze produced a crop of young rockers with dreams of playing professionally. Skiffle was a musical hybrid of African-American folk and blues mixed with "country" elements such as washboard percussion. It was popularized by Lonnie Donegan, whose hyperkinetic charisma, combined with skiffle's easy-to-play aspect, inspired boys and girls all over to Britain to take up the guitar in 1957 and 1958. Some, such as John Lennon and Norwich's Tony Sheridan, evolved into rock and rollers.[24] Koschmider also found talent when Liverpool's grandly named Royal Caribbean Steel Band spread the word about the money to be made playing in Hamburg. This piqued the interest of Allan Williams, who managed several Liverpool bands. In the spring of 1960 he met Koschmider at London's 2i's Coffee Bar and arranged residencies for his bands in St Pauli; Koschmider signed up 2i's acts as well. This became a good deal for all involved. The bands got steady work and could kick the can of adulthood further down the road. While a few had midlevel careers in Britain (such as Sheridan), most went from playing local dances to logging all-nighters on Europe's most sinful mile. Koschmider got competent, if unpolished, bands that could sing rock and roll in its native tongue—something fans demanded as a marker of quality and fidelity to the original.[25] And these young Brits came cheap. The Beatles played their first of over 250 nights in Hamburg in August 1960 at the Indra, then the Kaiserkeller, where they and other British acts built a vibrant local fan base for live rock and roll.[26]

The Kaiserkeller's success spawned a wave of other new venues in St Pauli. Twenty-one-year-old Peter Eckhorn converted the hippodrome his family had operated for decades at Reeperbahn 136 into the Top Ten; its large capacity and location on the main drag appealed to audiences put off by the sleazier Grosse Freiheit. Young entrepreneur Peter Denk later opened Club O.K., while the Hit Club opened in the former Ahoi cinema. Even Reeperbahn fixture Kaffeehaus Menke converted its basement into a Beat club. The scene's crown jewel was the Star Club, which opened in April 1962 in the former Stern-Kino at Grosse Freiheit 39. "Beat shacks" (as the local press dubbed them) were replacing older, proletarian-identified amusements like hippodromes as well as movie theaters, which were dying in droves as West Germans increasingly abandoned them for television.[27] The youth market was expanding, along with the market for sexualized entertainment. Indeed, several Beat clubs were underwritten by profits from the sexual commerce sector. Manfred Weissleder, for example, initially acquired the Star Club space as a fire exit for his Erotic Night Club and tapped his strip clubs for cash to cover Star Club expenses.[28] The entrepreneurs who opened these clubs did so to make money (though Weissleder evolved into a fierce advocate for an intelligent, ambitious youth culture). Yet the spaces they set up became lifelines to young people dreaming of alternatives to the period's sanitized pop music.

Dreams of Success, Dreams of Freedom: British Musicians in Hamburg

Many of the Brits hired to play in Hamburg hailed from Liverpool, itself a port city with rich cultures of making and listening to music, awash in black and white sounds from North America.[29] Most of these working-class or lower-middle-class musicians had never been outside Liverpool, much less abroad. Thus St Pauli, with its culture of sex, sleaze, and speed, represented not only an opportunity to play professionally but a school of life. Looking back after fifty years, they often invoke the language of dreams to describe Hamburg. Dressed in his school blazer, seventeen-year-old Gibson Kemp boarded a plane in 1962 to play drums at the Star Club for Rory Storm & the Hurricanes and, later, Kingsize Taylor & the Dominoes. "I went out of Liverpool once when I was on holiday to Wales. I'd never even been to Manchester."[30] He was blown away by the Reeperbahn, which he long mistook for Hamburg's main street, so little did he see of the rest of the city. While Kemp did not grow up poor (his father was a mechanical engineer), he described the Liverpool of his youth as "bomb sites and ration cards." Harold MacMillan's boast that Britons had "never had it so good" notwithstanding, Kemp and his generation remember the period as drab.[31] In contrast, Hamburg, which Kemp first saw from the air (Weissleder paid for his acts to fly over), "was just a dream, a complete dream." Liverpool had not come close to recovering from German bombing or postwar recession, while Hamburg's Economic Miracle was in full flower. Mary McGlory, bassist with the all-female Liverbirds, echoes this dream motif, stating that in 1964 her group had offers to go to America in the wake of Beatlemania, but chose Hamburg because it was "a dream of everybody in Liverpool to get that Star Club sticker on their guitar case."[32] A gig at the Star Club meant good wages, camaraderie, and street cred.[33] If Germany had been the land of Hitler for their elders, for these young Brits it became a place where dreams of stardom could come true.

Hamburg also offered the dream of freedom, particularly sexual freedom. At a time when marriage and fertility patterns in West Germany and Britain still resembled those of the conservative fifties,[34] St Pauli offered a smorgasbord of sexual opportunities. Local sex workers became fans, showering bands with drinks, meals, and sexual freebies.[35] Other fans, female and male, showed their musical appreciation sexually;[36] still others allowed musicians a more limited range of physical intimacies in exchange for the status of "girlfriend." Male musicians frequently highlight sex as a key aspect of their experience of Hamburg. Pete Best, the Beatles' first drummer, wrote in 2001, "birds, ready willing and able, were vying for our attention everywhere. … Hamburg was a young man's dream—we were surrounded by it and it was available around the clock."[37] John Lennon also had sex in mind when he famously quipped, "I was born in Liverpool but grew up on the Reeperbahn."

Such adventuring was to be expected from unchaperoned youths, many of whom (though not all) were virgins when they left home. But the timing of their tenure in Hamburg also had distinct historical aspects. They were the first British cohort not required to do military service, allowing them, as Cynthia Powell Lennon wrote, to be truly "youthful and unafraid."[38] St Pauli was also a particularly charged place to come of age sexually. Green youths encountered not just sexually available fans or sex for hire but non-normative sexualities on full display. Beatle Stu Sutcliffe wrote to his sister about how popular he had become with both local females and gay men, "who tell me I'm the sweetest, most beautiful boy. … When in Liverpool I would never have dreamt I could possibly speak to one without shuddering. As it is, I find the one or two I speak to more interesting and entertaining than any others."[39] The notion that Hamburg's atmosphere of sexual freedom expanded these young musicians' horizons more generally surfaces frequently in their memories. Kemp sums it up with characteristic Liverpool wit:

> Sex—in all its forms, the discovery thereof … [—was] the biggest single element that contributed to this so-called musical [revolution]. … Beat music, the incompetent copying of good American music, was the soundtrack to it. My

theory is that suddenly, there was a vehicle for young people to go and sort of let loose, out of parental control. And this new hypnotic Beat music ... was sexy, there were these young kids onstage who played good, and if they didn't play good they weren't allowed to play. And suddenly there was a whole sort of new mood. ... Between ... 1960 and 1970 the whole world changed. And music was a part of changing it.[40]

Even if such nostalgia glosses over unpleasant realities such as unplanned pregnancy, sexually transmitted disease, or men's frequent indifference to women's pleasure, Beat music became linked for participants with personal, physical liberation well in advance of the so-called sexual revolution. The cradle of that emotion was the music clubs, a counter-world that gave direct access to sensations of pleasure and happiness.[41] At a time when young people were caught between the dominant culture's demands for propriety and consumer capitalism's stimulation of all kinds of desires, musicians in the Hamburg scene could live out desire in a place of exile from the constraints of home.[42]

Dreams of Transcendence: German Fans

The Germans that came to cheer on these musicians dreamed of escape from their own country's culture of restraint. Growing up in 1950s West Germany, they had been socialized to believe that obedience was the child's first duty and family the only bulwark against chaos and communism. While democracy was the order of the day in politics, family life remained patriarchal and undemocratic—a poor fit with the general skepticism of adolescence and the particular skepticism of this generation, which had grown up under the cloud of potential nuclear annihilation and the Nazi past.[43] At the same time as parents and teachers prioritized security, economic expansion provided young women and men unprecedented access to higher education, social mobility, and disposable income in a consumer culture that encouraged mild indulgence.[44] Hamburg's music clubs became the perfect stage on which the drama of coming-of-age could play out among those desiring alternatives to the dominant culture. For those seeking "authenticity" and emotional truth, Beat music became a vehicle for self-discovery.

Audiences at the Kaiserkeller's first rock and roll shows were filled less with music fans than with St Pauli's typical rough mix of sailors, tourists, and workers in the entertainment economy. They sought release through dance, drink, and sex; as long as the music was wild, they did not care much about its content. But they were soon joined by others who did: working-class rockers, devotees of Elvis and Gene Vincent who made the club home for their spectacular subculture. They loved the music's punch, just as they loved fighting and posing in their black leather—"*they* were the stars," as photographer Jürgen

Vollmer put it.⁴⁵ Vollmer moved in a competing subculture of bourgeois students and young artists frequently dubbed "Exis" (Existentialists) for their "continental" look. Their black sweaters, androgynous haircuts, and preference for non-German music (French *chanson*, cool jazz) announced their own alienation from prevailing style and gender codes.

The Exis insinuated themselves into the Kaiserkeller audience in late 1960 after one of them, Klaus Voormann, chanced upon the club. Floored by the pounding beat and loose-limbed charisma of the band on stage, Voormann was instantly converted. He soon dragged along his friends Vollmer and Astrid Kirchherr, who was initially afraid to visit this disreputable street. And not without reason: she and her friends were easily identifiable as bourgeois, making them vulnerable to Rocker violence. But the lure of the music proved stronger than class anxiety as they staked out space at the club and became tolerated by the Rockers. They crossed another boundary—that of nation—when they became confidantes of the British musicians.

While many German fans moved through the Hamburg scene, Kirchherr was distinctly important for the ways she scrambled boundaries of class, gender, and nation through the aesthetic impulses she brought to the Hamburg scene.⁴⁶ She became famous for the black-and-white portraits she took of the Beatles in the early 1960s while apprenticing for Reinhard Wolf. Wolf was a successful advertising photographer who brought Kirchherr into the worlds of high fashion and Hamburg's gay elite.⁴⁷ She fused these influences with her own predilection for black and leather into a homemade bohemian style: "I just wanted to look different."⁴⁸ While Kirchherr responded to the music's beat on her first Kaiserkeller visit, it was the bands' visual aspect that sealed the attraction. She has spoken repeatedly of the "beauty" she saw on stage: she saw this gritty world through an aesthetic lens. It is not surprising she was most drawn to Sutcliffe, himself an artist with a strong sense of style (signaled, for example, by the black sunglasses he wore onstage). With earnest exuberance, she wove together impulses from high art and rock and roll, often using her lover Sutcliffe as her model. She dragged Wolf out to the Beat clubs, which Pop painter Eduardo Paolozzi (Sutcliffe's eventual tutor at the Hamburg College of Art) also visited with his students.⁴⁹ Kirchherr's skills as a photographer and designer made her a natural chronicler and stylist for musicians in the Hamburg scene.⁵⁰ She played with gender conventions by feminizing the men—for example, styling Stu's hair like her own, a look that later traveled the world as the Beatle mop top. She also masculinized the women, taking the Liverbirds from skirts and blouses to leather vests and trousers, giving them the gender neutrality of the male rocker who is free to just "get on with it."⁵¹ At a time when rock and roll was the epitome of *Unkultur*, Kirchherr saw art in it. While art-school dropout John Lennon strove to hide his artistic side behind a Rocker quiff and Hitler jokes, he and other Liverpool musicians drank in the impulses from their

German friends. Kemp declared that "from Astrid I learned the ability to think outside the limited horizon of the Liverpool box, appreciation of art, books, food, creases on your kecks and snogging properly."[52] Sharing enthusiasms and intimacies in their schoolbook English, Kirchherr and the Exis redefined Germany for the young Brits, who shed the anti-German prejudices they had grown up with.[53] Through their German friends, they learned to dream of broader possibilities for their music, and for themselves.

Kirchherr made a unique contribution by deploying the new impulses Beat music provided for what was essentially a grand art project with youth as its canvas. In another sense, however, Kirchherr was emblematic of her generation. Economic prosperity was weakening traditional milieus and giving young people unprecedented access to goods with which to fashion new identities and alliances. Such activities constituted an assertion of cultural power as a democratic right open to all who wished to claim it.[54] Fans' active role in this process was a crucial element in a larger transition away from the prevailing youth culture, conceived of by adults and designed to protect youth from "smut" and "moral dangers," to a new one generated by youth for youth. Music fans' consumption practices illustrated what David Chaney calls "a mode of radical democratization that put pursuit of pleasure at the heart of citizenship," especially if we accept a definition of citizenship that encompasses the right to speak through style and claim public space.[55]

These processes were not unique to Hamburg: youth-oriented consumer culture was on the march across the industrialized world and the rock–art school nexus was gathering its own momentum in Britain.[56] But certain elements were distinctly German. These modes of consumption advanced Germany's opening to the West. The use of English served key functions too as a sign of musical authenticity and a mark of "belonging" among fans of all classes who incorporated it into daily speech (a gesture that made particular sense in anglophiliac Hamburg).[57] English was also the language of the black American musicians revered by fans. Embracing it—and rock and roll in general—allowed young Germans to distance themselves from what Horst Fascher called the "old Nazis" who had once banned swing and now demonized rock.[58] Young Germans' avid consumption of Americanized popular culture both rode and drove their country's nascent shift toward a postmodern mass culture dominated by consumerism and mass media, promoting individualism and new, informal modes of behavior inimical to the spirit of authoritarianism still lingering in post-Nazi Germany.[59]

Conclusion

Considering the broader meanings of the Hamburg scene, we can see that while participants fervently embraced the Now, their actions also fall within certain cultural and historical continuities. The scene emerged out of a long line of entrepreneurial experimentation in the field of mass entertainment, with the new angle of catering to youth in an area known for adult-oriented sexual spectacle. It was also part of a long German engagement with African American musical forms and a simultaneous rejection by some of German-made popular music as emotionally inauthentic and redolent of a toxic nationalism.[60] Looking forward, the creative explosion in Hamburg's Beat music clubs was an early manifestation of the transnational imagined community of youth that historians call the "global sixties."[61] Detlef Siegfried sees the Hamburg scene as a catalyst of the student movement and liberalization processes more broadly, as the unconventional styles and ideas generated there gained national circulation through the city's powerful media outlets.[62]

Although the Beat clubs were born out of capitalist impulses, the cultural exchanges they facilitated transcended those mundane origins, generating "a democratic politics of self-invention from below."[63] What Gibson Kemp offhandedly dubbed "the incompetent copying of good American music" by Liverpool kids for German audiences actually meant a great deal more: respite from the weight of Germanness. At the same time, Germanness inflected who they were and what they brought to the scene, as exemplified by Kirchherr's seriousness and craft—the modernist blacks and whites as opposed to England's dull grays. The confidence she and her circle showed in the British musicians allowed them to transcend their own origins, cracking apart old certainties of class and nation and opening up new worlds of sex and art that were life altering.[64] Both sides in these cultural exchanges came from outward-looking port cities—multicultural outposts in wounded, nationalistic countries. Both sides sought spiritual escape from the countries they were born to, and both found it in American rock and roll, which to German fans meant the difference between life and a slow death in a land of airless conformity and monumental psychic repression. As they lived out their dreams of freedom and transcendence, they helped transform rock and roll from a niche "proletarian" taste into the lingua franca of youth that resonated across the global sixties.

Julia Sneeringer is professor of history at Queens College and the Graduate Center of the City University of New York. She is the author of *A Social History of Early Rock 'n' Roll: Hamburg from Burlesque to the Beatles, 1956–69* (Bloomsbury Academic Press, 2018) and *Winning Women's Votes: Politics* and *Propaganda in Weimar Germany* (University of North Carolina Press, 2002).

Notes

The ideas in this piece are developed from those in the original work *A Social History of Early Rock 'n' Roll in Germany: Hamburg from Burlesque to The Beatles, 1956–69*, published in 2018 by Bloomsbury Academic Press, an imprint of Bloomsbury Publishing Plc. This chapter was supported in part by a grant from The City University of New York PSC-CUNY Research Award Program. Thanks also to Tom Irvine, Neil Gregor, Belinda Davis, and the anonymous reviewers for their suggestions.

1. Ed Larkey, "Postwar German Popular Music: Americanization, the Cold War, and the Post-Nazi *Heimat*," in *Music and German National Identity*, ed. Celia Applegate and Pamela Potter (Chicago, 2002), 237–39.
2. Jon Savage dubs this style Pop Modernism; see his essay in Matthew H. Clough and Colin Fallows, eds., *Astrid Kirchherr: A Retrospective* (Liverpool, 2011), 100. The term "pop explosion" is from Greil Marcus, "The Beatles," in *The Rolling Stone Illustrated History of Rock & Roll*, ed. Jim Miller (New York, 1976), 175. See also Julia Sneeringer, "Meeting the Beatles: What Beatlemania Can Tell Us about West Germany in the 1960s," *The Sixties: A Journal of History, Politics and Culture* 6, no. 2 (2013): 172–98. "Youth" is defined here as those born between 1939 and 1950.
3. Sven Oliver Müller, "Analysing Musical Culture in Nineteenth-Century Europe: Towards a Musical Turn?" *European Review of History* 17, no. 6 (2010): 835–59.
4. British promoters adopted the phrase "Big Beat" around 1960 to distinguish the new style from skiffle. Skiffle used acoustic instruments like tea chests for rhythm, while post-skiffle bands used the drum kit and electric bass—hence Big Beat or just Beat. Dave Haslam, *Life after Dark: A History of British Nightclubs and Music Venues* (London, 2015), 105. Beat could also denote rhythm and blues performed by white artists. Keith Gildart, *Images of England through Popular Music: Class, Youth, and Rock and Roll 1955–76* (New York, 2013), 58. The German press used "rock and roll" and jazz interchangeably through 1960. Between 1961 and 1963, "Twist" became the dominant term while "Beat" circulated within the music scene. The Beatles' success cemented "Beat" as the main term after 1963. See Norbert Schneider, *Popmusik: Eine Bestimmung anhand bundesdeutscher Presseberichte von 1960 bis 1968* (Freiburg, 1978), 51–53.
5. Christopher Small, *Musicking: The Meanings of Performing and Listening* (Middletown, CT, 1998), 8.
6. The best overview of the scene is Ulf Krüger and Ortwin Pelc, *The Hamburg Sound: Beatles, Beat und Große Freiheit* (Hamburg, 2006). The fluid nature of this coming together around music complicates the issue of terminology; I prefer "scene," as it emphasizes the spatial element. See Sara Cohen, "Scenes," in *Key Terms in Popular Music and Culture*, ed. Thom Swiss and Bruce Horner (London, 1999), 239–49; and Andy Bennett, "Subcultures or Neotribes? Rethinking the Relationship between Youth, Style and Musical Taste," in *The Popular Music Studies Reader*, ed. Andy Bennett, Barry Shank, and Jason Toynbee (London, 2006), 106–13.

7. On clubs as sites of cultural production in West Germany, see Axel Schildt and Detlef Siegfried, *Deutsche Kulturgeschichte: Die Bundesrepublik von 1945 bis zur Gegenwart* (Munich, 2009), 188, 267.
8. Richard Langston, "Roll Over Beethoven! Chuck Berry! Mick Jagger! 1960s Rock, the Myth of Progress, and the Burden of National Identity in West Germany," in *Sound Matters: Essays in the Acoustics of Modern German Culture*, ed. Nora M. Alter and Lutz Koepnick (New York, 2004), 183–96.
9. On Adenauer-era sexual politics, see Dagmar Herzog, *Sex after Fascism* (Princeton, 2005), 101–28.
10. These ties persisted after 1945 as Hamburg fell within the British occupation and NATO sectors.
11. Local Nazis tried to contain St Pauli's sex trade and persecuted "asocials," habitual prostitutes, homosexuals, Swing Youth, and racial minorities. However, Nazism did not significantly curtail the pleasure economy, and entertainment was compatible with building Nazism. See Gaby Zürn, "Von der Herbertstrasse nach Auschwitz," in *Opfer und Täterinnen: Frauenbiographien des Nationalsozialismus*, ed. Angelika Ebbinghaus (Nördlingen, 1987), 91–101; Victoria Harris, *Selling Sex in the Reich: Prostitutes in German Society 1914–1945* (Oxford, 2010); Axel Schildt, "Jenseits der Politik? Aspekte des Alltags," in *Hamburg im dritten Reich*, ed. Forschungsstelle für Zeitgeschichte in Hamburg (Göttingen, 2005), 249–304; and Anne Berg, *In and Out of War: Space, Pleasure and Cinema in Hamburg 1938 – 1949* (Ph.D. diss., University of Michigan, 2011).
12. Julia Sneeringer, "'Assembly Line of Joys': Touring Hamburg's Red-Light District 1950–1966," *Central European History* 42, no. 1 (2009): 65–96. On sex and recovery, see Elizabeth Heineman, *Before Porn Was Legal: The Erotica Empire of Beate Uhse* (Chicago, 2011), 61–86.
13. See Uta Poiger, *Jazz, Rock, and Rebels: Cold War Politics and American Culture in a Divided Germany* (Berkeley, 2000), 165–93. It was not uncommon for West German commentators in the 1950s to use language reminiscent of Nazi campaigns against "degenerate music." This didn't keep the music off the big screen: a steady stream of rock-themed films played well into 1957, such as *The Girl Can't Help It*.
14. Peter Ziegler quoted in Krüger and Pelc, *Hamburg Sound*, 150. See also Rüdiger Bloemeke, *Roll Over Beethoven: Wie der Rock'n'Roll nach Deutschland kam* (Andrä-Wordern, 1996), 19–41.
15. On radio, see Detlef Siegfried, "Draht zum Westen: Populäre Jugendkultur in den Medien 1963–1971," in *Buch, Buchhandel und Rundfunk: 1968 und die Folgen*, ed. Monika Estermann und Edgar Lersch (Wiesbaden, 2003), 86. On records and juke-boxes, see Krüger and Pelc, *Hamburg Sound*, 76, 136; Horst Fascher, *Let the Good Times Roll: Der Star-Club Gründer erzählt* (Frankfurt, 2006), 65–67, 84–85; and Rüdiger Articus, *Die Beatles in Harburg* (Hamburg, 1996), 111. On the pop charts, see Bloemeke, *Roll Over Beethoven*, 13–14.
16. Germans were welcome in GI bars (especially females) though the bars' unsavory reputations limited their appeal. On GI bars generally, see Maria Höhn, *GIs and Fräuleins: The German-American Encounter in 1950s West Germany* (Chapel Hill, 2002), esp. 85–125. On early rock and roll outlets, see Hans-Jürgen Klitsch, *Shakin' All Over: Die Beatmusik in der Bundesrepublik Deutschland 1963–1967* (Düsseldorf, 2001), 27.

17. In 1960 the Mäuschen bar, for example, advertised Joe Dawkins' Cuban Rhythm Orchestra with promises of "negro dancing" and "ecstasy." The ad can be viewed at Jens Wunderlich, Hamburg Bildarchiv (www.hamburg-bildarchiv.de/XBA2371.jpg), accessed 14 January 2016. See also ad for "Das Golgosky Quartett, Dunkles Afrika–Neger-Show: Jazz, Tempo, Rhythm," *Hamburger Anzeiger*, 26 September 1953. On racialized display historically, see Eric Ames, *Carl Hagenbeck's Empire of Entertainments* (Seattle, 2009).
18. On this idea in the 1950s and 1960s, see Andrew Wright Hurley, *The Return of Jazz: Joachim-Ernst Berendt and West German Cultural Exchange* (New York, 2009), 60. For the 1920s, see Ivan Goll's 1926 essay "The Negroes Are Conquering Europe," reprinted in *Weimar Republic Sourcebook*, ed. Anton Kaes, Martin Jay, and Edward Dimendberg (Berkeley, 1994), 559–60; and Stephan Pennington, "Reading Uncle Bumba and the Rumba: The Comedian Harmonists and Transnational Youth Culture at the End of the Weimar Republic," *Journal of the Royal Musical Association* 140, no. 2 (2015): 371–84.
19. "Real feeling" is from Peter Bailey, "Jazz at the Spirella," in *Moments of Modernity: Reconstructing Britain, 1945–1964*, ed. Becky Conekin, Frank Mort, and Chris Waters (New York, 1999), 32. "Authenticity" correlated closely with "blackness." Hurley, *Return of Jazz*, 66–67.
20. The timing of this correlated with rock and roll's arrival and Cold War dynamics. Poiger, *Jazz, Rock, and Rebels*, 137–67. See also Heinz-Hermann Krüger, "'Exis, habe ich keine gesehen': Auf der Suche nach einer jugendlichen Gegenkultur in den 50er Jahren," in *"Die Elvis-Tolle, die hatte ich mir unauffällig wachsen lassen": Lebensgeschichte und jugendliche Alltagskultur in den 50er Jahren*, ed. Heinz-Hermann Krüger (Opladen, 1985), 129–51.
21. Barely 10 percent of West German youths identified as jazz fans, according to Michael Kater; cited in Hurley, *Return of Jazz*, 15. For contemporary takes on young Hamburg jazz fans, see Horst Günther, *Hamburg bei Nacht* (Schmiden bei Stuttgart, 1962), 177; and F. H. Miller, *St Pauli und die Reeperbahn: Ein Bummel durch die Nacht* (Rüschlikon, 1960), 33.
22. For example, in 1958 nearly 80 percent of Hamburg fifteen-year-olds earned full-time wages as workers or apprentices while still living at home. Axel Schildt, "Eine Großstadt nach dem Dritten Reich. Aspekte des Alltags und Lebensstils im Hamburg der fünfziger Jahre," in *Das Gedächtnis der Stadt: Hamburg im Umgang mit seiner nationalsozialistischen Vergangenheit*, ed. Peter Reichel (Hamburg, 1997), 85. On recovery generally, see Axel Schildt and Arnold Sywottek, "'Reconstruction' and 'Modernization': West German Social History during the 1950s," in *West Germany under Construction: Politics, Society, and Culture in the Adenauer Era*, ed. Robert G. Moeller (Ann Arbor, 1997), 414–39.
23. A brief history of Indorock is Lutgard Mutsaers, "Indorock: An Early Eurorock Style," *Popular Music* 9, no. 3 (1990): 307–20. For a local angle, see Articus, *Beatles in Harburg*, 19.
24. On skiffle, see Michael Brocken, *Other Voices: The Hidden Histories of Liverpool's Music Scenes 1930–1976* (Burlington, 2010), 19–20; David Simonelli, *Working-Class Heroes: Rock Music and British Society in the 1960s and 1970s* (Lanham, 2013), 12–13. Donegan was known in Germany as part of Chris Barber's trad combo, which was so popular in Hamburg that local fans dubbed their town the "free and Hanseatic Barber-

city." West Germany's skiffle craze hit middle-class students a year after Britain's. Ulf Krüger, then a young skiffler, writes that class divisions kept "purist" skiffle and trad fans from associating with working-class Rockers. Krüger and Pelc, *Hamburg Sound*, 76–84.
25. Fascher, *Let the Good Times Roll*, 85. Most of these bands were still quite raw, though this rawness became an asset in St Pauli's rowdy nightclubs.
26. They played several months-long stints between August 1960 and December 1962. By comparison, they logged 294 dates at their "home" club, Liverpool's Cavern.
27. On this *Kinosterben* in Hamburg, see Michael Töteberg and Volker Reissmann, *Mach dir ein Paar schöne Stunden: Das Hamburger Kinobuch* (Bremen, 2008), 112–19.
28. Günter Zint, *Grosse Freiheit 39: Vom Beat zum Bums* (Munich, 1987), 12–24.
29. These included sounds brought by members of various African and West Indian migrations, black and white GIs stationed at local air bases, and seamen. Liverpool also had record stores such as NEMS, which carried a wide selection of imports. See Sara Cohen, *Decline, Renewal and the City in Popular Music Culture: Beyond the Beatles* (Burlington, 2007), 31; Brocken, *Other Voices*, 29–30.
30. This and all Kemp quotes in paragraph from interview with the author, 15 June 2010.
31. Compare Ian Whitcomb, *Rock Odyssey: A Chronicle of the Sixties* (Garden City, NY, 1983), 3ff.; Adrian Horn, *Juke Box Britain: Americanisation and Youth Culture, 1945–60* (Manchester, 2009).
32. Mary McGlory, interview by Spencer Leigh, *On the Beat*, BBC Radio Merseyside, May 2011, retrieved 18 January 2016 from http://www.4shared.com/audio/2BI056HL/Talking_with_Mary_McGlory_of_t.html.
33. A steady gig in Hamburg paid over three times more than an office or factory job at home. Weissleder also gave his acts Star Club lapel pins, which granted them special status and kept toughs at bay in St Pauli.
34. Ute Frevert, "Umbruch der Geschlechterverhältnisse?," in *Dynamische Zeiten: Die 60er Jahre in den beiden deutschen Gesellschaften*, ed. Axel Schildt, Detlef Siegfried and Karl Christian Lammers (Hamburg, 2000), 655.
35. Paul McCartney called sex with strippers "members of the entertainment business getting together for social reasons." Barry Miles, *Paul McCartney: Many Years from Now* (New York, 1997), 71.
36. Members of various bands, for example, were treated for venereal disease in Hamburg; documentation in Star Club files, Sammlung Zint, Sankt-Pauli-Museum.
37. Pete Best with Patrick Doncaster, *Beatle! The Pete Best Story* (London, 2001), 53–56; see also David Pritchart and Alan Lysaght, *The Beatles: An Oral History* (New York, 1998), 35–55. Fascher's *Let the Good Times Roll* is a breathless compendium of sexual encounters between bands, fans, and sex workers. For contrasting female perspectives, see Thomas Rehwagen and Thorsten Schmidt, *Mach Schau! Die Beatles in Hamburg* (Braunschweig, 1992), 43–48, 91–94, 137–40.
38. Cynthia Lennon, *John* (New York, 2005), 12. She was John Lennon's first wife and an art student in this period.
39. Pauline Sutcliffe, *The Beatles' Shadow: Stuart Sutcliffe and His Lonely Hearts Club* (London, 2001), 80–81.
40. Interview with the author, 15 June 2010.
41. Music as a "counter-world" is from Müller, "Analysing Musical Culture," 845.

42. This "simultaneity of the unsimultaneous" was characteristic of the early sixties "Sex Wave," a time of growing media attention to issues like teen marriage and abortion in the years before the Pill. The Sex Wave also brought an increase in "sexy" content in advertising, even if full nudity was still taboo. See Sybille Steinbacher, *Wie der Sex nach Deutschland kam* (Munich, 2011), 295–316.
43. Ingeborg Weber-Kellermann, "Kindheit der fünfziger Jahre," in *Die Fünfziger Jahre: Beiträge zu Politik und Kultur*, ed. Dieter Bänsch (Tübingen, 1985), 163–70. Jeff Nuttall's *Bomb Culture* (London, 1970) posits the nuclear threat as the key source of the hedonism in the era's pop subcultures.
44. Detlef Siegfried, "Protest am Markt: Gegenkultur in der Konsumgesellschaft um 1968," in *Wo '1968' liegt: Reform und Revolte in der Geschichte der Bundesrepublik*, ed. Christina von Hodenberg and Detlef Siegfried (Göttingen, 2006), 48–78.
45. Jürgen Vollmer, *Rock 'n' Roll Times* (New York, 1983), n.p.
46. See Julia Sneeringer, *A Social History of Early Rock 'n' Roll in Germany: Hamburg from Burlesque to the Beatles, 1956–69* (London, 2018), 91–120.
47. On Wolf, see Clough and Fallows, *Astrid Kirchherr*, 35–36; and Michael Koetzle and Angelika Beckmann, *Twen: Revision einer Legende* (Munich, 1995), 16.
48. Clough and Fallows, *Astrid Kirchherr*, 51.
49. Ibid., 44. Sutcliffe quit the Beatles in 1961 to live in Hamburg with Kirchherr and resume his art studies (he had previously studied painting at Liverpool Art College, where he met John Lennon). He died of a cerebral hemorrhage in 1962.
50. Brian Epstein kept her on as a visual consultant when he took over the Beatles' management in 1961.
51. "Neutrality" is from Simon Reynolds and Joy Press, *The Sex Revolts: Gender, Rebellion and Rock 'n' Roll* (Cambridge, MA, 1995), 243. On the Liverbirds' style, see Stefanie Lohaus, "51 Jahre später – die Liverbirds sind zurück!," *Missy Magazine*, 2 October 2010.
52. Clough and Fallows, *Astrid Kirchherr*, 156. Kemp and Kirchherr were married from 1967 to 1974.
53. Pauline Sutcliffe writes that her brother initially hesitated to talk to German girls because of bad feelings about the war—feelings that Astrid and her circle helped him overcome. Sutcliffe, *Beatles' Shadow*, 102–3.
54. John Fiske, *Understanding Popular Culture* (New York, 1989), 147–48.
55. David Chaney, *Cultural Change and Everyday Life* (New York, 2002), 145. See also Nestor Garcia Canclini, *Consumers and Citizens: Globalization and Multicultural Conflicts* (Minneapolis, 2001), 15–16.
56. Simon Frith and Howard Horne, *Art into Pop* (London, 1987).
57. Ian Edwards of the Zodiacs claimed it was hard to learn German because Hamburg fans wanted to speak only English with them. Krüger and Pelc, *Hamburg Sound*, 129–30.
58. Fascher, *Let the Good Times Roll*, 65.
59. Kaspar Maase, "Establishing Cultural Democracy: Youth, Americanization, and the Irresistible Rise of Popular Culture," in *The Miracle Years: A Cultural History of West Germany 1949–1968*, ed. Hanna Schissler (Princeton, 2001), 428–50.
60. This stands in contrast to Celia Applegate's observation that no break with German music occurred across the 1945 divide in the classical world.

61. For an overview, see Timothy Scott Brown, *West Germany and the Global Sixties: The Antiauthoritarian Revolt, 1962–1978* (Cambridge, 2013), 3–12.
62. Siegfried, "Protest am Markt," 51.
63. Phrase borrowed from Brown, *Global Sixties*, 6.
64. Measured, for example, by the striking number who pursued culture industry careers or married Germans and settled there. Kemp, after an international career in the record industry, settled in Hamburg, where he now owns a British pub. McGlory married musician Frank Dostal and cofounded a music publishing company in Hamburg; her bandmate Valerie Gell moved to Munich, while singer Pam Birch settled in Hamburg after stints playing rock in Iran and the United Kingdom. See Spencer Leigh, "Pam Birch: Guitarist and Singer Who Helped to Break the Mould with the Sixties All-Girl Beat Group the Liver Birds," *Independent*, 4 December 2009. Sheridan fathered a child with Star Club barmaid Rosi Haitmann and lived intermittently in Hamburg for decades; barmaid Ruth Lallemann also married an English rocker. After divorcing his first German wife and retiring from a career as a Liverpool butcher, Kingsize Taylor moved back to Hamburg to marry his Star Club girlfriend Magda in 2001.

Bibliography

Ames, Eric. *Carl Hagenbeck's Empire of Entertainments*. Seattle: University of Washington Press, 2009.

Articus, Rüdiger. *Die Beatles in Harburg*. Hamburg: Christians, 1996.

Bailey, Peter. "Jazz at the Spirella." In *Moments of Modernity: Reconstructing Britain, 1945–1964*, edited by Becky Conekin, Frank Mort, and Chris Waters, 22–40. New York: Rivers Oram Press, 1999.

Bennett, Andy. "Subcultures or Neotribes? Rethinking the Relationship between Youth, Style and Musical Taste." In *The Popular Music Studies Reader*, edited by Andy Bennett, Barry Shank, and Jason Toynbee, 106–13. London: Routledge, 2006.

Berg, Anne. *In and Out of War: Space, Pleasure and Cinema in Hamburg 1938–1949*. Ph.D. diss., University of Michigan, 2011.

Best, Pete, with Patrick Doncaster. *Beatle! The Pete Best Story*. London: Plexus, 2001.

Bloemeke, Rüdiger. *Roll Over Beethoven: Wie der Rock'n'Roll nach Deutschland kam*. Andrä-Wordern: Hannibal, 1996.

Brocken, Michael. *Other Voices: The Hidden Histories of Liverpool's Music Scenes 1930–1976*. Burlington, VT: Ashgate, 2010.

Brown, Timothy Scott. *West Germany and the Global Sixties: The Antiauthoritarian Revolt, 1962–1978*. Cambridge: Cambridge University Press, 2013.

Canclini, Nestor Garcia. *Consumers and Citizens: Globalization and Multicultural Conflicts*. Minneapolis: University of Minnesota Press, 2001.

Chaney, David. *Cultural Change and Everyday Life*. New York: Palgrave, 2002.

Clough, Matthew H., and Colin Fallows, eds. *Astrid Kirchherr: A Retrospective*. Liverpool: Liverpool University Press, 2011.

Cohen, Sara. "Scenes." In *Key Terms in Popular Music and Culture*, edited by Thom Swiss and Bruce Horner, 239–49. London: Wiley-Blackwell, 1999.

———. *Decline, Renewal and the City in Popular Music Culture: Beyond the Beatles*. Burlington, VT: Ashgate, 2007.

Fascher, Horst. *Let the Good Times Roll: Der Star-Club Gründer erzählt*. Frankfurt: Eichborn, 2006.

Fiske, John. *Understanding Popular Culture*. New York: Routledge, 1989.

Frevert, Ute. "Umbruch der Geschlechterverhältnisse?" In *Dynamische Zeiten: Die 60er Jahre in den beiden deutschen Gesellschaften*, edited by Axel Schildt, Detlef Siegfried, and Karl Christian Lammers, 642–60. Hamburg: Christians, 2000.

Frith, Simon, and Howard Horne. *Art into Pop*. London: Methuen, 1987.

Gildart, Keith. *Images of England through Popular Music: Class, Youth, and Rock and Roll 1955–76*. New York: Palgrave Macmillan, 2013.

Goll, Ivan. "The Negroes Are Conquering Europe," *Die literarische Welt*, 15 January 1926. Reprinted in *The Weimar Republic Sourcebook*, edited by Anton Kaes, Martin Jay, and Edward Dimendberg, 559–60. Berkeley: University of California Press, 1994.

Günther, Horst. *Hamburg bei Nacht*. Schmiden bei Stuttgart: Franz Decker Verlag, 1962.

Harris, Victoria. *Selling Sex in the Reich: Prostitutes in German Society 1914–1945*. Oxford: Oxford University Press, 2010.

Haslam, Dave. *Life after Dark: A History of British Nightclubs and Music Venues*. London: Simon & Schuster, 2015.

Heineman, Elizabeth. *Before Porn Was Legal: The Erotica Empire of Beate Uhse*. Chicago: University of Chicago Press, 2011.

Herzog, Dagmar. *Sex after Fascism*. Princeton, NJ: Princeton University Press, 2005.

Höhn, Maria. *GIs and Fräuleins: The German-American Encounter in 1950s West Germany*. Chapel Hill: University of North Carolina Press, 2002.

Horn, Adrian. *Juke Box Britain: Americanisation and Youth Culture, 1945–60*. Manchester: Manchester University Press, 2009.

Hurley, Andrew Wright. *The Return of Jazz: Joachim-Ernst Berendt and West German Cultural Exchange*. New York: Berghahn, 2009.

Klitsch, Hans-Jürgen. *Shakin' All Over: Die Beatmusik in der Bundesrepublik Deutschland 1963–1967*. Düsseldorf: High Castle, 2001.

Koetzle, Michael, and Angelika Beckmann. *Twen: Revision einer Legende*. Munich: Klinkhardt & Biermann, 1995.

Krüger, Heinz-Hermann. "'Exis, habe ich keine gesehen': Auf der Suche nach einer jugendlichen Gegenkultur in den 50er Jahren." In *"Die Elvis-Tolle, die hatte ich mir unauffällig wachsen lassen": Lebensgeschichte und jugendliche Alltagskultur in den 50er Jahren*, edited by Heinz-Hermann Krüger, 129–51. Opladen: Leske + Budrich, 1985.

Krüger, Ulf, and Ortwin Pelc. *The Hamburg Sound: Beatles, Beat und Große Freiheit*. Hamburg: Ellert & Richter, 2006.

Langston, Richard. "Roll Over Beethoven! Chuck Berry! Mick Jagger! 1960s Rock, the Myth of Progress, and the Burden of National Identity in West Germany." In *Sound Matters: Essays in the Acoustics of Modern German Culture*, edited by Nora M. Alter and Lutz Koepnick, 183–96. New York: Berghahn, 2004.

Larkey, Ed. "Postwar German Popular Music: Americanization, the Cold War, and the Post-Nazi *Heimat*." In *Music and German National Identity*, edited by Celia Applegate and Pamela Potter, 234–50. Chicago: University of Chicago Press, 2002.

Lennon, Cynthia. *John*. New York: Three Rivers Press, 2005.

Lohaus, Stefanie. "51 Jahre später–die Liverbirds sind zurück!" *Missy Magazine*, 2 October 2010.

Maase, Kaspar. "Establishing Cultural Democracy: Youth, Americanization, and the Irresistible Rise of Popular Culture." In *The Miracle Years: A Cultural History of West Germany 1949–1968*, edited by Hanna Schissler, 428–50. Princeton, NJ: Princeton University Press, 2001.

Marcus, Greil. "The Beatles." In *The Rolling Stone Illustrated History of Rock & Roll*, edited by Jim Miller, 172–81. New York: Random House, 1976.

Miles, Barry. *Paul McCartney: Many Years from Now*. New York: Henry Holt, 1997.

Miller, F. H. *St Pauli und die Reeperbahn: Ein Bummel durch die Nacht*. Rüschlikon: Müller, 1960.

Mutsaers, Lutgard. "Indorock: An Early Eurorock Style," *Popular Music* 9, no. 3 (1990): 307–20.

Nuttall, Jeff. *Bomb Culture*. London: Paladin, 1970.

Pennington, Stephan. "Reading Uncle Bumba and the Rumba: The Comedian Harmonists and Transnational Youth Culture at the End of the Weimar Republic," *Journal of the Royal Musical Association* 140, no. 2 (2015): 371–84.

Poiger, Uta. *Jazz, Rock, and Rebels: Cold War Politics and American Culture in a Divided Germany*. Berkeley: University of California Press, 2000.

Pritchart, David, and Alan Lysaght. *The Beatles: An Oral History*. New York: Hyperion, 1998.

Rehwagen, Thomas, and Thorsten Schmidt. *Mach Schau! Die Beatles in Hamburg*. Braunschweig: EinfallsReich, 1992.

Reynolds, Simon, and Joy Press. *The Sex Revolts: Gender, Rebellion and Rock 'n' Roll*. Cambridge, MA: Harvard University Press, 1995.

Schildt, Axel. "Eine Großstadt nach dem Dritten Reich: Aspekte des Alltags und Lebensstils im Hamburg der fünfziger Jahre." In *Das Gedächtnis der Stadt: Hamburg im Umgang mit seiner nationalsozialistischen Vergangenheit*, edited by Peter Reichel, 81–100. Hamburg: Dölling und Galitz, 1997.

———. "Jenseits der Politik? Aspekte des Alltags." In *Hamburg im dritten Reich*, edited by the Forschungsstelle für Zeitgeschichte in Hamburg, 249–303. Göttingen: Wallstein, 2005.

Schildt, Axel, and Detlef Siegfried. *Deutsche Kulturgeschichte: Die Bundesrepublik von 1945 bis zur Gegenwart*. Munich: Hanser, 2009.

Schneider, Norbert. *Popmusik: Eine Bestimmung anhand bundesdeutscher Presseberichte von 1960 bis 1968.* Freiburg: Emil Katzbichler, 1978.

Siegfried, Detlef. "Draht zum Westen: Populäre Jugendkultur in den Medien 1963–1971." In *Buch, Buchhandel und Rundfunk: 1968 und die Folgen*, edited by Monika Estermann and Edgar Lersch, 83–107. Wiesbaden: Harassowitz, 2003.

———. "Protest am Markt: Gegenkultur in der Konsumgesellschaft um 1968." In *Wo '1968' liegt: Reform und Revolte in der Geschichte der Bundesrepublik*, edited by Christina von Hodenberg and Detlef Siegfried, 48–78. Göttingen: Vandenhoeck & Ruprecht, 2006.

Simonelli, David. *Working-Class Heroes: Rock Music and British Society in the 1960s and 1970s.* Lanham, MD: Lexington, 2013.

Small, Christopher. *Musicking: The Meanings of Performing and Listening.* Middletown, CT: Wesleyan University Press, 1998.

Sneeringer, Julia. "'Assembly Line of Joys': Touring Hamburg's Red-Light District 1950–1966," *Central European History* 42, no. 1 (2009): 65–96.

———. "Meeting the Beatles: What Beatlemania Can Tell Us about West Germany in the 1960s," *The Sixties: A Journal of History, Politics and Culture* 6, no. 2 (2013): 172–98.

———. *A Social History of Early Rock 'n' Roll in Germany: Hamburg from Burlesque to the Beatles, 1956–69.* London: Bloomsbury Academic, 2018.

Steinbacher, Sibylle. *Wie der Sex nach Deutschland kam.* Munich: Siedler, 2011.

Sutcliffe, Pauline. *The Beatles' Shadow: Stuart Sutcliffe and His Lonely Hearts Club.* London: Sidgwick & Jackson, 2001.

Töteberg, Michael, and Volker Reissmann. *Mach dir ein Paar schöne Studen: Das Hamburger Kinobuch.* Bremen: Edition Temmen, 2008.

Vollmer, Jürgen. *Rock 'n' Roll Times.* New York: Overlook, 1983.

Weber-Kellermann, Ingeborg. "Kindheit der fünfziger Jahre." In *Die Fünfziger Jahre: Beiträge zu Politik und Kultur*, edited by Dieter Bänsch, 163–70. Tübingen: G. Narr, 1985.

Whitcomb, Ian. *Rock Odyssey: A Chronicle of the Sixties.* Garden City, NY: Doubleday, 1983.

Zint, Günter. *Grosse Freiheit 39: Vom Beat zum Bums.* Munich: Heyne, 1987.

Zürn, Gaby. "Von der Herbertstrasse nach Auschwitz." In *Opfer und Täterinnen: Frauenbiographien des Nationalsozialismus*, edited by Angelika Ebbinghaus, 91–101. Nördlingen: F. Greno, 1987.

CHAPTER 3

"With Every Inconceivable Finesse, Excess, and Good Music"
Sex, Affect, and Techno at Snax Club in Berlin

LUIS-MANUEL GARCIA

This chapter explores the intersection of music, sex, travel, and affect in Berlin's electronic music scene. In particular, it focuses on a semiannual music event, "Snax Club" (hereafter "Snax"), where the intimate—and at times messy—entanglement of these phenomena is especially conspicuous. Snax is described by its organizers as a "pervy-party," an electronic dance music event held twice a year at the Berliner nightclub Berghain, in which the club harkens back to the queer sexual subcultures from which it initially emerged. Admission is restricted to men dressed in "fetish gear" (e.g., leather, rubber, latex, sports kit). The event has become one of the largest of its kind in Europe, attracting an international audience of fetish enthusiasts. Drawing from ethnographic interviews, observation, and media analysis, this chapter develops an account of encounters between travelers and locals of various affinities and affiliations, tracking the shifting tropes of queer sexual and musical conviviality. Of special interest is the central role music plays in both facilitating corporeal encounters and mediating between Berliner identity, fetish culture, and gay male sexuality. This chapter is also distinctly affective in its approach, focusing on how feelings are mobilized by various actors to articulate and negotiate complex constellations of musical affinity, sexual subjectivity, and local/national/cosmopolitan belongings.

This study strikes out in an orthogonal direction to established research on music and German identity. Celia Applegate and Pamela Potter frame their edited volume, *Music and German National Identity*, around the historical discourse of Germans as the "people of music," tracking the consolidation of a canon of elite art music that has served not only as a symbolic anchor for Germanness but also as the aesthetic-discursive material through which German identity has been collectively wrought.[1] But, like other contributions to this volume, this chapter examines a different set of musical practices—popular, subcultural, erotic, dance-focused—that have been left out of the "people of music" narrative. Of particular significance are the different spatial dimensions of contemporary popular music: its historical "centre of gravity," located in African-American musical practices of the early twentieth century, rather than among the cultural elites of emergent European nationalism; its global reach, disseminated through multiple media channels and consumed in a wide range of listening contexts; and, as a realm of musicking, its larger scale of participation tied to lower cultural and financial barriers to entry. With these factors in mind, it is noteworthy that "German" is not the primary "unit of identification" for Snax and the social world that surrounds it; neither the event organizers nor the clientele seem to be particularly keen on highlighting its specifically German qualities. Indeed, although Germany has been framed in the historiography of electronic dance music as fertile ground for electronics-driven popular genres, this cultural fertility has arisen out of contact with "foreign" influences such as African-American dance music, Italo-Disco, and pan-European synthpop.[2] On the one hand (as the cases covered in this chapter demonstrate), Snax appeals to a network of electronic music artists, professionals, and dancers that is transnational in practice and global in imagination. On the other hand, Snax is hyperspecific: it targets a specific range of sexual subcultures hosted in a specific venue as part of a specific local music scene situated in a specific city. In this regard, it seems to be associated more with the city of Berlin and with "Berlinness" than with the region or the nation.

As Berlin has emerged in the first decade of the twenty-first century as a global hub for the electronic dance music industry, the local actors, venues, music labels, and audiences have developed a strong identification with the city that prioritizes local frames of reference above national ones.[3] This resonates with some of the foundational theorizations of globalization and "glocalization," where global flows of culture and capital overflow national boundaries and undermine the sovereignty of the nation-state.[4] With the ongoing acceleration and intensification of human migration—including the "techno-tourists," touring artists, and expatriate creative workers of Berlin—group identification seems to be increasingly attached to an imaginative circuit between the local and the global that mostly bypasses the national.[5] Thus, many of Snax's participants express affinities that attach both to a cosmopolitan community of queer and kinky dance-music aficionados and to a specific urban music scene—even to a specific venue (i.e., Berghain).

With its focus on dreams, fantasies, and imagination, this volume departs from earlier research on Germanness in music that focused primarily on textual discourse, music-analytic representation, and other meanings accessible to semiotic practices. In keeping with this approach, this chapter highlights affect through the examination of a variety of modes of feeling arising from music-centric practices that can provide a sensory substrate for felt affinities.[6] I conceptualize affect as something akin to sonic vibration: waves of excitation that drive a sense of push in the lived world and form patterns that can be perceived as qualities, textures, atmospheres, and emotions.[7] Importantly, within the stream of affect theory that flows through Spinoza, Bergson, and Deleuze, affect is always inchoate, becoming, virtual and yet impactful—vaguely perceived but intimately felt.[8] Thus in this chapter attention is paid to how music, sex, built environments, travel, and crowded dance floors all contribute to moments of affective resonance and alignment that *feel like* identity, communion, and fellowship beyond the forms of national identity.

Finally, the research conducted for this study is primarily ethnographic in method, based on three extensive interviews as well as more informal oral histories, attendance at several Snax Club events, collection of related ephemera (e.g., flyers, online promotion, social media channels), and longtime immersion in Berlin's queer electronic music scene. The relative absence of such methods in earlier research on German musical identity can be partly traced to the foundation of *Musikwissenschaft* as a discipline, which separated "historical" from "systematic" research methods from the outset.[9] Although ethnographic methods have been more present in the systematic/comparative branch of music research (e.g., ethnomusicology, folklore), ethnography offers additional descriptive and analytic traction in the study of contemporary musical microcultures—especially when their actors and activities are absent from the historical record. What follows here is thus a set of three profiles of key stakeholders associated with Snax: Sergio, a regular attendee who has transitioned from "tourist" to "local"; Ralf, a bartender who has spent more than a decade working at Snax; and Marea a.k.a. the Black Madonna, one of only a handful of women DJs to have been booked for the event. Based on in-depth interviews, these profiles focus on the interviewees' perspectives on Snax, highlighting themes of musicality, sexuality, and mobility. These profiles are prefaced by a brief historical sketch of Snax, the club Ostgut, and Berghain, while the concluding section provides a comparative analysis of the role of music and affect in all three accounts.

Snax Club

Over more than two decades, Snax has become a combination of gay fetish sex-party and electronic dance music event, approaching both aspects with equal seriousness. With no trace of sarcasm or hyperbole, one can characterize Snax as a *Gesamtkunstwerk*. Although its organizers would likely be ambivalent about the Wagnerian associations, there is no denying their holistic, multisensory approach and their attention to detail. For example, the promotional copy for the 2015 Easter edition of Snax describes the event as "a Bacchanalian feast with every inconceivable finesse, excess, and good music."[10]

Indeed, "finesse, excess, and good music" could serve as Snax's motto, since it enumerates the event organizers' priorities: sexual playspaces are meticulously decorated according to yearly erotic themes; a carefully curated roster of world-class DJs are booked; and event-planning logistics are thoughtfully adjusted to the practicalities of having dance and sexual play share the same venue.

What is normally understood as the nightclub Berghain occupies only about one-third of the former DDR-era power plant in which it is housed. Snax, however, spills out into nearly every corner of the building, leaving only the second-floor "Panorama Bar" space closed off and accessible via a separate entrance for its straight/nonfetish clientele. The doors that usually separate the sex club, Lab.Oratory, from the main Berghain space are opened, as are the doors to the art/concert space Kubus and other rarely used rooms. The main Berghain space is located in the former turbine room on the second floor, accessible by a set of suspended steel stairs. With a ceiling eighteen meters in height and no external windows, this neoclassical-brutalist space lends a cathedral-like gravity to its dance floor, which usually features dark, thundering, and minimalist techno. Kubus, a similarly cavernous space, extends behind the rear wall of Berghain. The Lab.Oratory is located on the ground floor, deeper into the vast building (and partially underneath Kubus), comprised of a labyrinth of hallways and chambers surrounding a small concrete dance floor and wraparound bar. Lab.Oratory's warren includes spaces designed to serve nearly every sexual practice, including several open-plan chambers equipped with leather slings, a series of cages with slings and bunk beds, a row of glory holes, a tiled "wet room" located beneath a metal grate, an empty bathtub, a wide array of padded "sex furniture" in various shapes and forms, a handful of private cabins with lockable doors, and a dauntingly complex leather sex-swing hanging directly over the bar.

In its current incarnation, Snax takes place in the spring and autumn of every year: on Easter weekend and in November or early December. While the autumn edition of the event always adheres to the same sports-fetish theme ("FC Snax"), the Easter edition constantly selects new eroticized themes to guide the design of its spaces. The realization of these themes goes well beyond decorative accents; an immense investment of time, resources, and energy goes into thoroughly redesigning the dance- and playspaces according to these themes. For example, the 2014 edition featured a military setting, for which a complete military field camp was built in the Kubus area, including army-issue canvas tents representing various functions (medic, canteen, bunks, intelligence) filled with relevant furnishings and equipment. Throughout the sprawling sex-labyrinth built in the rearmost section of the building, camouflage canvas netting was draped along with other elements that evoked both a battlefield and a training obstacle course. An earlier edition of Snax took construction sites as its theme, using scaffolding to turn a large portion of the Kubus space into a multilevel play area while also installing the jobsite trailers usually found on construction sites and turning them into intimate orgy spaces. For the autumn "FC Snax" events, a full-size boxing ring is usually installed in the middle of the Berghain dance floor and the rear coat-check area is turned into a locker room. One year, the organizers built a doctor's office complete with an examination table, stirrup chair, (nonfunctioning) medical equipment, and a banal waiting room filled with popular-interest magazines from the 1980s.

Although this sprawling *Gesamtkunst*-Snax takes place as a "special event" within the framework of Berghain, it actually predates the club by a decade.[11] Snax began as an itinerant "pervert-party" in 1994, providing one of the few spaces where queer, fetish-focused sex play and underground electronic dance music intersected. It eventually found a permanent home at Ostgut, a fetish-friendly gay club that opened in 1999, when the operators of a neighboring sex club, Lab.Oratory, were given the opportunity to rent more space in the same building.[12] Ostgut was located in the empty Ostgüterbahnhof railway shipping warehouse near the Ostbahnhof S-Bahn/railway station in the Friedrichshain district, in former East Berlin. It was spatially marginal to Berlin's club culture—which was still mostly clustered in central Mitte—and far from any of the established gay areas of the city, such as Nollendorfplatz in Schöneberg or Greifenhagener Straße in Prenzlauer Berg. Nonetheless, its focus on somber, minimalist techno and festive sexual perversion drew a growing audience of straight clubbers. Ostgut and Lab.Oratory were forced to close in 2003, so that the building could be demolished to make way for the multi-use sports and entertainment arena O2 World, the naming rights to which were bought by mobile telecommunications company Telefónica O2 Germany in 2006. With some financial support from municipal government and outside investors, Ostgut reopened as Berghain in the autumn of 2004 in a DDR-era electrical plant near the northern side of Ostbahnhof's railway tracks. The new name, "Berghain," was a portmanteau taken from the final syllables of the names of the two districts that flank the location: Kreuz*berg* and Friedrichs*hain* (former West and East Berlin, respectively). The owners, Michael Teufele and Norbert Thormann, preserved, rebuilt, and/or expanded many of the defining elements of Ostgut, including the Snax Club series of parties.

The Tourist/Regular/Migrant: Sergio

When Sergio, a hairdresser in his early forties, first discovered Berghain in 2006, he "had no idea that [he] was going into a gay club." Considering that he is both queer and a long-time member of the fetish community in Paris, it is noteworthy that his queer/kink networks did not serve as the primary pathway to discovery. Instead, as a passionate lover of electronic music dissatisfied with Paris nightlife, what he had heard of the club focused exclusively on its reputation as a vanguard of techno music. Berghain's visibility was much lower at that time than it is now; *Rolling Stone* had not yet written its sensationalist feature article on the club's "sex-fuelled world," and Clare Danes had not yet sung the praises of the club on *The Ellen DeGeneres Show*.[13] Sergio came to find Berghain through a combination of indirect and subterranean channels: word-of-mouth reports from other techno-loving friends returning from Berlin; French electronic music magazines like *Trax* reporting on Berlin's vibrant scene; internet searches on Berlin nightlife that flagged Berghain as the city's foremost techno venue; and the realization that most of his favorite recent techno releases were issuing from Berlin-based labels and DJs with bookings at Berghain.

Sergio characterizes his moment of arrival and discovery as a *surprise géniale*, all the more *géniale* because of the circumstances that had inspired him and his partner, Jean, to travel to Berlin in the first place. "We came to Berlin," recounts Sergio, "because we are lovers of techno and we were really unsatisfied in Paris—with the music as well as with the clubs." He recognizes Rex Club as an important and long-standing Parisian institution of electronic music, but at that time he was yearning for a harder, darker style of techno than what was being programmed there. Furthermore, he identifies other frustrations that he sees as emblematic of Parisian nightlife: "Everything is forbidden; the clientele are kids in their early twenties; the bartenders are hostile; and the security personnel are more dangerous than the worst thugs of Paris." For Sergio and Jean, their first visit to Berghain revealed a club that seemed to both redress their dissatisfactions and far exceed their expectations.

Somewhat tongue-in-cheek, Sergio describes their emotional state in the aftermath of their first visit as "traumatized," but this traumatizing shock was one that awoke an appetite for repetition: "We returned two months later, because we had loved it so much. We then came back five weeks later, and then four weeks after that. And then we became regulars, going there every month." With their regular rhythm of visits to Berlin focused almost exclusively on participating in electronic dance music events, Sergio and Jean had joined the ranks of the "techno tourists" who visit the city in droves every weekend.[14] Approximately six months after their first visit, they adjusted their partying schedule to include a visit to Berghain's sex club, Lab.Oratory, where they had a similar epiphany. Sergio adored everything about the space, the atmosphere, and the crowd, but he highlighted the venue's luminosity as reflecting a more open and positive attitude toward sexuality. "What I love," he remarks, "is that people there aren't ashamed of their sexuality." He contrasts this with his experiences of Parisian sex clubs, which he associates with a retreat into pitch-black darkness to hide what one is doing, with whom, and how (e.g., the shame associated with receiving anal penetration). Although the Lab.Oratory has some darker corners available to those who prefer to play in near-anonymity, most of the space is illuminated with the kind of soft, moderately low lighting that one might expect to find in a dive bar—or one of Berlin's many *Eck-Kneipen*. Also, there are relatively few "private" cabins available for guests, thus encouraging sexual play "out in the open," as a communal activity. It was through their encounters at the Lab.Oratory (and ensuing friendships) that Sergio and Jean learned of Snax.

When asked to describe his impressions of Snax as if to a neophyte, Sergio characterizes it as, "a big techno-orgy in a fantastic club, with fantastic music and sexy men. For me, it's the best 100-percent-gay party in Europe." Throughout the interview, he returns repeatedly to this tripartite combination of venue, music, and erotic conviviality as the defining qualities of the Snax experience. Since the event now attracts men from all over Europe (and, to a lesser extent, the Americas and the Middle East), Sergio especially values the increased diversity of body shapes and ethnicities apparent in this pool of potential sexual partners:

> What's great about Snax is that you have the extravagance of the location—Berghain, the Lab: the most sublime of venues. You have guys from all over Europe ... there's every kind of guy: from the big blond, blue-eyed boys from Russia to the hairy, sexy little Spaniards. You have a pretty incredible mix as far as the clientele are concerned, and you have that music ... top-quality music.

As with Berghain and the Lab.Oratory, Sergio elucidates his view of Snax through comparisons to similar events and venues elsewhere in Europe. His perception of Snax's diversity, for example, is gauged against his experiences of more homogeneous crowds at national-scale fetish events. He nonetheless points to La Demence in Brussels as a monthly sex party that seemed to provide an enjoyable space for erotic play, but complains that the music was "unbearable," a complaint that he generalizes to most of the gay sex parties that he has attended outside of Berlin: "There were bad Madonna remixes and some sort of insipid, out-dated pseudo-tech-house." By contrast, he values Snax for providing an opportunity for both erotic and musical satisfaction. "Berliners pay attention to music," he asserts, making reference to the city's current status as a global hub for electronic dance music. Indeed, he locates Berliner identity in Snax's musical programming:

> There's a spirit there that is very Berlin. Even if the party attracts all of Europe, there's still this very Berliner venue and proper pounding techno [*musique bien techno qui tape*]. They don't adjust the music to the tastes of the Belgians, Spaniards, or Italians that will attend. They preserve the Berghain spirit with pounding techno. Snax still keeps its Berliner character, I find.

In this passage, "proper pounding techno" serves as the musical-stylistic anchor for place-specific identity, but Sergio's identifications slide from Berlin to Berghain to Snax. On the one hand, this speaks to Berghain's prominence at local, national, and international levels as not only a hub for musical production but also a locus of (sub)cultural export. But on the other hand, this also demonstrates how music can serve as a capacious and multithreaded relay between identity and place, allowing a particular style of music to articulate the identities of a city, a local music scene, and a specific club at the same time. For Sergio, "proper pounding techno" is all of these things at once.

Sergio also situates Snax's *esprit berlinois* within the extensive overlap of the city's techno and fetish scenes. "Fetishism is very, very important in Germany," he explains, citing not only the scale but also the wide age range of fetish events as an indication that "fetishism in Germany is much more developed than in France, in Paris." And so he sees the confluence of kink and techno as especially emblematic of Berlin:

> In Berlin, you'll see twenty-two-year-old kids already wearing harnesses. There's a culture here of nightlife and the discothèque, a place where people go out and meet each other. There's a social bond that forms out of this in a way you won't find anywhere else in the world.

"Fetish gear" such as harnesses play an important role in kinky communities as markers of belonging, expressions of erotic affinity, and cues guiding intercorporeal encounters. "People here love accessories," remarks Sergio, referring to the wide range of accoutrements associated with fetish practices; "everybody is in leather, latex, harnesses, and so on." Thus, the greater visibility of fetish gear in the sartorial repertoires of Berliner clubbers is meaningful to him as a hallmark of local identity to which he can also feel connected. He also reports that he and Jean are usually positively received when they show up in fetish gear to local techno clubs that are not associated with fetish or queer scenes, perhaps because their kinky presence serves as a mark of local authenticity. Sergio thus folds the erotic practices associated with fetish scenes into local electronic music culture; in his nocturnal world, dance and sex share prominence as corporeal modes of conviviality.

Sergio and Jean are now well-known *Stammgäste* [regular patrons] in Berghain and at Snax. As they continued to visit the city on a regular basis, their social world came to be located increasingly in Berlin. And so, after nearly seven years of monthly visits, they finally decided to emigrate—at least partially. They began to take German lessons. They sold their apartment in Paris and bought one in Berlin. Sergio closed and sold his hair salon in Paris and moved to Berlin to find work there. Jean continues to work in Paris, but he sleeps in a small rental flat during the week and "returns" to his home in

Berlin every weekend. "I'm single during the week and partnered during the weekend," quips Sergio, chuckling.

The Bartender: Ralf

Working as a bartender during the first year of Berghain's existence, Ralf heard his coworkers speaking excitedly about an upcoming event called "Snax." "I had no idea what was waiting for me there," he recalls. "I was only told, 'You're working the party and need to be there. You'll be doing such-and-such tasks and you need to be there at such-and-such time.'" And so, when he finally showed up for work to the first Snax party in the new Berghain venue, what he witnessed there came as "a complete surprise" [ein völliger Überraschungseffekt]. Although he had worked at other "pervy-parties" in Berlin at other venues in the past, the scale and intensity of Snax was overwhelming at first: "I was suddenly standing in the middle of the whole thing, stressed out, and thinking, 'Oh no, what I have gotten myself into?'" After the mini–culture shock of his first Snax shift, however, Ralf found himself joining his colleagues in their excited anticipation of Snax events. Like them, he would explicitly request to work the Snax party and would enjoy pre-event preparations such as assembling a fetish-appropriate outfit for work. Ralf recalls Snax as one of his favorite dates on the Berghain calendar.

With extensive knowledge of Berlin's gay nightlife, Ralf rates Snax as the largest event of its kind in the city. But it is not necessarily the scale of the event that impresses him:

> What I like the most about it is that the environment/décor [Ausstattung] is designed not only to provide a bare space—"get in there and get it on"—but instead attention is paid to music and music programming, playspaces, scenery, and so on. The effort invested in order to make the whole thing good is, I believe, incomparable.

Ralf nonetheless goes on to compare Snax to typical Berliner sex parties (where he often also worked as a bartender), noting that, even if they were located in interesting venues, other fetish events often "just threw all of the [sex play] equipment in there and called it a day—and often rather uncaringly [lieblos]." At Snax, however, "they create real playgrounds [Spielplätze] and theatrical environments, with an unbelievable eye for set design." Although he never attended Snax as a partygoer, Ralf enjoyed spending time during his breaks and after his shift meandering through the party space and enjoying the "scenery"; he would admire the sculptural installations and erotic playgrounds "because they simply look beautiful, because they're interesting, because they are made with humour and a great deal of reflexive irony." He notes that

Berghain's founders and owners (as well as a substantial portion of the club's staff) have long-standing roots in the local fetish scene and took part in the early years of Snax; and so, they have both a wry sense of humor about the event as well as the necessary practical and scene-specific knowledge to oversee the design of optimal, exciting, and captivating playspaces.

In contrast to Sergio's experience as a regular patron, Rolf's decade-long career as a Snax bartender enables him to provide not only insight into the labor and organization behind the event, but also observations of intriguing patterns among the party's clientele. For example, he notes somewhat bemusedly that drink orders at Snax involve far more "light," sugar-free soft drinks and alcohol-free beer than on regular Berghain nights. This pattern of consumption is common to fetish-oriented gay events anywhere, he suggests, remarking that, "you can't have a pervert-party without light drinks." Although he does not speculate on the factors influencing these event-specific drink preferences, one could see this as a side effect of the hypermuscular, "spornosexual," taut-fleshed body ideals that still predominate most gay sexual cultures—even though habitués of Snax repeatedly remark on the relative diversity of body shapes there in comparison to similar events elsewhere. In a similar vein, he also points to a scarcity of *Longdrinks* (i.e., cocktails composed of one alcohol and one mixer, such as the gin and tonic, usually served in a tumbler glass). "Things need to be practical," he notes wryly, hinting at the impracticalities of vigorously engaging in sexual activities with an open glass in hand.

But the most striking difference that Ralf has noticed at Snax is the increased presence of out-of-town participants, both over time and in comparison to other Berghain events. "There's been an incredible change," he observes; "at the beginning, it was primarily a Berliner affair, much like the techno scene ten years ago. There wasn't this party-tourism at the time." But as Snax grew in size and extraregional visibility, the crowd it drew soon shifted toward extra-urban visitors. According to Ralf, expectations were adapted accordingly: "Before, there were a lot of familiar faces [at Snax]. ... People would make plans to attend because they would see people they knew there. Now, people go because they won't know anybody!" From the perspective of the members of Berlin's sex-party scene, a roomful of kinky strangers signifies a vast increase in novelty, variety, and anonymity for one's pool of potential sexual partners. Ralf points out that, at smaller local events, "probably everyone has already had sex with one another"—a point that was also made by Sergio when our interview turned to the topic of tourism. In this case, the influx of strangers comes to be seen as an exciting expansion of erotic possibilities as well as a liberating break from the insular dramas of the local scene.

Local stakeholders usually refer to these eroticized strangers as "tourists," but this term is often taken to mean non-Germanophone, international travelers. This risks generating semantic slippage, especially since Berlin's techno, gay, and fetish scenes have all grown substantially over the past decade through an inflow of non-Germanophone migrants (mostly in the creative, "tech," and academic sectors) who may be mistaken for "tourists" at their events, even though many of them make vital contributions to the scene as organizers, artists, managers, journalists, and so on. Germanophone visitors are likewise overlooked, especially considering that the orgiastic setting of the party discourages the exchange of names—let alone life stories. Nonetheless, as a bartender whose weekly shifts have made him very familiar with the cosmopolitan membership of the city's electronic music scene, Ralf is perhaps best equipped to gauge the composition of Snax's crowd in relation to Berghain's "normal" crowd. According to him, the proportion of travelers at the event has grown steadily over the past decade. In recent years, he has noted a preponderance of Frenchmen in the crowd; pondering the possible reasons for this, he unwittingly echoes Sergio: "perhaps they don't have the same playspaces over there."

Despite complaints from some quarters of the local gay sex-party scene that Snax has become "too touristy," Ralf is sanguine about these out-of-town visitors, arguing that they bring an "extremely charming party atmosphere" to the event. In fact, he cites these Snax-tourists as a major factor in his eagerness to work there. "At most parties," explains Ralf, "there's always a bit of friction: some patrons are rude at the bar, there's this exchange of shouting [over the music] that can set an aggressive tone ... but this *never* happens at Snax." He plays on the contrast between the tough masculinity eroticized in gay fetish scenes and the gentleness of these encounters: "No matter how mean they look—big bears or rugged builds—they still come to the bar and they're friendly, they're super-nice [*übernett*]." For him, these out-of-town visitors lend not only novel excitement but also a "sweet" and "extremely relaxed" ambience.

Perhaps stemming from this influx of visitors, he notes that the temporal flow of Snax runs quite differently from that of regular nights at Berghain. To be precise, Snax runs "backwards":

> At a normal party, you meet and get to know each other, and maybe it leads to sex at the end. At Snax, you go there, you have sex, and then you party, dance, and hang out. ... At the start, people arrive and disappear quickly into the dark rooms and playspaces. Then they come to the bar afterwards to chat and relax.

As a result of this sex-first temporal organization, Ralf feels that the festive "party feeling" of Snax manifests toward the end of the event. Or, put differently, Snax starts as a fetish-sex party and turns into a techno party as the night unfolds.

Although it diverges from Berghain's regular festivities in many regards, Ralf still feels that Snax is an "essential facet" of Berghain. He situates it within the diverse array of spaces and experiential opportunities that Berghain offers—outdoor *Biergarten*, dance club, concert venue, art space, experimental salon—all of which appeal to different aspects of the city's "techno population groups" [*technoïde Bevölkerungsgruppen*]. But he also points out that Snax is the *Ursprung* of all of this: it was out of the Snax Club parties that first Ostgut and then Berghain developed. In this sense, Snax serves to periodically reauthenticate Berghain to its clientele and to reconsecrate it as a site of queer musical subculture by re-enacting its origins while also continually revising them for the present. This strategic use of a (felt, imagined, mythologized, collective) history as a "resource for the present" by Berghain and its *habitués* suggests that Snax has become an unconventional and highly localized heritage practice.[15]

Indeed, Snax's legacy is not taken lightly in these circles, as illustrated by Rolf's account of the debates that took place among its staff at the time that Berghain was first arising from the ashes of Ostgut in 2003 and 2004. As part of discussions about the identity of this new club, the continuation of Snax was brought into question. Although some of the uncertainty was logistical (i.e., which of the club's spaces to use; whether to keep a separate "straight" space running in parallel), a more fundamental concern was whether the event was still compatible with the changing clientele. Heterosexual participation was already increasing at the end of the Ostgut era, and their continued presence was much needed to ensure the success of Berghain's more ambitious scale. "It could have gone very wrong," notes Ralf. "The club was running the risk that the heterosexuals wouldn't accept Snax, that they would simply say, 'We're not going there anymore.' There was a lot of discussion and no certainty that it would work."

More than ten years later, it seems that Snax has done little to hinder the flow of straight clubbers to Berghain. If anything, the weekly intersection of fetish and electronic music scenes inside the venue has given rise to a hyperlocalized "contact culture" that is more accustomed to fetish practices, queer sexualities, and sex-positive spaces—although not without some concerns about the potential colonization of queer space. Snax's format has also changed over the years. Ralf notes that, in addition to growing larger, more intense, and more international, the music programming for the event has become more focused and more serious, thus coming into alignment with Berghain's regular (and world-famous) musical selections. Over time, Berghain's female resident DJs (e.g., Tama Sumo, Steffi) were also brought in to perform in the disco/house-oriented floor of the Lab.Oratory, and more recently this has come to include nonaffiliated women DJs such as Jennifer Cardini and The Black Madonna.

The DJ: The Black Madonna

Marea Stamper (a.k.a. The Black Madonna) is one of very few women DJs to have played at Snax. Now in her late thirties, this Kentucky-born artist first began spinning records during her college years, after having been very active in the UK Midwest rave scene during the 1990s. She moved to Chicago in 2006 and found a job working for Sole Unlimited, the distribution arm of the local house-music label Dust Traxx, helping to manage the company's entry into digital distribution. She continued to perform as a DJ and began producing dance music "tracks," and during the summer of 2013, she became both resident DJ and "talent buyer" (booking agent) for Chicago's highly respected and longest-running electronic music club, Smart Bar.

During that same summer, one of her releases, "A Jealous Heart Never Rests," became an international summer anthem at electronic dance music clubs—including Berghain/Panorama Bar, where it was frequently played by resident DJs such as Nick Höppner and nd_baumecker. That autumn, Marea was booked to play at Panorama Bar, which was the first international booking of her career. Her debut performance in the autumn of 2013 was well received by the club's crowd, staff, and management, and through the following year the club began to book her as an overseas guest on a quarterly basis. It is indicative of how quickly she built a rapport with the club's clientele and management that she was invited to play for Berghain's massive multiday *Silvester* [New Year's Eve] party only fourteen months after her debut.

It was then, shortly after her DJ set in Panorama Bar at the beginning of 2015, that Marea was booked for Snax. "When you finish up with your set," she recounts, "you think, 'Oh God, I hope they let me do that again!'" And so, even though she had just played at Berghain for the fifth time in a little more than a year, she was nonetheless elated when she received a message from her manager informing her that she had been invited back for a double-booking on Easter weekend: playing Panorama Bar with her Chicago colleague Derrick Carter and performing in the Lab.Oratory during Snax. "I was very happy just to be able to play twice in general," remarks Marea, "but also because I know that very few women have played at Snax. It is a very special honour for a woman to be asked to go into that space."

Unlike Sergio and Ralf, Marea had a good idea of what Snax had in store for her. Her long-time and close involvement with gay nightlife in Chicago and elsewhere in the United States provided her with an extensive network of former Snax attendees who could advise her. She was told to "expect Caligula-level sexual activity in the Lab during Snax," evoking images of wall-to-wall, writhing flesh. But, perhaps anxious not to discourage her, these same friends and colleagues insisted that she was "the right woman for the job," referring to her extensive experience playing records at sex-positive gay events in the United States.

Marea's account of Snax is particularly illuminating because, as a DJ who has played both Snax and "regular" events in Berghain, she can speak to the nuances of music, crowd, and affect in great detail. Unlike the dark, pounding, minimalist techno played in the main Berghain space during Snax, the Lab.Oratory space usually features disco, house, and early synthpop styles of dance music, which provides a high-camp contrast to the erotic exertions of partygoers. "I played the Patrick Cowley set of my imagination," she recalls, comparing her set to what she imagined Cowley would play, the legendary disco producer largely responsible for the San Francisco "Hi-NRG" sound that is associated with recording artists such as Sylvester. During his career, Cowley also produced electronic music soundtracks for gay pornographic films, which only came to light in recent years.[16] "I was trying to imagine: If I were on that dancefloor, what would I want to fuck to?" She answered her own question with a four-hour DJ set of "very slutty disco, Hi-NRG, a lot of sleaze, a lot of Eurodisco—even more obscure than I normally would." Perhaps inspired by Cowley's dual career in disco and porn, Marea sought to build a "soundtrack to this fantasy realm that kind of lives with one foot in dance and one foot in sexuality."

Soundtracks served as a recurring metaphor in Marea's reflections on her performance at Snax, for reasons that had a great deal to do with the spatial layout and affective dynamics of the performance space. Unlike the other rooms in the club, the Lab.Oratory's DJ booth is physically separated from the dance floor, elevated to a tiny mezzanine loft that hangs over the entrance to one of the darkened playspaces. When fully standing, the DJ's head and shoulders are hidden behind a concrete partition descending from the ceiling, while the turntables and other sound equipment nearly fill the rest of the space visible from the dance floor. "You're up in a birdcage above everyone," she says. "They can see your feet and you can see the tops of their heads and a bit of the bar." She contrasts this layout with that of Panorama Bar—the room in which she has played most often in Berghain—where the DJ booth is a corner of the dance floor marked out by a relatively slim metal railing, situating the DJ very much *inside* the crowd.

> Unlike in Panorama Bar, where there's an eye-to-eye, body-level exchange of energy and information, in the Lab you're more ... creating a soundtrack and playing inside your mind—and hoping that everyone comes along with you.

Like most DJs, Marea generally prefers to have direct sightlines and corporeal proximity to her audience, but she sees some advantages in being released from the expectation to sustain a constant exchange of affect with the crowd (which can be very exhausting for a DJ). Instead, she sets a particular musical mood and then holds it there until the rest of the room comes into affective alignment. According to Marea, this dynamic was facilitated by the density of the crowd during her set. Performing at the "peak" of the party (4:00 to 7:00 a.m.), she played to a dance floor that was so packed, "you could not get another dude in a harness into that room if you tried." As a result of this constant crowding, it became nearly impossible to "kill the floor" by losing the attention of the dancers: "you can kind of do no wrong; they're *trapped*." This enabled her to be more assertive in pushing the dancing crowd in particular aesthetic and affective directions, to "compel or enforce a sound," as she describes it. And so, Marea enjoyed the opportunity to take more risks during her set, selecting more obscure and adventurous tracks that took her "captive" audience on ero-to-psychedelic journeys.

Snax is an event that formally excludes women—that insulates homosexual play within men-only homosocial boundaries—and so Marea was hyperaware of her liminal position at the event. On the one hand, her role as a performing artist granted her exceptional access to a gender-segregated sexual space; on the other hand, she was dependent on participants' recognition of her exceptional status. She conscientiously avoided wandering into the areas where the sexual play was at its most intense, but nonetheless on two occasions her presence was questioned by individuals who did not recognize her as a performer. Fortunately, she was able to talk her way out of these encounters with minimal awkwardness. But on the whole, Marea reported feeling very welcome at Snax, which she has since described as a "turning point" for her career as well as for her sense of connection to her gay fans:

> In retrospect, I feel that Snax was such an important moment for me, in bonding with a whole group of men. Because, there are people that I see all over the world who are like, "I was at Snax! I flew from Brazil to Berlin to go to Snax, and I saw you there. I saw your feet, bouncing around!"

This moment of bonding, however, was made possible by a long historical chain of similar moments throughout Marea's personal life and performing career. Friendships with gay men have played a pivotal role in her life since adolescence, and her career as a producer and performer has always been tightly entwined with local queer dance-music scenes. As her DJ career began to gather momentum, many of her bookings were at established queer, sex-positive events such as Men's Room (Chicago), Hot Mass (Pittsburgh), Honey Soundsystem (San Francisco), and the Folsom Street Fair (San Francisco). By the time she was booked for Snax, she was already being booked regularly for queer dance events in Europe. This deep and ongoing involvement in queer nightlife provides her with invaluable "hands-on" experience playing for queer, sex-positive events, a familiar nonchalance in the presence of gay sex, an ever-expanding network of contacts and loyal fans, access to scene-specific information channels, and a deep knowledge of the musical repertoire affiliated with these scenes. Indeed, there is little doubt that her extensive queer-nightlife bona fides informed Berghain's decision to book her for Snax.

As a queer-identified woman who has dealt with discrimination, sexual oppression, and restrictive body ideals, Marea expresses a "deep kinship" with

Snax's queer, sex-positive crowd. She is an outspoken feminist who has used her recent success to make an impact in global club-culture discourses by calling attention to misogyny, racism, transphobia, and homophobia in the electronic dance music industry, insisting that it do justice to its historical origins in marginalized urban subcultures.[17] Notably, there is a markedly affective dimension to her kinship, which she characterizes variously in the interview as "falling in love with that kind of crowd," "a very special kind of romance," "a deep and abiding friendship," and "holding a very special place in my heart." "And no one on this earth," she insists hyperbolically, "has ever loved a big, huge, fat gay bear more than me. Those are my people." Although she cannot participate fully in the revelry, she cherishes the opportunity to play an essential role in building this temporary realm of erotic conviviality. Marea articulates a sense of queer solidarity with the utopian impulse that Snax represents, explaining, "I like to be around people following their bliss."

Conclusion: Belonging, Music, Affect

For these three "Snax-goers," music plays a central role in sensing and articulating belonging. It grounds their sense of identity, based on shared tastes and appetites. It draws them into scenes and communities that are anchored in specific places like Berghain and at specific moments like Snax. Notably, there is a strong affective dimension to how music works to create these sociocultural sutures between individual actors, a party, a former socialist-era power plant, a local scene, and a larger felt community of fellow queer music-lovers. Throughout the longer-term fieldwork that I have been conducting in Berlin's electronic dance music scenes, interviewees have generally been more articulate about how their (local, subcultural, urban) belonging *feels* than what social and cultural form it takes.[18] For many, experiences of affective resonance with their milieu come to signify belonging in the absence of more stable markers of affiliation. Here, belonging is presented primarily in sensory and affective terms, grounded in bodily (musical, erotic) practices.

For Sergio, music was in fact the pathway to discovering Berghain, the Lab.Oratory, and Snax. It was due to the club's reputation as a venue of techno music that he and his partner visited the club in the first place; the fact that it is also a fetish-oriented gay club came as a delightful surprise. After several years of near-monthly visits from Paris and a recent partial relocation to the city, Sergio reports feeling "at home" [*chez moi*] in Berlin, and especially at Berghain. Although there may be several factors contributing to his sense of being at home—such as social networks and scene-specific knowledge built up over years of monthly visits—Sergio immediately focuses on music: "I met people—gay or not—who love the same music I do; that wasn't easy in Paris."

He goes on to recount how in Paris he would often be disappointed to return to a new acquaintance's home for sex and/or socializing and be subjected to their selection of mainstream pop tunes or "commercial" dance remixes. But in Berlin, similar situations would be soundtracked by techno: "I would arrive to a friend's place and the music was *good*—even better than at my place!" For Sergio, "home" is not being disappointed by the musical tastes of your friends and lovers; it is the feeling of recognition and resonance routed through musical aesthetics and intimate scenes of listening/dancing.

Ralf continually returns to music during his interview to explain what makes Snax an exceptional event in Berlin. With more than a decade of experience bartending in Berlin's nightclubs (including sex parties), he identifies Snax's carefully considered, stylistically coherent, high-quality musical programming as a principal factor distinguishing it from other local fetish-focused events. At the same time, he also highlights the event's unique affective atmosphere, which he describes variously as festive, relaxed, sexually charged, and "almost sweet." Significantly, he values the presence of out-of-town visitors for their contribution to this "extremely charming party atmosphere," thus highlighting the role of stranger-sociability in generating a scene of capacious belonging. For Ralf, Snax would not be the same without its tourists.

Toward the end of our interview, Marea reflects at length on the "deep emotional bond between me and that building," a bond that has been forged through music. Indeed, her musical activities made her involvement in Snax possible in the first place. As a DJ, she is especially aware of how music can set a spatialized affective tone that drives corporeal encounters. For Marea, "that building" refers not only to Berghain (and the affective echoes of what has taken place within its walls), but also metonymically to the people who enliven the space with their bodies. She speaks at length about the "deep kinship" and "very special bond" that she feels with queer, sex-positive nightlife crowds, who enact utopian forms of eroto-musical sociality to which she claims a strong affinity.

All three interviewees identify "serious" connoisseurship of electronic dance music as a hallmark of Berliner nightlife and its denizens, pointing to Berghain and Snax as leading examples. In all three cases, music serves as a conduit—simultaneously metaphorical and literal—for affective resonance between individuals, communities, and spaces. At Snax, passion, euphoria, pleasure, abandon, conviviality, and friendly familiarity all course through the throng of bodies that move through Berghain's dark and humid passages. And these affective flows are channeled, organized, synchronized, and attuned by the pulsating music that fills the spaces between bodies.

Notably, this musical fellowship binds together a queer affective community that is both cosmopolitan and local, bypassing national imaginaries of musical "Germanness" while remaining grounded in the specificities of Berlin nightlife. Well before the rise of European nationalism, the "Grand Tour" of the seventeenth and eighteenth centuries functioned as an institution of cosmopolitan cultivation for young elites, guiding them along a circuit of travel through locales that were considered to represent the apex of European high culture.[19] Although there are vast differences in circumstances, the Grand Tour provides an intriguing prenational model of culture-driven cosmopolitan mobility and its significance for identity formation. Snax Club could perhaps be similarly situated in a "niche" erotic and musical Grand Tour, especially considering its growing visibility in queer communities abroad. Over the past decade, this event has become a yearly (or twice-yearly) pilgrimage for many queer fetish enthusiasts from across Europe and beyond. As it has developed into a "global underground" institution, has Snax Club become a destination for the musical cultivation of cosmopolitan queer identities?

Luis-Manuel Garcia is a lecturer in Ethnomusicology and Popular Music Studies at the University of Birmingham, with previous appointments at the Max Planck Institute for Human Development (Berlin) and the University of Groningen (NL). His research focuses on urban electronic dance music scenes, with a particular focus on affect, intimacy, stranger-sociability, embodiment, sexuality, creative industries and musical migration. He is currently conducting research on "techno tourism" and other forms of musical mobility in Berlin; he has also completed a book manuscript based on earlier research, entitled Together Somehow: Music, Affect, and Intimacy on the Dancefloor.

Notes

1. Celia Applegate and Pamela Potter, eds., *Music and German National Identity* (Chicago, 2002).
2. See, for example, Marcel Feige and Kai-Uwe Müller, *Deep in Techno: Die Ganze Geschichte Des Movements* (Berlin, 2000); Simon Reynolds, *Energy Flash: A Journey through Rave Music and Dance Culture* (London, 1998); and Dirk Waltmann, Sven Schäfer, and Jesper Schäfer, *Techno-Lexicon: Das Umfassende Nachschlagewerk Zur Größten Jugendkultur Europas* (Berlin, 1998).
3. Ingo Bader and Albert Scharenberg, "The Sound of Berlin: Subculture and the Global Music Industry," *International Journal of Urban and Regional Research* 34, no. 1 (2010): 76–91; Felix Denk and Sven von Thülen, *Der Klang Der Familie: Berlin, Techno und Die Wende* (Berlin, 2012); Feige and Müller, *Deep in Techno*; Luis-Manuel Garcia, "At Home, I'm a Tourist: Musical Migration and Affective Citizenship in Berlin," *Journal of Urban Cultural Studies* 2, no. 1–2 (2015): 121–34; Luis-Manuel Garcia, "Techno-Tourism and Postindustrial Neo-Romanticism in Berlin's Electronic Dance Music Scenes," *Tourist Studies* 16, no. 3 (2016): 276–95; Christina M. Heinen, *"Tief in Neukölln": Soundkulturen zwischen Improvisation und Gentrifizierung in einem Berliner Bezirk* (Bielefeld, 2013); Sean Nye, "Love Parade, Please Not Again: A Berlin

Cultural History," *ECHO: A Music-Centered Journal* 9, no. 1 (2009): 1–50; Sean Nye, "Minimal Understandings: The Berlin Decade, the Minimal Continuum, and Debates on the Legacy of German Techno," *Journal of Popular Music Studies* 25, no. 2 (2013): 154–84; Tobias Rapp, *Lost and Sound: Berlin, Techno und der Easyjetset* (Frankfurt, 2009); Reynolds, *Energy Flash: A Journey through Rave Music and Dance Culture*; Anja Schwanhäußer, *Kosmonauten Des Underground: Ethnografie Einer Berliner Szene* (Frankfurt, 2010); and Geoff Stahl, ed. *Poor, but Sexy: Reflections on Berlin Scenes* (Bern, 2014).

4. Anthony Giddens, *The Consequences of Modernity* (Stanford, 1990); Roland Robertson, "Glocalization: Time-Space and Homogeneity-Heterogeneity," in *Global Modernities*, ed. Mike Featherstone, Scott Lash, and Roland Robertson (London, 1995), 25–44.

5. Arjun Appadurai, *Modernity at Large: Cultural Dimensions of Globalization* (Minneapolis, 1996); Garcia, "I'm a Tourist"; John Urry, *Mobilities* (Cambridge, 2007).

6. Although the field of "affect theory" is far too broad and diverse to summarize here, one edited volume serves as an essential primer: Melissa Gregg and Gregory J. Seigworth, eds., *The Affect Theory Reader* (Durham, 2010).

7. Luis-Manuel Garcia, "Beats, Flesh, and Grain: Sonic Tactility and Affect in Electronic Dance Music," *Sound Studies* 1, no. 1 (2016): 59–76; Steve Goodman, *Sonic Warfare: Sound, Affect, and the Ecology of Fear* (Cambridge, MA, 2010).

8. Lauren Berlant, *The Female Complaint: The Unfinished Business of Sentimentality in American Culture* (Durham, 2008); Luis-Manuel Garcia, "Crowd Solidarity on the Dance Floor in Paris and Berlin," in *Musical Performance and the Changing City: Post-Industrial Contexts in Europe and the United States*, ed. Fabian Holt and Carsten Wergin (New York, 2013), 227–55; Brian Massumi, "The Autonomy of Affect," *Cultural Critique*, no. 31 (1995): 83–109; Kathleen Stewart, *Ordinary Affects* (Durham, 2007).

9. Guido Adler, "Umfang, Methode Und Ziel Der Musikwissenschaft," *Vierteljahrschrift für Musikwissenschaft* 1 (1885): 5–20.

10. Unless otherwise indicated, all translations are by the author. "*Ein bacchantisches Gelage mit allen undenkbaren Finessen, Ausschweifungen und guter Musik.*" Event listing retrieved 1 August 2018 from http://berghain.de/event/1281. See also the club's full monthly flyer, retrieved 1 August 2018 from http://berghain.de/media/flyer/pdf/berghain-flyer-2015-04.pdf.

11. For a more detailed history and description of Berghain, see Garcia, "Crowd Solidarity"; and Imre van der Gaag, "Function Follows Form: How Berlin Turns Horror into Beauty," *Failed Architecture*, 28 January 2014.

12. Alexis Waltz, "Nightclubbing: Berlin's Ostgut—Berghain before It Was Berghain," *Red Bull Music Academy Daily*, 24 September 2013.

13. Thomas Rogers, "Berghain: The Secretive, Sex-Fueled World of Techno's Coolest Club," *Rolling Stone*, 6 February 2014. Clare Danes mentioned the club when she appeared on *The Ellen DeGeneres Show* (28 September 2015) to promote the latest season of the television drama series *Homeland*, which was shot in Berlin.

14. Garcia, "Techno-Tourism."

15. Amanda Brandellero and Susanne Janssen, "Popular Music as Cultural Heritage: Scoping Out the Field of Practice," *International Journal of Heritage Studies* 20, no. 3 (2014): 224–40; Sara Cohen, "Musical Memory, Heritage and Local Identity:

Remembering the Popular Music Past in a European Capital of Culture," *International Journal of Cultural Policy* 19, no. 5 (2012): 576–94; Brian Graham, "Heritage as Knowledge: Capital or Culture?," *Urban Studies* 39, no. 5–6 (2002): 1003–17.
16. A brief biography and description of these new discoveries are available on the website of Dark Entries Records, the record label releasing his porn-related material posthumously. "Patrick Cowley – School Daze 2xLP," Dark Entries Records, n.d., retrieved 1 August 2018 from http://www.darkentriesrecords.com/store/dark-entries/patrick-cowley-school-daze-2xlp.
17. Some notable interviews with Marea on this topic include Eelco Couvreur, "The Black Madonna Manifesto," *DJ Broadcast*, 22 May 2015 (available at https://www.djbroadcast.net/article/121812/the-black-madonna-manifesto); and Kat Leinhart, "The Black Madonna Starts a Women's Movement in Dance Music," *Electronic Beats*, 13 March 2015 (available at http://www.electronicbeats.net/the-black-madonna-starts-a-womens-movement-in-dance-music/).
18. Garcia, "I'm a Tourist"; Garcia, "Techno-Tourism."
19. Rainer Babel and Werner Paravicini, *Grand Tour: Adeliges Reisen und europäische Kultur vom 14. bis zum 18. Jahrhundert: Akten der internationalen Kolloquien in der Villa Vigoni 1999 und im Deutschen Historischen Institut Paris 2000* (Ostfildern, 2005); John Towner, "The Grand Tour: A Key Phase in the History of Tourism," *Annals of Tourism Research* 12, no. 3 (1985): 297–333.

Bibliography

Interviews

Marea Stamper (The Black Madonna). Interview by the author. 4 November 2015.
Ralf (pseudonym). Interview by the author. 9 November 2015.
Sergio (pseudonym). Interview by the author. 6 November 2015.

Printed Sources

Adler, Guido. "Umfang, Methode und Ziel der Musikwissenschaft." *Vierteljahrschrift für Musikwissenschaft* 1 (1885): 5–20.
Appadurai, Arjun. *Modernity at Large: Cultural Dimensions of Globalization.* Minneapolis: University of Minnesota Press, 1996.
Applegate, Celia, and Pamela Potter, eds. *Music and German National Identity.* Chicago: University of Chicago Press, 2002.
Babel, Rainer, and Werner Paravicini. *Grand Tour: Adeliges Reisen und europäische Kultur vom 14. bis zum 18. Jahrhundert: Akten der internationalen Kolloquien in der Villa Vigoni 1999 und im Deutschen Historischen Institut Paris 2000* [in Italian, German, French, or English.]. Ostfildern: Thorbecke, 2005.
Bader, Ingo, and Albert Scharenberg. "The Sound of Berlin: Subculture and the Global Music Industry." *International Journal of Urban and Regional Research* 34, no. 1 (2010): 76–91.

Berlant, Lauren. *The Female Complaint: The Unfinished Business of Sentimentality in American Culture*. Durham, NC: Duke University Press, 2008.

Brandellero, Amanda, and Susanne Janssen. "Popular Music as Cultural Heritage: Scoping Out the Field of Practice." *International Journal of Heritage Studies* 20, no. 3 (2014): 224–40.

Cohen, Sara. "Musical Memory, Heritage and Local Identity: Remembering the Popular Music Past in a European Capital of Culture." *International Journal of Cultural Policy* 19, no. 5 (2012): 576–94.

Couvreur, Eelco. "The Black Madonna Manifesto." *DJ Broadcast*, 22 May 2015. Retrieved 1 August 2018 from https://www.djbroadcast.net/article/121812/the-black-madonna-manifesto.

Denk, Felix, and Sven von Thülen. *Der Klang der Familie: Berlin, Techno und die Wende*. Berlin: Suhrkamp, 2012.

Feige, Marcel, and Kai-Uwe Müller. *Deep in Techno: Die Ganze Geschichte des Movements*. Berlin: Schwarzkopf & Schwarzkopf, 2000.

Garcia, Luis-Manuel. "Crowd Solidarity on the Dance Floor in Paris and Berlin." In *Musical Performance and the Changing City: Post-Industrial Contexts in Europe and the United States*, edited by Fabian Holt and Carsten Wergin, 227–55. New York: Routledge, 2013.

———. "At Home, I'm a Tourist: Musical Migration and Affective Citizenship in Berlin." *Journal of Urban Cultural Studies* 2, no. 1–2 (2015): 121–34.

———. "Beats, Flesh, and Grain: Sonic Tactility and Affect in Electronic Dance Music." *Sound Studies* 1, no. 1 (2016): 59–76.

———. "Techno-Tourism and Postindustrial Neo-Romanticism in Berlin's Electronic Dance Music Scenes." *Tourist Studies* 16, no. 3 (2016): 276–95.

Giddens, Anthony. *The Consequences of Modernity*. Stanford, CA: Stanford University Press, 1990.

Goodman, Steve. *Sonic Warfare: Sound, Affect, and the Ecology of Fear*. Cambridge, MA: MIT Press, 2010.

Graham, Brian. "Heritage as Knowledge: Capital or Culture?" *Urban Studies* 39, no. 5–6 (2002): 1003–17.

Gregg, Melissa, and Gregory J. Seigworth, eds. *The Affect Theory Reader*. Durham, NC: Duke University Press, 2010.

Heinen, Christina M. *"Tief in Neukölln": Soundkulturen zwischen Improvisation und Gentrifizierung in einem Berliner Bezirk*. Bielefeld: transcript Verlag, 2013.

Leinhart, Kat. "The Black Madonna Starts a Women's Movement in Dance Music," *Electronic Beats*, 13 March 2015. Retrieved 1 August 2018 from http://www.electronicbeats.net/the-black-madonna-starts-a-womens-movement-in-dance-music.

Massumi, Brian. "The Autonomy of Affect." *Cultural Critique*, no. 31 (1995): 83–109.

Nye, Sean. "Love Parade, Please Not Again: A Berlin Cultural History." *ECHO: A Music-Centered Journal* 9, no. 1 (2009): 1–50. Retrieved 1 August 2018 from http://www.echo.ucla.edu/Volume9-Issue1/nye/nye1.html.

———. "Minimal Understandings: The Berlin Decade, the Minimal Continuum, and Debates on the Legacy of German Techno." *Journal of Popular Music Studies* 25, no. 2 (2013): 154–84.

Rapp, Tobias. *Lost and Sound: Berlin, Techno und der Easyjetset*. Frankfurt: Suhrkamp, 2009.

Reynolds, Simon. *Energy Flash: A Journey through Rave Music and Dance Culture*. London: Picador, 1998.

Robertson, Roland. "Glocalization: Time-Space and Homogeneity-Heterogeneity." In *Global Modernities*, edited by Mike Featherstone, Scott Lash and Roland Robertson, 25–44. London: Sage, 1995.

Rogers, Thomas. "Berghain: The Secretive, Sex-Fueled World of Techno's Coolest Club." *Rolling Stone*, 6 February 2014. Retrieved 1 August 2018 from https://www.rollingstone.com/culture/culture-news/berghain-the-secretive-sex-fueled-world-of-technos-coolest-club-111396/.

Schwanhäußer, Anja. *Kosmonauten des Underground: Ethnografie einer Berliner Szene*. Frankfurt: Campus, 2010.

Stahl, Geoff, ed. *Poor, but Sexy: Reflections on Berlin Scenes*. Bern: Peter Lang, 2014.

Stewart, Kathleen. *Ordinary Affects*. Durham, NC: Duke University Press, 2007.

Towner, John. "The Grand Tour: A Key Phase in the History of Tourism." *Annals of Tourism Research* 12, no. 3 (1985): 297–333.

Urry, John. *Mobilities*. Cambridge: Polity, 2007.

van der Gaag, Imre. "Function Follows Form: How Berlin Turns Horror into Beauty." *Failed Architecture*, 2014. Retrieved 1 August 2018 from https://failedarchitecture.com/berlin-horror-beauty/.

Waltmann, Dirk, Sven Schäfer, and Jesper Schäfer. *Techno-Lexicon: Das umfassende Nachschlagewerk zur größten Jugendkultur Europas*. Berlin: Schwarzkopf & Schwarzkopf, 1998.

Waltz, Alexis. "Nightclubbing: Berlin's Ostgut—Berghain before It Was Berghain." *Red Bull Music Academy Daily*, 24 September 2013. Retrieved 1 August 2018 from http://www.redbullmusicacademy.com/magazine/nightclubbing-ostgut.

PART II

The Local, the Regional, the National

CHAPTER 4

Bruckner, Munich, and the Longue Durée of Musical Listening between the Imperial and Postwar Eras

NEIL GREGOR

Few periods of German history challenge our ability to think of the plurality and diversity of musical identities across time, their capacity to weave in and out of the conventional periodizations of political history, and their tendency to inhabit simultaneously a multitude of indeterminate, overlapping cultural spaces as that of National Socialist Germany. Even as historians believe themselves to have long since jettisoned them, clichéd assumptions regarding the subordination of culture to dictatorship, and the continued insistence on Nazism's highly homogenizing dynamics, persist. These combine to imply that the multitude of imaginaries present in modern German history were brutally disrupted, if not completely broken down, following the Nazi seizure of power in 1933.[1]

Study of the reception of Anton Bruckner's music in the twentieth century has been a case in point. It has become axiomatic that after 1933 a "Nazi" way of hearing Bruckner supplanted the multiple ways of hearing the composer—as an Austrian, an Austro-German, a pious Roman Catholic, a Schopenhauerian, a mystic, a musician inspired by the mountain landscapes of his regional *Heimat*—that had existed before. A singularly nationalist, secular, and monumental reading of the composer bulldozed over all alternatives.[2] Bruckner's 1937 induction by the regime into the Walhalla monument near Regensburg—the nineteenth-century monument to "great Germans" in the form of a literal pantheon above the Danube—has become both a synecdoche for the more fundamental "nazification" of a specific cultural icon and a symbolic moment that carries, implicitly, a wider argument about how culture "worked" during the National Socialist era. Not for nothing has it been repeatedly referenced in both scholarly and popular constructions of that process down to the present day.[3]

Such ways of imagining the cultural history of the period are so persistent, in part, because they have become so naturalized within the language used to narrate the history of the period that they are no longer seen. In the extensive debate that occurred in the mid 1990s over Bruckner's place under the regime, for example, Bryan Gilliam spoke of the "annexation" of Bruckner, a metaphor that carried strong connotations of forceful occupation from outside and thus the assumption that "culture" is a space antithetical to "politics" under putatively "normal" conditions.[4] This is not to say that competing visions of Bruckner found no place in the narrative after 1933. Rather, in such readings, the Wagnerian, secular, "Greater German" Bruckner fêted by the regime was set in opposition to the Christian composer of church music emphasized by the International Bruckner Society (IBG) in a manner that assumed that the regime—understood as a unitary, homogeneous entity, populated by equally homogeneous "Nazis"—"manipulated" the image of Bruckner in a falsifying "propaganda." These processes of meaning-making were seen as being entirely top-down and constituted a "misuse" [*Missbrauch*]. They produced a "distorted" image of the composer that was at odds with a historical reality accessible (in implicitly unmediated form) in "normal" (i.e., non-Nazi) times.[5]

In a recent stimulating intervention on the conservative musical politics of the 1920s, however, Nicholas Attfield has demonstrated clearly how traces of different interpretive traditions surrounding Bruckner became interwoven, showing, in particular, how mystic, conservative, and nationalist vocabularies became fused.[6] This essay seeks to build on that insight by tracing the presence of that discursive interweaving through the period of the Third Reich (and beyond) too, for the cultural life of Nazi Germany was also considerably more open and varied than much inherited scholarship implies. There was significant regional variation: indeed, far from being shut down, the multiple federal traditions of German history were reanimated and became sites on which a variety of Nazi-compatible subjectivities could be mobilized. Towns and cities likewise drew on a diverse range of pre-existing civic traditions to become lively sites of cultural production, perpetuating, albeit in modified form, a wide range of discourses in which meaning continued to be produced through lively argumentation, not just conformist adaptation to an imagined single "Nazi" norm defined at the top.[7] This was produced by a multitude of different actors and speakers, whose voices and positions did not fall into a simple division of party supporters and nonsupporters, or otherwise map obviously onto a "Nazi"/"non-Nazi" divide.[8] They constituted a field of diverse opinions within a very general framework of permitted speech rather than a single ideological line.[9]

Many discourses surrounding Bruckner coursed through the "contained pluralist" environment of the National Socialist regime.[10] They were fashioned by a much larger variety of voices—those of popular biographers, program note authors, concert reviewers, and others—than a focus on Goebbels's speech at Walhalla in 1937 or the attendant publications in one or two prominent journals such as *Die Musik* would acknowledge. Indeed, the capacity of a number of different ways of thinking about Bruckner and his music to survive throughout the period and into the postwar era is indicative of substantial elements of continuity that were precisely part of what enabled the regime to naturalize itself so swiftly.

At the same time, 1945 was not the end of every story. As Karen Painter has demonstrated, it is easy enough to map the emergence of a language of symphonic monumentality through the early twentieth-century reception history of large-scale works onto broad moves in the direction of authoritarian politics and thus to demonstrate how the evolution of habits of thought in the sphere of musical culture performed cultural and political work on behalf of aggressive nationalist agendas.[11] But as Tim Mason argued long ago, where we begin and where we end a story does much to determine what we do and do not see, and a narrative organized around the conventional vanishing points of 1933 and 1945 can easily miss those stories that crossed those caesuras in more fluid and open ways.[12]

The examination in this chapter of both the flow and the persistence of such ideas across multiple caesuras is pursued via an exploration of the many voices that circulated between the late Wilhelmine period and the postwar era in and through Munich. Munich was a city long associated with Bruckner.[13] It was the site of the second performance of his seventh symphony, in 1885, an event subsequently mythologized as the moment when the composer made his public breakthrough. It hosted the first ever festival of Bruckner's music, in 1905. A series of conductors associated with the city and its musical institutions—most notably, Ferdinand Loewe, Siegmund von Hausegger, and Oswald Kabasta—had proselytized for Bruckner's music from an early stage. In the 1930s the city was a key site for the performance of the "original" scores of some of the symphonies, most notably when von Hausegger conducted back-to-back performances of both the published and the "original" scores of the ninth symphony in a single evening; the "original" score of the fifth symphony was likewise first performed by von Hausegger and the Munich Philharmonic Orchestra in 1935.[14] Members of Munich's local musical world fashioned these and other associations into an identity as a "Bruckner city" (*Brucknerstadt*) that emerged in the 1920s. This notion was strengthened during the National Socialist era and reanimated in after the war. The trope of the "Bruckner city" thus moved across successive periods of political rupture and provided a key element of continuity in local discourses centered on the composer, even as its inflections, valences, and resonances shifted from context to context.

Nationalism and Its Interlocutors in Interwar Munich

In Munich after World War I, one does not have to go far to find stridently nationalist constructions of Bruckner, with references both to "greater

German" cultural imaginaries and to overtones of racial thought. Paul Ehlers, who wrote for the *Münchner Neueste Nachrichten*, the city's main serious newspaper in the early 1920s, is a prime example. Ehlers later became the president of the Munich chapter of the Nazi-supporting Kampfbund für Deutsche Kultur, joined the Nazi party itself in 1933, and went on to write for prominent National Socialist music organs in the 1930s. In a review of a concert of Schubert and Bruckner symphonies given by von Hausegger and the Munich Philharmonic Orchestra in November 1922, for example, Ehlers wrote that "Schubert and Bruckner are not only ethnically [*völkisch*] but also spiritually musical sons of the same mother, the German-Austrian tribal community [*Stammesgemeinschaft*] (and the German-Austrian Siegmund von Hausegger is, to anticipate here, their wonderful prophet!)."[15] Such interventions can easily be placed in a linear narrative with any number of similar such texts published during the Nazi era that place the same "greater German" construction on Bruckner and cast his music in forceful, monumental language.[16] Upon the outbreak of World War II in particular, Bruckner was pushed aggressively into the service of nationalist politics. In a review of its concert season of 1939–40, local music publicist Wilhelm Zentner noted in the house magazine of the Munich Philharmonic Orchestra that "the programming was, naturally, determined by the needs of our profoundly eventful times, which forge all the forces of our national being into a unity. It sought and found its beating heart in the preferential treatment of German music. Beethoven and Bruckner, the two greatest German symphonists, were represented with almost all their symphonic creations."[17]

The dynamic of nationalization that unfolded at the level of civic cultural life took place in tandem, and in interaction, with the corresponding processes at national level. That the two processes were mutually implicated and co-constitutive is exemplified by the fact that, when Bruckner was inaugurated into the Walhalla monument, Hitler entrusted the Munich Philharmonic Orchestra with performing at the event. The orchestra celebrated this in subsequent promotional literature as a sign of its national commitment, noting proudly in a 1939 brochure that "in 1937 the Munich Philharmonic was engaged by the Reich and Bavarian State governments as the only festival orchestra for the International Bruckner Festival in Regensburg and for the state ceremony on the occasion of the erection of the Bruckner bust in Walhalla, and honoured on the occasion with the silver Bruckner medallion as the hitherto only orchestra to receive it."[18] Similarly, when, a year after the Walhalla event, von Hausegger retired as the Philharmonic's conductor-in-chief, Munich's mayor, Karl Fiehler, noted in his *laudatio* von Hausegger's achievement in "orientating Munich's musical life away from destructive Jewish and cultural Bolshevist influences," for which "his greatest reward ... was doubtless the engagement with his orchestra for the Reich Party Rally in 1937 to perform Bruckner's fifth symphony before the Führer on his command."[19] Conversely, the city's associations with the composer received material expression with the installation of a bust of Bruckner in the foyer of the Tonhalle, then the orchestra's home, in 1938.[20]

In other words: if one seeks, one finds. It is not difficult to take cumulative incidences of a nationalizing, racist, and anti-Semitic rhetoric attached to Bruckner and generate a narrative whereby at all levels, from the local and civic to the national, Bruckner was co-opted into a single "Nazi" vision. And yet, if nothing else, many of the same voices were regularly given to availing themselves of quite different vocabularies and registers. In his history of the advocacy of Bruckner by successive Munich-based conductors penned for the occasion of the Munich Bruckner Festival of 1930, for example, Ehlers noted that "when [Ferdinand] Loewe conducted Bruckner, one constantly had the feeling of attending a High Mass; unbeknown perhaps to him, something of the piety of Bruckner seemed to flow across to him."[21] Indeed, even at that most putatively "nazified" of moments, the induction into Walhalla, the festivities included a performance of Bruckner's *Te Deum* in the Minoritenkirche in Regensburg, on which occasion the same Wilhelm Zentner wrote, "Why, on the occasion of the evening concert in the wonderfully restored concert hall of the Minoritenkirche, does the Te Deum, interpreted by maestro Schrems, seize one with such forceful power? For sure, the builder of such massive cathedrals of sound, Anton Bruckner, hardly created anything greater."[22]

The ongoing presence of Bruckner's religious music, its performance in religious spaces, and its celebration by conventional nationalist critics such as Zentner at even the most high profile of ritual political events reminds that older discourses about the composer did not lose currency in the Nazi era. A variety of possibilities of imagining Bruckner remained both available and openly articulable in the language of the period. Indeed a cursory reading of the body of popular and semi-scholarly texts written by Munich-based authors, published in Munich, or otherwise regularly referenced by such texts as part of the emerging canon of literature on the composer in the first half of the twentieth century underlines not only that more than one tradition of thinking about the composer could manifest in the writings of a single author, but also, indeed, in one and the same text. Thus, the first biography of Bruckner, published in 1905 by the then music critic of the *Münchner Neueste Nachrichten*, Rudolf Louis, emphasized his "new German" musical heritage and, above all, his debt to Wagner, but also acknowledged his religious inspirations.[23] Max Auer, the influential president of the IBG, was likewise capable, simultaneously, of articulating aggressively nationalist approaches and of emphasizing the religious underpinnings not only of the sacred music but of the symphonies too.[24] Ernst Decsey, whose writings were widely referenced by Munich commentators, gave even more weight to Bruckner's deep religiosity.

But he simultaneously stressed the composer's rural anchorings and inspiration in the landscapes of the Alps.²⁵

The concurrent presence in such texts of tropes conventionally regarded as belonging to distinctive versions of what Bruckner's music stood for underscores that there was much overlap between different accounts. For all their differences, they tended to transport variations of a story rather than fundamentally competing versions of it. Their repetitiveness reinforced the stubborn longevity of these tropes once established.²⁶ This was particularly so when authors recycled their own writings from book to newspaper article to speech and back, sometimes across more than one political caesura; it was also reinforced by the intertextual relationship between writings by different authors, many of whom referred to and borrowed from—in ways both explicit and unacknowledged—the writings of one another, reproducing and transporting motifs through the literature and into contexts ever more removed from their original point of coinage.²⁷ Writers on Bruckner deployed them in diverse political, institutional, or literary contexts, which varied from academic volumes intended for close reading through popular handbooks designed for repeated consultation to program notes meant for cursory consumption. Readerships varied accordingly. Thus, Zentner's reference to "cathedrals of sound" in his review of the 1937 Regensburg performance of the Te Deum echoed an earlier formulation of Max Auer's; as late as 1946 Zentner was referring to Bruckner as "God's musician" [*der Musikant Gottes*], recycling a trope established in the literature in 1924 by Victor Léon and Ernst Decsey in their stage play of that name.²⁸

The difficulty of distinguishing competing constructions of Bruckner in a manner that sees them as embodiments of distinctive ideological positions and consumed as such in predictable, controlled ways by readers becomes most apparent, however, when one considers the polysemous qualities of the core terms that figured in the discourses surrounding the composer.²⁹ In his survey of the symphonies published for the Munich Bruckner Festival of 1930, for example, Erich Schwebsch described their consecutive emergence in terms of a series of stages in the finding of God: "thus we unconsciously experience the unity of the symphonic works as a tiered path of a higher nature, as necessary way stations of a musical communion"; by the completion of the fifth symphony, at which point "the entrances to his divine being are now always open to him," the music is described as the "music of one who bears the cross [*Kreuzträgermusik*]."³⁰ Yet it is also striking how easily such biblical language could segue into registers that owed more to nineteenth- and early twentieth-century languages of mysticism. Schwebsch described the expansiveness of Bruckner's symphonies using metaphors of spatial and temporal depth allied to a lexicon of "the eternal" that was not necessarily, or exclusively, metaphysical at all but could easily be imagined as connoting earthly power. Terms such as "giant" (*riesenhaft*), "immeasurable" (*unermesslich*), and "enormous" (*ungeheuer*) evoked multiple imaginaries of time and space that might easily be incorporated by different readers into both religious and secular ways of thinking and feeling at once. Similarly, in their mobilization of languages of struggle, inexorable power, vitalism, or inwardness, texts such as those of Schwebsch drew on semantic fields that lent themselves, variously and simultaneously, to Christian, mystical, Schopenhauerian, martial, and nationalist appropriations according to choice, dependent not only on the convictions of the author but also on the mental frames of the individual reader. The multivalent quality of such vocabularies was precisely what gave the many overlapping cultural imaginaries that moved through and across this period their openness, their nebulousness, and their longevity and enabled them to resist too direct or exclusive a colonization by any one obvious set of ideological positions.

1933: A Moment of Rupture?

A comparison of the two Bruckner festivals that took place in Munich in 1930 and 1933 can be a useful starting point for considering what did and did not change in the transition from Weimar to Nazi Germany. The first followed immediately in the wake of the 1929 formation of the Munich chapter of the IBG, which had been formally constituted in Vienna earlier that year. The founding chair of the Munich chapter was Siegmund von Hausegger, whose pan-German political sensibilities placed him within one broad reception tradition. The choice of cathedral choir director Ludwig Berberich and cathedral organist Josef Schmid as his two deputies, however, underlines the strong emphasis placed by Munich's Bruckner community on the composer's sacred music.[31]

Hausegger had worked hard to bring the first international Bruckner festival of the IBG to Munich in 1930. In addition to performances in the Tonhalle of the fifth and sixth symphonies under Franz Schalk and the eighth symphony under Hausegger, the F-minor mass was given—also in the Tonhalle—by local conductor Adolf Mennerich (alongside the ninth symphony). Ludwig Berberich conducted the E-minor mass in the Odeon concert hall; the whole festival opened with an additional celebratory mass in the cathedral.[32]

For all of this sacred music a simultaneous staging of Wagner's *Rienzi* in the state theater gestured at the same time toward a cultural nationalist reading of the composer that stressed his affinities with Wagnerian tradition. As the speeches that accompanied the event—and the local reportage—suggest, however, the variety of discourses that circulated simultaneously through the festival was as wide as ever. Reporting on a speech given by the Viennese court councillor Max von Willenkovich entitled "Bruckner's Mission," for example, the *Münchner Neueste Nachrichten* noted how "following comments on the esteem in which Bruckner was held by Richard Wagner and on the role of Munich in the breakthrough of the master the speaker showed how Bruckner's music had brought us back to our connection with the divine, something that has never been needed more greatly than in our own time."[33] In this way, Wagnerizing constructions of Bruckner, local civic associations, Bruckner's own deep religiosity, and implicitly conservative anti-Republican sentiments were referenced simultaneously in the space of a few lines, demonstrating again the entangled quality of the many rhetorics surrounding the composer.

Yet the emphasis in this first festival was ultimately on the sacred music, reflecting how central religious ways of imagining the composer were to the event. This was not born merely of the curatorial preferences of the festival organizers, but spoke to the deeply ingrained religious, and specifically Roman Catholic, sentiments among the intended audience. Indeed, the festival was timed to coincide with the Oberammergau Passion Play of 1930.[34] The festival program's front page featured a poem entitled "Anton Bruckner" whose stanzas similarly testified, in their repeated invocations of the saints, to a specifically Roman Catholic sensibility informing the event.[35] Not only did the sacred compositions figure prominently in the official program of events, but a number of other performances were given in churches around the city to coincide. The requiem was given in the Theatinerkirche by the Munich Bruckner Association for the Cultivation of Spiritual Music, where it was performed by the mass choirs of several local churches.[36] Neither were such performances exceptional moments in the musical life of a city that otherwise ignored Bruckner's sacred music—in its review of the performance of the E-minor mass, for example, the *Münchner Neueste Nachrichten* noted that "it must be said that, to the credit of the practice of church music in Munich, this piece is in the repertoire not only of the cathedral but also of other churches."[37]

The contrast between the emphasis on Bruckner's religious identity at the 1930 festival and the nationalizing rhetoric that surrounded the 1933 event is unmistakable and testifies to an obvious shift in political climate. The October 1933 festival was held under the motto "A Demonstration of German Spirit" [*Eine Kundgebung Deutschen Geistes*].[38] Such language resonated with the generic nationalist discourse of the "national uprising" that characterized much of the public culture of that year, but the organizers went to considerable lengths to strike a more stridently "National Socialist" tone too. The Munich Philharmonic Orchestra, one of the mainstays of the festival, suggested that either Hitler or Reich President Hindenburg be offered the position of honorary patron of the festival.[39] On new Nazi mayor Karl Fiehler's direction the post was offered instead to the *Reichsstatthalter* of Bavaria, Franz Ritter von

Epp, and to Bavarian minister president Ludwig Siebert, yet the list of honorary recipients of tickets to the festival concerts—which included Bavarian ministers of state Adolf Wagner, Hans Frank, and Hermann Esser—read like a Who's Who of prominent Nazi dignitaries.[40]

In his draft program notes, likewise, IBG President Auer took the opportunity to align the festival with an overtly "National Socialist" cultural-historical critique, noting how "the hypermodernity of the postwar era was based on a thoroughly Bolshevik tendency; contempt for everything inherited, for rules and laws; this lawlessness, introduced by racially alien elements, also poisoned the creativity of German youth, and there emerged that unpersonal music, lacking any rootedness, that sought to call itself 'international music.'"[41] These sentiments were reinforced in his opening remarks to the annual meeting of the IBG, in which he proclaimed that "with hardly any other great master of the art of composition is it likely to have been as possible as it has been for Bruckner to prove his German blood lines back through four hundred years with unbroken documentation." Bruckner's remote ancestors, Auer continued, hailed from the "Nibelungengau." They were in what was now Lower Austria "as settlers and farmers on German soil. Thus his art reaches back into the primal origins of the Germanic people, of the human soul."[42]

As far as the programming of the festival was concerned, there was also a tangible, though partial, shift away from the sacred music and toward the symphonies. In the enlarged program for 1933 the F-minor mass and *Te Deum* were given in one concert by von Hausegger; a mass was held in the cathedral on the middle Sunday of the festival (figuring, in contrast to 1930, as one event among many, rather than as the festive opening). Berberich gave a further a cappella concert with the cathedral choir in the Odeon that included minor choral works by Bruckner; an additional performance of the D-minor mass was given in the Michaels-Hofkirche under the direction of Adolf Singer.

Nonetheless, whatever this may suggest about attempts by either the new local arbiters of cultural policy or sections of the local Bruckner society to rebalance veneration of the composer away from the sacred music and toward the notionally secular, attendance at the performances of the religious music remained high. According to the account of the festival printed immediately afterward in the IBG's newsletter, "all the concerts in the Tonhalle and the Odeon were completely sold out, and at some the demand could only be met by quickly adding additional seating in at the last minute. The demand was just as great at the performances in church, in the cathedral and St Michael's church."[43] Moreover, not only did the commitment to performing the sacred music remain, but there was palpable resistance to the increasing habit of doing so in the concert hall rather than in the context of the celebration of mass. In his account of the festival penned for the *Zeitschrift für Musik*, Zentner noted that "there was also an opportunity to hear the three masses again. Of these the D-minor and E-minor masses sounded out in their fitting place within the liturgical frame of the Sunday service, the former in the cathedral under Professor Ludwig Berberich, the latter in the Michaels-Hofkirche under Professor Alfons [sic] Singer, and were able in this environment to exude their unbroken magic that is not to be measured by aesthetic criteria alone."

Such remarks indicate a strongly intact religious sensibility that, in the case of Zentner, was entirely compatible with his nationalist perspective on Germany's cultural patrimony. He complained, indeed, that "the F-Minor mass, which is perhaps the most suited to a concert performance, was not quite in the right place in the sober environment of the Tonhalle. The experience of 1930 repeated itself: it was as if the work was resisting its separation out from its liturgical context and its removal from the space of the church." While some of the absent effect may have been due to the choir not having performed at its best, Zentner conceded, "the reason why the mass did not have the same powerful effect as those of its sister pieces played in their proper place is not to be found solely in external factors but lies in the nature of the creations themselves."[44] Indeed, for all the greater emphasis prominent Bruckner commentators now placed on the symphonies, and for all that commentators such as Auer downplayed any religious content in these, Bruckner's sacred music remained in the repertoire throughout the period of the Third Reich, in both church and concert hall settings.[45]

The continued performance of Bruckner's sacred music did not simply express the persistence of a *resistent* religious sentiment and practice in the period. Rather, it reflected the ongoing presence of a variety of cultural-spatial discourses that had not been dissolved by the more powerful forces of a simple, unitary "nationalizing" rhetoric on the part of the regime that dominated from 1933 onwards. Elements of an apparently straightforward "greater German" nationalist rhetoric that appeared, at first sight, simply to legitimate Nazism's "annexation" of both the composer and his country of origin tended to overlay deeper-seated ways of imagining cultural space and affinity that were not synonymous with a uniform National Socialist "greater German" vision, but rather existed within, alongside, and underneath it.

The Munich Philharmonic Orchestra's tour to Austria in 1936 is a case in point. In his account of the tour, the orchestra's administrator Otto Mayer placed the trip firmly within an aggressively "greater German" nationalist framework and identified it as a piece of cultural diplomacy in line with the foreign policy agendas of the National Socialist movement. "From Kärnten," he wrote, "and indeed from the Steiermark, we have brought with us as a souvenir the conviction that there stands, on the threatened outpost of the greater German border, a people hardened in defensive struggle who stake life and possessions for the defence of Germandom, face forward but feeling the powerful strength of the entire German *Volksgemeinschaft* behind it, in order that they may always be able to draw upon it anew." In this way, he continued, the visit to Austria was not only a great artistic success but also a "most deeply felt expression of the powerful German blood-brotherhood not to be destroyed by any enemy powers."

Yet such language was intertwined with another register, that of a shared Bavarian-Austrian *Heimat*. This distinctive rhetoric simultaneously evoked, through a quite different repertoire of images, a sense of cultural and historical affinity with a much deeper archaeology. Describing the orchestra's crossing of the border at Salzburg, Mayer explained that it was "a joy, of course, to be able once more to tread after many long years on brother Austrian soil, to which our relationships and personal connections as citizens of Munich in particular, as immediate neighbors, mountain comrades and war comrades, have always been heartfelt, I would almost say familial in nature."[46] Such evocations of shared geography, culture, and history, anchored in a sense of shared experience and patrimony, bespoke the presence of a diffuse but palpable southern German-Austrian ethnic and cultural space that transcended the vicissitudes of nineteenth- and twentieth-century politics and successive state formations.

Traces of this imaginary reproduce themselves in multiple variants in fragments of discourse across the literary ephemera attached to Bruckner in Munich before and after 1933. Their variety underlines that of all the semantic fields upon which Bruckner criticism drew in the first half of the twentieth century, the language of "Germanness" was the most diffuse. Mayer's account of the tour to Austria is interesting to read, for example, alongside Ludwig Berberich's description of the E-minor mass penned for the 1930 Munich Bruckner festival. He noted, first, that "today the mass enjoys 'house rights' [*Heimatrecht*] not only in the cathedrals of South Germany but also in those of the more austere North," in a manner that reflected clear assumptions regarding the absence of a homogenous German cultural space. Moreover, his subsequent comments appeared not only to suggest a distinctive south German patrimony, but to imply that this included Austria too. Noting, for example, that in the opening kyrie of the mass "Bruckner departs completely from the Haydn and Mozart traditions of upper Austria, with their celebratory, intoxicating introductions," Mayer remarked of the Credo that "whoever does not understand the *et incarnatus est* in all its devoutness and warm sentimentality simply does not understand southern German nature at all, should leave Bruckner be and—emigrate!"[47] In this manner, "southern German" was imagined not as a politically defined and bordered entity but rather as a synonym for a loosely defined southern-central European German cultural space of the same kind to which Mayer alluded in his ostensibly very different account of the orchestra tour six years later.

Nationalism and Mysticism: Listening to Bruckner in World War II

The most obvious moment of "nationalizing" rhetoric came with the outbreak of war in 1939. The Munich Philharmonic Orchestra's concert journal was typical in its pronouncement that "one cannot imagine that the people of a Bach, Mozart, Beethoven, Schubert and Bruckner should have anything to fear, as long as the ethos of these great figures, with their courage in struggle, their trust, their enthusiasm and their joy burns in people's hearts."[48] Similarly, at the end of the first season of the war, the same publication insisted that "the war demands not only the greatest external unleashing of force imaginable; its successful prosecution is also inseparable from the mobilization of the inner, spiritual and moral forces of a people. Where, however, would one become more forcefully and proudly aware of the latter than in art, in which the sum of a people's spirit is unified?"[49]

Such remarks testify simultaneously to a moment of intensified nationalist commitment and to the institutional needs of orchestras such as the Munich Philharmonic to justify their ongoing activities as "war essential."[50] As the war progressed, however, the language of music criticism and concert reviews also resonated with a poetic concern for last things and the mysteries of the cosmos. These continued, sometimes, to be inflected with the inherited language of Christian faith, but often owed an obvious debt to secular traditions of metaphysical thinking that had their roots in late nineteenth- and early twentieth-century vulgarizations of Schopenhauerian philosophy. Again, this habit of mind predated the National Socialist seizure of power and embodied a discourse that was widely drawn upon in the interwar era. In 1930, for example, the then music critic of the *Münchner Neueste Nachrichten*, Oskar von Pander, wrote in respect of a performance of Bruckner of the "breathtaking, thrill-inducing sinking of the sound into the nothingness" that evoked an understanding of music's relationship to the noumenal with its clear origin in Schopenhauerian aesthetics.[51] Pander retained his post at the *Münchner Neueste Nachrichten* through the National Socialist era; in the war, in particular, his criticism resonated with such Schopenhauerian allusions. Of Bruckner's fourth symphony, for example, he wrote in October 1939 that "both the listening for mystical connections within the cosmos and the tragedy of subjectivity are already present here."[52] The Munich Philharmonic Orchestra, similarly, reached specifically for Schopenhauerian constructions of music and its status as a conduit for the underlying drives of the noumenal world during the war, foregrounding a lengthy set of extracts of the philosopher's writing "On the Nature of Music" from *The World as Will and Representation* in its concert journal of November 1940: "The effect of music is far more powerful and penetrating than that of the other arts, for these speak only of the shadow, whereas it speaks of the actual thing. Music gives the innermost core of a being prior to its being given form, or the heart of things. ... The composer reveals the innermost nature of the world and expresses the deepest wisdom in a language that his reasoning self does not comprehend."[53]

In the second half of the war, Pander, in particular, reached for such language more and more. In July 1943, for example, he wrote of the "unfathomable depths" of Bruckner's music.[54] Of the eighth symphony, he opined only a few months later that "here 'the tragic' is presented in all its universal validity, of which only music, with its capacity to give meaning beyond time and space, is capable."[55] As with both the continued elements of religious thinking and the resonances of the deep cultural-spatial imaginary of southern Germany in the criticism of the era, such metaphysical thought was interwoven with other discourses, including nationalist ones. Thus, in a review of a September 1943 concert that paired Hans Pfitzner's *Das Dunkle Reich* with Bruckner's ninth symphony, Pander wrote that "if [Pfitzner's] choir of the dead felt like a greeting from beyond, so did the closing Bruckner's Ninth give one a sight of that beyond, an insight into secrets of such wonderful depth and beauty as can only be received in a state of overcome awe by the rational listener."[56] Pander's evocations of the mysteries of the universe intertwined unmistakably with national pathos in the wake of defeat at Stalingrad, reminding forcefully that whatever configurations of tropes were present in successive accounts of Bruckner's music, they gained their force not only from what was actually articulated, but also from the context in which it was said.[57]

Between the Catholic and the Civic: (Re)Constructing Bruckner after 1945

As shown by the examples of the Bruckner festivals of 1930 and 1933, the orchestra's tour to Austria in 1936, and popular writings about the composer in the war, the stridently nationalist constructions associated with the Nazi regime were almost always infused with echoes of other ways of thinking about music, be they Christian, regionalist, Schopenhauerian, or something else again. How did this habit of continuous intermingling of tropes fare across the political and moral rupture of 1945? What is initially striking, again, is the apparent discontinuity, most obviously in the shift toward decidedly Christian, and specifically Roman Catholic, readings. Zentner, whose career survived the political reckoning of 1945 entirely unscathed, embodying the well-known element of biographical continuity that has done so much to shape discussion of German musicology's mid twentieth-century history, was a case in point.[58] He lost no time in repositioning his voice as an exponent of the overtly

"Catholic" reading of the composer, issuing a short account of Bruckner's life that foregrounded piety as the source of his musical inspiration.[59] By the time the Munich Philharmonic Orchestra had firmly re-established its main concert series in 1950, with Zentner as its main publicist, the emphasis in his writing for audiences was also very much on Bruckner's music as an expression of deep faith.

Thus, when the seventh symphony—a piece broadcast by the German Reich radio service upon the announcement of Hitler's death, and thus freighted with a peculiar nationalist baggage for contemporaries—was performed in March 1950, Zentner's note observed that "the seventh symphony represents, in its overall outlook, the highest unison between mankind, the world and God."[60] Likewise, his accompanying text for the fifth symphony, performed by the Munich Philharmonic in December 1951, noted that the work embodied "an almost unprecedented force of synthesis, the synthesis between heaven and earth, man and God, time and eternity."[61] The reanimation of something specifically Roman Catholic in Zentner's postwar account was captured in his description of the ninth symphony as Bruckner's "ultimate confession [*Lebensbeichte*]."[62] Zentner's own repositioning was underlined by a greater tendency to write about the sacred works, for instance, his contribution of a pamphlet on the F-minor mass to a series entitled "The Christian Heritage in Music" that he himself edited.[63] Other, newer commentators, unencumbered by previous statements and thus with less strategic need to claim different positions, also stressed the personal piety and the peculiarly Roman Catholic quality in Bruckner's music. Alfons Ott, who was to become the director of the city's public music library and an influential voice in the local musical establishment, described a performance of the eighth symphony by the Bavarian Radio Symphony Orchestra in terms of humanity caught between "the chasms of darkness and the immeasurable heights of the world of divine light."[64] Elsewhere in the same brochure he underlined that Bruckner composed from the perspective of a "practicing Catholic."

If the forceful "re-Christianization" of Bruckner in post-1945 Munich suggested a dynamic of postwar reorientation and discontinuity from that which had gone before, other aspects of the postwar discourse surrounding the composer stood out for their apparent continuity. The most obvious of these pertained to Bruckner's relationship with the city. The program notes for a performance of the seventh symphony in November 1950, for example, contained an essay entitled "Bruckner's Seventh Symphony and Munich" that recounted exactly the same stories of the 1885 Munich premiere of the symphony and its role in the composer's public breakthrough that had been the standard fare of concert programs for the previous twenty years. The notes observed not only that "the early reputation and fame of Munich as a site of deep understanding of Bruckner dates from this remarkable performance," but that "we who come after are filled with a particular pride that our Munich was the site of the first comprehension of Bruckner and has remained true to this spirit down to the present day!"—placing themselves, without self-reflexivity or critical distance, in a direct line of continuity with a long tradition of Bruckner reception.[65]

These civic associations are repeated with a frequency and forcefulness across the archive of Bruckner reception in postwar Munich. Such local linkage suggests a proclivity not only to ignore the way the composer was framed during the Nazi era but also to see in the city's Bruckner traditions a set of positive alternative traditions that distanced Munich, its musical life, and its politics from those of the National Socialist regime. In other words, only shortly after the celebration of associations between the city and the composer had served to suture the local culture to that of the regime, these were now mobilized to do the opposite—the unspoken assumption being that anything anchored in civic tradition must necessarily have stood in conflict with the "totalizing" dynamics of a centralizing Nazi state.[66] While the forceful reaffirmation of Bruckner's Christian identity sat within a wider reanimation of aspects of political and cultural tradition that could be imagined, with very strong doses of selectivity, to have embodied "non-Nazi" or even "anti-Nazi" habits of thought, the simultaneous re-embrace of pre-existing rhetorics anchored in the civic was much more ambiguous, as traditions of governance and identity formation that had been highly implicated in National Socialist politics were simply reimagined after the event to have been an untainted space of thought and action.

Between them, the reanimation of the religious and civic rhetorics surrounding Bruckner appear to carry that blend of pragmatic distancing, continuity, and denial that many scholars have seen as dominating the immediate postwar reckoning, such as it was, with the legacies of the Nazi era. Yet such a reading sells short the complexities of the postwar emotional landscape. Performing the music of Bruckner carried far more complex layers of meaning and, in some ways, a more intractable set of historical encumbrances. Certainly, to experience Bruckner in the early 1950s was to do something more than act out a banal continuity. To mount a Bruckner symphony cycle in an environment in which Karl Amadeus Hartmann's postwar project of "Musica Viva" was articulating its forceful critique of the Romantic canon in Munich was, if nothing else, a forcefully pointed gesture of its own—a "negation of the negation" for which the modernist "Musica Viva" itself stood. But in the case of the Munich Philharmonic Orchestra's performance of Bruckner in the immediate postwar period, there were layers of memory and meaning that went considerably deeper still.

Here it is instructive to focus on the orchestra's relationship to its principal conductor from 1938 to 1945, Oswald Kabasta. Kabasta, like his predecessor

Siegmund von Hausegger an Austrian, had been appointed on account of both his status as a distinguished interpreter of Bruckner and his strong German nationalist proclivities. Once in Munich, he proved himself a loyal conformist whose political sensibilities appeared entirely in tune with the regime. His first performance with the Munich Philharmonic, at what amounted to an audition, in 1937, was of Bruckner's eighth symphony; he developed a particular reputation over the course of his six-and-a-half-year tenure with the orchestra for his performances of the piece, which was also the centerpiece of his final concert with them, in August 1944, just before the orchestra was closed down by the regime.[67] Kabasta's emotional attachment to this music was captured in a handwritten note of 5 April 1945, in which he described "this incomparable symphony, with the greatest, deepest Adagio ever written for orchestra."[68] Banned from performing by the denazification authorities, Kabasta committed suicide in February 1946. Two days before this he wrote to Munich mayor Karl Scharnagl asking the Munich Philharmonic Orchestra to remember him and his wife the next time they played "his" Bruckner's eighth symphony.[69]

Far from dissociating themselves from their politically tainted conductor, the orchestra celebrated his memory repeatedly in the early 1950s: in 1951, indeed, it traveled to Kufstein, Austria, where he was buried, specifically to perform a memorial concert.[70] Similarly, in May 1950 a performance of Bruckner's eighth symphony was framed as a memorial event, the program carrying a photo of him with the caption "In memory of Oswald Kabasta." Noting Kabasta's particular affinity for "his Eighth," the program note explained that "this love was of such a deeply ingrained nature, that it accompanied Oswald Kabasta not only through his earthly life: he wanted to know himself accompanied by its mystery even on his journey into the dark realm [*dunkle Reich*]." It continued: "some of our orchestra members will remember the words of the master, absorbed by thoughts of death, to whom a life without music meant no life at all: 'when you play the Eighth, think of me!'"[71]

On the face of it, the declaration that "we mourn the loss of a great conductor, a good and noble man" carries the tendency, typical of the period, and indeed much subsequent music history writing, to divorce the aesthetic achievements of the person from their ideological commitments. This seems symptomatic of the era's allegedly amnesic pragmatism. The statement, however, that "only we can feel ourselves at one with him and his soul as this 'Eighth' resounds, which none aware of the context will listen to without being deeply moved" transported something different, born of experiences that seemed now to echo across from a distant and yet highly present past. Indeed, it referenced hauntings that carried both a residue of national pathos and a sense of emotional community born of powerful shared memories. The emotional legibility of this moment for all concerned depended in turn on the recognition of the profound impact of wartime violence, dislocation, and collapse in the period between Kabasta's directorship and the present, five years after his suicide, of the concert given in his memory. Performing a work so central to him became, in other words, a highly significant act. Far from embodying an "unpolitical" continuum that bore no relation to the changing frameworks of the "political" world, its meaning emerged from a profound knowledge of the shocking things that had happened very recently in a world of which the orchestra, its conductor, and their audiences had been so integral a part.

Listening across the Longue Durée

Such nationalist residues echoed in a landscape of rubble, haunted by the violence of the recent past. Whatever reconfigurations of the discourse surrounding Bruckner took place after the war, they were suffused with the complex inheritances of an earlier period. If one looks at popular publications of the immediate postwar era, residual nationalism is present enough and lends itself to easy political critique, not least where the traces of seemingly overt National Socialist language are obvious. It would, however, be too easy to see the ongoing discursive connections between origin, appearance, temperament, predisposition, and talent as a rearticulation of racial anthropological pseudoscience derived specifically or immediately from National Socialist repertoires of thought.

Rather, such ways of explaining the talents of individuals had a considerably deeper archaeology and formed part of the set of discourses into which National Socialism had successfully inserted itself. Thus Anton Gräflinger's essentially anecdotal sketch of Bruckner's biography—published in 1911— opened with remarks concerning Bruckner's birthplace, his tribal affiliations, his allegedly inborn character traits, tied to an account of his ancestry, all of which anchored the explanation of his later-to-unfold musical career in heredity tied to locale.[72] Gräflinger was not a lone outrider for habits of thought that became mainstream only later: Munich music critic Rudolf Louis had reached for the same regional ethnographic essentialism in his biography of 1905.[73] The prominence and longevity of such habits remind us that ways of explaining musical "genius" that show ideological traces seemingly reminiscent of specifically National Socialist thought were considerably less peculiar to the Third Reich that one might assume.

These patterns are particularly visible in the practice, common in the first half of the twentieth century, of reissuing, with modifications, texts originally published under different regimes. It has become commonplace to point to the usually minor, but crucial, insertions and excisions to scholarly and popular texts published during the National Socialist and postwar eras as evidence of the trimming and tacking of authors toward the ideology of the regime and their subsequent self-distancing from it. These readings are usually freighted, in turn, with assumptions regarding the "propagandistic," and thus inauthentic, nature of whatever version appeared in the Nazi era and the dishonest pragmatism that governed postwar alterations.

Such accounts capture a partial truth. It mattered who was in power, and music critics, no less than anyone else, had to navigate changes of regime while seeking to gloss silently over past political indiscretions. Yet if one examines, for example, the three versions of Munich-based cultural commentator Oskar Lang's biography of the composer published, respectively, in 1924, 1943, and 1947, one is struck not only by the coterminous presence of a multitude of tropes conventionally associated with competing discourses, but also by the fact that so little of the text changes from version to version.[74] This holds true, most notably, for Lang's nationalist reification of Bruckner and for the retention in the 1947 issue of the biological and medical imagery in which Lang's account of modernism and "cultural decay" had been framed in the 1924 and 1943 versions. But it becomes even clearer when one considers the underlying assumptions concerning the object of study itself. Near-identical as they are, all three versions are governed by the same ideology of creativity and "genius." They are all given to a linear history of musical culture that reifies the conventional Austro-German canon. Each version also reiterated, through its republication, the insistent cultural habit of substituting poetic analogy for musical analysis. All of this transported the same ingrained assumptions about "what music is" and what the practice of music criticism entails that had been in evidence since before World War I.

Insofar as the ostensibly more austere analytical practices of the post-1945 musicological academy started to make their way into popular discourses surrounding the composer—in genres such as newspaper reviews and program notes—it was arguably the 1960s and 1970s, rather than immediately after 1945, that such a shift began to present itself in Munich. Commentaries written by figures such as Manfred Wagner for concerts of the Bavarian Radio Symphony Orchestra started then to demonstrate a sense of distance to the hermeneutic traditions that had characterized local writing on Bruckner since the turn of the century.[75] Even here the shift was partial rather than absolute. As the writings of other commentators, such as Walter Abendroth, demonstrate, a slightly greater interest in formal and structural issues continued to sit alongside deep-seated composer-centered habits of popular writing that anchored their explication in biography rather than in a discussion, however simple, of the musical material itself.[76]

Indeed, the same underlying habits of thought structure popular communication regarding the composer to this day, transporting and reanimating a set of imaginaries that are less interesting for the ways in which they change than for their stubborn recurrence. In the elucidatory notes to its performance of the third symphony in September 2012, for example—a performance paired with Wagner's *Prelude and Liebestod* from *Tristan und Isolde*—the Munich Philharmonic Orchestra offered a biographical sketch of the relationship between the two "masters," an account of the "fiasco" of the premiere of Bruckner's symphony that implicitly underlined the importance of his early local champions in establishing his reputation, and a long history of the piece's performance by the orchestra that stressed the role of its successive conductors in proselytizing for the composer and promoting different versions of the work. The list was now lengthened to include not only Loewe and Kabasta but postwar conductors Fritz Rieger, Eliahu Inbal, Sergiu Celibidache, and Christian Thielemann.[77] If the spirited partisanship of some of the earlier, long-dead acolytes has given ground to the sober distance of contemporary commentary, earlier ways of imagining the composer in the city echo, resonantly, still.

Neil Gregor is professor of modern European history at the University of Southampton, UK. He has published widely on the economic, social, and cultural history of twentieth-century Germany, including *Daimler-Benz in the Third Reich* (Yale University Press, 1998) and *Haunted City: Nuremberg and the Nazi Past* (Yale University Press, 2008), both of which won the Fraenkel Prize for Contemporary History. He is currently writing a book on the symphony concert in Nazi Germany.

Notes

1. Pamela Potter raised the question of how the long legacies of totalitarianism theory constrained exploration of the musical cultures of the Third Reich a decade ago in "Dismantling a Dystopia: On the Historiography of Music in the Third Reich," *Central European History* 40, no. 4 (2007): 621–51. A decade on, little has changed. For stimulating reflections on how this image emerged, see, more recently, Pamela Potter, *Art of Suppression: Confronting the Nazi Past in Histories of the Visual and Performing Arts* (Chicago, 2016). I have offered more extensive reflections on the possibilities and limitations of writing the cultural history of Nazi Germany; see Neil Gregor, "Die Geschichte des Nationalsozialismus und der Cultural-Historical Turn," *Vierteljahrshefte für Zeitgeschichte* 65, no. 2 (2017): 233–45.
2. On the range of inherited framings of Bruckner's music, see Christa Brüstle, *Anton Bruckner und die Nachwelt: Zur Rezeptionsgeschichte des Komponisten in der ersten Hälfte des 20. Jahrhunderts* (Stuttgart, 1998); on the fascists' allegedly total appropriation, see, for example, Mathias Hansen, "Die faschistische Bruckner-Rezeption und ihre Quellen," *Beiträge zur Musikwissenschaft* 28 (1986): 53–61.
3. See, for example, Alexander Rehding, *Music and Monumentality: Commemoration and Wonderment in Nineteenth-Century Germany* (Oxford, 2009), 180–6; on more

popular representations that transport the same trope, see the front cover of Fred K. Prieberg, *Musik im NS-Staat* (Frankfurt, 1982); and, much more recently, Neil MacGregor, *Germany: Memories of a Nation* (New York, 2015), 168.
4. Bryan Gilliam, "The Annexation of Anton Bruckner: Nazi Revisionism and the Politics of Appropriation," *Musical Quarterly* 78, no. 3 (1994): 584–604; in a similar vein, see Benjamin Marcus Korstvedt, "Anton Bruckner in the Third Reich and After: An Essay on Ideology and Bruckner Reception," *Musical Quarterly* 80, no. 1 (1996): 132–60.
5. Such assumptions are carried, for example, in the title of Erik Levi, *Mozart and the Nazis: How the Third Reich Abused a Cultural Icon* (New Haven, 2010).
6. Nicholas Attfield, *Challenging the Modern: Conservative Revolution in German Music, 1918–1933* (Oxford, 2017).
7. Emblematic of this new wave of research is Chris Szejnmann and Maiken Umbach, eds., *Heimat, Region and Empire: Spatial Identities under National Socialism* (Basingstoke, 2012).
8. On ideology as an open field of argument in this context, see, above all, Lutz Raphael, "Pluralities of National Socialist Ideology: New Perspectives on the Production and Diffusion of National Socialist *Weltanschauung*," in *Visions of Community in Nazi Germany: Social Engineering and Private Lives*, ed. Bernhard Gotto and Martina Steber (Oxford, 2014), 73–86.
9. As such, they displayed similar characteristics to those discerned by recent scholarship on musical culture under other twentieth-century dictatorships. See, for example, Elaine Kelly, *Composing the Canon in the German Democratic Republic: Narratives of Nineteenth-Century Music* (Oxford, 2014); and Pauline Fairclough, *Classics for the Masses: Shaping Soviet Musical Identity under Lenin and Stalin* (New Haven, 2016).
10. I borrow the term "contained pluralism" from Martina Steber, "Region and National Socialist Ideology: Reflections on Contained Plurality," in Szejnmann and Umbach, *Heimat, Region and Empire*, 25–42.
11. Karen Painter, *Symphonic Aspirations: German Music and Politics, 1900–1945* (Cambridge, MA, 2008).
12. Tim Mason, "Ends and Beginnings," *History Workshop Journal* 30, no. 1 (1990): 133–50.
13. The following draws on Gertrude Quast-Benesch, *Anton Bruckner in München* (Tutzing, 2006).
14. Wilhelm Zentner, "München," *Zeitschrift für Musik* (December 1935), 1407–9. On the historical editing of Bruckner's symphonies, see, above all, Wolfgang Doebel, *Bruckners Sinfonien in Bearbeitungen: Die Konzepte der Bruckner-Schüler und ihre Rezeption bis zu Robert Haas* (Tutzing, 2001).
15. Paul Ehlers, "Münchner Konzertverein. 2 Konzert im Abonnement," *Münchner Neueste Nachrichten* (hereafter *MNN*), 16 November 1922. All translations are mine.
16. See also the many examples in Painter, *Symphonic Aspirations*.
17. Wilhelm Zentner, "Die Münchener Philharmoniker im Konzertjahr 1939/40," *Konzertanzeiger der Münchener Philharmoniker, Tonhalle*, (Nr. 31, 1940).
18. *Die Münchener Philharmoniker: Orchester der Hauptstadt der Bewegung*, Konzertverein München, e.V., Tonhalle (n.d.[1939]).
19. Stadtarchiv Munich (StadtAM), KA 208, Konzertverein München / Aktennotiz betr. Hausegger-Ehrung, (n.d. [April 1938]). (Concert Association Munich, Memorandum on Hausegger Celebration, undated, April 1938).

20. "Bruckner-Plastik in der Tonhalle," *Münchner Abendblatt*, 31 October 1938.
21. Paul Ehlers, "Der Münchener Dirigentenkreis und Bruckner," *Bruckner-Blätter: Mitteilungen der Internationale Bruckner-Gesellschaft* 2, no. 4 (1930): 1; Internationale Bruckner-Fest München 1930, Festschrift und Programm, 68–69.
22. Wilhelm Zentner, "Anton Bruckners Einzug in die Walhalla," *Kölnische Volkszeitung*, 9 June 1937.
23. Rudolf Louis, *Anton Bruckner* (Munich and Leipzig, 1905).
24. See, most obviously, Max Auer, *Anton Bruckner als Kirchenmusiker* (Regensburg, 1924).
25. Ernst Decsey, *Anton Bruckner: Versuch eines Lebens* (Berlin, 1919).
26. Wolfgang Partsch, "Die Bruckner-Rezeption," in *Bruckner-Handbuch*, ed. Hans-Joachim Hinrichsen (Stuttgart, 2010), 340.
27. This comes across forcefully in the excellent overview provided by Dominik Höink, *Die Rezeption der Kirchenmusik Anton Bruckners: Genese, Tradition und Instrumentalisierung des Vergleichs mit Giovanni Pierluigi da Palestrina* (Göttingen, 2011), esp. 77–181.
28. Wilhelm Zentner, *Anton Bruckner: Leben und Werk 1824–1896* (Munich, 1946), 55; the reference is to Victor Léon and Ernst Decsey, *Der Musikant Gottes* (1924). For an example of such language entering the interwar newspaper review culture, see Oscar von Pander, "Das Münchner Brucknerfest: Schalk dirigiert die 6. und 5. Symphonie," *MNN*, 29 October 1930.
29. Here I am drawing on Paul Ricoeur, *Interpretation Theory: Discourse and the Surplus of Meaning* (Fort Worth, TX, 1976).
30. Erich Schwebsch, "Zu den Symphonien des Münchener Bruckner-Festes," *Beilage zur Festschrift München. Den Teilnehmern des 1 Internationalen Bruckner-Festes in München (27. Mit 31. Oktober 1930) überreicht von der Internationalen Bruckner-Gesellschaft* (1930): 2, 7.
31. StadtAM, Kulturamt 104, Abschrift: Internationale Bruckner-Gesellschaft, Ortsgruppe München. Protokoll über die Gründungsversammlung am 12 Juni 1929. (Copy of: International Bruckner Association, Munich Chapter: Minutes of the Founding Meeting on 12 June 1929).
32. StadtAM, Kulturamt 104, Internationales Bruckner-Fest, Ausgaben, Süddeutsche Konzertdirektion Otto Bauer (o.D., 1930). (International Bruckner Festival, Expenses, South German Concert Directorate Otto Bauer, undated, 1930).
33. "Das Münchner Bruckner-Fest," *MNN*, 1–2 November 1930.
34. StadtAM, KA 104, Oberbürgermeister Scharnagl an Max Auer 9 October 1929. (Mayor Scharnagl to Max Auer, 9 October 1929).
35. *Bruckner-Blätter. Mitteilungen der Internationale Bruckner-Gesellschaft*. II. Jg 1930, no. 4 (October-December): 1. Internationale Bruckner-Fest München 1930, Festschrift und Programm.
36. "Das Münchner Bruckner-Fest – Requiem in d-moll," *MNN*, 1–2 November 1930.
37. "Das Münchner Bruckner-Fest – Streichquintett und Messe e-moll," *MNN*, 1–2 November 1930.
38. StadtAM, Kulturamt 269, Aktennotiz: Bruckner-Fest vom 23. Mit 30. Oktober 1933. (Memorandum on Bruckner Festival of 23 to 30 October 1933).
39. StadtAM, Kulturamt 269, Vorstandschaft des Konzertvereins München e.V. an Hausegger, 8 April 1933 (Board of the Munich Concert Association to Hausegger,

8 April 1933). I have analyzed the experience of the Munich Philharmonic Orchestra in this period in greater detail in Neil Gregor, "Siegmund von Hausegger, the Munich Philharmonic Orchestra and Civic Musical Culture in the Third Reich," *German History* (forthcoming, 4, 2018).

40. StadtAM, Kulturamt 269, Ehrenkartenempfänger zum Brucknerfest (undated, 1933) (List of Recipients of Honorary Tickets for the Bruckner Festival, undated, 1933).
41. StadtAM, Kulturamt 269, "Warum ist die Bruckner-Gesellschaft international und weshalb tagt sie in München?," MS, Max Auer (II. Brucknerfest in Verbindung mit der Hauptversammlung der Internationalen Brucknergesellschaft. Eine Kundgebung deutschen Geistes). ("Why is the Bruckner Society international and why is it meeting in Munich?" MS, Max Auer (II. Bruckner Festival in Cooperation with the Annual General Meeting of the International Bruckner Society. A Demonstration of German Spirit).
42. "Zweites Bruckner-Fest in München, 23.–30. Oktober 1933," *Bruckner-Blätter: Mitteilungen der Internationalen-Bruckner-Gesellschaft*, no. 3–4 (1933), 19.
43. Ibid., 17.
44. Wilhelm Zentner, "Bruckner-Fest in München," *Zeitschrift für Musik* (December 1933), 1277–78.
45. In 1941, for example, Ludwig Berberich conducted the Munich cathedral choir in a performance in the Tonhalle of Bruckner's setting of Psalm 150, alongside sacred music by Rossini and Verdi. "Rossini – Verdi – Bruckner," *MNN*, 20 February 1941.
46. Otto Mayer, "Österreichfahrt der Münchner Philharmoniker (Oktober 1936)," *Zeitschrift für Musik* (January 1937), 68–70.
47. Ludwig Berberich, "Messe E moll von Anton Bruckner," *Bruckner-Blätter*, 1; Internationale Bruckner-Fest München 1930, Festschrift und Programm, 78.
48. Wilhelm Zentner, "Die Zweite Reihe der Philharmonischen Konzerte," *Konzertanzeiger der Münchner Philharmoniker, Tonhalle*, no. 23 (20 December 1939).
49. "Die Münchener Philharmoniker im Konzertjahr 1939/40," *Konzertanzeiger der Münchener Philharmoniker, Tonhalle*, no. 31 (1940).
50. Neil Gregor, "Listening as a Practice of Everyday Life: The Munich Philharmonic Orchestra and Its Audiences in the Second World War," in *The Oxford Handbook of Music Listening in the 19th and 20th Centuries*, ed. Christian Thorau and Hansjakob Ziemer (Oxford, 2019), 123-141.
51. Oscar von Pander, "Das Münchner Brucknerfest. Schalk dirigiert die 6. und 5. Symphonie," *MNN*, 29 October 1930.
52. Oscar von Pander, "Beethoven und Bruckner im zweiten Philharmonischen Konzert," *MNN*, 9 October 1939.
53. Arthur Schopenhauer, *Die Welt als Wille und Vorstellung*, in *Arthur Schopenhauers sämtliche Werke*, vol. 1, ed. Paul Deussen (Munich, 1911), 304–12 (sec. 52) ["Die Musik gibt den innersten, aller Gestaltung vorhergängigen Kern oder das Herz der Dinge ... der Komponist offenbart das innerste Wesen der Welt und spricht die tiefste Weisheit aus, in einer Sprache, die seine Vernunft nicht versteht."].
54. Oscar von Pander, "Ein Bruckner Abend," *MNN*, 5 July 1943.
55. Oscar von Pander, "Bruckners Tragische Symphonie. Im 1. Jubiläumskonzert der Münchner Philharmoniker," *MNN*, 20 September 1943.

56. Oscar von Pander, "Sympathie mit dem Tode…," *MNN*, 15 March 1943.
57. The emotional landscape of German society after Stalingrad is a subject that awaits its historian. For compelling first accounts, see Malte Thiessen, *Eingebrannt ins Gedächtnis: Hamburgs Gedenken an Luftkrieg und Kriegsende 1943 bis 2005* (Munich, 2007); and Jörg Arnold, *The Allied Air War and Urban Memory: The Legacy of Strategic Bombing in Germany* (Cambridge, 2011).
58. David Monod, *Settling Scores: German Music, Denazification and the Americans, 1945– 1953* (Chapel Hill, 2005).
59. Wilhelm Zentner, *Anton Bruckner 1824–1896* (Munich, 1946).
60. Programm: *Die Münchener Philharmoniker. Aula der Universität, 5. Großes Konzert*, 22 March 1950.
61. Programm: *Die Münchener Philharmoniker. 7 Philharmonisches Abonnementskonzert. Leitung: Fritz Rieger. Aula der Universität*, 21–22 December 1951.
62. *Festschrift zum XII. Internationales Bruckner-Fest 1954 anläßlich des 130. Geburtstages von Anton Bruckner (München, 29 April-14 Mai)*. The reference is to a concert conducted by Fritz Rieger on 5 and 6 May 1954.
63. Wilhelm Zentner, *Anton Bruckner: Messe in F-Moll* (Das christliche Gut in der Musik, ed. Wilhelm Zentner, Heft 4) (Munich, 1948).
64. *Festschrift zum XII. Internationales Bruckner-Fest 1954 anläßlich des 130. Geburtstages von Anton Bruckner (München, 29 April–14 Mai)*. The reference is to a performance conducted by Eugen Jochum, 29 and 30 April 1954.
65. Programme: *Deutsches Museum: Kongress-Saal, München, Philharmoniker, Ltg Adolf Mennerich (Sonderkonzert der Theatergemeinde)*, 16 November 1950.
66. Gregor, "Siegmund von Hausegger."
67. Gabriele Meyer, "Oswald Kabasta und die Münchner Philharmoniker," in *"… mögen Sie meiner still gedenken": Die Beiträge zum Oswald Kabasta-Symposion in Mistlbach vom 23. Bis 25. September 1994*, ed. M. Exl Engelbert and Michael Nagy (Viennas, 1995), 29–42, 29.
68. Ibid., 31.
69. Ibid., 34.
70. Programme: *Oswald-Kabasta-Gedenkkonzert der Münchener Philharmoniker am 12 Juli 1951 um 20 Uhr in den Neuen Hirschen-Lichtspielen in Kufstein*.
71. Programme: *Münchener Philharmoniker. 11. Philharmonisches Konzert Ltg. Fritz Rieger. Aula der Universität* 24/25 May 1950.
72. Anton Gräflinger, *Anton Bruckner: Bausteine zu seiner Lebensgeschichte* (Munich, 1911), 1–4.
73. Louis, *Anton Bruckner*, 88.
74. Oskar Lang, *Anton Bruckner: Wesen und Bedeutung* (Munich, 1924; 1943; 1947).
75. See, for example, the notes by Manfred Wagner for a performance of Bruckner's ninth symphony in Programme: *Bayerischer Rundfunk: Symphonie-konzerte 1977–78 / 12. Konzert des Symphonieorchesters, Herkulessaal der Residenz: Leitung Rafael Kubelik*, 22–23 June 1978.
76. See, for example, Abendroth's notes for a performance of Bruckner's Eighth symphony in Programme: *2. Konzert des Symphonieorchesters, Herkulessaal, Munich, Leitung: Karl Böhm*, 21–22 October 1971.
77. Programme: *Die Münchener Philharmoniker. Das Orchester der Stadt*. 7 September 2012.

Bibliography

Arnold, Jörg. *The Allied Air War and Urban Memory: The Legacy of Strategic Bombing in Germany*. Cambridge: Cambridge University Press, 2011.

Attfield, Nicholas. *Challenging the Modern: Conservative Revolution in German Music, 1918–1933*. Oxford: Oxford University Press, 2017.

Auer, Max. *Anton Bruckner als Kirchenmusiker*. Regensburg: Gustav Bosse Verlag, 1924.

Brüstle, Christa. *Anton Bruckner und die Nachwelt: Zur Rezeptionsgeschichte des Komponisten in der ersten Hälfte des 20. Jahrhunderts*. Stuttgart: M & P Schriftenreihe für Wissenschaft und Forschung, 1998.

Decsey, Ernst. *Anton Bruckner: Versuch eines Lebens*. Berlin: Schuster & Loeffler, 1919.

Doebel, Wolfgang. *Bruckners Sinfonien in Bearbeitungen: Die Konzepte der Bruckner-Schüler und ihre Rezeption bis zu Robert Haas*. Tutzing: Publikationen des Instituts für österreichische Musikdokumentation, 2001.

Engelbert, M. Exl, and Michael Nagy, eds. *"... mögen Sie meiner still gedenken": Die Beiträge zum Oswald Kabasta-Symposion in Mistlbach vom 23. Bis 25. September 1994*. Wien: Vom Pasqualatihaus, 1995.

Fairclough, Pauline. *Classics for the Masses: Shaping Soviet Musical Identity under Lenin and Stalin*. New Haven, CT: Yale University Press, 2016.

Gilliam, Bryan. "The Annexation of Anton Bruckner: Nazi Revisionism and the Politics of Appropriation." *Musical Quarterly* 78, no. 3 (1994): 584–604.

Gräflinger, Anton. *Anton Bruckner: Bausteine zu seiner Lebensgeschichte*. Munich: R. Piper, 1911.

Gregor, Neil. "Siegmund von Hausegger, the Munich Philharmonic Orchestra and Civic Musical Culture in the Third Reich." *German History* (forthcoming, 4, 2018).

———. "Die Geschichte des Nationalsozialismus und der Cultural-Historical Turn." *Vierteljahrshefte für Zeitgeschichte* 65, no. 2 (2017): 233–45.

———. "Listening as a Practice of Everyday Life: The Munich Philharmonic Orchestra and Its Audiences in the Second World War." In *The Oxford Handbook of Music Listening in the 19th and 20th Centuries*, ed. Christian Thorau and Hansjakob Ziemer, 123-141. Oxford: Oxford University Press, 2019.

Hansen, Mathias. "Die faschistische Bruckner-Rezeption und ihre Quellen." *Beiträge zur Musikwissenschaft* 28 (1986): 53–61.

Höink, Dominik. *Die Rezeption der Kirchenmusik Anton Bruckners: Genese, Tradition und Instrumentalisierung des Vergleichs mit Giovanni Pierluigi da Palestrina*. Göttingen: V & R, 2011.

Kelly, Elaine. *Composing the Canon in the German Democratic Republic: Narratives of Nineteenth-Century Music*. Oxford: Oxford University Press, 2014.

Korstvedt, Benjamin Marcus. "Anton Bruckner in the Third Reich and After: An Essay on Ideology and Bruckner Reception." *Musical Quarterly* 80, no. 1 (1996): 132–60.

Lang, Oskar. *Anton Bruckner: Wesen und Bedeutung*. Munich, 1924; 1943; 1947.
Léon, Victor, and Ernst Decsey. *Der Musikant Gottes*. N.p.: Steyrermühl-Verlag, 1924.
Levi, Erik. *Mozart and the Nazis: How the Third Reich Abused a Cultural Icon*. New Haven, CT: Yale University Press, 2010.
Louis, Rudolf. *Anton Bruckner*. Munich and Leipzig: Georg Müller, 1905.
MacGregor, Neil. *Germany: Memories of a Nation*. New York: Knopf, 2015.
Mason, Tim. "Ends and Beginnings." *History Workshop Journal* 30, no. 1 (1990): 133–50.
Meyer, Gabriele. "Oswald Kabasta und die Münchner Philharmoniker." In *"… mögen Sie meiner still gedenken": Die Beiträge zum Oswald Kabasta-Symposion in Mistlbach vom 23. Bis 25. September 1994*, ed. M. Exl Engelbert and Michael Nagy, 29–42. Vienna: Pasqualatihaus, 1995.
Monod, David. *Settling Scores: German Music, Denazification and the Americans, 1945–1953*. Chapel Hill: University of North Carolina Press, 2005.
Painter, Karen. *Symphonic Aspirations: German Music and Politics, 1900–1945*. Cambridge, MA: Harvard University Press, 2008.
Partsch, Wolfgang. "Die Bruckner-Rezeption." In *Bruckner-Handbuch*, ed. Hans-Joachim Hinrichsen, 339–72. Stuttgart: J. B. Metzler, 2010.
Potter, Pamela. "Dismantling a Dystopia: On the Historiography of Music in the Third Reich." *Central European History* 40, no. 4 (2007): 621–51.
———. *Art of Suppression: Confronting the Nazi Past in Histories of the Visual and Performing Arts*. Chicago: Chicago University Press, 2016.
Prieberg, Fred K. *Musik im NS-Staat*. Frankfurt: Fischer Verlag, 1982.
Quast-Benesch, Gertrude. *Anton Bruckner in München*. Tutzing: Hans Schneider, 2006.
Raphael, Lutz. "Pluralities of National Socialist Ideology: New Perspectives on the Production and Diffusion of National Socialist *Weltanschauung*." In *Visions of Community in Nazi Germany: Social Engineering and Private Lives*, ed. Bernhard Gotto and Martina Steber, 73–86. Oxford: Oxford University Press, 2014.
Rehding, Alexander. *Music and Monumentality: Commemoration and Wonderment in Nineteenth-Century Germany*. Oxford: Oxford University Press, 2009.
Ricoeur, Paul. *Interpretation Theory: Discourse and the Surplus of Meaning*. Fort Worth, TX: TCU Press, 1976.
Schwebsch, Erich. "Zu den Symphonien des Münchener Bruckner-Festes," *Beilage zur Festschrift München: Den Teilnehmern des 1 Internationalen Bruckner-Festes in München (27. Mit 31. Oktober 1930) überreicht von der Internationalen Bruckner-Gesellschaft* (1930).
Steber, Martina. "Region and National Socialist Ideology: Reflections on Contained Plurality." In *Heimat, Region and Empire: Spatial Identities under National Socialism*, edited by Chris Szejnmann and Maiken Umbach, 25–42, Basingstoke: Palgrave Macmillan, 2012.
Szejnmann, Chris, and Maiken Umbach, eds., *Heimat, Region and Empire: Spatial Identities under National Socialism*. Basingstoke: Palgrave Macmillan, 2012.

Thiessen, Malte. *Eingebrannt ins Gedächtnis: Hamburgs Gedenken an Luftkrieg und Kriegsende 1943 bis 2005*. Munich: Dölling und Galitz, 2007.
Zentner, Wilhelm. "München." *Zeitschrift für Musik* (December 1935): 1407–9.
———. *Anton Bruckner: Leben und Werk 1824–1896*. Munich: Schnell & Steiner, 1946.
———. *Anton Bruckner: Messe in F-Moll*. Munich: Schnell & Steiner, 1948.

CHAPTER 5

Female Musicians and "Jewish" Music in the Jewish Kulturbund in Bavaria, 1934–38

DANA SMITH

Music, "the most German of the arts," has held a particular place of honor in the German cultural pantheon since at least the nineteenth century, when the appreciation of music became an important component of a "German" national identity.¹ The trope guided multiple generations as they navigated the varying tides of what it meant to be "German"—through a monarchy, an attempt at democracy, and a dictatorship. It also distinguished who was not "German." For German Jews, "the most German of the arts" represented both the optimism of national inclusion and the disillusionment of national exclusion. It was also the means through which segments of the German Jewish population strove to rebuild their own internal representations of "Jewishness" in the face of National Socialist persecution.

The simultaneous experiences of German unification and Jewish emancipation at the end of the nineteenth century appeared to open new doors for Germany's Jews. This abstract notion of national acceptance through cultural appreciation was for many an appealing idea, not least because it offered straightforward guidelines on how to be included in the national community: go to concerts, read about music, converse about music, immerse yourself in the canon. Yet the emergence of anti-Semitism at the end of the century threatened this nascent sense of cultural-national belonging. Changes in the contemporary art world left many conservative cultural ideologues looking for answers. According to reactionary voices of the time, it was none other than "the Jew"—an omnipresent yet indeterminate cultural villain—who was responsible for this supposed decline of "German" art. This argument found a contemporary voice in Richard Wagner's now infamous polemic *Das Judenthum in der Musik*.² According to Wagner, Jews were unable to produce authentic art and instead could only mimic the art traditions of other people; in the process, he claimed, they debased the so-called national music with inadequate imitations. Following such arguments, German anti-Semites argued that Jews be excluded from the national community because they were incapable of producing or properly appreciating music. By the time of the rise of National Socialism, "the Jew" was no longer a figure merely unable to appreciate "German" music, but an agent of its corruption.

Legislative assaults on the presumed "Jewish" influences on "German" culture began shortly after Adolf Hitler assumed power in 1933. After the passage in April 1933 of the Law for the Restoration of the Professional Civil Service (commonly known as the Civil Service Law), all "politically unreliable" civil servants (including, among other groups, Jews and "leftists") were dismissed from employment in state cultural venues.[3] The development of Nazi cultural policy that followed has been well documented. Nazi cultural understandings built on pre-existing interpretations of a "national" art that represented the "health" of the national "body." Such ideas were first developed by cultural ideologues as a component of Romanticism; this vocabulary was later re-energized by a new generation of cultural thinkers in the post–World War I era, a regeneration now termed Neo-Romanticism.[4] Under National Socialism, cultural life was politicized by the state, and as such it was a component of the regime's overall ideology and worldview: "the struggles for racial, political, and cultural renewal would be identical. The politics of art would be integral to the creation of the 'people's community.'"[5] National Socialist cultural plans did not include Jews within this newly envisioned community of "Germans."

German Jews came together in Berlin to reorganize Jewish cultural life in the summer of 1933 as a response to Nazi cultural exclusion. The Jewish neurologist, conductor, and musicologist Kurt Singer and the young Jewish theater director Kurt Baumann led the initial effort. In July 1933, Singer gathered a number of respected Jewish academics and cultural figures in his Charlottenburg home. The group consisted of "a serene, older generation, all men with long beards," and one woman, the young musicologist Anneliese Landau—whom the men initially assumed to be Singer's secretary.[6] These individuals developed the Kulturbund Deutscher Juden (Cultural League of German Jews; later the Jüdischer Kulturbund in Deutschland, or Jewish Cultural League in Germany), the lone state-approved Jewish cultural organization in Nazi Germany. Over time, eighty-two German cities, towns, and villages had a local Kulturbund branch.[7]

On 1 October 1933 the Berlin Kulturbund staged its inaugural performance: Gotthold Ephraim Lessing's humanist classic *Nathan the Wise*. The choice to stage *Nathan the Wise* was fraught with symbolism. As Jeanette R. Malkin argues, *Nathan the Wise* was a "cultural object which for 150 years symbolized both Enlightenment gravitas and the ideal of a German/Jewish 'symbiosis.' ... Indeed, for many German Jews, *Nathan* was far more than a play; it became a credo and platform of Jewish aspirations for inclusion and acceptance in Germany."⁸ Lessing's *Nathan* came to represent the ideals of a German-Jewish symbiosis: the three Mosaic faiths (represented in the play by Nathan, the Sultan, and the Templar) embrace as the curtain falls. The story is one of religious coexistence, of individuals rising above theological divides.

That a play dating from the Enlightenment and written by a non-Jew maintained such leverage in the minds of 1930s German Jews is hardly surprising. German Jews are often noted for their "assimilation" into "German" society, even if this meant distancing themselves from Jewish culture and religious practice or beliefs. As theater historian Rebecca Rovit writes, the Kulturbund in Berlin was composed of "'assimilated' Jews more in touch with humanist, secular values and literary classics than with religious precepts of Judaism and Eastern European or Hebrew-language drama."⁹ This interpretation rests upon an image of German Jewry predicated upon particular class and gender markers. Indeed, the prevailing description of the modern German Jewish experience is that of middle-to-upper-middle-class assimilation. In the late nineteenth and early twentieth centuries, portions of the German Jewish community sought entry into the public sphere of an educated German middle class (*Bildungsbürgertum*) through their commitment to German educational and cultural traditions.¹⁰ Accordingly, it was through the tradition of *Bildung* (cultural self-edification) that one developed the supposedly correct set of morals and self-comportment. These morals were indicative of a properly educated and enlightened person who was dedicated to the ideals of German *Kultur* (high culture). Great works of "German" art were seen as monuments testifying to the strength of "German" culture and civilization—and the appreciation of these great works seen as a chief means of entering the collective "German" national body. For the post-emancipation Jewish middle class, cultural appreciation was a means of not only asserting national belonging, but also establishing a connection to Germany, however tenuous and abstract, that rose above discriminatory politics and prejudices.¹¹ Chief among these high arts used as a bridge to German culture was music.

The majority of the Berlin Kulturbund's original founders, those older men gathered in Singer's Charlottenburg apartment, were members of this educated and middle-class post-emancipation generation. They maintained an "unswerving support" of the ideals of German high culture and civilization. Indeed, they sustained a belief that the same ideals that seemingly opened the doors to German society in the nineteenth century would not fail Germany's Jews in the face of National Socialism. As the Berlin Kulturbund dramaturge Julius Bab wrote in 1933, many of these men believed that if the Kulturbund upheld a high level of cultural production "the Germans will have to be ashamed" of their anti-Semitic legislation.¹² The early Berlin program was guided by an attempt to be, as the adage goes, "more German than the Germans."

Scholarship on the general scope of Jewish cultural life in the Third Reich, and on the Kulturbund more specifically, remains invested in the image of an assimilated German Jewish community. Their taste is almost uniformly described as aligning with traditional "German" or western European humanist traditions until the Nazi regime forced Kulturbund leadership into a more "Jewish" (meaning, in practice, Eastern European) repertoire in the late 1930s. This movement toward "Jewish" cultural production was, scholarship holds, generally interpreted as an unwelcome development. Lily Hirsch's recent study of the Jewish Kulturbund orchestra in Berlin claims that the Kulturbund's impetus toward "Jewish" art was "in many ways forced" and emerged only after 1936.[13] Herbert Freeden, a former dramaturge for the Berlin Kulturbund and an early author on the organization's history, shared a similar sentiment when he wrote that the Kulturbund was a "Jewish Cultural League without Jewish culture."[14]

This interpretation poses certain problems. First and foremost, a monolithic "German Jewish" cultural narrative has been based almost entirely on the experiences of a specific portion of the German Jewish community: educated, middle-class men in Berlin. Singer's Berlin Kulturbund was, in many ways, exceptional—but it has been represented by scholars as the norm. Berlin was, without question, an important center of Jewish life in the first decades of the twentieth century. Nearly one-third of German Jews, or approximately 160,000 individuals, called Berlin home.[15] Yet there were important regional differences in the variety of Jewish experiences during National Socialism. The cosmopolitan northern metropolis offered a level of anonymity not available to Jews elsewhere. Berlin's Kulturbund—located in the city with the largest Jewish population and the largest concentration of Jewish artists—was itself an atypical cultural experience. Weimar Berlin's art scene was exceptional in modern German Jewish cultural history; its impact did not immediately disappear in 1933. Nowhere else in Germany was there such a large congregation of professional and skilled amateur Jewish artists as in the capital. Berlin's Kulturbund was thus a distinctive endeavor with unmatched professional potential.

Not only has scholarship remained focused on Berlin, but it has also overlooked the contributions of Jewish women. These two factors are intertwined. As outlined above, Berlin's cultural resources could sustain a professional-scale cultural organization in ways that the cities in which other Kulturbund branches were located could not. Yet what often goes unstated is that this professionalized atmosphere of German high culture was the sphere of bourgeois men. It was educated men, Marion Kaplan writes, who "felt more at home with culture and politics" and who "cherished what they regarded as German culture."[16] And it was these same men who maintained active membership in the Berlin Kulturbund (as members of its leadership committees or as artists). The number of male artists active in Berlin was nearly double the number of female artists (1,326 to 717).[17] However, this gender imbalance did not hold true everywhere. In Bavaria, for example, it was women who formed the majority of Kulturbund members.

Still, Landau's experience of finding herself the lone woman in Singer's living room remains the dominant image of activity in the Jewish Kulturbund. Women feature as aberrations rather than the norm. Outside of an essay by Gabriele Fritsch-Vivié, analysis of the role of female contributions to Jewish cultural life under Nazism remains unexplored. In her work, Fritsch-Vivié describes the often-overlooked efforts of "the women of the Kulturbund" in Berlin, including Ruth Abelsdorf, the director's secretary; Hildegard Brillig, the telephone operator; and the countless other women who worked from morning until night organizing the office paperwork, setting appointments for the administration, working in the ticket office and the coat check— and then in the evening filling in as members of the choir if someone suddenly fell ill.[18] These women performed the daily tasks that kept the league's doors open. Jewish women were more than Kulturbund secretaries, however. Women were also Kulturbund artists. While female artists were outnumbered in Berlin, in Bavaria the local Kulturbund audience was just as likely to see a female artist on stage as a male artist. Female Kulturbund artists in Bavaria outnumbered their male counterparts in every area of activity except adult education.[19]

Approximately two-thirds of Bavarian Kulturbund musicians were women. Further, the vast majority (nearly 80 percent) of musicians in a Bavarian Kulturbund branch outside of Munich were women. These women performed a musical program oriented toward their own self-defined interpretations of "Jewish" music within the confines of their time and place—in direct contradiction to the traditional western European canon performed on stages in Berlin. Bavaria's early Kulturbund musical programming tackled issues of "Jewishness" head on; the program focused extensively (although not exclusively) on issues related to individual heritage, liturgy, and "Jewish" folk music (here meaning folk music from eastern Europe or the British mandate in Palestine).[20]

Grappling head on with the topic of "Jewish" music was an important component of the Jewish community's redefinition of its own identity in the face of Nazi persecution. Kulturbund members were Germans. Dealing with issues related to individual or community "Jewishness" neither diminished nor negated their "Germanness." Yet, in Bavaria there was also little illusion that a strict adherence to "German" culture, or to the supposed "German-Jewish symbiosis," was going to overcome Nazism's exclusionary aims. As Bavarian Kulturbund chairman Fritz Ballin put it in February 1934 during a speech prior to the local Munich Kulturbund Orchestra's inaugural concert,

German Jews had been fused into German cultural life for 150 years, particularly since the Emancipation. Even in contemporary times, this symbiosis within German society was very strong. ... Our entire political and cultural lives are now being excluded from the specifically German *Volksgemeinschaft*. Jews must now create public spaces and working possibilities for our artists, authors, and intellectuals.[21]

According to Ballin, the key to moving forward was for Bavarian Jews to create their own public spaces for the consumption of their own art. Accordingly, shared cultural experiences helped the Kulturbund membership create new internal understandings of "Jewishness" under external Nazi persecution in Bavaria.

Amos Funkenstein argues that Jews in modern Germany developed their understandings of "Jewishness" as an "idiom always acquired from their environment."[22] In this case, Kulturbund artists and audience members were part of a social fabric that wove together a group identity with shared cultural threads. Musical production and consumption seemingly created a community of "Germans" out of disparate German states in 1871, and to many Jews it carried with it the promise of acceptance in German society after emancipation.[23] In the Bavarian Kulturbund after 1933, music again became a means for community building. This time, however, music was employed in the service of the local Jewish community's own terms of self-redefinition. In the Bavarian Kulturbund's musical department, it was a process heavily influenced by Jewish women.

To bring into better focus women's contributions to organized public Jewish culture under Nazism is to challenge the existing narrative of an assimilationist German Jewish middle-class cultural elite—a narrative based almost entirely on the male experience. This is not to say the existing scholarship on Berlin is wrong; however, to base a general "German Jewish" cultural narrative on the Berlin example is misleading. Jewish men and Jewish women experienced German nationalism, Judaism, and National Socialist persecution in diverse ways. As such, it is crucial to draw attention to the wide expanse of Jewish experiences and modes of self-representation throughout the Reich in the 1930s. These differences include a variety of regional and gendered experiences.

A Jewish Kulturbund in Bavaria

After 1933, anywhere in Germany, Kulturbund performances were closed, meaning audience membership was limited to Jews (as reflected in the legal definition at the time). State oversight of the Kulturbund was placed in the hands of Hans Hinkel, an underling of Goebbels in the Ministry of Public

Enlightenment and Propaganda.²⁴ In principle, National Socialist anti-Jewish cultural policy was meant to limit the Kulturbund program to non-"German," apolitical, and "Jewish" performances.²⁵ The regime felt it could control the shape of a new "Jewishness" through strict censorship and extensive surveillance.²⁶ In practice, however, these ideals were limited by the regime's own shortcomings. Cultural policy was prone to "administrative chaos and aesthetic inconsistencies between purported ideals and actual artistic endeavours."²⁷

Jewish community support for the Kulturbund spread quickly. The *Nürnberg-Fürther Israelitisches Gemeindeblatt*, the main Jewish newspaper for Franconia, concluded, "within its two weeks of activities [the Kulturbund Deutscher Juden] has far exceeded expectations."²⁸ By the early spring of 1935 there were sixty-one Jewish Kulturbund branches located in cities and towns throughout the Reich—including the regional Kulturbund Rhine-Ruhr (this eventually consisted of eleven cities: Aachen, Bonn, Cologne, Dortmund, Duisburg, Düren, Essen, Gelsenkirchen, Krefeld, Recklinghausen, and Wuppertal) and the Kulturbund Rhine-Main in Frankfurt.²⁹ Most of these Kulturbund offices were affiliated with Singer's original Kulturbund office in Berlin. After April 1935, however, these loosely affiliated sixty-one locations were brought into a centralized Kulturbund office (based in Berlin); Singer and Hinkel remained at their respective helms. By the late summer of 1935, this newly reorganized national Kulturbund had branches in eighty-two locations.³⁰ The Kulturbund remained active throughout Germany until Kristallnacht in November 1938. From January 1939 until the eve of deportations in 1941, Kulturbund activity was limited to Berlin.

However, a small number of Jewish cultural organizations existed outside of the Berlin Kulturbund's administrative domain prior to April 1935. The most extensive of these was the Jewish Kulturbund in Bavaria (Jüdischer Kulturbund in Bayern). Erich Erck submitted his proposal for an independent Kulturbund for Bavarian Jews to the Bavarian State Ministry of Education and Culture and the Bavarian Political Police in October 1933. Erck was a conductor who had relocated to Munich in 1931 after a few decades away from the Bavarian capital.³¹ He informed Bavarian Minister of Education and Culture Hans Schemm that his proposed Kulturbund, although modeled on the Berlin example, would be different in key respects. According to Erck, the Bavarian Kulturbund would "secure bread through work for Jewish artists" by easing the financial constraints imposed by the Civil Service Law.³² Further, Erck stressed that his proposed Kulturbund was to exist under the umbrella of the Bavarian Jewish Community (Bayerische Israelitische Kultusgemeinde). So, unlike its counterpart in Berlin, the Bavarian Kulturbund was not a separate organization.³³ Erck's proposal was approved in January 1934. Its first event, a concert performed at Munich's Main Synagogue, took place in March.

Bavaria's Kulturbund originally served seven cities: Augsburg, Bamberg, Fürth, Kitzingen, Munich, Nuremberg, and Würzburg (the branch in Kitzingen closed shortly after its founding). Later expansions added Bad Kissingen (February 1934), Aschaffenburg (February 1934), Regensburg (May 1934), and Memmingen (February 1935).[34] Membership was extensive. During the 1935–36 season, a total of 4,710 Bavarian Jews registered as Kulturbund members. As a proportion, this represented from one-third of the Jewish communities in Munich and Nuremberg to two-thirds of the Jewish community in Regensburg.[35] Events were divided into three categories: adult education (essentially a lecture series), visual arts (including the popular Munich Marionette Theatre of Jewish Artists), and music. Of these three areas of activity, the music department was the most active.

Women and a "Jewish" Musical Program in 1930s Bavaria

In all of its various forms, the Kulturbund did not develop within a vacuum. It drew from pre-existing cultural traditions, particularly nineteenth- and twentieth-century preoccupations with "national" music and the related effort to define a community of "Germans" through music.[36] Yet the long-term impact of these traditions on Germany's Jews was twofold. For the German Jewish middle-class, musical participation resulted in both acculturation and, eventually, dissimilation. By the Weimar era, these same methods of creating communal cohesion through shared musical participation were being used to foster a sense of being "Jewish" in Germany. The broader processes of dissimilation and an internal renewal of "Jewish" cultural forms were shaped out of the "raw materials of German culture."[37] The 1920s witnessed what Michael Brenner has deemed the "renaissance of Jewish culture"—a "renaissance" crafted, at least in part, by the same sense of shared cultural traditions that decades earlier helped to shape the notion of a "German" culture.[38]

Indeed, some Kulturbund institutions were continuations of earlier initiatives. In 1927, Franz Kleinbauer and Heinrich Lamm, two local youths, founded the Jewish Chamber Orchestra in Munich (Jüdisches Kammerorchester München). This was the first "Jewish" orchestra in the Bavarian capital. The two young men described their new orchestra as a "serious" musical undertaking that would facilitate community building through cultural participation. Articles in the local Jewish press stressed the leaders' desire to use music and the Jewish Chamber Orchestra as a means to "bring together a Jewish circle" and foster a *collegium musicum*."[39] Erck took over leadership of the chamber orchestra in 1931; according to reviews in the Jewish press, he expanded the orchestra from its original twenty-two members to forty and increased the orchestra's level of talent.[40] In the spring of

1934 the Jewish Chamber Orchestra began performing under a new name: Munich's Kulturbund Orchestra. It became a leading endeavor of the Jewish Kulturbund in Bavaria.[41]

Musical performance and consumption played an important role in the Kulturbund structure as Jews were again forced to reimagine themselves within new community boundaries after 1933. The Bavarian Kulturbund staged more concerts than any other form of cultural event. Further, musicians comprised nearly three-fourths of all affiliated Bavarian Kulturbund artists. Local Kulturbund musical groups included Munich's thirty-member orchestra, Nuremberg's twenty-five-member orchestra, Munich's synagogue choir, Nuremberg's synagogue choir, Munich's Jewish vocal quartet, and Munich's chamber music trio. In addition, there were a number of individual musicians who were hired either to perform solo events or to act as musical accompaniment to visiting lecturers or authors.

Nearly two-thirds of Bavarian Kulturbund musicians were women. Outside of Munich, however, the percentage of female musicians in Bavaria was even greater: well over three-fourths of all Bavarian Kulturbund musicians in cities or towns other than Munich were female. Only a small number of these Bavarian women were professional musicians prior to being forced into unemployment as a result of the Civil Service Law. Included among the small ranks of professional female musicians were Irma Stern, Alma Weiss, and Emma Färber-Strasser. Stern was employed at the Staatsoper in Munich; Weiss was well known in the Bavarian capital for her Master Class at the Akademie der Tonkunst;[42] and Färber-Strasser was a former opera singer.[43] Many, such as Sonja Ziegler, were not professionals. Ziegler, for example, had a performance background that existed entirely within the confines of the Jewish community.

Rather than being marginal—as the solitary image of Landau in Berlin suggests[44]—Bavaria's women were at the center of the regional Kulturbund's music department. Taking this one step further, not only were women the majority of the Bavarian Kulturbund's musicians, but they also constituted the majority of Bavarian audience membership—at least in Würzburg, the only Kulturbund branch with a surviving membership list. According to the 1935–36 membership application forms for Würzburg, the average Kulturbund member in the Lower Franconian city was a thirty-eight-year-old woman. Indeed, approximately two-thirds of the city's Kulturbund general membership applicants were women.[45]

Female Bavarian musicians performing in the Kulturbund worked within two spheres that had traditionally relegated women to subordinate positions: the secular cultural-intellectual sphere and the religious sphere. German Jewish women (indeed, all German women) were conspicuously absent from organized public cultural life. By the Weimar era, public careers and higher levels of education came to mark the male Jewish sphere of participation in this life. Such aspects of male lives fostered an experience rooted in both a physical "Germany" built upon engagement in the public sphere and an abstract "Germany" built upon Enlightenment ideals, such as a dedication to humanism and reason.[46]

Women, on the other hand, were not afforded the same opportunities for formal advanced higher education. German universities were late to open their doors to female students; women could not enroll in German universities until the first decade of the twentieth century.[47] Even after women were granted entrance to German universities in 1908, however, Jewish women still faced a double discrimination in the form of both anti-Jewish and antifemale sentiments. Women were also traditionally cut off from active public involvement within the religious world—particularly within the walls of the synagogue. After all, men, not women, are required by religious texts to participate actively in religious worship.

Thus, in the pre-1933 society in which these future female Kulturbund musicians lived, their traditional experiences of a secular "Germanness" and a religious "Jewishness" existed almost entirely in the private sphere of the home. As Harriet Pass Freidenreich has argued, "for women, who were largely excluded from the public domain of synagogue and community and whose documented Jewish life-cycle events were most likely to be marriage and burial, Jewish identity was expressed mainly in the private sphere of the home and was often hidden from general view."[48] When women did enter the religious public sphere, it was mostly through efforts at social relief or specific women's events publicized within the Jewish community structure (such as attending lectures organized by their local branch of the Jüdischer Frauenbund).[49]

However, after 1933 Jewish daily life was altered. National Socialist persecution during this early phase of the regime largely targeted the public lives of men. Dalia Ofer claims that "Nazi policies had an important, gendered impact on internal Jewish life" and, as a result, "the victims also crossed gender boundaries."[50] Accordingly, "gender roles in Jewish families shifted because of devastating economic, social, and emotional realities—forcing families to embrace strategies that they would never have entertained in ordinary times."[51] Among these strategies were women taking employment outside the home. The high number of female Kulturbund musicians in Bavaria may be a result of women taking the initiative to provide their families with an additional—although likely quite limited—source of money.

Munich's Sonja Ziegler was the most active female Jewish musician in Bavaria. Ziegler (née Sura Fleischer) was born in 1898 as the third of eight children to Max and Ida Fleischer in Odessa. Ziegler's family moved to Munich when she was a young child. She undertook private vocal training and by 1924 was a frequent soloist for Munich Main Synagogue's Synagogue Choir. In April 1925 she married Josef Ziegler, the director of the Synagogue

Choir. The couple had two children: Manfred Kurt, in 1928, and Hannelore, in 1929. Her performance repertoire was overwhelmingly, although not exclusively, composed of Jewish liturgical music and Yiddish folk songs. Further, her pre-Kulturbund musical career appears to have been limited to "Jewish" musical spheres: specifically, Munich's synagogue choir and Munich's Hebrew Theater. In 1929 Ziegler performed Yiddish folk songs in Munich for an evening of Hebrew theater.[52]

As a member of the Bavarian Kulturbund, Ziegler was noted in the local Jewish press for her performances in Hebrew and Yiddish—including liturgical solos in the 21 November 1934 Munich Kulturbund Synagogue Concert and Yiddish solos in a March 1935 quartet concert.[53] A review in Munich's Jewish newspaper of Ziegler's March 1935 performance was favorable. The critic admitted "surprise" at Ziegler's "excellent presentation of Yiddish folksongs, not only vocally but also in her character, which famously came out with fully graceful humor."[54] What exactly surprised the reviewer about the performance is unclear—whether it was the quality of Ziegler's performance or that the reviewer enjoyed Yiddish folk music. Ziegler remained active in the Bavarian Kulturbund until its "liquidation" in December 1938.[55]

Significantly less is known about the public cultural endeavors of many other female musicians. Würzburg's Marie Schlamme-Sprinz, who was born in the small Franconian village of Burghaslach before moving to the city later in life, played violin for the local Kulturbund. Schlamme-Sprinz, along with her husband, Leo, and son, Otto, eventually fled Nazi Germany for the United States; she later played violin for the Houston Symphony.[56] Else Rypinski (née Buchbinder) was an alto and also performed in Würzburg's Kulturbund. Rypinski's sister, Rose Buchbinder, was a professional harpist who was also employed by city theaters in Würzburg, Memel, and Nuremberg before her dismissal in 1933; it is unclear whether Rose was a performing member of the Kulturbund.[57] The Würzburg pianist Herthe Gotthilf, along with her husband, Alfred, and son, Heinz Michael, left Franconia for Edam, a declining fishing town in the Netherlands.[58] Aschaffenburg's chamber pianist Hilde Freund, born in 1915, also eventually fled Bavaria and settled in Chicago, Illinois, in 1939. Freund remained an active musician in Chicago, performing and teaching.[59] For still others even less is known. Bamberg's Hilde Marx and Regensburg's Suse Lehemann both performed in the Kulturbund musical department, yet it is not clear if they were singers or played an instrument.

The predominantly female composition of the Bavarian Kulturbund may have influenced the main programmatic difference between Bavaria and Berlin: Bavaria's early engagement with "Jewish" music. Women possibly found it easier to navigate between various "German" and "Jewish" spheres due to their previous experiences. Anti-Semitism and patriarchal antifemale sentiment both impacted the daily lives of Jewish women and shaped their perceptions of community and self. As Judith Szapor has argued, the double emancipation of Jewish women (as Jews *and* women) resulted in a complexity of experiences that allowed many to exist fluidly within multiple mental frameworks.[60] Or, in other words, women adopted multifaceted identities as a direct result of their "multiply coded" experiences (meaning their gendered confrontations with anti-Semitism, antifeminism, nationalism, etc.).[61] Bavarian Jewish women, who would have been influenced by both cultural and religious public spheres yet fully included in neither, may have felt less of an ideological commitment to maintaining the rigid structures of the "culture of the German Enlightenment" than their male counterparts. Jewish men could attempt to find solace in a strict adherence to that ideological realm as their former worlds contracted around them.[62] For Jewish women, however, that ideological realm had never provided a comparable level of opportunity—and this was perhaps reflected in the fluid nature of female maneuvering between "German" and "Jewish" cultural forms in ways that did not occur in the male-dominated atmosphere of the Berlin Kulturbund.

In addition, the Jewish Kulturbund in Bavaria may have been conceptualized by its membership as a social-cultural division of the Jewish community rather than, as in Berlin, a more professional cultural institution—suggesting that a main aim was to foster communal bonds rather than strictly uphold the rigid Enlightenment ideals of German *Kultur*. It was, after all, comprised mostly of amateurs rather than professionals. This is not to suggest the Bavarian leadership and artists did not hold themselves to high artistic standards. Yet there are practical cultural concerns to take into account in small cities and towns that are not relevant in the large metropolises—chief among them being a more limited talent pool. Further, as Erck stated in his initial proposal for a Bavarian Kulturbund, the league was envisioned as a subsidiary of the Jewish community with a particular social aim: "to provide help for all Jewish individuals affiliated with artistic creation through the generation of religious, artistic and scientific events available only to closed Jewish circles."[63] These social efforts extended beyond the events themselves. In Bamberg, for example, Kulturbund performances were followed by a social hour with cake and coffee.[64] Second, as argued above, women's social and cultural experiences were different than men's; undoubtedly the variety of experiences resulted in varied self-representations of being "German" and "Jewish." Since the Imperial era, as Kaplan notes, it was women who "saw no conflict between affirming their German heritage and retaining their religious and cultural legacy."[65]

Indeed, the musical program of the Bavarian Kulturbund reflected both a "German" and "Jewish" cultural heritage—a musical representation of cultural Zionism.[66] In "the more traditional south," there was an immediate engagement with what was categorized at the time as "Jewish" music.[67] Bavarian self-definitions of "Jewish" music encompassed composers of Jewish heritage (both German- and foreign-born), biblically inspired themes, liturgical music, and Jewish folk music (i.e., Yiddish or Hebrew folk music originating from eastern Europe or Palestine). These modes of classification were part of the wider musicological discussion on "national" music that had begun in the wake of German unification. According to Pamela Potter, the role of liturgy and folk music in establishing what was then viewed as "authentic" "German" musical expression was by the 1930s a common component of contemporary musical scholarship. Further, the Romantic and later neo-Romantic movement fostered research on folk art in its search for a supposedly "authentic" culture. The parallel search for an "authentic" Jewish liturgy or folk music only emerged within the confines of the Jewish communities in Germany.[68] As Brenner has shown, this search for "authentic" "Jewish" music, defined as both liturgical and folk music, did take place during the Weimar years—and in Bavaria it continued during the 1930s, albeit under extremely different political circumstances.[69] Already during the 1934–35 season, over 80 percent of the musical program consisted of music by Jewish or foreign composers. Yet this orientation toward "Jewish" music did not develop without community discussion. Nor did the various Bavarian communities always align in their representations of "Jewish" music. What developed in Munich was a "Jewish" musical program more focused on composers of Jewish heritage whose music was entrenched largely within nineteenth-century western European traditions. In larger urban areas, "Jewishness" was generally defined in terms of individual heritage and not in terms of religious belief or practice.

In smaller communities, such as Würzburg and Regensburg, however, the Kulturbund presented a program with a much greater presence of liturgical and folk music. In these cities, the 1934–35 season began with concerts featuring Hebrew, liturgical, and Jewish folk songs.[70] The events in Würzburg were well received and, according to a review, "every seat in the Gotteshaus was filled."[71] Jewish folk songs were also more common in the Würzburg programs. Würzburg staged four separate performances (of a total of nine concerts) featuring Jewish-Yiddish folk songs in the 1934 and 1934–35 seasons. This orientation toward folk and liturgical music represented understandings of Jewishness based on heritage and religious practice. These smaller locales were, as a whole, more traditional, with larger conservative and Orthodox Jewish congregations. In addition, it was these communities that saw the most active participation of female musicians.

The question remains, then, as to why such programming occurred in Bavaria and did not occur in Berlin—or, in other words, why Bavaria had more female musicians who played a more "Jewish" musical program than the predominantly male musicians did in Berlin. A potential answer may be found in the composition of the communities themselves. In the smaller communities, such as Aschaffenburg, Bamberg, or even Munich, there simply were not as many professional Jewish musicians. Less competition with professionals may have translated to more opportunity for those amateurs willing to participate, which Bavarian Jewish women did at a higher rate than Bavarian Jewish men.

In addition, the presence of fewer professionals may have resulted in an environment less shaped by the traditionally male-dominated bourgeois public sphere of *Kultur*, opening cultural performance to amateurs at precisely the same time Jewish women were required to take on a more active role in public life. And it was women who had been successfully negotiating between their various "German" and "Jewish" traditions and self-understandings since the Imperial era, albeit in the private sphere of the home.[72] What changed under Nazism was that the persecution of Jewish men forced Jewish women from the private into the public sphere. Yet the previous terms of their "German" and "Jewish" experiences, traditions, and self-understandings did not suddenly shift. Instead, Jewish women continued to perform the same balancing act. After 1933 it was increasingly played out in public arenas—including on the Kulturbund stage.

For the musical performances of the Bavarian Kulturbund, audiences in prewar National Socialist Germany were confronted with a complicated heritage. These performances represented contemporary realities of exclusion and inclusion. Their expulsion from the "German" cultural world was just one of the ways in which the National Socialist regime sought to remove Jews: they were fired from their jobs in culture venues; they were banned from performing "German" music (the definition of which changed almost annually); and they were barred from German concert halls and theaters. Yet the role of music for Jews in the Third Reich was not merely one of exclusion. Nor was it one of desperately clinging to an illusionary belief in humanism and *Kultur*. The Kulturbund was not merely a "catastrophic misunderstanding, in which Jews had been abused for the Nazi cause."[73] Rather, as the Bavarian example shows, there were efforts at utilizing cultural performance and consumption, particularly music, as a mode of self-definition. These performances, and the debates that occurred as a result, were important acts in the process of coming to terms with the rapidly changing realities of persecuted Jewish life. Efforts at performing "Jewish" music as a means of internal Jewish community self-conceptualization were especially strong in smaller cities, towns, and villages—the very places where women maintained an active and notable presence in the local Kulturbund music departments. Shifting attention toward women suggests an interpretation of organized Jewish cultural life more rooted in acculturation than assimilation. These musicians were Germans, yet they were also Jews. As Germans, they were still the "people of music." But as Jews facing the daily onslaughts of life in Nazi Germany, they also sought to use music in their search for what it now meant, to them, to be "Jewish."

Dana Smith received her Ph.D. from Queen Mary, University of London, where she held a doctoral fellowship with the Leo Baeck Institute. Her dissertation explored the intersection of gender and regionalism in self-conceptualizations of Jewish art in the Jewish Cultural League (Jüdischer Kulturbund) in Bavaria from 1934 through 1938. She is currently an assistant professor in the department of Holocaust and Genocide Studies at Keene State College in New Hampshire.

Notes

1. Celia Applegate and Pamela Potter, "Germans as the 'People of Music': Genealogy of an Identity," in *Music and German National Identity*, ed. Celia Applegate and Pamela Potter (Chicago, 2002), 1.
2. Richard Wagner, *Das Judenthum in der Musik* (Leipzig, 1869). The essay was originally published, to little critical fanfare, under a pseudonym in 1850. Nearly two decades later, in 1869, the essay was republished with an expanded addendum under Wagner's own name.
3. Rebecca Rovit, "Jewish Theatre: Repertory and Censorship in the Jüdischer Kulturbund, Berlin," in *Theatre under the Nazis*, ed. John London (Manchester, 2000), 187, 196; Alan E. Steinweis, *Art, Ideology and Economics in Nazi Germany: The Reich Chambers of Music, Theater and Visual Arts* (Chapel Hill, 1996), 44–46.
4. For more recent work on the topic of artistic trends during National Socialism, see Richard Etlin, ed., *Art, Culture, and Media under the Third Reich* (Chicago, 2002); Peter Paret, *An Artist against the Third Reich: Ernst Barlach, 1933–1938* (Cambridge, 2003); Eric Michaud, *The Cult of Art in Nazi Germany* (Stanford, 2004); Joan Clinefelter, *Artists for the Reich: Culture and Race from Weimar to Nazi Germany* (Oxford, 2006); and Neil J. Levi, *Modernist Form and the Myth of Jewification* (New York, 2014).
5. Steinweis, *Art, Ideology and Economics*, 21.
6. Lily E. Hirsch, *A Jewish Orchestra in Nazi Germany: Musical Politics and the Berlin Jewish Cultural League* (Ann Arbor, 2012), 17.
7. Sonderbeauftragter des Reichsministers Dr. Goebbels to the Jüdischer Kulturbund in Deutschland, 29 July 1935, 8, Doc 575 Reel 54/29/I, Wiener Library.
8. Jeanette R. Malkin, "Introduction: Break a Leg!," in *Jews and the Making of Modern German Theatre*, ed. Jeanette R. Malkin and Freddie Rokem (Iowa City, 2010), 7.
9. Rebecca Rovit, *The Jewish Kulturbund Theatre Company in Berlin* (Iowa City, 2012), 4.
10. Michael Brenner, Vicki Caron, and Uri R. Kaufmann, eds., *Jewish Emancipation Reconsidered* (Tübingen, 2003).
11. Shulamit Volkov, "The *Verbürgerlichung* of the Jews as a Paradigm," in *Bourgeoisie Society in Nineteenth Century Europe*, ed. Jürgen Kocka and Allan Mitchell (Oxford, 1993), 367–91. See also Marian Kaplan, *The Making of the Jewish Middle Class: Women, Family and Identity in Imperial Germany* (Oxford, 1991).
12. Bab, quoted in: Saul Friedländer, *Nazi Germany and the Jews*, vol. 1, *The Years of Persecution, 1933–1939* (New York, 1997), 66; Henryk Broder, "Business As Usual" in *Premiere und Pogrom: der Jüdische Kulturbund 1933–1941*, ed. Eike Geisel and Henryk Broder (Berlin, 1992), 10.

13. Hirsch, *A Jewish Orchestra*, 44.
14. Herbert Freeden, *Jüdisches Theater in Nazideutschland* (Tübingen, 1964), 55.
15. Avraham Barkai and Paul Mendes-Flohr, *Renewal and Destruction, 1918–1945*, vol. 4 in *German-Jewish History in Modern Times*, ed. Michael Meyer and Michael Brenner (New York, 1998), 226.
16. Marion A. Kaplan, *Between Dignity and Despair: Jewish Life in Nazi Germany* (New York, 1998), 65.
17. Gabriele Fritsch-Vivié, "Der Bund – Soziales, Solidarität, Verbundheit: Der Jüdische Kulturbund 1933–1941 in seiner Entwicklung, Aufgabenstellung und Wirkung," in *Der Vertreibung des Sozialen*, ed. Ariane Feustel, Inge Hansen-Schaberg, and Gabriele Knapp (Munich, 2009), 187.
18. Ibid., 187–88.
19. The vast majority of local lecturers were rabbis or academics with doctorates; opportunities for advanced formal higher education still eluded many women at the time.
20. For various definitions and debates surrounding the terms of "Jewish" music in Bavaria, see Kulturbund advertisements placed in the *Bayerische Israelitische Gemeindezeitung* (hereafter *BIG*) on 1 November 1934 and 15 November 1934; Ba., "Synagogenkonzert des Kulturbundes," *BIG*, 1 December 1934, 506; Ba., "Konzert des Münchner jud. Vokalquartetts," *BIG*, 1 April 1935, 158; "Kulturbundabend," *Die Laubhütte*, 30 May 1934; "Nachrichten für die bayerischen Gemeinden," *Die Laubhütte*, 25 June 1934, 4; "Vermischtes. Regensburg," *Der Israelit*, 28 June 1934, 10; "Nachrichten für die bayerischen Gemeinden," *Die Laubhütte*, 18 October 1934, 3; and "Süddeutschland: Würzburg," *Israelitisches Familienblatt*, 18 October 1934, 14.
21. Fritz Ballin, "Der Jüdische Kulturbund in Bayern gegründet," *BIG*, 15 February 1934, 68.
22. Amos Funkenstein, "The Dialectics of Jewish Assimilation," *Jewish Social Studies* 1, no. 2 (1995): 9.
23. Michael Brenner, *The Renaissance of Jewish Culture in Weimar Germany* (New Haven, 1996).
24. Hinkel was an "Old Fighter" who first joined the National Socialist movement as a university student in Munich in 1921. He quickly ascended the political ranks and by 1933 was state commissioner for the "Entjudung" of German cultural life in Prussia; in April 1933 he was named the head of the Prussian Theatre Commission. See Völker Dahm, "Kulturelles und geistiges Leben," in *Die Juden in Deutschland: 1933–1945*, ed. Wolfgang Benz (Munich, 1989), 75-267; Alan E. Steinweis, "Hans Hinkel and German Jewry, 1933–1941," *Leo Baeck Institute Year Book* (1993): 209–20; Ernst Klee, *Das Kulturlexikon zum Dritten Reich: Wer war was vor und nach 1945* (Frankfurt, 2007), 249–50.
25. Schemm, Addendum in "Gesuch um Genehmigung," 7. MK 15382, BHStAM.
26. Ibid., 7.
27. Pamela Potter, "The Arts in Nazi Germany: A Silent Debate," *Contemporary European History* 15, no. 4 (2006): 587.
28. E.D. "Ein Abend im Theater des jüdischen Kulturbundes in Berlin," *Nürnberg-Fürther Israelitisches Gemeindeblatt*, 1 November 1933, 127.
29. Kulturbund Deutscher Juden, ed., *Almanach* (Berlin, 1935).
30. Goebbels to the Jüdischer Kulturbund, 29 July 1935, 8.

31. Andreas Heusler, "Verfolgung und Vernichtung (1933–1945)," in *Jüdisches München: Von Mittelalter bis zur Gegenwart*, ed. Richard Bauer and Michael Brenner (Munich, 2006), 173; Waldemar Bonard, *Die gefesselte Muse: Das Marionettentheater im Jüdischen Kulturbund 1935–1937* (Munich, 1994), 46.
32. Erich Erck to Minister Hans Schemm, "Gesuch um Genehmigung eines Jüdischen Kulturbunds in Bayern als vordringliche Aktion der sozialen Winterhilfe," 10 October 1933, 2. MK 15382, BHStAM.
33. Ibid.
34. Bayerisches Staatsministerium für Unterricht und Kultus, "Gesuch um Genehmigung eines Jüdischen Kulturbundes in Bayern, I. 6671," 9 February 1934; Bayerische Politische Polizei (BPP), "Bad Kissingen, I8763," 17 February 1935; BPP, "Aschaffenberg, I9586," 21 February 1934; BPP, "Regensburg, I. 26801," 17 May 1934, all MK 15382, BHStAM.
35. By comparison, Kulturbund membership in Berlin hovered at approximately 10 percent of its Jewish population. Hirsch, *Jewish Orchestra*, 19. For information on Bavarian Kulturbund membership, see "Aus den Gemeinden: Nürnberg," *Israelitisches Familienblatt*, 22 July 1937, 15; Isr. Kultusgemeinde Bamberg, "Jüdischer Kulturbund in Bayern," November 1935, D/Ba/378, CAHJP; "Aus den Gemeinden: Nürnberg," *Israelitisches Familienblatt*, 23 December 1937, 4; "Konzerte und Vorträge: Nürnberg-Fürth," *Central Verein Zeitung*, 30 December 1937; M. Ltz., "Regensburg," *BIG*, 15 January 1937, 32; and "Jüdisches Leben in Nürnberg: Kulturbund," *Israelitisches Familienblatt*, 20 October 1938, 10.
36. Celia Applegate and Pamela Potter, "Germans as the 'People of Music': Geneology of an Identity," in *Music and German National Identity*, ed. Celia Applegate and Pamela Potter (Chicago 2002), 1-35.
37. Sharon Gillerman, *Germans into Jews: Remaking the Jewish Social Body in the Weimar Republic* (Stanford, 2009), 4.
38. Brenner, *Renaissance of Jewish Culture*.
39. "Das Jüdische Kammerorchester," *BIG*, 23 May 1927, 163; "Das Jüdische Kammerorchester München," *BIG*, 13 December 1927, 377.
40. "Symphoniekonzert des Jüdischen Kammerorchesters München," *BIG*, 1 December 1931, 361; I. Z., "Das Konzert des jüdischen Kammerorchesters," *BIG*, 1 December 1932, 360.
41. Heusler, "Verfolgung und Vernichtung," 173–74.
42. "Chanukka-Konzert des Jüdischen Kammerorchesters München," *BIG*, 1 December 1931, 361; "Konzert des verstärkten Jüdischen Kammerorchesters München am 27. Juni im Museumsaal," *BIG*, 15 July 1932, 214.
43. "Konzert des Münchner Jüdischen Vokalquartetts," *BIG*, 1 June 1934, 228.
44. Hirsch, *Jewish Orchestra*, 17–18.
45. The majority of application forms were submitted as a household—generally as a couple. However, women were more likely to apply for an individual membership outside of a family structure. "Mitgliedsanmeldungen zum Jüdischen Kulturbund in Bayern," 1935. D/Wu2/380, CAHJP.
46. See Steven E. Aschheim, *Brothers and Strangers: The East European Jew in Germany and German Consciousness, 1800–1923* (Madison, 1982); Steven E. Aschheim, *Culture and Catastrophe: German and Jewish Confrontations with National Socialism and Other Crises* (Basingstoke, 1996); Shulamit Volkov, *Germans, Jews and Antisemites:*

Trials in Emancipation (New York, 2006); Brenner, Caron, and Kaufmann, Jewish Emancipation Reconsidered; and Kaplan, Dignity and Despair.
47. Kaplan, Jewish Middle Class, 137.
48. Harriet Pass Freidenreich, Female, Jewish, and Educated: The Lives of Central European University Women (Bloomington, 2002), 134.
49. For a complete overview of women in German-Jewish historiography, see Benjamin Maria Baader, "Jews, Women, and Germans: Jewish and German Historiographies in a Transatlantic Perspective," in Gendering Modern German History: Rewriting Historiography, ed. Karen Hagemann and Jean H. Quataert (New York, 2007), 169–89. Sharon Gillerman discusses the increasingly visible role of Jewish women in Jewish social bodies (e.g., welfare, social relief) during the Weimar years. Gillerman, Germans into Jews: Remaking the Jewish Social Body in the Weimar Republic (Stanford, 2009). See also Kaplan, Jewish Middle Class, 4.
50. Dalia Ofer, "The Contribution of Gender to the Study of the Holocaust," in Gender and Jewish History, ed. Marion Kaplan and Deborah Dash Moore (Bloomington, 2011), 124, 132.
51. Marion A. Kaplan, "The Jewish Response to the Third Reich: Gender at the Grassroots," in Jews and Gender: The Challenge to Hierarchy, ed. Jonathan Frankel (Oxford, 2001), 71–72.
52. Samuel Taubes, "Hebräischen Theaterabend," BIG, 15 March 1929, 87; "Das hebräische Theater in München," Münchener N.N., 1928, 41A.
53. Ba., "Synagogenkonzert," BIG, 1 November 1934, 506; Ba., "Konzert," BIG, 1 April 1935, 158.
54. Ba., "Konzert," 1 April 1935, 158.
55. Sonja Ziegler was amongst the approximately one thousand Jewish men, women, and children from Munich who were murdered by Einsatzkommando 3 in the forest around Kaunas, Lithuania, in late November 1941. See Biographisches Gedenkbuch der Münchner Juden, 1933–1945, ed. Stadtarchiv München, retrieved 24 March 2015 from https://www.muenchen.de/rathaus/Stadtverwaltung/Direktorium/ Stadtarchiv/Juedisches-Muenchen/Gedenkbuch.html.
56. Gestapostelle Würzburg 12404, StAW; Audiovisual Records, AV/016, Houston Symphony Archives.
57. Matthias Pasdzierny, "'Der Ozean, der mich seit jener Zeit von dem Geburtslande trennt, hat wieder zwei Ufer...': Der Künstlerfonds des Süddeutschen Rundfunk und das deutsch-jüdische Musikerexil," in Kulturelle Räume und ästhetische Universalität: Musik und Musiker im Exil, ed. Dörte Schmidt (Munich, 2008), 195–231.
58. Ron Grossman, "Holocaust Mystery Is Solved in Chicago," Chicago Tribune, 30 May 2006, retrieved 24 March 2015 from http://articles.chicagotribune.com/2006-05-30/ news/0605300211_1_edam-dutch-town-parents.
59. Lawrence B. Johnson, "Hyphenated Careers Link Young Pianists," Milwaukee Sentinel, 28 March 1975, 15.
60. Judith Szapor, Andrea Pető, Maura Hametz, and Marina Calloni, eds., Jewish Intellectual Women in Central Europe, 1860–2000 (Lewiston, 2012), ix, 1.
61. See Michael Herzfeld, Cultural Intimacy: Social Poetics in the Nation-State, 2nd ed. (New York, 2005).
62. Kaplan, Dignity and Despair, 65; Freeden, Jüdisches Theater, 3.
63. Erck to Schemm, "Gesuch und Genehmigung."

64. Willy Cohn, *Kein Recht, nirgends: Tagebuch vom Untergang des Breslauer Judentums, 1933–1941* (Cologne, 2006), 318.
65. Kaplan, *Jewish Middle Class*, 4.
66. Philip V. Bohlman, *"The Land Where Two Streams Flow": Music in the German-Jewish Community of Israel* (Chicago, 1989); Brenner, *Renaissance of Jewish Culture*; Sander L. Gilman, "Are Jews Musical? Historical Notes on the Question of Jewish Musical Modernism and Nationalism," *Modern Judaism* 28, no. 3 (2008): 239–56.
67. Jews in Bavaria, particularly in the more Orthodox Franconia, were generally more religiously traditional and conservative than those in Berlin. Jacob Borut also points to the need for a more regionally diverse study of *Kulturbund* activity: "It should be added that the discussions on the Jewish content of the *Kulturbund* activities refer almost exclusively to Berlin. The activities of the other *Kulturbünde*, especially in the more traditional south, are still open to research." Borut, "Struggles for Spaces: Where Could Jews Spend Free Time in Nazi Germany?," *Leo Baeck Institute Year Book* 56, no. 1 (2011): 344.
68. Pamela Potter, "Jewish Music and German Science," in *Jewish Musical Modernism, Old and New*, ed. Philip V. Bohlman (Chicago, 2008), 88.
69. Brenner, *Renaissance of Jewish Culture*, esp. 37, 130, 155–57.
70. "Nachrichten," 18 October 1934, 3.
71. "Süddeutschland: Würzburg," 18 October 1934, 14.
72. Kaplan, *Jewish Middle Class*, 4.
73. Henryk M. Broder, "Selbstbehauptung in der Sackgasse," *Berliner Zeitung*, 27 January 1992, 25. Broder maintains a similar stance in Broder, "Business As Usual."

Bibliography

Applegate, Celia, and Pamela Potter. "Germans as the 'People of Music': Genealogy of an Identity." In *Music and German National Identity*, edited by Celia Applegate and Pamela Potter, 1–35. Chicago: University of Chicago Press, 2002.

Aschheim, Steven E. *Brothers and Strangers: The East European Jew in Germany and German Consciousness, 1800–1923.* Madison: University of Wisconsin Press, 1982.

———. *Culture and Catastrophe: German and Jewish Confrontations with National Socialism and Other Crises.* New York: New York University Press, 1997.

Baader, Benjamin Maria. "Jews, Women, and Germans: Jewish and German Historiographies in a Transatlantic Perspective." In *Gendering Modern German History: Rewriting Historiography*, edited by Karen Hagemann and Jean H. Quataert, 169–89. New York: Berghahn Books, 2007.

Barkai, Avraham, and Paul Mendes-Flohr. *Renewal and Destruction, 1918–1945.* Vol. 4 of *German-Jewish History in Modern Times*, edited by Michael Meyer and Michael Brenner. New York: Columbia University Press, 1998.

Bohlman, Philip V. *"The Land Where Two Streams Flow": Music in the German-Jewish Community of Israel.* Urbana: University of Illinois Press, 1989.

Bonard, Waldemar. *Die gefesselte Muse: Das Marionettentheater im Jüdischen Kulturbund 1935–1937.* Munich: Buchendorfer Verlag, 1994.

Borut, Jacob. "Struggles for Spaces: Where Could Jews Spend Free Time in Nazi Germany?" *Leo Baeck Institute Year Book* 56, no. 1 (2011): 307–50.

Brenner, Michael. *The Renaissance of Jewish Culture in Weimar Germany*. New Haven: Yale University Press, 1996.

———. Vicki Caron, and Uri R. Kaufmann, eds. *Jewish Emancipation Reconsidered*. Tübingen: Mohr Siebeck, 2003.

Broder, Henryk. "Business As Usual." In *Premiere und Pogrom: der Jüdische Kulturbund 1933–1941*, edited by Eike Geisel and Henryk Broder, 7–35. Berlin: Siedler, 1992.

Clinefelter, Joan. *Artists for the Reich: Culture and Race from Weimar to Nazi Germany*. Oxford: Oxford University Press, 2006.

Cohn, Willy. *Kein Recht, nirgends: Tagebuch vom Untergang des Breslauer Judentums, 1933–1941*. Cologne: Böhlau Verlag, 2006.

Dahm, Völker. "Kulturelles und geistiges Leben." In *Die Juden in Deutschland: 1933–1945*, edited by Wolfgang Benz, 75–267. Munich: C.H. Beck, 1989.

Etlin, Richard, ed. *Art, Culture, and Media under the Third Reich*. Chicago: University of Chicago Press, 2002.

Freeden, Hebert. *Jüdisches Theater in Nazideutschland*. Tübingen: Mohr Siebeck, 1964.

Freidenreich, Harriet Pass. *Female, Jewish, and Educated: The Lives of Central European University Women*. Bloomington: Indiana University Press, 2002.

Friedländer, Saul. *Nazi Germany and the Jews*. Vol. 1, *The Years of Persecution, 1933–1939*. New York: Harper Collins, 1997.

Fritsch-Vivié, Gabriele. "Der Bund—Soziales, Solidarität, Verbundheit: Der Jüdische Kulturbund 1933–1941 in seiner Entwicklung, Aufgabenstellung und Wirkung." In *Der Vertreibung des Sozialen*, edited by Ariane Feustel, Inge Hansen-Schaberg, and Gabriele Knapp, 178–99. Munich: Edition Text + Kritik, 2009.

Funkenstein, Amos. "The Dialectics of Jewish Assimilation," *Jewish Social Studies* 1, no. 2 (1995): 1–14.

Gillerman, Sharon. *Germans into Jews: Remaking the Jewish Social Body in the Weimar Republic*. Stanford: Stanford University Press, 2009.

Gilman, Sander L. "Are Jews Musical? Historical Notes on the Question of Jewish Musical Modernism and Nationalism." *Modern Judaism* 28, no. 3 (2008): 239–56.

Herzfeld, Michael. *Cultural Intimacy: Social Poetics in the Nation-State*, 2nd ed. New York: Routledge, 2005.

Heusler, Andreas. "Verfolgung und Vernichtung (1933–1945)." In *Jüdisches München: Von Mittelalter bis zur Gegenwart*, edited by Richard Bauer and Michael Brenner, 161–84. Munich: C. H. Beck, 2006.

Hirsch, Lily E. *A Jewish Orchestra in Nazi Germany: Musical Politics and the Berlin Jewish Cultural League*. Ann Arbor: University of Michigan Press, 2012.

Kaplan, Marion A. *The Making of the Jewish Middle Class: Women, Family and Identity in Imperial Germany*. New York: Oxford University Press, 1991.

———. *Between Dignity and Despair: Jewish Life in Nazi Germany*. New York: Oxford University Press, 1998.

———. "The Jewish Response to the Third Reich: Gender at the Grassroots." In *Jews and Gender: The Challenge to Hierarchy*, edited by Jonathan Frankel, 70–87. Oxford: Oxford University Press, 2001.

Klee, Ernst. *Das Kulturlexikon zum Dritten Reich: Wer war was vor und nach 1945*. Frankfurt: Fischer Verlag, 2007.

Kulturbund Deutscher Juden. *Almanach*. Berlin: Kulturbund Deutscher Juden, 1935.

Levi, Neil. *Modernist Form and the Myth of Jewification*. New York: Fordham University Press, 2014.

Malkin, Jeanette R. "Introduction: Break a Leg!" In *Jews and the Making of Modern German Theatre*, edited by Jeanette R. Malkin and Freddie Rokem, 1–20. Iowa City: University of Iowa Press, 2010.

Michaud, Eric. *The Cult of Art in Nazi Germany*. Stanford: Stanford University Press, 2004.

Ofer, Dalia. "The Contribution of Gender to the Study of the Holocaust." In *Gender and Jewish History*, edited by Marion Kaplan and Deborah Dash Moore, 120–38. Bloomington: Indiana University Press, 2011.

Paret, Peter. *An Artist against the Third Reich: Ernst Barlach, 1933–1938*. Cambridge: Cambridge University Press, 2003.

Pasdzierny, Matthias. "'Der Ozean, der mich seit jener Zeit von dem Geburtslande trennt, hat wieder zwei Ufer…': Der Künstlerfonds des Süddeutschen Rundfunk und das deutsch-jüdische Musikerexil." In *Kulturelle Räume und ästhetische Universalität: Musik und Musiker im Exil*, edited by Dörte Schmidt, 195–231. Munich: Edition Text + Kritik, 2008.

Potter, Pamela. "The Arts in Nazi Germany: A Silent Debate." In *Contemporary European History* 15, no. 4 (2006): 585–99.

———. "Jewish Music and German Science." In *Jewish Musical Modernism, Old and New*, edited by Philip V. Bohlman, 81-101. Chicago: University of Chicago Press, 2008.

Rovit, Rebecca. "Jewish Theatre: Repertory and Censorship in the Jüdischer Kulturbund, Berlin." In *Theatre under the Nazis*, edited by John London, 187–221. Manchester: Manchester University Press, 2000.

———. *The Jewish Kulturbund Theatre Company in Berlin*. Iowa City: University of Iowa Press, 2012.

Steinweis, Alan E. "Hans Hinkel and German Jewry, 1933–1941." In *Leo Baeck Institute Year Book* (1993): 209–20.

———. *Art, Ideology and Economics in Nazi Germany: The Reich Chambers of Music, Theater and Visual Arts*. Chapel Hill: University of North Carolina Press, 1996.

Szapor, Judith, Andrea Pető, Maura Hametz, and Marina Calloni, eds. *Jewish Intellectual Women in Central Europe, 1860–2000*. Lewiston: Edwin Mellen, 2012.

Volkov, Shulamit. "The *Verbürgerlichung* of the Jews as a Paradigm." In *Bourgeoisie Society in Nineteenth-Century Europe*, edited by Jürgen Kocka and Allan Mitchell, 367–91. Oxford: Oxford University Press, 1993.
———. *Germans, Jews, and Antisemites: Trials in Emancipation*. New York: Cambridge University Press, 2006.
Wagner, Richard. *Das Judenthum in der Musik*. Leipzig: J. J. Weber, 1869.

CHAPTER 6

Pride of Place
The 1963 Rebuilding of the Munich Nationaltheater

EMILY RICHMOND POLLOCK

On 10 November 1955, the journalist Johann Lachner published an essay in the *Süddeutsche Zeitung* under the title "Das Phantom unserer Oper."[1] The "phantom" to which Lachner referred was not a masked, opera-obsessed kidnapper of sopranos, but rather a more symbolic "ghost": Lachner was haunted by his memories of attending opera performances at the Nationaltheater, a building buried since 1943 in a pile of rubble on Max-Joseph-Platz in Munich. The cultural past symbolized by the destroyed opera house was mourned as much as the loss of the building itself. Lachner wrote poignantly of seeing, after more than a decade, the "blessed ruins of our Nationaltheater," even as other landmark buildings in Munich had already been rebuilt and other opera houses in other cities had by then been built anew or reconstructed (Lachner mentioned Hamburg and Vienna in particular).[2] He felt the Nationaltheater's comparative neglect very keenly and ached to see it restored. Even as a ruin, he explained, the Nationaltheater called to mind the majestic building of the past, which he imagined reconstructing to correspond exactly to his architectural apparition. Because "the opera is a traditional institution," Lachner explained, he felt a sense of responsibility both to the site itself and to the history it represented.[3] He begged his fellow citizens to commit to reconstructing the opera house by Munich's "jubilee" year of 1958, ending his plea with these lines:

> The spirit of compromise must not be allowed to broaden. The inauguration of a worthy Nationaltheater in the year 1958 must be promoted. From now on, we will no longer be too tired to beat the drum for it and to watch over it. Because it is ten minutes to twelve.[4]

The sense of spiritual commitment and urgent dedication embodied in Lachner's essay was representative of a discourse that came to dominate the movement to rebuild Munich's opera house in the postwar period, resulting finally in the "reopening" of a reconstructed house in 1963. This huge architectural project was motivated primarily by a sense of loss and a yearning for the traditions of the past, combined with civic or regional pride and the fear of its degradation. While opera houses have commonly been regarded as essential institutions for the solidification of civic identity, the particular combination of traditionalism and pride surrounding Munich's Nationaltheater takes on a different connotation when it is acknowledged (as Lachner would not have) that the "tradition" evoked at the time was one bound up with the horrors of a war just over a decade in the past. With the word "tradition" one may audiate echoes of performances in the past—imagine a timeline extending from the building's first premieres to Wagner's *Tristan und Isolde* in 1865 to watershed performances of operas by Richard Strauss in the first quarter of the twentieth century—now rendered not only ephemeral but ghostly and discomfiting, estranged. It is important, too, that the "imagined" past here was not generally German but specific to Munich and Bavaria (Wagner and Strauss also being, of course, an essential part of that local and regional heritage). In the process of rebuilding, Lachner imagined restoring that cherished tradition to an unbroken state (that is, to unbreak the building would be to reconnect a shattered timeline), thereby granting Munich the continuity of artistic greatness that was its perceived due.

The singing ghosts in Munich's ruins remind us that, long after 1945, and well beyond what are usually thought of as "the rubble years," major structures in German cities that had previously served as cultural icons and landmarks remained in their bombed state. The home of the Bayerische Staatsoper was one such landmark, and only after two decades of missed deadlines, official processes, broken promises, and competing values was a faithful reconstruction of the original Nationaltheater finally achieved. The occasion was celebrated with a grand festival in November 1963, hailing the future of the arts in Munich and the restoration of an illustrious past tradition that adumbrated much more than opera itself.[5] In the postwar (re)construction of buildings designated for the preservation (and, sometimes, renewal) of the operatic tradition, architecture stood metaphorically for the status of opera as a genre, revealing fault lines between restoration and modernity, between the power of the past and a critique of conservatism. The discursive questions surrounding the structure amplified the problems of preserving or advancing the arts in an era in which projects of rebuilding were always politically charged, if rarely conducive to specific generalizations about political affiliation. Conservative politics and a conservative return to past artistic traditions were not strictly correlated. The Social Democratic Party (SPD) held power in Bavaria in the mid 1950s, even though "conservative" in the region eventually came to be associated with the Christian Social Union; likewise, with the exception of the three immediate postwar years, the mayoralty of Munich was held by the SPD throughout. That a "conservative" project of operatic and architectural restoration was undertaken in the context of Social Democratic city government reminds us of the hazards of correlating political terminology to affiliations in the arts (that is, "progressive" versus "conservative"), as if the arts were neatly analogous to party politics.[6] In practice, both in architecture and in the performance and creation of musical works, ideas about opera's proper future were divided untidily between a desire for opera to progress and a conception of opera as traditional and worthy of intense reinvestment. That the Bavarian case eventually subscribed so strongly to the latter reflects cultural values that cannot be reduced to simple conservatism or a stubborn opposition to change.

The Reconstruction of German Cities and Opera Houses

Reconstruction after World War II occurred within a complex matrix of architectural discourse, bureaucratic processes, material scarcity, and cultural memory.[7] A landscape of rubble in German cities was the backdrop not only for death but also for hunger, political displacement, and violence. Under these conditions, the architectural destruction took on synecdochic status; in the words of Tony Judt, "ruined cities were the most obvious—and photogenic—evidence of the devastation, and they came to serve as a universal visual shorthand for the pity of war."[8] The act of mourning the loss of symbolic German cultural buildings was arguably tinged, however, with a problematic nostalgia or even a sense of misdirected (and uncritical) grief. When destroyed landmarks were reconstructed in full, the new edifices became monuments in their own way, memorializing the destruction of cities through their renewed glory. Building projects and the events that celebrated them were but one way to come together to articulate a collective historical narrative that could be purposely amnesiac or even narcissistic. Neil Gregor has identified a tendency to remember the achievements of rebuilding in place of memorializing the bombing itself (and certainly not acknowledging the global situation of war and suffering), just as Jeffry Diefendorf has referred to the "mythmaking" inherent in such narratives of struggle and "heroic recovery" in reconstruction.[9]

Postwar public debate continuously politicized decisions about architectural style for new and reconstructed buildings.[10] On a purely logistical plane, these processes were complicated enough. The policies that governed building priorities, set initially by the occupying Allied forces, were often in conflict, and projects were often further confounded by clashing local, state, and federal guidelines.[11] Building materials were scarce and were commonly procured on the black market. There was also no consistent logic to prioritization. Although it was reasonable to focus first on essential infrastructure and utilities, on housing for the homeless and displaced, or on new administrative buildings, bureaucracies in different locations invested in certain "nonessential" projects (such as theaters, churches, and other symbolic buildings) despite ongoing housing shortages and persistent piles of rubble. The project of publicly accounting for and remedying the destruction of landmarks and cultural buildings thus proceeded haphazardly and often controversially, with few consistently applied principles in place.

Debates about architectural style had a particularly strong capacity to polarize when it came to Germany's *Altstädte*, or old city centers, many of which had been repeatedly bombed and were seen, as Diefendorf puts it, to "physically embod[y] Germany's urban history and culture. Hence debates about reconstructing the old inner cities were as much about historical symbols and values as about architectural elements or the technical dimensions of modern planning."[12] Opera houses and other cultural buildings (such as museums and universities) could take on similar status, featuring iconic architecture that was tied to urban identity and evoking a sense of cultural heritage that needed to be "preserved" (even when "preservation" really meant "wholesale reconstruction from the rubble"). In addition, many debates about the status, meaning, and preservation of old buildings originated well before the specific destruction of World War II. As Rudy Koshar has documented, postwar debates sat within a longer twentieth-century history of argument over priorities around national heritage, modernity, and preservation activities. As he notes, the first wave of discourse around reconstruction after 1945 was gradually absorbed into a concept of "normal" rebuilding and renovation, rather than evoking a specifically "postwar" condition.[13]

These discourses were largely rearticulated in the case of West Germany's opera houses, even as opera houses had certain characteristic elements. Opera houses were subject to the same regulatory tangles and bureaucracies as all building projects in the postwar period, and because opera houses in Germany are public institutions, they were subject to public opinion and investment in a way that large commercial buildings, for example, were not. Contemporary theaters required functional upgrades to enable modern stagecraft and a more comfortable audience experience, and it was often more expedient to raise a new modern opera house than it was to rebuild a historic façade.[14] On the other hand, those opera houses that *were* rebuilt had the cachet of seeming "well preserved" and "historic," which from a historical and material perspective is ironic.

Nearly all German opera houses were destroyed in the war. Even in Stuttgart, where the "Großes Haus" of the State Theater was one of the only theaters of that size in Germany to sustain minimal damage, a large number of repairs and renovations proved necessary.[15] Munich, with its attempt at a complete reconstruction, was quite unusual; most cities opted for modern options. For example, a brand-new opera house opened in Hamburg in 1955, designed in a modern style by Gerhard Weber, and West Berlin's Deutsche Oper opened in 1961, built as a continuation of the previous Charlottenburg Opera / Städtische Oper (architect: Fritz Bornemann). In Cologne, the neo-Gothic "Neues Theater" was burned out but widely thought reparable; the antipathy of the people toward what they saw as an artefact of Prussian domination, however, meant that it was ultimately demolished and replaced with a modern building. Designed by Wilhelm Riphahn, it opened in 1957.[16] Frankfurters saw their destroyed 1880 opera house as a relic of its time whose reconstruction would be dishonest. The city erected modern buildings to house the city's opera and theater companies in 1951.[17]

Even as the plan to rebuild Munich's Nationaltheater according to "original" specifications became solidified as a matter of public conception, then, such a strong sense of conviction should not be mistaken for a "default" or natural mode for German opera houses. All of these modern opera houses debuted well in advance of Munich's "reconstructed" opera house, as did the closest analog for Munich's project, the Staatsoper in Vienna, which had reopened in 1955.[18] Nor was the plan for the Munich Nationaltheater so easily settled in the first years after the war: there had even been calls for the Nationaltheater to be built in a modernized fashion elsewhere, with the ruins preserved as a permanent memorial.[19] That the Nationaltheater was eventually reconstructed in such an "exact" style can be best understood as part of the particular cultural context for rebuilding in Munich in the postwar period, which eventually consolidated a restorationist agenda.

Munich and Restorationism

Munich's exceptionally restorationist opera house project should be put into two different contexts. The first is the general concept of "restoration" in the postwar period, which had both political and material dimensions; the second is the specifically and explicitly traditionalist attitude toward reconstruction in Munich, which was more complicated than a label such as "conservative" might imply. The intersections of these two "work ethics" provide the foundation for understanding how the rebuilding project of the opera house in Munich was discursively framed over the project's two decades (for example, in references to the theater being "restored to its former glory").

Traditionally, the historic preservation of architectural landmarks had been accompanied by a rhetoric of authenticity that enabled the age of a building to show, thus not allowing full reconstructions to stand in falsely for original historic buildings. A strand of thought persisted that held that, while it was valid to preserve buildings that had been only moderately damaged, to completely reconstruct landmarks from the ruins was a falsehood because "original buildings were works of art ... [and] a reconstructed building would necessarily fail to achieve the originality, beauty, and value of its prototype."[20] However, in Munich in particular, these otherwise dominant standards were shifted radically, so that the effacement of material loss took priority over authenticity.[21] Citizen groups and popular opinion encouraged this shift, even as "experts" would decry it, as Diefendorf explains:

> This change from a narrow view of preservation and restoration, in which only individual buildings largely undamaged should be saved or restored, to one which emphasized the character of an area or quarter as an ensemble, even if that meant complete reconstruction of a totally destroyed building, ... matched the sentiments of the citizenry better than the narrower, purist position.[22]

Practical matters also required consideration: "restoring" an old building did not preclude the interior from being entirely modernized, even as the façades were meticulously recreated.[23]

Some modernists continued to critique such forms of *Wiederaufbau* (reconstruction), based in part on the idea that the trajectory of German tradition had led to National Socialism and that only with brand-new architectural ideas could Germany be sure to avoid its recurrence.[24] One of the most controversial articulations of this conflict may be seen in a project that directly contributed to the debates around the Nationaltheater: the dual (re)building of Munich's Residenztheater, originally a small rococo theater by François de Cuvilliés. In the war, the exterior had been damaged beyond repair, but the lavish interior had been disassembled and moved to the countryside. Despite that preservation, early postwar plans led to the erection of a brand-new Residenztheater, built on the original site in a modern style and opening in 1951 (this, incidentally, was the stage used for many postwar opera productions of the Bayerische Staatsoper while the company waited for the Nationaltheater to be rebuilt). The outcry among Munich's traditionalists, however, was so severe that money was raised by a group of concerned citizens to "rebuild" the destroyed theater on a different nearby site, complete with the restored interior; this brand-new structure, which opened in 1958, was thenceforth known as the "Altes Residenztheater."[25] In this case, a modern building had to be "corrected" by the meticulous reconstruction of an original, which then became "old," even though it was actually newer.

Historian Gavriel Rosenfeld has attributed this dominance of traditionalism in the rebuilding of Munich's landmarks to an unusual reading of the "dangers" of modernism. Munich's traditionalists saw National Socialist ideology as having been concerned with technical progress and drive; in their view, then, an emphasis on continuity and tradition would connect the people to their roots and conserve a lost, specifically *Bavarian* heritage that had been threatened by "the Nazis'" modern ideas.[26] Rosenfeld has argued that this was an explicit strategy to "forget" the city's identity as the *"Hauptstadt der Bewegung"* (capital of the movement) during the Third Reich by characterizing National Socialism as an anomalous rupture.²⁷ As Rosenfeld writes,

> By blaming modernity for all of the century's urban destruction, the *Heimat* groups relativized the important contribution of Munich's traditionalism to the rise of the Nazis and, by extension, the destruction caused by the Second World War. ... While the desire to view Bavaria and its regional traditions as historically innocent was indispensable to the *Heimat* groups' revision of memory, it led them to reiterate ideas that, along with others, were implicated in the disastrous course of recent history.²⁸

Modernism itself was thereby seen as a threat to local identity and integrity; a concern with authenticity had been revised to signify innocence, in a manner that seemingly disowned the fact that similar ideas of authenticity had themselves been deployed as a part of the naturalization discourses of National Socialism. Traditionalist tendencies consequently dominated, particularly among the upper middle class and the elites—the social classes that arguably were both most invested in "high culture" conceptions of Munich and most nostalgic and affirmative regarding the idea that the city could "arise once more in its old brilliance."²⁹

While practical factors also undeniably fed into reconstructionist projects, the overall "traditionalist" approach in Munich must be seen as part of what Rosenfeld calls "its citizenry's strategies of coming to terms with the past."³⁰ This involved the reiteration of a deeply ingrained view of Munich and Bavaria as distinct from the north, with a thousand-year history worthy of celebration. As a result, Munich succeeded in becoming one of the most completely restored cities in Germany, ironically earning a reputation with tourists for being well preserved.³¹ This rehabilitation of tradition brings to mind parallels with the situation of "high art" itself, which, as scholars of music under denazification have documented, was considered to be apolitical, a universal good that had persisted in spite of National Socialism.³² Just as the politicization of urban space by "the Nazis" could later be positioned as having deviated from the continuity of Munich's "true" identity as the Bavarian capital, the politicization of composers such as Wagner was constructed to have been a perversion of Bavarian musical heritage now to be readopted, for example, by emphasizing the Nationaltheater's continuity as a center for this tradition. Thus, many opera fans in Munich repeatedly requested throughout the 1950s that more Wagner be played, precisely to counter the idea that Wagner had been permanently politicized:

> What is the reason for this apparent rejection of Wagner? Is he still the representative of "Germanness" in some circles? Such people should be taught that the pacifist Richard Wagner was never a nationalist.³³

Articulations of this kind drew on an "older history" that predated the Third Reich. These efforts to recast the significance of opera as simultaneously apolitical, traditional, and worthy of preservation suggest parallels with Munich's self-image in its reconstruction more generally.

The Reconstruction of the Munich Nationaltheater

Munich's Nationaltheater sustained heavy damage from the air war. The bombing of 3 October 1943 resulted in a level of heat so high that the iron in the stage melted. Only the façade and the entrance hall remained, and the interior ruins were exposed to the weather over subsequent years, eventually requiring complete demolition. After the war's end, the opera house was part of the rubble landscape of Munich. While it might be tempting to think of that landscape as undifferentiated, materially reduced to a kind of stony, elemental meaninglessness, the destruction of the opera house was freighted with particular symbolic importance. Richard Strauss's elegiac *Metamorphosen*, for example, has been strongly associated with the destruction of monuments and opera houses, and specifically that of the Nationaltheater, which Strauss described as "the greatest catastrophe that ever occurred in my life."[34] After essential projects had taken priority, the question remained of what to do about the destroyed opera house. Financing the project was a considerable challenge, and worries were persistently articulated, both in press coverage and in letters to the opera company, that the ruin would be entirely demolished and lost for all time (watching modern edifices be built in other major cities certainly did not allay these fears). Plans for changes to traffic patterns around the center of the city and the cost overruns on the Cuvilliés-Theater all threatened the project throughout the 1950s.

To the extent that financing the project was the main problem, some concerted effort was made to raise money for the project through donations, air shows, raffles, benefit concerts, and a tax on beer. Many of these efforts were carried out by an organization eventually formalized in 1952 as the Freunde des Nationaltheaters (Friends of the National Theater).[35] With missions in both fundraising and publicity, this group of Munich's everyday opera fans and high-culture connoisseurs—conspicuously independent of the bureaucracies of either the opera house or the city—created an implied first-person plural around the project: the "we the people" of Munich.[36] Given the suspicious attitude with which top-down state decisions were regarded in the postwar period, it was essential that this campaign took the "grassroots" form it did, even though more conservative aesthetic decisions were the result.[37] Integral to the group's identity were two assumptions: that the project would be a *Wiederaufbau*, not a modern building, and that it needed to be completed in time for the 1958 jubilee year. The deadline was significant because, as Rosenfeld has shown, the 1958 celebrations were geared toward proving that "Munich had remained Munich" in spite of the devastation.[38] A pronounced sense of urgency consequently pervaded the group's marketing materials and the press coverage around this time (recall as well Lachner's line about "ten minutes to twelve" in his 1955 article, quoted above). This insistent tone was reinscribed visually, as well—for example, in sinister cartoon images depicting the machinery set to demolish the ruins in the absence of progress, with a caption threatening, "If nothing happens within a year, the excavator is coming!"[39] In 1955, a sign draped on the ruin (see Figure 6.1) stated that the building *had* to be finished before the 1958 jubilee year, with the plea, "Help the Friends of the National Theater!"[40]

With fundraising not nearly reaching the levels necessary to meet the 1958 deadline, a watershed moment was nonetheless reached in 1957: a call for signatures in the *Süddeutsche Zeitung* asked citizens to send in a small form lending their names to support the cause (Figure 6.1).[41]

"We want the National Theater!" proclaimed the headline above an article explaining the project, giving testimonials and background information and asking for support. As accusatory comparisons, dates for reopened opera houses in other cities are listed as "good examples," along with the question, in capital letters, "AND WHEN DOES MUNICH FOLLOW?"

This timeline of other cities' reopenings presented an interesting chronological counterpoint to the article's timeline of the "tragedy" of the ruins, which accounted for the project's successes and lags. But even more than that, it deployed the rhetoric of competition between Munich, as an erstwhile but restorable city of culture and music, and other cities. Why did Munich have to live with a ruin, when other (less worthy?) cities' houses had reopened? Similar rhetoric could be found in fan letters. One supporter wrote to a city official to assert,

> Now is really the time to begin. ... Cities like Vienna, Berlin, and Hamburg, not to mention smaller cities like Düsseldorf, Hagen, etc., have already long had their new houses, and now Stuttgart is starting to renovate their *Großes Haus* and to build a new *Kleines Haus*. Therefore, somehow or other a solution must also be found for Munich.[42]

What this fan's formulation implied was actually quite nuanced: while the heritage of opera to be restored with the Nationaltheater was positioned as simultaneously German, regional, and civic, the latter of the three was the form that dominated, driven by competition and comparison among putative musical "centers." A sense of indignation at the prospect of falling behind other large *and small* German cities betrayed the fear of "losing face" on the

Figure 6.1. Full-page call for support for the Nationaltheater (*SZ*. 23/24 February 1957. Source: DIZ München GmbH. Used with permission).

national and international stage due to the perceived and presumed centrality of elite artistic culture in any city of consequence.

With the newspaper's call for signatures, the campaign gained considerable momentum. Celebrating these developments, the opera company's *Intendant*,

Rudolf Hartmann, wrote a letter to a fellow *Intendant* to describe the rising tide of popular support for the opera:

> In the question of the rebuilding of our opera, a decisive development began in these last few weeks. The *Süddeutsche Zeitung* in Munich has called for a huge petition. ... The point is to get as many people as possible who are interested in culture to express their desire that the tradition-rich Munich Opera House should finally rise again [*wiederstehen*].[43]

The triumphant *"wiederstehen"* used by Hartmann shows how firmly the popularity of the campaign rested on an ideology of restoring something felt to be lost. From this point on, the company would always be lauded in terms of its continuity. The official discourse surrounding the opera house's *Wiederaufbau* made repeated reference to "restoring" Munich to its former state, cementing a sense that opera was an essential part of a cultural heritage that needed to be supported and reconstructed.

The call in the *Süddeutsche Zeitung* replicated another familiar trope from this period: photographs showed the glory days and the ruined building in a "then and now" comparison (*"so war's einmal ... so ist es heut"*). Rhetorical force accumulated through the repeated visual presentation of images of the ruins in the postwar era, recalling both the nineteenth-century aesthetic romanticization of ruins and National Socialist ideas about how monumental buildings were meant eventually to decay and provide evidence of their former greatness.[44] Similarly, in an official book published by the Freunde des Nationaltheaters after the project was completed, pairs of images showed the restored condition next to the destroyed artifacts, conveying a sense of heroic accomplishment by emphasizing just how severe the damage had been.[45] The "before" then became the "after," with the ruins standing as an aberration between a mythologized past and a gleaming reconstruction of the present.

On 9 April 1957, the campaign's triumph was announced, bearing the headline "195097 want the Nationaltheater!"[46] Although the project would not be completed until 1963, the momentum had decidedly turned in favor of reconstruction. Sure enough, by November 1963, the Nationaltheater in Munich had been rebuilt as exactly as possible to the specifications of the original building of 1811, even removing some revisions dating from the first time the building had been rebuilt, after a fire in 1823. It was a triumph of restorationism.

No one celebrated, or was celebrated, more than the Freunde des Nationaltheaters when the new opera house finally opened. In 1964, the Freunde published a book about the reconstruction in which the project was enshrined and fetishized in astonishing detail.[47] The entire process of fundraising and campaigning was cataloged. The architectural and design plans were intricately detailed in both prose and photographs. The book reproduced plans from every entry of the architectural competition and documented plumbing and stage machinery. It listed every firm involved in the building project, alongside countless ministries, committees, bureaucrats, artisans, designers, and other stakeholders. Photographic evidence showed the painstaking reconstruction by skilled craftsmen of decorative elements out of the evidence of the ruins. Nostalgic testimonies appeared from people of all walks of life who remembered the old house and were thrilled that it had been rebuilt. This overwhelming nostalgia was sanitized as a version of the past distinct from the horrors of recent decades, conveniently focusing instead on the echoes of a supposedly unbroken and artistically glorious nineteenth-century opera heritage that had continued up through Wagner and Strauss—in the process, ironically celebrating the legacy of a more "courtly" authoritarianism. A triumphant crescendo mounted in an essay by Ludwig Wismeyer:

> *Habemus theatrum novum!* We have a (our) new opera theater. … Who is still talking about the millions that the house cost (and until the other buildings are finished, will still cost)? The word of a simple Munich taxi driver as a *vox populi* should be cited, who said that the money was well spent and "Munich needed 'er opera house fer a right long time." Or consider as even better and more powerful evidence for the necessity of this building that evening after evening, the youth are waiting at the box office for their standing tickets, just as it was in the old Nationaltheater; that moreover Munich's residents can traverse the Max-Joseph-Platz with pride, to discover that here the tradition and artistry of the past harmonize with Munich's reputation as the "City of Art"? "Friends of the Nationaltheater" helped to build this house. … As long as opera is played here, then good, that accords with the great operatic tradition in Munich, which Munich achieved with honor and which makes it worth it to come to Munich to visit the Nationaltheater and the Bavarian State Opera—and thereby to find Friends of the Nationaltheater the whole world over.[48]

Overall, the volume told an epic saga of the rectification of a tragic mistake (the passive voice is often used to describe the destruction, as for a natural disaster), with little sense of historical causality or reconciliation. The affirmatively restorationist ideology contained within this account was undoubtedly both sincere and self-serving, presenting the reconstructed result as self-evidently "correct" rather than contingent or potentially political. And this "victorious" teleological narrative has carried forward into other publications about the history of the Munich opera house, becoming a standard trope. Not only the 1964 book but many more-recent publications by the Bavarian State Opera were underwritten by the Freunde des Nationaltheaters.[49] These publications were invariably richly illustrated with dazzling photos of the opera house's reconstructed exterior and interior, as well as with black-and-white photos of its destroyed state.[50] Such photos of the house's architecture were used to show both the company's symbolically central place in the life of the city and the triumph of its physical reinstatement *at* the center.

This attitude toward the opera house also owed its character to the tenor of Rudolf Hartmann's administration (1952–67), which has been appropriately described as a time of "conservation and rebuilding."[51] The reopening became a symbol of the way in which Hartmann generally guarded and restored the legacy of Munich's opera company during the postwar period (the first few postwar years, led by Georg Hartmann, were negatively received by audiences). Perhaps acknowledging his conservative orientation, Rudolf Hartmann once described himself as "born for the task" of rebuilding the theater, which rose triumphantly "like a phoenix from the ashes."[52] At the time, this attitude of restorationism probably seemed divorced from any relationship to the recent past, since Hartmann—whose career had been extremely strong during the Third Reich, who had belonged to National Socialist political and theatrical organizations from 1933 on, and who had benefited from copious financial support and access to party officials—had, like so many other artists, later claimed to have been apolitical.

Contemporary criticism of the restorationist position generally went unacknowledged in the official discourse. However, the occasional critique surfaced, most trenchantly expressed in the architectural journal *Baumeister* in essays by editor-in-chief Paulhans Peters and several other architects. Peters, who condemned the reconstruction as a "pseudo-*Aufbau*" inconsistent with professional architectural values, decried the lack of open and informed public debate and criticized the architectural establishment for not speaking out more.[53] An editorial by two young architects explicitly critiqued the restoration for covering up the circumstances of the opera house's destruction, calling the reconstructed house a "museum" and a "prison" for opera that prioritized a superficial festivity and tourist optics over truth.[54] By the same token, Johanna Schmidt-Grohe wrote an opinion piece in the *Süddeutsche Zeitung*, "Journey into the Past?," that critiqued the rebuilt theater as "surreal" and "akin to children playing Olden Times."[55] She bemoaned the lost opportunity to show the best of Munich's contemporary designers and artisans and characterized the attitude of the Freunde des Nationaltheaters as "the sentimental desire to arouse blessed memories by means of a copy of the old house."[56]

But the voices that decried reconstruction as a falsehood and reconstructed buildings as Potemkin villages were not heeded, nor was the old idea that the ruins might be architecturally preserved in the service of historical awareness. Despite these critical strains, then, and despite the political implications of postwar conservatism, it is actually primarily the restorationist discourse that is current in the Bavarian State Opera's culture and self-fashioning today. As recently as 2001, an essay in one of Munich's opera books repeated a 1992 assertion that "nothing has changed in 350 years. ... [C]ulture wants to be taken care of as a traditional value, above all in the Munich Nationaltheater. From there came the decision to rebuild the house after the Second World War in the form and function of the romantic monumental building."[57] The author did not mean this as a critique.

Analyzing the original campaign's self-mythologizing discourse, then, is not merely a question of reading between the lines. Such discourse forges an explicit connection between civic identity—the implied first-person plural of Munich, Bavaria, and the Freunde des Nationaltheaters—and the arguably dishonest premise of the project, the "reopening" of a Nationaltheater that for every practical purpose was a brand-new building. A history that elided the years of the Third Reich to preserve a sense of pride in collective greatness and cultural accomplishment was by necessity a *rewriting* through discourse; in the rebuilding of the opera house, this civic identity was articulated through high art and through the discourse of the friends (as well as the Friends) of the National Theater.

November 1963: The Gala Reopening

The opera house, central to Munich's self-cultivation as a *Künstlerstadt* for over a century before the war, had been restored and along with it a connection to a more perfect past. The "reopening" festival in November 1963 was a predictably huge, multiweek, and star-studded event. It was also framed by other significant events, both musical and political. In West Berlin, the iconic modern Philharmonie, designed by Hans Scharoun, opened on 15 October 1963, with Herbert von Karajan conducting Beethoven's Ninth Symphony. As one of the great architectural and musical events of the period, this concert served as an ongoing symbolic articulation of classical music's glory on the "democratic" side of the divided city. On the second day of the Munich festival, the American president John F. Kennedy—a wildly popular figure in West Germany, especially since his speech at the Berlin Wall earlier that same year—was assassinated in Dallas. In December 1963, while the opening festival continued to mount new productions, the German music community also mourned the deaths of Winfried Zillig and Karl Amadeus Hartmann. These two important figures in postwar musical life, both born in 1905, were members of the generation that had seen the Third Reich through adult eyes (and Hartmann, of course, had been an important modernist voice in Munich in the immediate postwar period, with his Musica Viva festival). Finally, just before Christmas, on December 20, the Frankfurt Auschwitz trials began. A consciously "postwar" era of restoration wound down, and a new cultural era was dawning.

The nature of the reopening gala as an "event" was evidenced by the media blitz beforehand. This ranged from the historical and weighty to the practical and the frivolous. The *Süddeutsche Zeitung* printed a lengthy and detailed history of opera in Munich, written by Walter Panofsky, in twenty-five-part serialization between mid October and the week of the opening gala.[58] This print run connected the festival event to the long history of the company and its previous buildings, celebrating the famous voices and conductors who had performed there. Journalists covered the rehearsal process—but also the new parking garage, recording studio, coat-check personnel, and other preparations: the champagne glasses, it was reported, "stood at the ready."[59] Proclaiming "Curtain Up!" and calling the gala the "event of the decade," the fashion industry also got in on the act in the fall style section, with special showings of formalwear in all of Munich's best stores (the columnist recommended floor-length evening dresses and feathers in one's hair, with long tails, of course, for men).[60] The events were exclusive; many opera fans and well-wishers who had wanted tickets to the opening could not obtain them because the first day's events were "invitation only"; this state of affairs was caricatured in a cartoon by Ernst Hürlimann, which showed a working-class man asking, in Bavarian dialect, "Were you not invited, either?" ("*San Sie aa net eingladn worn…?*").[61]

Pomp and ceremony were cultivated in spades at this opening gala, which comprised a concert in the afternoon and the premiere of *Die Frau ohne Schatten* in the evening. The concert on the morning of 21 November predictably consecrated the house with Beethoven's "Weihe des Hauses" Overture—originally written for a Viennese theater opening in 1822—and the "Hallelujah" Chorus (see transcribed program in Figure 6.2). To close the concert, the orchestra played the national anthem and the Bayernhymne (the Bavarian anthem).[62]

The use of the German and Bavarian anthems in this concert was eerily echoed later in the week by the festival's response to the Kennedy assassination: before the premiere of a new production of *Die Meistersinger von Nürnberg* on 23 November, the orchestra played the American national anthem. "The shadow of a death hangs over this evening," one newspaper report about that evening began, "but on the Max-Joseph Platz stand over a thousand people," arriving in limos and dressed to the nines.[63] As the opera was supposed to begin, the *Ministerpräsident*, Alfons Goppel, stood before the closed curtain and lauded Kennedy as having "dedicated his life to us and our future freedom."[64] Then, "The Star-Spangled Banner" was played, followed by more than a minute of silence, and then the conductor began the overture. The use of the three national anthems that week—stranger still, with "The Star-Spangled Banner" played directly before an overture that had been performed so often during the Third Reich that it was almost a secondary anthem of the regime—perhaps metaphorically emphasized the complicated connections between Bavaria (or regional identity), Germany (or national identity), and the occupier-turned-ally, the United States.

> **FESTAKT**
> Aus Anlass der Eröffnung des wiederaufgebauten Nationaltheaters in München am Donnerstag, den 21. November 1963, um 10:30 Uhr.
>
> LUDWIG VAN BEETHOVEN
> "Die Weihe des Hauses"
> Dirigent Hans Knappertsbusch
>
> Ansprache des Bayerischen Ministerpräsidenten Alfons Goppel.
> Schlüsselübergabe an den Bayerischen Staatsminister
> für Unterricht und Kultus Dr Theodor Maunz
> Ansprache des Staatsintendanten Rudolf Hartmann
> nach Übernahme des Schlüssels
>
> GEORG FRIEDRICH HÄNDEL
> Einleitung und zwei Chöre aus dem Oratorium "Der Messias"
> "Dank sei dir Gott"
> "Halleluja, Halleluja!"
> Dirigent Robert Heger
> Der Chor der Bayerischen Staatsoper
> Das Bayerische Staatsorchester.
>
> Das Orchester spielt zum Abschluss der Feier die Nationalhymne und die Bayernhymne

Figure 6.2. Transcribed festival concert program from the opening of the rebuilt Nationaltheater.

After the opening night, a celebratory atmosphere was sustained in Munich for several weeks, even as the world turned. The festival's overall program was diverse, consisting of an opening concert, eight productions, and a run of ballet performances (Table 6.1), with premiere events occurring over the course of a month.

To feature a new production of *Fidelio* was almost stereotypical by 1963, echoing both the first opera performance in Berlin after the surrender in 1945 and the reopening of the Vienna State Opera in 1955, as well as reopening celebration productions of *Fidelio* in Düsseldorf, Kiel, and Kaiserslautern, among other houses. The choice to create a technically sophisticated production of the somewhat rare *Die Frau ohne Schatten*, on the other hand, acknowledged the appetite for rarer works by Strauss in a community that had had a sustained historical relationship with that composer, thereby invoking and reaffirming a sense of pride in regional tradition as well as an appropriately Bavarian representation of modern music. Meanwhile, the premiere of a new, yet extremely traditional, production of *Die Meistersinger* reflected the reality that even in a completely historicized staging, the work by Wagner had long

Table 6.1. Timeline of the "Opening Festival for the Rebuilt National Theater," Munich, 1963.

Date	Event	Notes
21 November (am)	Concert and opening ceremony	see Figure 6.2
21 November (pm)	Strauss, *Die Frau ohne Schatten*	new production. invited guests only
23 November	Wagner, *Die Meistersinger von Nürnberg*	new production
27 November	Egk, *Die Verlobung in San Domingo*	commissioned for the festival
1 December	Beethoven, *Fidelio*	new production
3 December	Ballets by Heinz Rosen to Copland, Hartmann, and Orff	mixed premiere of music and choreography
7 December	Verdi, *Aida*	new production
11 December	Mozart, *Don Giovanni*	revival
21 December	Orff, *Carmina Burana, Catulli Carmina, Trionfo di Afrodite*	revival
22 December	Handel, *Julius Cäsar*	revival

since become cleansed of its National Socialist associations. Works by three major living Bavarian composers—Werner Egk, Carl Orff, and Karl Amadeus Hartmann—framed a new postwar canon of contemporary composers who were considered important enough, artistically moderate enough, and regionally cherished enough to be safely housed in a large-scale institution.

Many of the new productions took advantage of modern staging techniques, enabled by the house's up-to-date technology and modern lighting, and indulged a sense of dramatic grandeur that used the large stage to its fullest effect. Production photographs show that a slightly pared-down, abstracted, or symbolic version of realism was in vogue, as in the Strauss, though a detailed historical approach was also common (as in *Die Meistersinger* and *Aida*). Only a few productions (*Don Giovanni, Trionfo*, and *Julius Cäsar*) had been imported from the smaller theater that had served as the company's provisional home. Runs of each of the premiered productions continued over weeks, catering to thousands of opera fans. The casting and musical direction were luxurious: famous singers and conductors involved in the festival included Dietrich Fischer-Dieskau, Fritz Wunderlich, Herbert von Karajan, Christa Ludwig, Aaron Copland, Karl Böhm, and Lisa Della Casa. Critical praise, especially for the acoustics and the star performances, abounded, and the whole occasion was a patriotic triumph.

Given this, it is worth reflecting on what exactly had been accomplished here: a wildly expensive project to painstakingly reconstruct a temple to the musical heritage of a city and region whose relationship to the past was far from benign. In rebuilding the Nationaltheater, the citizens and opera fans of Munich did not even need to squint to imagine their operatic legacy as one of unending and unbroken glory. Destruction had been an aberration, a glitch, the complication of which had been erased through their loving and meticulous attention to detail. Phantoms of the opera past, now, could be treated as if laid to rest, recalling a common trope in ghost stories that the "haunting" ends when the spirit in question has had its scores settled. As a project and a narrative, the rebuilding of the Nationaltheater was just such a settling of scores, if not a true reconciliation with the past.

The first night's gala was, of course, front-page news, reproducing many images of the new hall's outer and inner beauty. Program booklets and other printed materials for the festival likewise reproduced distant and recent visions of the past (the original nineteenth-century design next to the opera house's destroyed interior and façade), alongside the present and presumed future (images of the reconstruction). Such images implied a teleology of rightful restoration. A dual declaration of victory over wartime destruction and optimism about the future was here concretized in material form—velvet, gold, and stone—and preserved in presumed perpetuity. Not despite but rather abetted by the emphasis on its monumental physicality, the Nationaltheater was more than just a building. By materially manifesting Munich's particularly restorationist ideas about history and the importance of tradition, the theater was given "pride of place": a place for cultural tradition, built in expression of civic and regional pride.

Emily Richmond Pollock is associate professor in the Music and Theater Arts Section of the Massachusetts Institute of Technology. Her book, Opera after the Zero Hour: The Problem of Tradition and the Possibility of Renewal in Postwar West Germany, was published by Oxford University Press in 2019. Her research has been supported by the German Academic Exchange Service (DAAD), the Paul Sacher Stiftung, and the Class of 1947 at MIT.

Notes

1. Johann Lachner, "Das Phantom unserer Oper," *Süddeutsche Zeitung* (hereafter SZ), 10 November 1955. "Johann Lachner" was a pseudonym for Hans Mollier.
2. Ibid. All translations are mine unless otherwise noted.
3. Ibid.
4. Ibid.
5. In my reading of the ideology built into this occasion, I draw on Peter Stachel, "'Das Krönungsjuwel der österreichischen Freiheit': Die Wiedereröffnung der Wiener Staatsoper 1955 als Akt österreichischer Identitätspolitik," in *Bühnen der Politik: Die Oper in europäischen Gesellschaften im 19. und 20. Jahrhundert*, ed. Sven Oliver Müller and Jutta Toelle (Vienna, 2008), 90–107; and Neil Gregor, "Beethoven, Bayreuth and

the Origins of the Federal Republic of Germany," *English Historical Review* 76, no. 521 (2011): 835–77.
6. On the general context of postwar Bavarian politics, see Maximilian Lanzinner, *Zwischen Sternenbanner und Bundesadler: Bayern im Wiederaufbau 1945–1958* (Regensburg, 1996).
7. Gavriel D. Rosenfeld, *Munich and Memory: Architecture, Monuments, and the Legacy of the Third Reich* (Berkeley, 2000), 47.
8. Tony Judt, *Postwar: A History of Europe since 1945* (New York, 2005), 16.
9. Neil Gregor, *Haunted City: Nuremberg and the Nazi Past* (New Haven, 2008), 3; Jeffry M. Diefendorf, *In the Wake of War: The Reconstruction of German Cities after World War II* (New York, 1993), xx.
10. Jeffry M. Diefendorf, "Introduction: New Perspectives on a Rebuilt Europe," in *Rebuilding Europe's Bombed Cities*, ed. Jeffry M. Diefendorf (New York, 1990), 1–15.
11. Diefendorf, *In the Wake of War*, 31–42. The remainder of this paragraph further paraphrases the conditions for rebuilding as documented by Diefendorf.
12. Ibid., 67.
13. Rudy Koshar, *Germany's Transient Pasts: Preservation and National Memory in the Twentieth Century* (Chapel Hill, 1998), 199–287. For a history, though specific to Cologne, similarly focused on a timeline that extends far beyond the "divide" of 1945, see Johanna M. Blokker, "(Re)Constructing Identity: World War II and the Reconstruction of Cologne's Destroyed Romanesque Churches, 1945–1985" (PhD diss., New York University, 2011), ProQuest (AAT 3466856).
14. Diefendorf, *In the Wake of War*, 43.
15. Building inspector's report, 24 June 1945, EL 221/1 Bü 8, Verwaltungsakten I: Instandsetzung der Gebäude, archive of the Württembergisches Staatstheater Stuttgart, Staatsarchiv Ludwigsburg. There were also several smaller opera houses that had been relatively undamaged by Allied bombing, such as the opera house in Hanover, which were rebuilt in their original style and reopened relatively quickly.
16. Diefendorf, *In the Wake of War*, 97.
17. Ibid., 77–78. The "backlash" against the postwar modern aesthetic, however, was manifested in the fact that the "old" opera house was in fact eventually rebuilt. Opened in 1981, it is now used as a concert hall; it is still known—apparently unironically—as the "Alte Oper" (literally, the old opera).
18. Stachel, "Die Wiedereröffnung."
19. Ulrike Hessler, "Die Oper in München und ihre Theater," in *Kraftwerk der Leidenschaft: Die Bayerische Staatsoper*, ed. Ulrike Hessler (Munich, 2001), 91. See also Rosenfeld, *Munich and Memory*, 47.
20. Diefendorf, *In the Wake of War*, 71.
21. Rosenfeld, *Munich and Memory*, 176.
22. Diefendorf, *In the Wake of War*, 73.
23. Ibid., 69. See also Koshar, *Germany's Transient Pasts*, 261–62.
24. Rosenfeld, *Munich and Memory*, 52.
25. Ibid., 39–40.
26. Ibid., 7.
27. Ibid., 8–9
28. Ibid., 160, 252–53.
29. Meitinger Plan quoted in ibid., 31.

30. Ibid., 49.
31. Ibid., 15. See also Diefendorf, *In the Wake of War*, xiii.
32. David Monod, *Settling Scores: German Music, Denazification, and the Americans, 1945–1953* (Chapel Hill, 2005).
33. Hermann Steinberger to Rudolf Hartmann, fan letter, 15 June 1953, V-Nr. 284: correspondence S, Sch, St., archive for the Staatliche Theater (Nationaltheater and Prinzregententheater) 1945–1963, Hauptstaatsarchiv Munich.
34. Richard Strauss to Willi Schuh, 8 October 1943, in *Richard Strauss: Briefwechsel mit Willi Schuh*, ed. Willi Schuh (Zurich, 1969), 50; quoted and translated in Neil Gregor, "Music, Memory, Emotion: Richard Strauss and the Legacies of War," *Music and Letters* 96, no. 1 (2015): 62.
35. "Die Stadt spielt mit beim Opernbau," *SZ*, 11 May 1955.
36. For all that the Nationaltheater is "national" to Bavaria, there is little evidence that many members of the working classes or rural Bavarians were involved with the project. Nonetheless, I see their language as employing a "grassroots" rhetoric that implies a synecdochic relationship between the fans involved in the Freunde and some construction of "the populace" as a whole.
37. Diefendorf repeatedly describes the tensions between volunteer citizen groups and various levels of centralized governmental authority. Diefendorf, *In the Wake of War*.
38. Rosenfeld, *Munich and Memory*, 48.
39. Freunde des Nationaltheaters, *Festliche Oper: Geschichte und Wiederaufbau des Nationaltheaters in München* (Munich, 1964), 40 ["Wenn nicht innerhalb eines Jahres was geschieht, dann – kommt der Bagger!"].
40. Hans Zehetmair and Jürgen Schläder, eds., *Nationaltheater: Die Bayerische Staatsoper* (Munich, 1992), 238.
41. "Wir wollen das Nationaltheater!" *Süddeutsche Zeitung*, 23/24 February 1957.
42. Helmuth Katz, industrialist and opera supporter, to the Bavarian Ministerpräsident Wilhelm Hoegner, cc: Rudolf Hartmann, letter, 4 April 1956, V-Nr. 282: correspondence K, archive for the Staatliche Theater (Nationaltheater and Prinzregententheater) 1945–1963, Hauptstaatsarchiv Munich.
43. Rudolf Hartmann to Paul Rose, Generalintendant in Karlsruhe, letter, 14 March 1957, V-Nr. 283: correspondence O, P, Q / R, T, archive for the Staatliche Theater (Nationaltheater and Prinzregententheater) 1945–1963, Hauptstaatsarchiv Munich.
44. Diefendorf, *In the Wake of War*, 3.
45. See, for example, Freunde des Nationaltheaters, *Festliche Oper*, 258–59. For more, see Johanna M. Blokker, "Remembering and Experiencing German Cities in Photographic Books after World War II," in *Paper Cities: Urban Portraits in Photographic Books*, ed. Susana S. Martins and Anne Reverseau (Leuven, 2016), 191–214.
46. "195097 wollen das Nationaltheater!," *SZ*, 9 April 1957.
47. Freunde des Nationaltheaters, *Festliche Oper*.
48. Ibid., 310.
49. Other publications include Zehetmair and Schläder, *Nationaltheater*; Hessler, *Kraftwerk der Leidenschaft*; and Hermann Friess, *Dreihundert Jahre Münchner Oper* (Munich, 1953).
50. Hessler, *Kraftwerk der Leidenschaft*, 2–5; Hessler, 90–92; and Hessler, 156–59; Ulrike Hessler and Jürgen Schläder, eds., *Macht der Gefühle: 350 Jahre Oper in München* (Berlin, 2003), 130–33; Zehetmair and Schläder, *Nationaltheater*, 220–21.

51. Andreas Backöfer, "'Intendant zu sein ist eine Zumutung': Über die Regisseure Günther Rennert, Rudolf Hartmann und August Everding," in Zehetmair and Schläder, *Nationaltheater*, 143–44.
52. Ibid., 143–45.
53. Paulhans Peters, "Nationaltheater nach 'Vorlagen,'" *Der Baumeister* (1962): 471; Paulhans Peters, "Nationaltheater – zweiter Akt," *Der Baumeister* (1964): 51.
54. Peter Debold and Thomas Herzog, "Die Touristenkulisse," *Der Baumeister* (1964): 51–52. Some of these same sources are quoted in Rosenfeld, *Munich and Memory*, 182–83, 368–69n16.
55. Johanna Schmidt-Grohe, "Reise in die Vergangenheit?," *Süddeutsche Zeitung*, 11 December 1963.
56. Ibid. More recently, Rosenfeld critiqued the Nationaltheater project as a "denial of the past" that was "not only aesthetically anachronistic but historically dishonest." He has also described the Nationaltheater as a paradigmatic example of the "conflict between modernists and traditionalists." Rosenfeld, *Munich and Memory*, 180–83.
57. Jürgen Schläder, "Kontinuität der Geschichte: Die Oper in München, ihre Veranstalter und ihr Publikum," in Hessler, *Kraftwerk der Leidenschaft*, 33–72. This is a reprint of an essay from Zehetmair and Schläder, *Nationaltheater*, 9–20.
58. Walter Panofsky, "Eine Chronik der berühmten Münchner Oper," *SZ*, serialized in twenty-five parts, 19/20 October 1963 through 23/24 November 1963.
59. "Auch kein Meistersinger fällt vom Himmel: die letzten Probenarbeiten vor der Galapremiere des Nationaltheater," *SZ*, 19 November 1963; "Tiefgaragenbau in Höchstgeschwindigkeit: Der unterirdische Parkplatz an der Oper wird vor den vereinbarten Terminen fertig," *SZ*, 16/17 November 1963; "Sie spielen in der Oper die Dienerrolle: Gespräche mit alten Einlaßdienern und Garderobenfrauen," *SZ*, 16/17 November 1963; "Die Sektgläser stehen bereit—die Pause kann beginnen" (caption), *SZ*, 21 November 1963; "Die Oper—das reinste Lichtspielhaus," *SZ*, 15 October 1963.
60. *SZ*, 27 September 1963.
61. Ernst Hürlimann, cartoon, *SZ*, 23/24 November 1963.
62. Theaterzettel, archive for the Staatliche Theater (Nationaltheater and Prinzregententheater) 1945–1963, Hauptstaatsarchiv Munich.
63. Hans Krammer, "Schatten über dem Premierenglanz," *SZ*, 25 November 1963.
64. Ibid.

Bibliography

Blokker, Johanna M. "(Re)Constructing Identity: World War II and the Reconstruction of Cologne's Destroyed Romanesque Churches, 1945–1985." PhD diss., New York University, 2011. ProQuest (AAT 3466856).

———. "Remembering and Experiencing German Cities in Photographic Books after World War II." In *Paper Cities: Urban Portraits in Photographic Books*, edited by Susana S. Martins and Anne Reverseau, 191–214. Leuven: Leuven University Press, 2016.

Diefendorf, Jeffry M. "Introduction: New Perspectives on a Rebuilt Europe." In *Rebuilding Europe's Bombed Cities*, ed. Jeffry M. Diefendorf, 1–15. New York: St. Martin's Press, 1990.

———. *In the Wake of War: The Reconstruction of German Cities after World War II*. New York: Oxford University Press, 1993.

Freunde des Nationaltheaters. *Festliche Oper: Geschichte und Wiederaufbau des Nationaltheaters in München*. Munich: Verlag Callwey, 1964.

Friess, Hermann. *Dreihundert Jahre Münchner Oper*. Munich: Gotteswinter, 1953.

Gregor, Neil. *Haunted City: Nuremberg and the Nazi Past*. New Haven, CT: Yale University Press, 2008.

———. "Beethoven, Bayreuth and the Origins of the Federal Republic of Germany." *English Historical Review* 76, no. 521 (2011): 835–77.

———. "Music, Memory, Emotion: Richard Strauss and the Legacies of War." *Music and Letters* 96, no. 1 (2015): 55–76.

Hessler, Ulrike, ed. *Kraftwerk der Leidenschaft: Die Bayerische Staatsoper*. Munich: Prestel, 2001.

Hessler, Ulrike, and Jürgen Schläder, eds. *Macht der Gefühle: 350 Jahre Oper in München*. Berlin: Henschel, 2003.

Judt, Tony. *Postwar: A History of Europe since 1945*. New York: Penguin, 2005.

Koshar, Rudy. *Germany's Transient Pasts: Preservation and National Memory in the Twentieth Century*. Chapel Hill: University of North Carolina Press, 1998.

Lanzinner, Maximilian. *Zwischen Sternenbanner und Bundesadler: Bayern im Wiederaufbau 1945–1958*. Regensburg: Verlag Friedrich Pustet, 1996.

Monod, David. *Settling Scores: German Music, Denazification, and the Americans, 1945–1953*. Chapel Hill: University of North Carolina Press, 2005.

Rosenfeld, Gavriel D. *Munich and Memory: Architecture, Monuments, and the Legacy of the Third Reich*. Berkeley: University of California Press, 2000.

Stachel, Peter. "'Das Krönungsjuwel der österreichischen Freiheit': Die Wiedereröffnung der Wiener Staatsoper 1955 als Akt österreichischer Identitätspolitik." In *Bühnen der Politik: Die Oper in europäischen Gesellschaften im 19. und 20. Jahrhundert*, ed. Sven Oliver Müller and Jutta Toelle, 90–107. Vienna: Oldenbourg, 2008.

Zehetmair, Hans, and Jürgen Schläder, eds. *Nationaltheater: Die Bayerische Staatsoper*. Munich: Bruckmann, 1992.

PART III

Globalizing Musical Germanness

CHAPTER 7

Was ist Japanisch?
Wagnerism and Dreams of Nationhood in Modern Japan

BROOKE MCCORKLE OKAZAKI

In their introduction to *Music and German National Identity*, Celia Applegate and Pamela Potter proclaim, "For musical audiences today, the words 'German' and 'music' merge so easily into a single concept that their connection is hardly ever questioned."[1] The seeds of this fantasy of the convergence of music and Teutonicism stretch back into the eighteenth century, they argue, and came to particular prominence with the consolidation of the German nation in 1871. By the end of the nineteenth century, no composer so clearly represented the German *Geist* as did Richard Wagner. Wagner himself perpetuated his reputation as "most German composer," a claim carried onwards by his disciples, many of whom projected their own notions about art and politics back onto him and his legacy.[2] Wagner's potency as a template for cultural nationalism held sway across Europe, Russia, and the United States, as evidenced by numerous reception studies.[3] By the end of the nineteenth century, Wagner's music and ideologies had arrived in a very different part of the world: Tokyo. More than Beethoven or Mozart, Wagner was the composer most significant in the evolution of Japan's imperial ideology in connection to Western music.

German culture arrived in Japan in 1868, when rebels overthrew the ruling samurai government and reinstated the imperial system. Early on, the Meiji emperor (r. 1868–1912) ended a centuries-long period of isolation. In opening its doors to the West, the country welcomed a flood of foreign technology and culture, particularly from Germany. Many in Japan's bureaucratic upper echelons considered Germany a European corollary to Japan. Both were young, imperial nations with long cultural histories seeking to flex newly founded military might. Japanese scholars went to study in Europe, most notably Berlin, planning to return home with utilitarian knowledge as well as Western-style aesthetic refinement. The import and appropriation of all things foreign was so dramatic that the process of Westernization quickly became conflated with the idea of modernization.⁴ This conflation would echo throughout East Asia in the coming decades, with nations like China grappling with forging modernity vis-à-vis Western music.⁵ As Japan rose to prominence and, taking its cue from the West, established itself as a colonial power, this interweaving of the Occidental with the modern persisted. While the collective goal for turn-of-the-century Japan was to fulfil the imperial slogan "rich nation and strong army," intellectuals there increasingly lost faith with the government and its promises. These "ideologues," as Carol Gluck calls them, came from a variety of backgrounds, including academic, bureaucratic, and religious.⁶ Dispersed pockets of these ideologues sought to create a new mythology for the Meiji state.⁷

It was in this social and political crucible that Wagnermania caught fire in Japan. Japanese Germanophiles sought to transplant Wagner's ideals and cultivate them to suit their own nation-building pursuits. Some of these intellectuals reinvented Wagner in order to articulate their perspective of the process of modernization and nation building in the late nineteenth and early twentieth centuries. Thus the importation of Wagner-related philosophies, including those of Nietzsche and Schopenhauer, along with Wagner's own prose and musical works was more than appropriation; it was also a political action.⁸ An examination of early incarnations of Wagnerism in Japan can thus shed light on the complex skein of Japan's modernization.⁹

I will discuss four cases to demonstrate the diverse ways in which this occurred. The first is the religious scholar Anesaki Chōfū's published letters from Germany; in them, Anesaki connects ideas on Wagner, Nietzsche, and Japan. Soon after, an attempt by Tokyo conservatory students to stage *Tannhäuser* emphasized a conviction among young people regarding Wagner's value to a revolutionary cause. A few years later, literature both high and low also blended Wagner and autochthonous ideals. Finally, the poet Akimoto Rofū translated and adapted the *Tannhäuser* libretto into classical poetic form for a literati journal while collections of short stories based on Wagner's operas circulated in more popular realms.

It is important to recognize, however, that in Japan Wagner's outlook and aesthetics were emphasized more than his music, so much so that sheet music of Wagner's pieces did not circulate until 1918 and there were no complete stagings of any of his operas until the 1940s, when both Wagnerism and Japanese imperialism reached their apogee. In sum, Japan's reception of Wagner was, for all of its intensity, astoundingly silent. Very few Japanese Wagnerians had ever heard a Wagner opera.¹⁰ But this lack of musical engagement early on was not entirely unique. Like many Western Wagnerians, Japanese followers first encountered Wagner not through his music but through its echoes in the writings of Nietzsche.¹¹ In these they tended to favor pro-Wagnerian texts such as *Also sprach Zarathustra* and *The Birth of Tragedy*; those few with any knowledge of Nietzsche's later break with Wagner conveniently ignored it.[12] In this, Wagner supporters in Tokyo mostly resembled their Russian counterparts. In the milieu of Russia's "Silver Age," Nietzsche was considered "a mystic and a prophet, a progenitor of a new culture of freedom and beauty," while Wagner was "the modern bearer of the 'spirit of music' itself."[13] Though Nietzsche had certainly inspired France's Wagnerian symbolists, it was in Russia and beyond, to the east, that the philosopher and composer were most inextricable.

Yet despite Nietzsche's own fascination with *Tristan*, it makes sense that it was *Tannhäuser* that captured the Meiji imagination. Many factors likely contributed to this, including accessibility. Carolyn Abbate and Roger Parker point out that "*Tannhäuser* was by far the most popular of Wagner's operas throughout the entire nineteenth century and well into the twentieth, with glowing reviews that evidently softened impresarios and theatre directors worldwide."[14] The same held true in Japan. Musically, *Tannhäuser* is less challenging and more purely lyrical than the later music dramas. The *Venusbergmusik*, Pilgrims' Chorus, and "Song to the Evening Star" are performable as excerpts. As I will argue here, the libretto's monumentalization of pseudohistorical figures resonated with the Japanese tendency to do likewise in literature and drama, both ancient and contemporary.[15]

In Japan, the lack of discourse specifically on Wagner's music suggests that Wagnerism there had less to do with opera and more to do with disillusionment on the part of the Japanese Wagnerians. In this I concur with Takenaka Toru, though I wish to take things a step further by examining not just the elite Wagnerians but also Wagnerism in popular culture in the late Meiji era.[16] The import of Wagner to Japan has only recently been acknowledged and sheds important light on Japanese political and aesthetic culture in the long nineteenth century. Wagner emblematized a fantasy of Germanness. But he also served as a totem for ideologues dreaming of a new global position for a modern Japan that utilized Western tools, both philosophical and technological, in service of a broader imperial mission. The articulation of Wagnerism in Japan was part of an invented ontology that managed an equilibrium between modernity and autochthonous values.[17]

Rousing a Nation

The trauma of being compelled to open to the West defined Japan's international relations and nation-building pursuits through the end of World War II.[18] In concert with this trauma notions of modernity developed that echoed throughout the twentieth century. Thus, the events leading to what is called the Meiji Restoration are worth considering briefly.

From 1600 up to the mid nineteenth century, a samurai government (*bakufu*) ruled Japan from its political center, Edo (modern-day Tokyo). This government, dominated by the Tokugawa samurai clan, adhered to a policy of strict isolationism.[19] Thus, until the 1860s, Japan radically limited its contact with the outside world. The long reign of the Tokugawa created a stable atmosphere for internal development of traditional Japanese art forms. But this stability was disrupted in the mid nineteenth century.

In the years prior to the Civil War, the United States was eager to expand its global position. It acquired California in the war with Mexico, and Manifest Destiny—the belief that an America blessed by God was fated to stretch its borders across the continent—led it west, across the Pacific. Trade with China and the lure of plentiful whaling had beckoned American ships across the water. Naturally, the Americans soon turned their eyes toward Japan. After an unsuccessful mission in 1845, the United States redoubled its efforts to "open" Japan. Commodore Matthew C. Perry was in command of the mission; nominally his goal was to gain port trading rights and safe transport for shipwrecked sailors.[20] Marius Jensen describes Perry's arrival off the shore of Edo: "Perry entered Edo Bay on July 2, 1853, with four ships mounting sixty-one guns and carrying 967 men.... The American warships were six or more times the size of any ship in Japan, and their dark hulls earned them their 'black ships' (*kurofune*) name in Japanese lore."[21] The arrival of the black ships served to weaken what was an already feeble *bakufu*. Isolationism was clearly no longer a viable policy.[22]

The Japanese public was in an uproar—it was unthinkable that foreigners could dictate native policy. Many of the provincial rulers demanded war with the United States, despite the obvious disparity in military might. The resulting backlash to the treaty with the Americans led to internal strife and rebellion, culminating in what became an axiom of the era: *sonnō jōi*, or "revere the emperor, expel the barbarians." In little over a decade, the *bakufu* was overthrown and the emperor, until then a mere figurehead, was reinstated as both head of state and national spiritual leader. In 1868, the Meiji era—named posthumously after the restored emperor—began in earnest.

Ironically, Japan's experience with Perry's black ships in the previous decade had revealed that foreign goods and knowledge were essential to maintaining independence from colonial invaders. Many believed that it had been superior military technology that had led to the forced treaties. So, for the next twenty years there was a dramatic upheaval in Japanese politics, society, education, and industry as the government adopted and adapted Western culture and technology.[23]

By the late 1880s a backlash against this modernization arose among politicians and intellectuals. The distress at the abrupt change and fragmentation of a Japanese society overwhelmed by foreign culture brought about a wave of ideological writings from scholars. Riding that wave, however, was a curious crest of Teutonic influence.[24] The decades following the restoration were socially and politically tumultuous and the haphazard importation of foreign culture problematic. Japan needed to settle on one country to emulate, and that country was Germany. In the 1870s, the Japanese army slowly shifted from a French-style system to a Prussian one. This shift, possibly induced by the outcome of the Franco-Prussian War, included everything from conscription laws to drill training. The pivot to Germany extended beyond the military realm. In 1886, after testing several Western education structures, including French and American models (the former too centralized and the latter too localized), the Meiji government settled on a hybridized German-style state system. A decade later, after a lengthy examination and rejection of British and French civil codes, the Japanese government decided to enact ones based on Germany's. French and British ones, politicians argued, clashed with native values.

These policies trended toward a Prussian approach that suited the prevailing desire to establish a sense of national unity. The successful wars against China in 1894–95 and Russia a decade later contributed much to the formation of a new Japanese national consciousness, to which the Prussian model had contributed effectively.[25] But along with the practical imports of Western culture came other facets—literature, fashion, cuisine, and music. A taste for bourgeois, and particularly German, culture all but satiated a Japanese hunger for the foreign. Japanese who studied in Germany returned home with ideas that were quickly absorbed into Meiji culture. Nakagawa Seibei, founder of Sapporo beer, cultivated German brewing techniques to suit Japanese tastes. Authors such as Natsume Sōseki, Nagai Kafū, Mori Ōgai, Ueda Bin, and Tsubouchi Shōyō found inspiration in Germany and its music.[26] In 1872, the Ministry of Education issued a directive requiring schools to teach Western-style vocal music.[27] Some of these school songs were contrafacts of Western folk melodies of the early 1870s. Japanese court musicians began studying Western music and soon military bands became a staple at national and local fêtes.[28]

In 1880 the Imperial Household hired Franz Eckert, a German, as a music consultant. His job was to "correct" a native composition called "Kimigayo" by Hayashi Hisamori—a composition that would become the Japanese national anthem.[29] A Germanic music tradition, from the start, then, was co-opted without friction into the most politically potent song in Japan. Additionally, many Germans found positions in Japan teaching music at a university level. As Luciana Galliano points out,

> The first exchanges for serious academic musical studies were established with Germany. German teachers were resident in Japan for lengthy periods and composition students were given grants to study in Germany. This became an

established tradition and German influence also made itself felt in the way the musical world became organized (the running of the new symphony orchestras and of the newly established seasons of concerts open to the public, the publication of magazines, etc.).[30]

In sum, between 1870 and 1945 "everything to do with German musical history and culture was very much revered."[31]

Naturally, this kind of music required a proper venue. Concurrent with the influx of German culture, a Western-style concert hall and ballroom called the Rokumeikan (Deer-cry pavilion) was built under the aegis of British architect Josiah Conder in 1883. The building, a French Renaissance–style structure, accommodated the fashion for foreign sounds; it was a place where diplomats, their guests, and native elite could meet and mingle, adorned in cosmopolitan costumes and enveloped in a European atmosphere.[32] This venue, with its amalgamation of native and foreign design and visitors, was one of the first places in Japan to echo with Wagner's music. Military bands played excerpts from *Tannhäuser* and *Lohengrin* there and at the Japanese music-training pavilion in 1887 and 1893, respectively.[33]

But what was the special allure of German culture? Why not French, American, British, or Russian?[34] Many intellectuals and officials felt that Germany was Japan's European counterpart. The Japanese saw themselves as facing problems similar to those of Germans. Both countries experienced significant political changes under imperial rule and both struggled to establish a unified national ideology at the turn of the century. Itō Hirobumi, Japan's first prime minister, noted these parallels and traveled to Germany to study constitutional theory and observe Otto von Bismarck's role in the government. He was so taken with Bismarck that "he was later chided for trying to mimic his mannerisms."[35] In this case of Itō and the government as a whole, mimicry was the highest form of flattery.[36] As Bernd Martin puts it, once German influence was "solidly anchored in the constitution, the military and education systems could not easily be repudiated and soon the Japanese people as well identified with it. In 1889, Japan stood definitively on German bedrock."[37] Though Germany and Japan were vastly different in many respects, the ideological goals of their ruling elites were very similar. Both sought to unify a country via a strong central government and a convincing national ideology; both nations wanted to establish themselves as international powers on the basis of cultural uniqueness.

For Japanese Wagnerians, Wagner, along with Nietzsche, was a social symbol.[38] They appropriated Wagner's and Nietzsche's critiques of German society and valorization of the distant past (imagined or real). At the same time, they assimilated them, adding Confucian values of a "family state" with the emperor as father.[39] Even if Japanese ideologues recognized that reversal of modernization was impossible, they clung to the sanctification of the premodern, emblematized by a concept of folk (*minzoku*). Significantly, this term can be "spelled" multiple ways. One version uses the characters 民 (*min*) 俗 (*zoku*); in this word, the first character conveys the "people in general" while the second means "common" or "popular." So, this version of *minzoku* expresses the idea of a common people in a nostalgic sense. It hints at a non-cosmopolitan population that represents the bastion of an untainted traditional culture. This *minzoku* is a common prefix attached to music, dance, and literature to indicate a folk source.

The alternative way of spelling *minzoku* uses the same first character, 民 (*min*), but a different second character, 族 (*zoku*). This latter character, most familiar in its appearance in the word *kazoku*, or family, gives a different orientation to the word. This spelling of *minzoku* suggests a "family of people"— that is, a race. And in Japan, race is intertwined with notions of the nation and the myth of ethnic homogeneity. This *minzoku* is also occasionally attached as a prefix to music, but translates as "ethnic music" rather than "folk music." "Ethnic music" implies a music based on racial rather than geographical origins.

This etymological explanation touches on the Japanese conception of folk. From this, the connection to Wagner's own ideas on the topic becomes apparent. In German, *das Volk* can mean "common people" or people in an ethnic or national sense. Like *minzoku*, it portrays the two notions in tandem. Wagner acted as a musical spokesman for the *Volk*, defining the term as such: "The 'folk' is the epitome of all those men *who feel a common and collective want*. To it belong, then, all those who recognize their individual want as a collective want, or find it based thereon." Conversely, "All those *who feel no want*, whose lifespring therefore consists in a need which rises not the potence of a want, and thus is artificial, untrue, and egoistic," are not folk.[40]

Wagner's *Volk* is predominantly defined by a communal goal; those who pursue individual goals (e.g., luxuries) are not part of the folk. In Wagner's ideal, everyone can become part of the community, part of the folk, and it is through mythos that expression of community can be created.[41] Of course, this hints at Wagner's anti-Semitism, but also at something more: the defining of a community by its antithesis. It is not a unique concept, but it was one that Japanese ideologues could easily latch on to for their own purposes. This mythos of the folk appealed to the early Japanese ideologues hoping to weave together the political and the aesthetic in their vision for a modern Japan that balanced native and foreign ideals. They sought, as Gluck points out, "not only national unity but also an 'inner spiritual revival' to help protect the nation against potentially threatening social results of modernization."[42] In a powerful strain of German cultural and philosophical critique, the Japanese discovered a shared dream: to build a nation rooted in mythic fantasy but emboldened by the trappings of modernity.

A Reverie: Anesaki Chōfū

By 1900, German culture was thoroughly naturalized in Japan. Many young men were obsessed with German literature and philosophy; scattered essays on German thought appeared in various journals.[43] This helped spur the first translations of Nietzsche and Schopenhauer into Japanese in 1911: *Also sprach Zarathustra* by Ikuta Chōkō and *Die Welt als Wille und Vorstellung* by Anesaki Chōfū.[44] A pilgrimage to Berlin was also in order for many young men of mind and means. The translator of Schopenhauer, Anesaki (1873–1949), was one of these young men. Born in Kyoto to a middle-class family that performed Buddhist liturgy at ceremonies, he had very little knowledge of Western classical music outside of some school songs that used Western tunes to Japanese text.[45]

Yet, in his youth, Anesaki was clearly enchanted by Wagner. In 1897, at the age of twenty-four, he wrote an article for the Japanese literary magazine *Taiyō* (Sun), which was already a leading voice in intellectual circles that typically consisted of young men who had received a Western-oriented education. The article's title, "Gakugekiron über Musikdramen Wagners" (Opera essay on Wagner's music dramas), is a curious mix of Japanese and German. As Takeuchi Fumiko has argued, this article introduced a select generation of Japanese readers to the composer.[46] Anesaki followed this up in 1898 with the first Japanese essay on Nietzsche, also published in *Taiyō*.[47] The essay draws parallels between Buddhism and Nietzschean philosophy, encouraging readers to draw on the German's thoughts in order to defend Buddhism from an imagined threat posed by Christianity.[48] In 1901, while studying theology in Berlin, Anesaki attended a performance of *Das Rheingold* and was enthusiastic about it.[49] Later, *Taiyō* published Anesaki's letters from Berlin to his friend Takayama Chogyū in Tokyo.[50] They reveal an interest in Wagner, philosophy, and their relevance to Japanese social concerns.[51] In a 1902 letter, Anesaki examines Schopenhauer, Nietzsche, and Wagner. For him, Wagner's music dramas were the artistic realization of the philosophers' ideologies.[52] Anesaki begins with an analysis of Nietzsche's discussion on Wagner in *The Birth of Tragedy*. He clarifies the essence of "will" according to the works of Nietzsche, Schopenhauer, and Wagner. He then discusses the connection between Nietzsche and Schopenhauer.[53]

For Anesaki, Wagner's works are the consummation of the two philosophers' writings.[54] He examines three early works—*Der fliegende Holländer*, *Lohengrin*, and *Tannhäuser*—emphasizing the connection between love and death as the predominant literary theme. In another letter, from 26 December 1902, Anesaki tells Takayama about the numerous Christmas Eve festivals that carried on in Berlin despite the cold weather. At one of the festivals,

Anesaki attended a performance of *Tannhäuser*. He compares it with the Ring cycle, suggesting that Brünnhilde's immolation and Siegfried's death are admirable and heroic, and implies that Tannhäuser and Elisabeth are their predecessors.⁵⁵ Moving on to the *Tannhäuser* performance, he outlines the plot, briefly noting points where the music caught his attention. He remarks that a life like Tannhäuser's, given to Venusian pleasures, is a life of suffering, making a point of quoting Tannhäuser in the original German, "*Nicht Lust allein liegt mir am Herzen. Aus Freuden sehn' ich mich nach Schmerzen*" ("Not pleasure alone lies close to my heart. In the midst of joy I crave after pain"). Anesaki was captivated by Tannhäuser's redemption through the conquering of lust—it is only through the escape from carnal desire that Tannhäuser is saved.⁵⁶ The death scene particularly enthralled him. In his only comment on the music, Anesaki finds the joyous sounds of *Tannhäuser*'s finale to be the sounds of death, and thus the end of suffering.⁵⁷ For Anesaki, then, Wagner's hymn of Christian redemption is the sound of nirvana. Despite the Western religious elements at the end of *Tannhäuser*, the chorus of voices combined with the title character's redemption in death is, for Anesaki, a reflection of Buddhist thought. In this, Anesaki reads Buddhist values onto Wagner's works from the time period before the composer had become familiar with the religion.⁵⁸

Although Anesaki finds the music moving, he makes little attempt to describe and interpret it. Furthermore, there is practically no description of the performance's visual elements. The only mention is a short note that Venus had been illuminated by soft red light that brought to mind a sunset filtering through maple leaves.⁵⁹ At first this might seem odd. After all, for most Wagnerians in the golden age of Wagner and beyond, what matters is the music. Without it, Wagner would be another late-Romantic aesthete with a narcissistic streak. Nevertheless, Anesaki writes, "I cannot suppress the feeling that I want to see this (*Tannhäuser*) in Japan."⁶⁰ How is it possible that Anesaki was enthralled not with the music, but instead with *Tannhäuser*'s story and subtext? Or was this even truly the case? Just because Anesaki does not write specifically about the music does not mean he was not enthralled by it. Indeed, it could easily be the contrary; perhaps for Anesaki, the music's aura was inexpressible, and thus he did not attempt to describe it. Moreover, being a musical dilettante, Anesaki might have felt uncomfortable writing in depth about musical details he did not fully understand.⁶¹

Takenaka Toru offers another suggestion: "Anesaki's Wagner-worship was accordingly more the result of coinciding ideals than that of musical enthusiasm."⁶² Recall that Anesaki was born into a Buddhist family and thus was expected to become a priest at the conclusion of his studies. Indeed, he went on to become a well-known religious scholar who founded modern religious studies in Japan.⁶³ But after the publication of his essay and letters in *Taiyō*,

Anesaki never wrote about Wagner again, save for one reference in his memoirs. Takenaka points out that in the earlier May letter, the discourse on Schopenhauer, Nietzsche, and Wagner is preceded by a visceral critique of Wilhelm's Germany, namely, its rampant materialism and class tension.[64] Given the parallel many Japanese saw between Imperial Germany and late Meiji Japan, Anesaki's critique of Germany can easily be read a critique of his own country.[65] The Meiji revolution, such critics believed, had turned out to be an empty promise. The first two decades of the Meiji era saw rapid shifts in civil codes, governmental structure, and technological development, all under the aegis of equality.[66] Yet, in truth, society changed very little. Economic stratification became more pronounced; tangible aspects of "progress" had failed to unite society.[67]

One answer to this crisis was nationalism. In Wagner, Anesaki perceived a savior, an ideological figurehead who could offer a path of redemption via high art.[68] Indeed, this was essentially Wagner's belief of himself, particularly at the time of composing *Tannhäuser*, during his "revolutionary years." Abbate and Parker note that, as an opera, *Tannhäuser* is not terribly revolutionary; yet, it was around this time that "Wagner was an optimist, still young, barely into his thirties. His optimism rhymes with the philosophies that engrossed him up to that point, in particular the 'Young Germany' movement with its energy and faith in future betterment."[69] Perhaps in *Tannhäuser* Anesaki sensed some of early Wagner's faith and energy in service of a political cause. If only Japan had its own Wagner, Anesaki implied, true change could occur.[70] Anesaki's "Wagner fever" was a symptom of his critique of turn-of-the-century society. The ideals of the Meiji Restoration had withered, and Anesaki, like so many of his generation, was searching for something to fill an ideological void. Who could answer his summons for a spiritual breakthrough?

Wagnerian Aspirations

Around the same time as Anesaki's epistles, peculiar clubs started popping up at various Tokyo universities. In 1901, students at Keio University established a Wagner society.[71] The following year, inspired in part by Anesaki's published letters, a student named Ishikura Kosaburo (1881–1965) founded a Wagner study group at Tokyo Imperial University.[72] A similar club at the national conservatory soon followed.[73] The members of these groups had at least two things in common: first, they loved Wagner; and second, they had never seen a Wagner opera. This is not to say it was impossible that they had heard or seen excerpts of his works. We know, for example, that in 1887 a traveling slide show that depicted Wagner's operas toured Japan, but it is unclear if Wagner's music accompanied the slides. We also know from historical accounts that, the same year, excerpts from *Lohengrin* arranged for brass band entertained the Empress at a concert, and later, in 1894, an amateur opera night to benefit the Red Cross took place at the Tokyo School of Music's performance hall.[74] There, Austrian and Italian bandsmen performed excerpts of Gounod's *Faust* as well as Wotan's Farewell ("Leb' wohl").[75] But such musical *amuses-bouche* lacked the sustenance the young Wagnerian students craved.

Ishikura, along with his cohorts Okkotsu Saburō, Yoshida Toyokichi, and Kondō Itsugorō got to work.[76] Like many of their colleagues, they were familiar with German culture. Mori Ōgai had just translated some of Goethe's writings, and Anesaki, along with his letter recipient, Takayama, had introduced Schopenhauer and Nietzsche to a wider Japanese audience through a series of articles.[77] Japan's love affair with Germany was at its height. What better way to consummate that passion than with a staging of a Wagner opera? Beyond Wagner representing a pinnacle of German musico-dramatic achievement, Anesaki's interpretation of Wagner as a revolutionary was inspiring young intellectuals disenchanted with political stagnation.

The students at the Imperial University collaborated with those at the conservatory. Together they were determined to stage *Tannhäuser*. Thanks to their many foreign music professors, including Raphael von Koeber, they had access to a score as well as the libretto.[78] But Noel Peri, a French missionary turned professor and orchestra conductor, recognized the impossibility of doing the work justice despite the students' enthusiasm.[79] In lieu of *Tannhäuser*, he suggested Gluck's *Orfeo ed Euridice*. Peri convinced the young Wagnerites that Gluck's opera was an important reform work that set the stage for Wagner's future music dramas. The students wanted to embody revolutionary social and aesthetic ideals on stage, ideals that reflected their own sources of inspiration, the philosophies of Nietzsche and Schopenhauer. But they accepted Peri's assessment.[80] Ishikura and his colleagues set about translating the Gluck libretto (of which they had a German version) into Japanese, and on 23 July 1903, Gluck's *Orfeo ed Euridice* became the first opera to be performed by native Japanese.[81] The performance was recognized as a national cultural success despite several shortcomings in the production.

The attempt at *Tannhäuser* was not a total loss. Later that year, on 6 December, students and teachers at the Tokyo Music School performed an orchestral suite from *Carmen* and, with the addition of a choir, the Pilgrim's Chorus from *Tannhäuser* set to Japanese text.[82] The winter program's combination of Bizet and Wagner was a quintessential echo of Nietzsche's trajectory from the latter to the former if nothing else. The following year, the society at Keio University had about as much success. Though founded in 1901, it was not able to muster a performance of Wagner's music until

1906. Akiba Junichirō, who was graduating that spring, was determined to perform Wagner before he left. He selected instrumental portions from *Tannhäuser* and *Lohengrin* (presumably the overture and prelude). With the musical instrument club, he practiced the pieces for half a year in order to do them justice by the spring graduation ceremony and concert. In 1907, the group performed the *Tannhäuser* selection again, at the fiftieth anniversary of Keio's founding.[83] But they were not allowed to continue their operatic pursuits much longer. By 1908 all university-related opera performances were banned on moral grounds; board members at the Ministry of Education considered it immoral for men and women to spend long hours rehearsing together.[84]

Another Germanophile poet, Akimoto Rofū, completed his own translation of *Tannhäuser* around the same time.[85] He began working on it in the summer of 1907 and in November of that year it was published in the journal *Kokoro no Hana* (The spirit's bloom).[86] After the speedy translation and publication, Akimoto discovered several discrepancies between his translation and the original libretto. He was determined to fix these points in a 1911 reprint by the literary group *Seikanshōin*.[87] In his preface to the reissue, Akimoto writes that in spite of his poor translation, "It will be good if it is able to reach a kind of purpose, a goal."[88] What that goal was, exactly, is less clear than in previous examples. Clearly Akimoto had some goal in mind; why else undertake the burdensome task of editing and translating Wagner?

It is evident, however, what Akimoto's goal was *not*. His translation is utterly incompatible with the music; the libretto was never intended for actual performance. In the final paragraph of the preface, Akimoto even confesses, "I myself am not acquainted with the music."[89] Given this lack of attention to the musical aspects of *Tannhäuser*, one would assume that this translation was rather intended to be a *Lesedrama*, in the tradition of Goethe's *Faust*— that is, a book written in the form of a drama but not actually intended to be staged. Wagner's libretto can easily be appreciated this way. In the third act of *Tannhäuser*, the Pilgrim's Chorus and "Song to the Evening Star" in particular serve as ideal points of comparison: both are easily excerpted and are among some of the earliest Wagner excerpts published in Japan. So, these excerpts are an ideal starting point from which to examine the peculiar weaving together of Japanese and German art forms.

At the opening of the third act, Wagner gives an extensive description of the setting and place. The directions read as follows: "The curtain rises. The valley of the Wartburg, to the left Hörselberg, as in the first act. It is autumn. Evening is falling. On a small hill to the right Elisabeth prays before the shrine of the Virgin Mary. Wolfram comes from a higher wooded area. He stops halfway, waiting for Elisabeth."[90] Akimoto, however, forgoes much of the description, writing only "A valley in front of the Wartburg castle and to the left of Hörselberg."⁹¹ Akimoto omits information about the season and what Wolfram and Elisabeth are doing.

This kind of abbreviated description is typical. Moreover, Akimoto deletes any stage directions within the dialogue. This exclusion particularly hinders the effect of the Pilgrim's Chorus, one of the most musically dynamic moments in any Wagner opera. Beginning quietly and offstage, the chorus rises in dynamic as it enters the stage and decrescendos at its exit. This combination of dynamics and staging creates an aural spatiality that extends beyond the visible stage.⁹² At first the pilgrims seem to be distant, their soft song rousing Elisabeth from intense prayer. She and Wolfram converse over the chorus in a kind of aural close-up. As the pilgrims enter, their voices overtake those of Elisabeth and Wolfram.

Akimoto, in eliminating the stage directions, tampers with this stirring entrance. We do not even receive an insertion of dialogue amidst the chorus. Instead, Elisabeth "hears" the pilgrims before their song actually occurs on the page. In an attempt to indicate the simultaneity of the texts, Akimoto separates them with a thin line. Thus, the Chorus, instead of being broken up by Wolfram and Elisabeth's line, is presented as an intact whole. The lack of stage directions and this manipulation of text dispersal suggest that Akimoto does not intend for his translation to necessarily function as a *Lesedrama* after all. Instead, his preference for complete textual forms without disruption hints at the transformation of *Tannhäuser* into a Japanese epic poem, something that makes sense given that many of the ancient epics were originally presented as musical narratives.⁹³

Several other qualities in the translation augment this notion of the *Tannhäuser* translation as Japanese epic poetry. First, Akimoto eschews any kind of Wagnerian rhyme scheme. Instead, his translation follows a pattern that alternates lines of seven and five syllables. True throughout the libretto, the translation of the Pilgrims' Chorus is particularly well executed:

A`a, fu`ru`sa`to`yo/u`re`shi`ku`mo/ma`ta`mo i`ma`shi`to/a`i`mi`ru`ka. I`ma`shi yu`ka`shi`no/ ku`sa`ba`ra`yo/ u`re`shi`ya ma`ta`mo/ko`sho ni a`u.⁹⁴

[Beglückt darf nun dich, o Heimat,
ich schauen und grüssen froh deine lieblichen Auen]

The setting of the translation in the traditional Japanese poetic style gives Akimoto's *Tannhäuser* the veneer of ties to ancient poetry, not of German-speaking lands but of Japan. The words he uses complement the syllabic setting. Some of the word choices and their readings are uncommon. For example, Akimoto uses the Chinese *kanji* character *imashi* to correspond to "*dich*" and "*deine*" in the original German. Yet the use of this character to mean "you" and "your" is not common in the Japanese language contemporary to Akimoto. Instead, this word with this pronunciation originates from a collection of ancient Japanese poetry called the *Manyōshū*. *Imashi* is a word used in spoken Japanese until the end of the sixth century and it appeared in classical literature until the end of the twelfth.[95] Akimoto's seemingly simple use of an alternate pronoun gives his translation the flavor of a classical text despite the foreign subject of *Minnesingers*, Christianity, and Roman goddesses. The translation's language exists at the crossroads of tradition and modernity, its grammar a poetic rendition of late Meiji Japan's own ideological positioning. Likewise, the association of the revered aesthetic of classical poetry with modern German opera resonated philosophically. Chastity, restraint, and repentance—moral values ostensibly upheld in *Tannhäuser*—resonated with the Confucianist backlash to the diseases of modernity (among them materialism and carnal hedonism).

"Song to the Evening Star" is also littered with words gesturing toward Japanese cultural traditions. Akimoto, though unable to directly translate Wagner's own peculiar German into Japanese, effectively captures the aura of the song via use of such words. Most notable is the translation of *Abendstern* to the Japanese word *hoshikage*, literally "starlight." The word first appeared in a 1509 collection of poems by Sakurai Motosuke describing spring: *Haru: Yama kadura mata hoshikage ni uguisu no hane tatakitenaku ume no eda matsuni* (Spring: In starlight through mountain and vine, a nightingale beats its wings and cries at the end of a plum branch).[96] Clearly *hoshikage* carries a different weight in the Japanese language than *Abendstern* does in German, or "evening star" in English. For the latter two languages, the word means a specific astronomical body, one whose brightness outshines other stars and whose light provides guidance to night-time travelers. In Wolfram's song, the evening star will guide Elisabeth's soul to heaven; in Akimoto's translation, the light of the star is the light of heaven. The final line of Akimoto's translation reads *"amatsu hoshikage"* (heaven's starlight). Through translation, Akimoto aligns the starlight with the divine. In this way, he adapts the spiritual outlook of Wagner's Wolfram while maintaining a Japanese mood.

As we can see from these examples, Akimoto took some liberties with the translation, which he readily admitted, yet the work succeeds in taking something that ought to be utterly foreign and transfiguring it into something that appears native. The omission of stage directions as well as the use of traditional poetic forms and lexicon enabled Akimoto to modify Wagner's work into something that emulates classical poetry. Consequently, the emphasis is again on text and the appropriation of it to serve literary motivations. If Wagner declared his music dramas to be deeds of music made visible, Akimoto's *Tannhäuser* translation is a deed of music made invisible. Of course, the practical side to this is the fact that Wagner was unperformable in this era of

Japanese opera history. But there is something more to Akimoto's translation: by placing Wagner in this ancient context, Akimoto synthesized a Japanese perspective of Wagner that melded the weightiness of cultural pasts with modern fantasies.

Minagawa Masaki's translation of J. Walker McSpadden's English-language collection of prose adaptations of Wagner's operas is a final relic of the Meiji Wagner boom.[97] In the Meiji era the Japanese language itself went through a major transformation. Early on, dialects and different kinds of written language made communication with the nation as a whole impossible.[98] After a linguistic "period of chaos," government officials and scholars agreed "to adopt the language spoken by the ruling elite in Tokyo as the standard written language."[99] This shift to a written vernacular was a sharp change from previous reliance on Chinese characters and classical grammar based on the language of the Heian period (794–1185). The unification of written and spoken Japanese promised likewise to unify the Japanese people, or so the government believed. Language was a crucial part of Meiji ideology, and this chapter's final Wagnerian artefact exemplifies this. Obviously, a lot of anxiety over linguistic matters was in the air, as exemplified by Akimoto's preface to *Tannhäuser*. Not only did Minagawa have to deal with the weightiness of translating Wagner; he was also compelled to engage with Japanese linguistic history and contemporary ideological currents.

Minagawa's short stories abandon Wagnerian weightiness in favor of a fairy tale–esque, vernacular prose. In strong contrast to the *Tannhäuser* libretto and the writings of Ishikawa and Anesaki, they are made for a popular audience, as evidenced by the linguistic style and the advertisements in the back matter, featuring books such as Sewell's *Black Beauty*, Swift's *Gulliver's Travels*, and Paolo Mantegazza's *The Art of Choosing a Husband*.

The aforementioned scene from Act Three of *Tannhäuser*, in which Wolfram sings his "Song to the Evening Star," illustrates this more popular style. The grammar is mostly modern; the sentences lack the complexity of the other writings discussed in this chapter. Also notable is a reversion to a pseudo-classical style akin to Akimoto's when Wolfram "sings." Below is an excerpt, translated into English:

> The sun went down quickly. Twilight was enveloping his body. Despite this, Wolfram wandered, finding it difficult to leave the crucifix whose virtue was lent to the maiden. Around the distant hill the Evening Star gave off a soft glow. The light of the star made Wolfram think of Elisabeth's soul and a poem sprung forth, to which he set a short song to send up to the star. "Oh you, great and beautiful Evening Star," he sang. While doing so, the figure of a lone pilgrim appeared, walking, drawing closer. Clothes tattered, feet cracked, he dejectedly stumbled. Wolfram recognized him in a single glance. "Tannhäuser," he called.[100]

This passage, like the rest of the book, is not set in the five-seven syllabic pattern of poetic writing. Even Wolfram's song is adumbrated to a single sentence. Yet, the translator still hints toward the classical style of Akimoto and others, using, in the song, more classical word choices, beginning with the same reading of *imashi* meaning "you" in Wolfram's ode. So, despite being written for a general audience, traditional language, with its mytho-historical weightiness, still haunts the Wagner-inspired text.

The tales themselves are twice removed from Wagner's works, first by McSpadden's adaptation and then by Minagawa's translation. Wagner has become less ideologically important than the stories and the manner of their telling. The popular medium of the vernacular short-story collection helped popularize and, in turn, Japanify Wagner. Minagawa admits in his short introduction that such adaptations cannot convey Wagnerian music drama in full; rather, they are an introduction to Wagner meant to reach a broader audience. These adaptations were a gateway to the ideology espoused by the intellectual Wagnerians.

What does it tell us about Wagnerism as both the Meiji period and the Wagner boom drew to a close?[101] First, it is apparent that the emphasis again is on the narrative rather than the music. But here there is no pretence even of being true to Wagner's own words. Moreover, the translator and the publisher must have believed the stories would resonate with a popular audience. The heroic and the historical, the mythic and the mystical—all these topoi suit the ideologues' push toward reclaiming the folk. Wagner's stories could serve by example—what was needed were similar such stories of a Japanese variety. In this way, the Japanese imagining of Wagner was not limited to its impression of Germany. The Meiji-era perspective on Wagner was actually a dream for Japan, a vision in which the aesthetic could be politically harnessed to bring about a national community.

The title of the collection in Japanese, *Waguneru Monogatari* (Wagner stories), does likewise. By using the term *monogatari* (literally "spoken things"), the translator and publisher align the collection with a long tradition of Japanese narrative and storytelling that was often performed as musical recitation. In the classical Heian period, several *monogatari* circulated and solidified as artistic works, including the famous *Genji Monogatari* (The Tale of Genji) and *Heike Monogatari* (The Tale of the Heike).[102] Using the term *monogatari*, Minagawa places Wagner's stories in this genre. Despite the obvious foreignness of Wagner's settings and characters, the formal markings of the stories resemble Japanese ones suitable for the emerging Japanese petit bourgeois. Wagner's dramas, with their historical characters obscured to the point of mythologization, female self-sacrifice, and magic, thus gain a Japanese literary doppelgänger.

Yet, there is something very peculiar about the title *Waguneru Monogatari*. In the Japanese examples, *The Tale of Genji* is about a prince named Genji; likewise, *The Tale of the Heike* is about the Heike war. Someone unfamiliar with

Wagner would assume *Waguneru Monogatari* to be about Wagner and his life and accomplishments, not his libretti. In the case of this collection, the stories *are* Wagner's life and accomplishments. Instead of narrating Wagner's personal deeds, the composer's adapted libretti become the deeds themselves. By configuring them for a Japanese audience, Minagawa and his publisher display a certainty that the people will find a reflection of their own mythos in Wagner's tale.

Awoken

For all the Meiji Wagnerians' efforts, their movement never gained momentum. Instead, the tendrils of Wagnerism lingered for decades, dormant until the premiere of *Lohengrin* in 1942. Still, for the ideologues at the turn of the century, Wagner's ideas encapsulated the spirit of the era—an era that revolved around the coalescing of a modern Japanese national ideology through a blending of native and foreign, ancient and modern. Wagner and his works illustrated the possibility of reconciling these dichotomies in the guise of social revolution. Despite an absence of an audible Wagnerism in Japan, the movement's impetus was similar to those of other nations. The filtered impressions of Wagner that trickled into Japan allowed ideologues to project their values and goals onto the composer and his works. The porous nature of ideology allowed for the transmutation of Wagner into a composer symbolizing the Japanese spirit. Wagner and his works, like Germany itself, represented simulacra of Japanese dreams of self in the late Meiji era, dreams brimming with hopeful fervor and nightmarish potential.

Brooke McCorkle Okazaki is an Assistant Professor of Music at Carleton College in Northfield, Minnesota. She specializes in opera of the nineteenth and twentieth centuries, film music, and the music of modern Japan. In addition to numerous articles, McCorkle Okazaki is the co-author of Japan's Green Monsters: Environmental Commentary in Kaijū Cinema (2018) and the author of Shōnen Knife's Happy Hour: Food, Gender, Rock and Roll(2020). In the 2019-20 academic year, she received a Japan Foundation Fellowship to complete her monograph Searching for Wagner in Japan.

Notes

1. Celia Applegate and Pamela Potter, "Germans as the 'People of Music': Genealogy of an Identity," in *Music and German National Identity*, ed. Celia Applegate and Pamela Potter (Chicago, 2002), 1.

2. Ibid., 11–12.
3. Beyond Germany, French receptions of Wagner dominate the field, though there are monographs addressing Wagner reception in the United States, England, Russia, Italy, Poland, the Netherlands, and Nordic countries. See Steven Huebner, *French Opera at the Fin de Siècle: Wagnerism, Nationalism, and Style* (New York, 1999); Ute Jung-Kaiser, *Die Rezeption der Kunst Richard Wagner in Italien* (Regensburg, 1973); Anne Dzamba Sessa, *Richard Wagner and the English* (Rutherford, 1979); Rosamund Bartlett, *Wagner and Russia* (Cambridge, 1995); Josine Meurs, *Wagner in Nederland, 1843-1914* (Zutphen, 2002); Hannu Salmi, *Wagner and Wagnerism in Nineteenth-Century Sweden, Finland, and the Baltic Provinces: Reception, Enthusiasm, Cult* (Rochester, 2005); Karol Musioł, *Wagner und Polen = Wagner a Polska* (Bayreuth, 1980); Joseph Horowitz, *Wagner Nights: An American History* (Berkeley, 1994); Edgard de Brito Chaves Jr., *Wagner e o Brasil* (Rio de Janeiro, 1976).
4. Carol Gluck, *Japan's Modern Myths: Ideology in the Late Meiji Period* (Princeton, 1985), 7.
5. See Joys H. Y. Cheung, "Riding the Wind with Mozart's 'Jupiter' Symphony: The Kantian and Daoist Sublimes in Chinese Musical Modernity," *Music and Letters* 96, no. 4 (2013): 534–63.
6. Gluck, *Japan's Modern Myths*, 9–10.
7. Ibid., 9.
8. Here I am drawing on ideas of globalization and Enlightenment discussed in Sebastian Conrad, "Enlightenment in Global History: A Historiographical Critique," *American Historical Review* 117, no. 4 (2012): 999–1027.
9. This represents an attempt at considering the spread of Wagnerism from the perspective of *histoire croisée*, as laid out in Michael Werner and Bénédicte Zimmerman, "Beyond Comparison: *Histoire Croisée* and the Challenge of Reflexivity," *History and Theory* 45, no. 1 (2006): 30–50.
10. The few Japanese that had heard a Wagner opera are documented below as well as sheet music releases and recordings. In addition to sheet music publications, music journals also released piano reductions and reviews of recordings of Wagner's music. According to Luciana Galliano, a music journal called *Ongaku Shinchō* journal did so while it was active between 1924 and 1941. Galliano, *Yōgaku: Japanese Music in the Twentieth Century*, trans. Martin Mayes (Lanham, 2002), 97.
11. For more on the importation of Nietzsche in Japan, see Graham Parkes, "The Early Reception of Nietzsche's Philosophy in Japan," in *Nietzsche and Asian Thought*, ed. Graham Parkes (Chicago, 1991), 177–99.
12. Ibid., 185–87. Most Japanese intellectuals relied on secondary literature for information regarding Nietzschean philosophy.
13. Bernice Glatzer Rosenthal, "Wagner and Wagnerian Ideas in Russia," in *Wagnerism in European Culture and Politics*, ed. David C. Large and William Weber, in collaboration with Anne Dzamba Sessa (Ithaca, 1984), 202.
14. Carolyn Abbate and Roger Parker, *A History of Opera* (New York, 2012), 304.
15. The most prominent examples of this are the literary works *The Tale of Genji* and *The Tale of Heike* discussed later in this essay.
16. Takenaka Toru, "Wagner-Boom in Meiji Japan," *Archiv für Musikwissenschaft* 62, no. 1 (2005): 13–31.

17. This importation of Wagnerism in the Meiji era closely parallels Conrad's discussion of the globalization of the Enlightenment. See Conrad, "Enlightenment in Global History," 1005–6.
18. At first glance, some might consider the Japanese experience of Westernization to be less traumatic than that of India or China, since Japan was never officially colonized by a Western power. This assessment is inaccurate. The combination of soft and hard power used by American military to compel Japan's opening was one that had repercussions throughout the first half of the twentieth century and arguably beyond. Scholars of Meiji Japan have clarified this experience in their many works. See Kenneth B. Pyle, *The New Generation of Meiji Japan: Problems of Cultural Identity, 1885–1895* (Stanford, 1969); and Marius B. Jansen, ed., *The Emergence of Meiji Japan* (New York, 1995).
19. This time period is referred to as either the Tokugawa era, after the ruling samurai family, or the Edo period. Generally, the latter is used in discussion of social and cultural histories.
20. Marius B. Jansen, *The Making of Modern Japan* (Cambridge, 2000), 275–77.
21. Ibid., 277.
22. Jansen relates that the checks and balances placed on the shogun by this time made strong leadership almost impossible. Furthermore, a string of sickly or young shoguns ensured that there was not a strong central ruler. Ibid., 279.
23. Gluck, *Japan's Modern Myths*, 7.
24. The following two paragraphs draw on ibid., 19–20.
25. On the other hand, the Sino-Japanese War weakened relations between Japan and Germany. Germany was a member of a tripartite alliance (with Russia and France) that interfered with the treaty ending the war, contending that that the Japanese must return some territories on the mainland. See Christian W. Spang and Rolf-Harald Wippich, "Introduction – from 'German Measles' to 'Honorary Aryans': An Overview of Japanese-German Relations until 1945," in *Japanese-German Relations 1895–1945: War, Diplomacy, and Public Opinion*, ed. Christian W. Spang and Rolf-Harald Wippich (New York, 2006), 2.
26. Sōseki was a great fan of Beethoven, while Ōgai and Kafū were opera devotees. Both Ōgai and Kafū were Wagner fans; Ōgai saw *Tannhäuser* and *Der fliegende Holländer* during his time studying abroad in Germany in 1884. He made notes in the margins of his libretti to these operas, conveying his astonishment at the visual elements of the production. He also made note of Elisabeth and Senta's love and self-sacrifice, apparently much moved by this. See Takii Reiko, *Sōseki ga kiita Betovuen: Ongaku ni miserareta bungōtachi* (Tokyo, 2004), 5–6. Ueda Bin and Tsubouchi Shōyō were more interested in Wagner's aesthetics and the possibilities of a national theater movement. They were especially interested in concepts like endless melody, leitmotif, and *Gesamtkunstwerk* in relation to Japanese theater. See Shinoda Harumi, "Waguna no juyō ni tsuite oboegaki," *Taishō engeki kenkyū Meijidaigaku Taishō engeki kenkyūkai kaishi*, no. 1 (1980): 76–81.
27. Nomura Kōichi, "Occidental Music," in *Japanese Music and Drama in the Meiji Era*, ed. Komiya Toyotaka, trans. Edward G. Seidensticker and Donald Keene (Tokyo, 1956), 464.
28. Galliano, *Yōgaku*, 28. The most ubiquitous Japanese contrafact of a Western tune is "Hotaru no Hikari," which is set to the melody of "Auld Lang Syne."

29. Ibid., 29.
30. Ibid., 41.
31. Ibid.
32. Ibid., 28.
33. Shinoda, "Waguna no juyō," 69.
34. Gluck, *Japan's Modern Myths*, 159–62.
35. Jansen, *Making of Modern Japan*, 390. As an outspoken statesman, Itō became known in pro-Japanese German circles as "the Bismarck of Japan." See Takii Kazuhiro, *Itō Hirobumi: Japan's First Prime Minister and Father of the Meiji Constitution*, ed. Patricia Murray, trans. Takechi Manabu (New York, 2014), 35.
36. Jansen, *Making of Modern Japan*, 391.
37. Bernd Martin, "The German Role in the Modernization of Japan—The Pitfall of Blind Acculturation," *Oriens Extremus* 33 (1990): 85.
38. Parkes, "Early Reception," 177–99.
39. Ibid., 180.
40. Richard Wagner, "Definition of the Folk," in *Wagner on Music and Drama: A Compendium of Richard Wagner's Prose Works*, eds. Albert Goldman and Evert Sprinchorn, trans. H. Ashton Ellis (New York, 1964), 85–86.
41. Richard Wagner, "Myth as it Relates to the Folk and to Art," in *Wagner on Music and Drama: A Compendium of Richard Wagner's Prose Works*, eds. Albert Goldman and Evert Sprinchorn, trans. H. Ashton Ellis (New York, 1964), 87–89.
42. Gluck, *Japan's Modern Myths*, 38.
43. Friedrich Nietzsche, *Niche goroku*, trans. Ikuta Shōkō (Tokyo, 1911), 10.
44. Ibid., 9–11.
45. Takenaka, "Wagner-Boom," 23.
46. Takeuchi Fumiko, "Bemerkungen zur Rezeptionsgeschichte von Mozarts Opern in Japan," in *Festschrift Christoph-Hellmut Mahling zum 65. Geburtstag*, ed. Axel Beer, Kristina Pfarr, Wolfgang Ruf (Tutzing, 1997), 1404.
47. Parkes, "Early Reception," 181.
48. Ibid.
49. While in Germany, Anesaki studied under Deussen, Oldenberg, Garbe, and Weber. His primary focus seemed to be a reconciliation of Buddhism with Western philosophy. See Joseph Kitagawa, "Review of Masaharu Anesaki's *History of Japanese Religion*," *Journal of Religion* 44, no. 3 (1964): 274.
50. Takayama was an author and leading nationalist literary voice (Gluck, *Japan's Modern Myths*, 136). He also wrote quite a few essays on Nietzsche around this time. See Takayama Chogyū, Anesaki Masaharu, and Sasakawa Rinpū, *Gendai Nihon bungakuzenshū*, vol. 13 (Tokyo, 1928), 223–24.
51. Takenaka, "Wagner-Boom," 20. In 1905, Anesaki translated Wagner's final diary entries from Venice. See Takayama, Anesaki, and Sasegawa, *Gendai Nihon bungakuzenshū*, 412–17.
52. Anesaki Chōfū, "Futatabi Chogyū ni kotafuru sho," in *Meiji bungaku zenshū*, vol. 40 (Tokyo, 1970), 225, 228–34.
53. Ibid., 229–31.
54. Ibid., 231.
55. Anesaki Chōfū, "Takayama kun ni okuru," in *Meiji bungaku zenshū*, vol. 40 (Tokyo, 1970), 222.

56. Ibid., 222–23.
57. Ibid., 222.
58. Buddhist values via Schopenhauer are typically read onto some of Wagner's later works, such as the Ring cycle and *Parsifal*. Indeed, Wagner was not introduced to Schopenhauer until 1854, long after the premiere of *Tannhäuser*.
59. Anesaki, "Takayama kun ni okuru," 222.
60. Ibid., 223.
61. Rachel Epstein brought this point to my attention. I am grateful for her observation, particularly regarding this peccadillo of Japanese culture.
62. Takenaka, "Wagner-Boom," 24.
63. Ibid.
64. Ibid.
65. Anesaki's colleague Takayama Chogyū offers a similar critique in his 1901 essay, "The Literateur as Culture-Critic" (*Bunmen hihyōka toshite no bungakusha*). In it, he draws on Nietzsche's scathing assessment of decadent European culture and applies it to the Japanese situation. See Parkes, "Early Reception," 183.
66. Gluck, *Japan's Modern Myths*, 17.
67. Ibid., 29
68. Takenaka, "Wagner-Boom," 28.
69. Abbate and Parker, *History of Opera*, 303.
70. Takenaka, "Wagner-Boom," 28–29.
71. *Keiogijuku Waguneru sosaietei 100 nenshi* (Tokyo, 2002), 2.
72. Takeuchi, "Bemerkungen zur Rezeptionsgeschichte," 1404.
73. Ibid.
74. Masui Keiji, *Nihon opera-shi – 1952* (Tokyo, 2003), 35. The performance raised 1414 yen and 80 sen.
75. Ibid.
76. Galliano, *Yōgaku*, 101 and Takii Keiko, *Sōseki ga kiita Betovuen: Ongaku ni miserareta bungōtachi* (Tokyo, 2004), 33.
77. Takii, *Sōseki ga kiita*, 33.
78. Galliano, *Yōgaku*, 101. Koeber taught piano and philosophy. He arranged the piano accompaniment for the performance of *Orfeo ed Euridice*.
79. Peri was a French missionary who became a docent at the leading music school *Ongaku Gakko*. See Takeuchi, "Bemerkungen zur Rezeptionsgeschichte," 1404.
80. In their desire to perform *Tannhäuser*, it is possible that the students displayed their own ignorance of the music and the requirements for its production.
81. Galliano, *Yōgaku*, 101.
82. Nomura Kōichi, "Occidental Music," 496. I found no evidence of a publication of this setting. I believe it was part of Ishikura and Okkotsu's original attempt to translate *Tannhäuser*.
83. *Keiogijuku Waguneru sosaietei 100 nenshi*, 5.
84. Masui, *Nihon opera-shi*, 40; Galliano, *Yōgaku*, 101.
85. Akimoto also translated Goethe and Schiller, in addition to writing poetry himself. See Johann Christophe Friedrich von Schiller, *Shirureru shishū*, trans. Akimoto Rofū (Tokyo, 1906); Johann Wolfgang von Goethe, *Enōkyoku*, trans. Akimoto Rofū (Tokyo, 1907); and Akimoto Rofū, *Kita no sora: Shishū* (Tokyo, 1911). This final

entry, published by the "German poetry study group," shows that Akimoto was considered an important figure in bringing German poetry to a Japanese audience.
86. Akimoto Rofū, preface to *Gakugekiron: Tanhoizeru* (Shiga, 1911), 1.
87. This reprint is the libretto referred to in this essay.
88. Akimoto, preface, 1.
89. Ibid., 4. Translated literally, Akimoto writes, "I myself am in the dark about the music."
90. Richard Wagner, *Tannhäuser* (New York, 1984), 344 ["Der Vorhang geht auf. Tal vor der Wartburg links der Hörselberg, wie am Schluss des ersten Aufzuges, nur in herbstlicher Färbung. Der Tag neigt sich zum Abend. Auf dem kleinen Bergvorsprunge rechts liegt Elisabeth vor dem Muttergottesbilde betend ausgestreckt. Wolfram kommt links von der waldigen Höhe herab: auf halber Höhe hält er an, als er Elisabeth gewahrt"].
91. Akimoto Rofū, *Gakugekiron: Tanhoizeru* (Shiga: Seikashoin, 1911), 73 ["ヘルゼルヒの左方ソルトブルヒ城前の谷地"].
92. Many scholars have addressed components of this effect, dubbed "phantasmagoria" by Theodor Adorno. For insights on this, see Adorno, *In Search of Wagner* (New York, 2005); Nicholas Vazsonyi, introduction to *Wagner's Meistersinger: Performance, History, Representation*, ed. Nicholas Vazsonyi (Rochester, 2003), 1–20; Adrian Daub, *Tristan's Shadow: Sexuality and the Total Work of Art after Wagner* (Chicago, 2014), 96–126.
93. See Komoda Haruko, "The Musical Narrative of *The Tale of the Heike*," trans. Alison Tokita, in *The Ashgate Research Companion to Japanese Music*, ed. Alison McQueen Tokita and David W. Hughes (Burlington, 2008), 77–104.
94. Akimoto, *Gakugekiron: Tanhoizeru*, 76.
95. *Nihon Kokugo Daijiten* [Japanese language dictionary], s.v. "imashi," retrieved 4 August 2013 from https://japanknowledge.com/library/en/.
96. *Nihon Kokugo Daijiten*, s.v. "hoshikage," retrieved 4 August 2013 from https://japanknowledge.com/library/en/.
97. See J. Walker McSpadden, *Stories from Wagner* (New York, 1905). *Parsifal*, though included in the original, is omitted in the Japanese version of the book.
98. Paul H. Clark, *The Kokugo Revolution: Education, Identity, and Language Policy in Imperial Japan* (Berkeley, 2008), 3.
99. Ibid., 4.
100. Minagawa Masaki, *Waguneru Monogatari* (Tokyo, 1908), 107.
101. The Meiji period ended in 1912 with the death of the emperor.
102. Murasaki Shikibu, a court woman, wrote *The Tale of Genji* in the eleventh century. The collection is often identified as the world's first novel. *The Tale of the Heike* is a collection of sung epic poems concerning the twelfth-century battle between the Taira and Minamoto clans. The monk Kakuichi compiled the poems in the fourteenth century. See Murasaki Shikibu, *The Tale of Genji*, trans. Edward Seidensticker (New York, 1978); and *The Tale of the Heike*, trans. Helen Craig McCullough (Stanford, 1988).

Bibliography

Abbate, Carolyn, and Roger Parker. *A History of Opera*. New York: W. W. Norton, 2012.
Adorno, Theodor. *In Search of Wagner*. New York: Verso, 2005.
Akimoto Rofū. *Kita no sora: Shishū*. Tokyo: Doitsu Shibun Gakkai, 1911.
———. Preface to *Gakugekiron: Tanhoizeru*. Shiga: Seikashoin, 1911.
———. *Gakugekiron: Tanhoizeru*. Shiga: Seikashoin, 1911.
Anesaki Chōfū. "Takayama-kun ni okuru." In *Meiji bungaku zenshū*, volume 40, edited by Okitsu Kaname, 221–224. Tokyo: Chikuma Shobō, 1970.
———. "Futatabi Chogyū ni kotafuru sho." In *Meiji bungaku zenshū*, volume 40, edited by Okitsu Kaname, 225–41. Tokyo: Chikuma Shobō, 1970.
Applegate, Celia, and Pamela Potter. "Germans as the 'People of Music': Genealogy of an Identity." In *Music and German National Identity*, edited by Celia Applegate and Pamela Potter, 1–35. Chicago: University of Chicago Press, 2000.
Cheung, Joys H. Y. "Riding the Wind with Mozart's 'Jupiter' Symphony: The Kantian and Daoist Sublimes in Chinese Musical Modernity." *Music and Letters* 96, no. 4 (2013): 534–63.
Clark, Paul H. *The Kokugo Revolution: Education, Identity, and Language Policy in Imperial Japan*. Berkeley: Institute of East Asian Studies, 2008.
Conrad, Sebastian. "Enlightenment in Global History: A Historiographical Critique." *American Historical Review* 117, no. 4 (2012): 999–1027.
Daub, Adrian. *Tristan's Shadow: Sexuality and the Total Work of Art after Wagner*. Chicago: University of Chicago Press, 2014.
Takeuchi, Fumiko. "Bemerkungen zur Rezeptionsgeschichte von Mozarts Opern in Japan." In *Festschrift Christoph-Hellmut Mahling zum 65. Geburtstag*, edited by Axel Beer, Kristina Pfarr, and Wolfgang Ruf, 1403–1415. Tutzing: Hans Schneider, 1997.
Galliano, Luciana. *Yōgaku: Japanese Music in the Twentieth Century*. Translated by Martin Mayes. Lanham, MD: Scarecrow Press, 2002.
Gluck, Carol. *Japan's Modern Myths: Ideology in the Late Meiji Period*. Princeton, NJ: Princeton University Press, 1985.
Goethe, Johann Wolfgang von. *Enōkyoku*. Translated by Akimoto Rofū. Tokyo: Yanagi Shobō, 1907.
Jansen, Marius B., ed. *The Emergence of Meiji Japan*. New York: Cambridge University Press, 1995.
———. *The Making of Modern Japan*. Cambridge, MA: Harvard University Press, 2000.
Keiogijuku Waguneru sosaietei 100 nenshi. Tokyo: Seikōsha, 2002.
Kitagawa, Joseph. "Review of Masaharu Anesaki's *History of Japanese Religion*." *Journal of Religion* 44, no. 3 (1964): 274.
Komoda Haruko. "The Musical Narrative of *The Tale of the Heike*," translated by Alison Tokita. In *The Ashgate Research Companion to Japanese Music*, edited

by Alison McQueen Tokita and David W. Hughes, 77–104. Burlington, VT: Ashgate, 2008.

Martin, Bernd, and Peter Wetzler. "The German Role in the Modernization of Japan—The Pitfall of Blind Acculturation." *Oriens Extremus* 33, no. 1 (1990): 77–88.

Masui Keiji. *Nihon opera-shi – 1952*. Tokyo: Suiyōsha, 2003.

McSpadden, J. Walker. *Stories from Wagner*. New York: Thomas Y. Crowell, 1905.

Minagawa Masaki. *Waguneru monogatari*. Tokyo: Nagai Shuppan Kyōkai, 1908.

Murasaki Shikibu. *The Tale of Genji*. Translated by Edward Seidensticker. New York: Knopf, 1978.

Nietzsche, Friedrich. *Niche goroku*. Translated by Ikuta Shōkō. Tokyo: Genōsha, 1911.

Nomura Kōichi. "Occidental Music." In *Japanese Music and Drama in the Meiji Era*, edited by Komiya Toyotaka, translated by Edward G. Seidensticker and Donald Keene, 451-508. Tokyo: Ōbunsha, 1956.

Parkes, Graham. "The Early Reception of Nietzsche's Philosophy in Japan." In *Nietzsche and Asian Thought*, edited by Graham Parkes, 177–99. Chicago: University of Chicago Press, 1991.

Rosenthal, Bernice Glatzer. "Wagner and Wagnerian Ideas in Russia." In *Wagnerism in European Culture and Politics*, edited by David C. Large and William Weber, in collaboration with Anne Dzamba Sessa, 198–245. Ithaca: Cornell University Press, 1984.

Pyle, Kenneth B. *The New Generation of Meiji Japan: Problems of Cultural Identity, 1885–1895*. Stanford, CA: Stanford University Press, 1969.

Schiller, Johann Christophe Friedrich von. *Shirureru shishū*. Translated by Akimoto Rofū. Tokyo: Tōadō, 1906.

Shinoda Harumi. "Waguna no juyō ni tsuite no oboegaki." *Taishō engeki kenkyū: Meiji daigaku Taishō engeki kenkyūkai kaishi*, no. 1 (1980): 69–81.

———. "Waguna no juyō ni tsuite oboegaki." In *Taishō engeki kenkyū*, 76–81. Tokyo: Meiji University Taishō engeki kenkyūkai, 1980.

Spang, Christian W., and Wippich, Rolf-Harald. "Introduction – from 'German Measles' to 'Honorary Aryans': An Overview of Japanese-German Relations until 1945." In *Japanese-German Relations 1895–1945: War, Diplomacy, and Public Opinion*, edited by Christian W. Spang and Rolf-Harald Wippich, 1–18. New York: Routledge, 2006.

Takayama Chogyū, Anesaki Masaharu, and Sasakawa Rinpū. *Gendai Nihon bungakuzenshū*. Vol. 13. Tokyo: Kaizōsha, 1928.

Takenaka Toru. "Wagner-Boom in Meiji Japan." *Archiv für Musikwissenschaft* 62, no. 1 (2005): 13–31.

Takii Kazuhiro. *Itō Hirobumi: Japan's First Prime Minister and Father of the Meiji Constitution*. Edited by Patricia Murray, translated by Takechi Manabu. New York: Routledge, 2014.

Takii Reiko. *Sōseki ga kiita Betovuen: Ongaku ni miserareta bungōtachi*. Tokyo: Chuokōronshinsha, 2004.

The Tale of the Heike. Translated by Helen Craig McCullough. Stanford, CA: Stanford University Press, 1988.

Vazsonyi, Nicholas. Introduction to *Wagner's* Meistersinger: *Performance, History, Representation*, edited by Nicholas Vazsonyi, 1–20. Rochester: University of Rochester Press, 2003.

Wagner, Richard. "Definition of the Folk." In *Wagner on Music and Drama: A Compendium of Richard Wagner's Prose Works*, edited by Albert Goldman and Evert Sprinchorn, translated by H. Ashton Ellis, 85-86. New York: E. P. Dutton, 1964.

———. "Myth as It Relates to the Folk and to Art." In *Wagner on Music and Drama: A Compendium of Richard Wagner's Prose Works*, edited by Albert Goldman and Evert Sprinchorn, translated by H. Ashton Ellis, 87–89. New York: E. P. Dutton, 1964.

———. *Tannhäuser*. New York: Dover Publications, Inc., 1984.

Werner, Michael, and Bénédicte Zimmerman. "Beyond Comparison: *Histoire Croisée* and the Challenge of Reflexivity." *History and Theory* 45, no.1. (2006): 30–50.

CHAPTER 8

Hubert Parry, Germany, and the "North"

THOMAS IRVINE

Teutons at the Gates

In the autumn of 1914 Sir C. Hubert H. Parry, director of the Royal College of Music (RCM), formerly Heather Professor of Music at Oxford University, and one of the British Empire's most distinguished composers, stood before the assembled students of the RCM to give one of his termly addresses. It was the first in wartime. "If, ultimately, the imperial bird of Prussia...," he proclaimed, "waves over our towers in the place of the Union Jack, all the people belonging to [the RCM] will prefer extermination to submission."[1]

It was a bitter moment for him. No British musician had done more than Parry to integrate Britain into a cosmopolitan, liberal, and most of all German world order of music. The "great" German composers—Bach, Haydn, Mozart, Beethoven, Schubert, Schumann, Wagner, and Brahms—had been his lodestars across a career that traversed composition, the teaching and writing of history, and the creation of new institutions of music-making in Britain.

As the war settled into bloody stalemate, Parry admitted to his students, many of whom would soon be in uniform, "that he had been for a quarter of a century and more a pro-Teuton." He had not believed that Germany "could be imbued with the teaching of a few advocates of mere brutal violence and material aggression [and] with the extravagance of those who talked about super-morality."[2] Now the time had come to resist—not the Germans, but the "Prussians," who were dragging Germany though the mud with their aggressive behavior. The reference to popular interpretations of Nietzsche's philosophy ("super-morality") is hard to miss. Indeed, for Parry, war demanded the setting aside of "frivolous and purposeless amusement." The "great thoughts of real composers, to which we devote ourselves, are as valuable to the world as great victories." In times of war, music should be inspired by heroism. In a dig at Germany's leading modern composer, Richard Strauss, Parry explains that he means "not the fussy, aggressive, blatant heroism of the Prussian *Heldenleben*, but the heroism we hear of daily in stories from the front. Real heroism is chivalrous and frank, modest and unaggressive, cheerful in adversity and unboastful in success. True music can be inspired by such qualities."[3]

For many years Parry's legacy was eclipsed by the reputations of his younger contemporary Edward Elgar and composers in the generation of his protégé Ralph Vaughan Williams. Many of the latter were graduates of the RCM and leading lights of the "English Musical Renaissance," the efflorescence of English composition that gathered steam just before World War I. When this new generation claimed for itself the mantle of the first important group of "native" composers since Purcell, Parry's stock declined accordingly. Critics such as George Bernard Shaw—never a fan of Parry's when the composer was alive—made a habit of caricature when it came to a man who had been South Kensington's guiding musical force. They portrayed him as an eminent academic Victorian whose decades of serious but conservative composition—symphonies, oratorios, chamber music, songs—weighed little in a new age. Soon Parry's critical reputation rested on a few works: the ode *Blest Pair of Sirens* (1887), the coronation anthem "I was Glad" (1902), and, most of all, the hymn to a text by William Blake, "Jerusalem" (1916), now a mainstay of party conferences and the Last Night of the Proms.

Parry—an unbeliever who refused to attend his own daughter's christening—would spin in his grave in St. Paul's Cathedral at the thought of his music being sung by members of the Conservative Party, let alone its playing a central role in a globally televised orgy of flag waving. He was a lifelong liberal, internationalist, vigorous proponent of home rule for Ireland, and women's suffragist. He was what Stefan Collini has called a Victorian "public moralist."[4] Indeed, his allergy to jingoism and imperial fantasy led him to oppose the Boer War and withdraw the dedication of "Jerusalem" to the patriotic organization Fight for Right after he observed the nationalist frenzy the hymn provoked when it was first performed at a rally in the Albert Hall in 1917.

It took until 1998 for a serious scholarly biography to appear, in the form of Jeremy Dibble's authoritative *C. Hubert H. Parry: His Life and Music*.[5] Around the same time, historians Robert Stradling and Meirion Hughes put the cat among the musicological pigeons with a revisionist account of the English Musical Renaissance.[6] In their view this renaissance was primarily a symptom of British nervousness about German economic and military superiority, simultaneously aping German musical structures and "arming" the nation against them.[7] It coalesced around an exclusive club of musical opinion-makers—mostly male, musically conservative, and independently wealthy—focused in London institutions such as the RCM (which they called "the Goodly House") and later the BBC. This concentration of musical power allowed the renaissance, they claimed, to write its own history and to shape the paths on which future members of the British musical establishment would have to travel. In fact their attack on the "Goodly House" echoes an assault on Parry by Shaw less than two years after Parry's death. Parry, Shaw wrote in the inaugural issue of the journal *Music and Letters*, was the "centre" of "the London section of the Clara Schumann-Joachim-Brahms clique in Germany; and the relations between the two were almost sacred." One of the worst crimes of this "clique" was that they found the young Elgar—an interloper from the West Midlands—insufficiently polished. In end, Shaw wrote, Elgar was the winner: "his Enigma Variations took away your breath. The respiration induced by their [the clique's] compositions was perfectly regular, and occasionally perfectly audible."[8] Shaw's implication that "almost sacred" relations with Schumann, Joachim, and Brahms made Parry the leader of an anti-Wagner and anti-Elgar party in London is unfair: in his youth Parry had been an enthusiastic Wagnerian; later on he enjoyed cordial relations with Elgar. But history proved Shaw right about the music, even if in recent years Parry's critical reputation has improved slightly, helped by prominent public exposure at royal weddings and in BBC television documentaries. Some confusion about Parry's "national" style remains. In John Bridcut's 2010 film *The Prince and the Composer*, the prince in the title, Prince Charles, insists vehemently to a somewhat bemused conductor of the BBC Symphony Orchestra after a rehearsal of Parry's Brahmsian Fifth Symphony that Parry's music is quintessentially "English."[9]

This chapter returns to, and complicates, Hughes and Stradling's overdrawn statement of the "German problem" in British music history around 1900. Its aim is a better understanding of Parry's relationship with "German music," or, to put it more in the spirit of this volume, "Germanness" in music—one that takes account, however, of other intellectual networks in which Parry was enrolled. Focusing on his music history writings and the wartime *College Addresses*, I will argue here that Parry—at the time surely one of Britain's most influential musicians—acted as a mediator of ideas about music often taken to be "German." Consciously or unconsciously, however, he attached these to concerns with less of a connection to German national identity. In keeping with his optimistic brand of political liberalism, these included ideologies of progress, or, as Parry often put it, "evolution." But one of Parry's strongest music-historical principles, perhaps the strongest, was that race determines a person's or nation's musical possibilities. For all of his egalitarian instincts, Parry, like so many of his contemporaries, was a white supremacist in the spirit of "scientific" racism. His vision of music history, laid out in decades of widely read publications and countless hours of lecturing at the RCM and across the country, rested on the superiority of whiter "northern" races over darker "southern" ones. Indeed, Germany's special role in Parry's music history was to have assimilated the musical "instincts" of "southerners" and turned these into "self-reflective," "northern" art. More than the extent of Parry's commitment to one or another brand of "Germanness" it is with his white supremacism, with which his commitment to Germany is inextricably linked, that we must come to terms.

Early Career

Hubert Parry was born in 1848 into a wealthy landowning family in rural Gloucestershire.[10] Like his father, who was an amateur painter, he attended Eton College and the University of Oxford. His musical talent was recognized at Eton, where he studied music as much as the curriculum allowed. Oxford had no formal course in the subject; nonetheless, Parry spent much of his time there following musical pursuits. His father sponsored a summer in Stuttgart after Parry's first year to enable him to study with Henry Hugo Pierson (originally Pearson), an English composer who lived as a freelance composer in Germany. Parry's main aim that summer was to study orchestration, but the most important consequence was that he learned very adequate German.

After he left Oxford in 1870 he worked in the City of London in the insurance industry. The necessity to earn a living stemmed from his courtship of Lady Maude Herbert, an aristocrat whose family objected to Parry's relative poverty—he was not then expected to inherit his father's fortune, although he eventually did. While still working as an underwriter, Parry continued composing. In 1873 Walter Stewart Broadwood, of the piano-making family, arranged for Parry's work to be shown to Joseph Joachim, who suggested lessons with Johannes Brahms (Brahms declined). Parry then sought tuition with the émigré pianist and composer Walter Dannreuther, who also directed London's Wagner Society; Dannreuther arranged for his new pupil to attend the inaugural cycle of the Ring in Bayreuth in 1876. Parry helped to host Wagner on the composer's visit to London in 1877.

The acquaintance that changed Parry's career, however, was with the writer and educator George Grove. Grove, an engineer by profession, became a central figure in British musical circles through his involvement in the move of the Crystal Palace from Hyde Park to South London and his subsequent role as secretary of the company that operated it there.[11] In 1875, Grove engaged Parry as a major contributor and subeditor on the first edition of his new *Dictionary of Music and Musicians*. Parry wrote dozens of articles for Grove, including most of the major ones on forms and concepts (he edited hundreds more). The *Dictionary* featured substantial contributions by German-speaking scholars, including Philipp Spitta and Ferdinand Pohl, and focused heavily on recent "progress" in British music.[12] Indeed, the *Dictionary*'s 1874 "Prospectus" reveals Grove's almost technoscientific ambitions for it. Grove assured the reader of information in language an "intelligent inquirer … can understand" about "what is meant by a Symphony or Sonata, a Fugue, a Stretto, a Coda, or any other technical terms." In addition he promised "a succinct account of the history of the various branches of the art [and] the use and progress of the pianoforte or other instruments."[13]

Parry's work for Grove allowed him to leave insurance and work full time as a musician. Soon he celebrated his first major commission, a setting of Shelley's *Prometheus Unbound* for the Three Choirs Festival in 1880. The premier, in Gloucester Cathedral, in which the young Elgar played the violin in the orchestra, was only a mixed success. Yet twenty-five years later Elgar recalled the first performance as "a practical starting point for anything that may be usefully considered in relation to present day music."[14]

In 1883 Grove appointed Parry to the faculty of the newly formed Royal College of Music. The RCM was founded in the wake of the failure of the National Training School for Music (NTSM), which was established in South Kensington in the wake of the Great Exhibition of 1851. The organizers of the Exhibition wished for their legacy to include a conservatory to rival continental institutions. The NTSM took more than fifteen years to open, under the direction of Arthur Sullivan, and failed quickly. In 1881 a group of influential patrons including the Prince of Wales (the future Edward VII) brought in Grove to organize a replacement.[15] The RCM flourished from the start under Grove's direction.

Parry was the RCM's inaugural professor of music history, a position he retained after succeeding Grove as director in 1895. Parry's music history—much in the spirit of Grove's *Dictionary*—was a story of progress. In one of his earliest draft lectures for the RCM (1884–85) he discusses changes to piano design around 1800. Parry observes that "it is not merely the necessity of adapting the music to a given instrument which comes prominently before us, but the law that men can only build on what they know." In other words, technology is a determining factor in music history. Indeed, Parry continues, "all the music we have in the world is only the old story of one generation of men building upon and improving the results of the work of their predecessors, [which we see in every department of human life. Engineering, mechanics, chemistry, politics etc.]"[16] The added reference (a later insertion to the text) to "every department of human life" underscores Parry's suggestion that all musical practices (instrument building, performance, and composition) are subject to the rules of progress. The students to whom he spoke at the brand-new RCM were to be agents of such progress in exactly the same way as students at the Royal College of Science next door in South Kensington.

A final formative set of experiences in the early stages of Parry's career were occasioned by his growing commitment to liberal, even radical, politics. Victorian liberalism, or any liberalism for that matter, is notoriously difficult to define.[17] Parry's liberalism started with frustration at the limits of his immediate environment. Once, after a difficult afternoon at his wife's family's estate, he wrote in his diary, "it is enough to make one a bitter democrat to belong in the company of people brought up in luxury ... as uselessly ornamental and injuriously bigoted about their 'rights' and 'position' as it is possible to be."[18] A little later he vented his dislike for the way in which "the part of English country gentlemen grovelled in obeisance before this utterly fortuitous fetish—the Semitic Disraeli." There follows a shockingly anti-Semitic outburst couched in terms that could have been lifted directly from the pages of Wagner's *Das Judenthum in der Musik*. Disraeli, Parry writes, was "cunning, crafty, mean, unscrupulous, artificial, a poser. ... He had the Semitic gift of mere technique in the fullest measure." This, Parry continues, Disraeli used "to hoodwink and cajole the unintelligent, the simpletons, the party folks who were glad of a man with such supreme facility ... to express their shibboleths, their hatreds, and their interests."[19]

It is easy to be horrified by this passage, which Dibble includes in his book but does not discuss at length. Instead, Dibble sees Parry's aversion to Disraeli as "only one of several catalysts on the way to radicalism."[20] In his published writings Parry never returned to open anti-Semitism—although this was not uncommon in liberal circles, for instance, as embodied by the Oxford historian Goldwin Smith, who held the Regius Professorship just before Parry's studies at the university and later was instrumental in the foundation of Cornell University in the United States.[21] As an educator, however, Parry campaigned tirelessly against the artificiality he felt marked both his Tory in-laws and their "crafty" political hero. Of a piece with this attitude was his aversion to organized religion, which led eventually to a painful break with his father, Thomas Gambier Parry.[22] As he grew older Parry did not shy away from politically liberal positions. He vigorously supported home rule for Ireland and, later, the efforts of the suffragettes, even at their most radical.[23] Parry made his most frequently quoted political statement in a piece of compositional advice to the young Ralph Vaughan Williams, who studied at the RCM from 1890 to 1892 and again from 1895 to 1869: "write choral music as befits an Englishman and a democrat."[24] Parry's Wagnerian tirade against Disraeli may not have been reflected in the egalitarian habitus for which he was well known. Yet judging a person by their ethnic origin remained second nature: the next section of this chapter will show, indeed, that Parry's progressive approach to music history was inextricably entwined with ugly racism. His liberalism had a profoundly dark side.

Music Historian

Parry taught music history at the RCM from his original appointment in 1882 until his death in 1918. He was elected Heather Professor of Music at Oxford

Table 8.1. Hubert Parry's Writings on Music History.

---

123 articles for Grove's *Dictionary of Music and Musicians* (1879–89). Articles in *Proceedings of the Musical Association*, *Musical Quarterly*, *Musical Times* and other contemporary journals.

Lectures at the Royal College of Music, Royal Institution, Oxford University, Musical Association and other institutions. Drafts in the RCM Archive and Bodleian Library.

Seven books: *Studies of the Great Composers* (1886), [*The Evolution of*] *The Art of Music* (1893/1896), *Summary of the Development of Medieval and Modern European Music* (1894), *The Music of the Seventeenth Century* (vol. 3 of *The Oxford History of Music*) (1902), *Johann Sebastian Bach: The Story of the Development of a Great Personality* (1909), *Style in Musical Art* (1912), *College Addresses* (1920).

University in 1899 and served in this position, concurrently with the directorship of the RCM, until he resigned from Oxford on health grounds in 1908. Taken together, the platform afforded by these two posts, and his voluminous writings on music-historical topics, made him one of the most prolific and influential writers on the subject in Britain around 1900 (Parry's output as a music historian is summarized in Table 8.1).

In the opening pages of his main contribution to music history, *The Evolution of the Art of Music*, Parry begins with the "primeval savage" who only begins to make anything like music "when a few definite notes were made to take the place of vague, irregular shouting." Speech, Parry claims, is "music in the rough." Progress toward "higher" expression begins when "the ear is trained to distinguish niceties which have distinct varieties of meaning; so the resources of music increased as the relations of more and more definite notes were established."[25] Crucially, some groups begin their evolution at a "higher" stage. "Harmony represents the higher standard of intellectuality in mankind," he writes, "and the Germans have always had more feeling for it than southern races." Their tendency towards harmonic construction is evident, for example, in the prominence of arpeggios in some German folk music. "The Tyrolese," he continues, "adopt arpeggios for their singular jodels, which are the most ornamental forms of vocal music in Teutonic countries. In their case, however, the excess of decoration does not so much imply low organization or superficial character" but the "exuberance and joy of life in the echoing mountains."[26] Two key elements of Parry's philosophy of music history stand out in these passages. The first is that music history flows like a river, in one direction: from chaos to order, from "irregular shouting" to "higher intellectuality." The second is that environment always makes a difference. German yodelling does not imply superficiality. It is a product of "life in the echoing mountains."

These are typical tenets of historicism; they have roots in late eighteenth-century German thought, particularly the writings of Johann Gottfried

Herder.²⁷ But Parry drew equally on contemporary evolutionary thought, especially, as Bennet Zon has shown, on Herbert Spencer's models of organic development.²⁸ Spencer was one of the first to adapt Darwinian ideas about natural selection and evolution to what we today would describe as sociology and psychology. He proposed that societies evolved like organisms, from the simple to the complex (or from "homogenous" to "heterogenous"). As such, he is often credited as the father of "Social Darwinism," that is, of the idea that some people (or peoples) are superior to others on account of naturally occurring traits or qualities and that these traits and qualities can be passed onward through the generations. As Duncan Bell has written, "the popularity of [Spencer's] evolutionary thought stemmed, at least in part, from their ability to crystallise the hopes and anxieties of educated Victorians, as well as quenching their thirst for knowledge of self and society."²⁹ So would it have been for Parry, who found in Spencer's thinking an explanation for the superiority of the music he thought of as "true art."

The opening gesture of the *Evolution of the Art of Music* is a paradigmatic example of how Parry adapted Spencerian thought. The fact that Tyrolese Germans yodel in arpeggios—in melodies that also imply harmonies—demonstrates that Germans as a people are born with more "heterogeneous" musical natures. Thanks to this head start, they reach "higher" forms sooner. In his inaugural lecture as Heather Professor at Oxford, given in 1902, Parry suggests that "the style of an untutored savage in a very hot climate might be quite picturesque and appropriate in his own country, but if any ill-regulated being were to adopt it in the streets of a cool and civilized city he would probably have to be suppressed." The binary opposition cold/warm gives way to "broad distinctions between the tastes of the southern and the northern races."³⁰ Southerners "delight in what is voluptuous." They "enjoy their art with indifferent promiscuity," while northerners "look for qualities of virginal purity upon which they can dwell with constant loving contemplation." Northerners "love to make every part of their artistic work vital and interesting, so that nowhere shall commonness and the insincerity of indolence or convention be visible."³¹ In the *Evolution of the Art of Music* Parry's assessment of music from the global "south" was similarly negative. Pentatonic Chinese music was both too simple and too florid (full of "excessive unmeaning decoration"). Indian music, which draws on richer melodic materials, was more interesting, if still too ornamental.³² Only Western scales, Parry concludes, "sifted and tested" by a thousand years of "instinct," represent "a thing which is most subtly adapted to the purposes of artistic expression." This "thing" has "afforded Bach, Beethoven, Schubert, Wagner, and Brahms ample opportunities to produce works which in their respective lines are as wonderful as it is conceivable for any artistic works to be."³³

Parry transferred his racial thinking easily from large to small scales. He was particularly proud of the RCM's internationally celebrated Afro-British graduate Samuel Coleridge-Taylor. Coleridge-Taylor's early death moved Parry to lament the loss of a "life brimming with artistic activity." Yet even Parry's heartfelt obituary in the *Musical Times* focuses on race. "It is to the general credit," Parry writes, "that people accepted command and criticism from one whose appearance was so unoccidental."[34] In his student days at the RCM, Parry recalls, Coleridge-Taylor's work "poured out in a spontaneous flood, showing the influence of composers who appealed to him most at different periods," until he came under the influence of Dvořák, "between whom and himself there was some racial analogy." The first performance of his pupil's most famous work, "Hiawatha," at the RCM in 1898, "was one of the remarkable events in modern English musical history." The secret of this "universally beloved" work lay in the fact that Coleridge-Taylor was "particularly fitted by racial combination to produce an exception to the conventional tendency" of the narrative cantata. "Like his half-brothers of primitive race," Parry continues, "[Coleridge-Taylor] loved plenty of sound, plenty of colour, simple and definite rhythms, and above all plenty of tune." Even (or especially) when it came to celebrating one of the RCM's most successful alumni, Parry, the proud director, chose whiteness and blackness as critical categories with which to locate him in music history.

There is a German component to Parry's definition of the "north." It lies in the music history of the seventeenth century, when German instrumental music took the exuberance of the south and turned it into something "greater," thus inaugurating a specifically German music history. "Organ music," Parry writes, "may indeed be said to be the first branch of art in which Germany asserted herself as an independent musical nation."[35] It is only a short jump to Germany's greatest organist, Johann Sebastian Bach. Here again the "northernness" of German instrumental music brings order to "southern" vocal composition. In his discussion of the duet "Komm, mein Jesu" in the cantata "Ich hatte viel Bekümmernis," BWV 21 Parry observes the use of dialogue techniques that might have been at home in an Italian opera. "The transference of an Italian artistic device," he writes, "is seen to minister to the carrying out of an essentially Teutonic, or at least northern, conception; for the dialogue form had been just as popular with English composers of the latter part of the seventeenth century as with the Germans."[36] Parry's attention to Italian influences reflects a typical line of thinking in nineteenth-century German music historiography, summed up in what Carl Dahlhaus called the "two cultures" debate.[37] It also echoes British unease around 1800 about the substantial presence of Italians in London's musical life.[38] But it seems that, overall, Parry wished to transcend a European north/south divide with a more global one—one that also, willy nilly, invokes categories of race alongside those of nation.

The first culmination of musical "evolution" arrives with Mozart and Beethoven, who create a "self-dependent" music that disciplines spontaneous inspiration and southern vocality. In secular song the high point was reached with Schubert, Schumann, and Brahms, who "fill up almost the whole range of the higher type of songwriting," uniting "direct utterances of musical feeling" with technical command and disciplined construction.[39] Their national triumph transcends national labeling. "Composers of different nations impart the flavours of Slav, English, Norwegian, and French to their songs," Parry writes, "but make them, if they have any sense, on the same general terms as the great Germans."[40] In Parry's liberal panorama, his use of the "north" as a guiding concept elides any differences between good music of German or other origin. Behind cosmopolitanism lurks whiteness.[41]

War Clouds

As war clouds gathered, Parry seemed at first not to take the danger seriously. In 1913 he accepted a commission from the Oxford University Dramatic Society (OUDS) to provide incidental music to its annual production of a Greek play, in this case Aristophanes's comedy *The Acharnians*. The comic plot involves maintenance of the peace between quarreling Athens and Sparta. Parry draws on current events in the music: in the overture alone, the score references "Rule Britannia," "The British Grenadiers," "We don't want to fight, but by jingo if we do," Schumann's "Merry Peasant," and a persiflage of Elgar's "Pomp and Circumstance" (in his program note Parry indicates he had included a "parody on patriotic effusions"), all crowned by a climactic mashup of "God Save the King" and "La Marseillaise."[42] Throughout it all, the tune of "Oh dear, what can the matter be" appears again and again like a comic leitmotiv (music example in Figure 8.1).

The performance was not entirely a success. Parry noted in his diary that the audience seemed restrained in their reaction to the overture's comic references, "as if they were afraid it wasn't quite proper."[43] Perhaps this signaled the breakdown of a certain liberal optimism. Parry seems to have thought the idea that Germany and Britain—brothers in musical northernness or whiteness—would go to war literally laughable. His faith in social, psychological, and cultural evolution, forged in decades of service to cosmopolitan ideals and a deep belief in rational solutions to almost any problem, was to be shaken profoundly. The OUDS gave *The Archarnians* in the winter and spring of 1914. By the end of the summer the laughs were over. Parry had a particularly close view of the political run-up to the war through his son-in-law Arthur Ponsonby, a liberal backbencher who was one of only five MPs to speak out in

Figure 8.1. Incidental music to *The Acharnians of Aristophanes as Written for Performance by the Oxford University Dramatic Society* (1914). 1. Prelude: "War and Peace," mm. 54–59.

the Commons, in the war debate of 3 August 1914, against Britain's involvement in the war.[44]

Parry spent the war years mostly at his desk in South Kensington, holding the RCM together as its male students and younger staff departed one by one for the front. Many, including the phenomenally talented George Butterworth, never returned. Others, such as Ivor Gurney, who was gassed at Passchendaele, returned broken.[45] During the war the rhythms of British musical life that had shaped Parry's career, particularly the yearly choral festivals in the provinces, came to a halt. In the summers, Parry tended to his farm properties in Gloucestershire and tried to compose. Chronically ill with heart problems, he knew his strength was slipping. In 1915 he completed a set of choral motets, the *Songs of Farewell*, on which he had been working periodically since 1906. These richly harmonized works, some for double choir in eight voices, seem at first to speak an idiom familiar from the nineteenth-century English cathedral. But they likewise invoke the monuments of the German tradition that meant so much to Parry, from Bach to Brahms and Parry's younger contemporary Max Reger.[46] All of these composed exquisite choral motets, and it is their example against which Parry wished himself to be measured. In their wartime performances they must have sounded like a requiem for a lost world.

As the war dragged on Parry was approached from time to time with commissions for patriotic music. Even if he supported the war—at the cost of some tension with his pacifist son-in-law Ponsonby—jingoism made Parry nervous.[47] Nonetheless, the commission for his final major work, a patriotic hymn on a text by William Blake, came from the Fight for Right movement—a group founded by the explorer and religious eccentric Sir Francis Younghusband—which argued that the war needed to be prosecuted more vigorously.[48] The result was "Jerusalem," which was first performed at a rally in the Albert Hall in May 1916. Its immediate success led him to withdraw his dedication of the piece to Fight for Right. Parry was delighted when the work was taken up by the women's suffrage movement, who made it the Women Voters' Hymn.

Culture vs. Civilization

On the other side of the western front, Parry's younger contemporary Thomas Mann was fashioning his own views on music, national identity, and conflict into a sprawling series of interlocking essays, *Betrachtungen eines Unpolitischen (Reflections of an Unpolitical Man)*.[49] In the *Reflections* Mann formulates a specifically "musical" identity for Germany: in Hans Rudolf Vaget's words, Mann "grounded" his arguments for Germany's right to wage war "in the uniqueness of Germany's music-centered culture."[50] Mann believed the war "was being waged for Germany's right to be different from the Western democracies and to maintain a culture in which music, not politics, would rule."[51] To be German is to draw one's identity from the "musical," an irrational other to politics, literature, and civilization; it is this musicality that allows for drastic action such as war. Mann's polemical opponent is the *Zivilisationsliterat*, a figure who represents both a foreign enemy and the German Reich's liberal and cosmopolitan bourgeoisie, who are unable to surrender themselves to music's irrational power. People of music know better. "It is understandable," Mann writes, that any thinking German musician "is prepared to oppose the progressive plans of the *Zivilisationsliteraten* ... to replace the national supremacy of music with the democratic regime of politics and literature."[52] Mann's musical ideal "is art as sounding ethics, fugue and counterpoint, as [both] lighthearted and serious piety, as a building not dedicated to the profane, where one thing reaches into another, intelligent and held together without mortar."[53] His polemical enemies, on the other hand, understand "music to be a political cantilena, tenor aria with brass accompaniment *unisono*, in the Italian taste, — and as national dumbing-down potion and tool of quietism." Note the north-south axis.

Parry's diagnosis of Germany's "musicality" and its relation to the war was not so different. As we saw earlier, Parry believed Germany's war aims were driven by a minority who advocated "mere brutal violence and material aggression" while talking of their "super-morality." The German attitude to the war, he writes, "is arrogance run mad." Its main driver "is the hideous militarism of the Prussians that has poisoned the wells of the spirit throughout Germany ..., cynical manipulation of the Press, and all the channels through which enlightenment can flow to the millions."[54] War-mongering Prussians (throughout the war sections of the *College Addresses* Parry avoids the word "German") hold "up to general worship the fetish formula of 'Blood and Iron.'"⁵⁵ Parry's analysis betrays his socially progressive instincts: the "Prussian Junkers," he explains, "must be a great fount and source of stupidity, since they still batten upon the worn-out theory of class privilege; which tries still to induce men to believe that the world was made for the few, and that when the few think it for their advantage the many are to be driven to kill one another in hundreds of thousands and to suffer every kind of torment without any one except the few gaining any advantage."⁵⁶ Yet he soon clarifies that German "musicality" cannot be to blame. Although their music suggests that Germans too should possess great reserves of character, the war proved otherwise. "If the Germans had been content to devote themselves to metaphysics and music," Parry observes, "the world might have been spared the painful and offensive exhibition they have made of themselves." For the coming peace, after all the carnage, Parry holds out hope, "that the Germans may go back to their music too, and leave alone the business of dominating the world by any other means but peaceful art; which, in truth, until this evil day of their own miscontriving, they had nearly accomplished."⁵⁷

The war inspired Parry to reflect on the mission of the RCM. "It is a time like this," he writes, "that tests the genuineness of our work."⁵⁸ Besides being a battle against an external enemy, the war, Parry believed, was a test of the RCM's campaign against those in Britain who did not appreciate the role that serious music should play in national life. Indeed, in the opening paragraphs of one address ("The College in Peace and War") Parry speculates that Germany might have thought it possible to defeat Britain because of coverage in the popular press of Britain's taste for "frivolous" music.

The establishment of the RCM, Parry explains, was key to systematic efforts to remedy this problem.⁵⁹ From its first years, the RCM offered training in every orchestral instrument; its orchestra toured the provinces. In time its graduates were numerous enough that cities and towns far from London were able to field their own orchestras. The RCM required chamber music, "thereby sustaining the appreciation of a lofty form of art which meets but scanty encouragement in modern times." Soon RCM graduates were performing this repertoire to audiences who had never heard it before, "diffus[ing] the taste for [it] far and wide through the country, and even in the slum districts of our overgrown cities." The RCM produced one opera a year, "afford[ing] us opportunities of ... training a good many singers who have ultimately attained to very high positions among operatic artists in countries besides England." The college's obligatory training in music history and literature meant that organist graduates could "take the lead in any provincial town ... encouraging people to take enlightened interest in music outside the limited range of their church services and choral societies." The same broad curriculum, finally, allowed composition students to hear "a vast amount of music of every period and style ..., to experiment hard and wide, and to watch modern developments and learn and assimilate what is worthy in the name of art, and to dispense with such things as are made merely for vain show and popularity with the thoughtless herd." Parry's war aim, then, was first to defeat Germany and then to harness the national seriousness of purpose the war had engendered in order to win the musical peace. "There never was a time," he concludes, "when it was more needful to take our art seriously. ... [A]s long as we aim steadfastly at the best we can concentrate ourselves on our College work in wartime as in peacetime with clear consciences."

Discounting Mann's attraction to the irrational sides of German "musicality" (Parry might have referred to these as symptoms of "arrogance" and "Prussian super-morality") both men—on opposite sides of a brutal conflict—shared congruent goals: first, a commitment to music as earnest process ("fugue and counterpoint," as Mann put it) and not entertainment; second, the idea that serious music made for a more serious country and that this seriousness could make the difference in the conflict; and third, the notion that the music they stood for, however much it could make a nation, was also universal. Finally, their respective enemies (the *Zivilisationsliterat* and the "frivolous" well-to-do classes) had more than a little in common.

Networks

One might even conclude that Mann and Parry belong to the same network of thinkers about Germanness in music and, since Parry himself was not German, that—for all of his bitter disappointment with Germany over the war—he acted as a "representative" or "ambassador" in Britain of German musical thought. In some ways he did have this function, as he himself admitted ("I have been for a quarter century and more a pro-Teuton") and as Shaw observed after his death. On a more granular level, however, the ideologies to which Parry and Mann claimed allegiance were profoundly different. Parry, his early Wagnerism notwithstanding, was not committed in any serious way to the mysteries of musical Germanness that his younger contemporary Mann was. Nor was he at all conflicted about his liberal belief in "progress," a notion Mann distrusted deeply. Mann, likewise, did not share Parry's capacious notions of "north" and "south," concentrating instead on Germany as the "north's" sole representative. Parry, on the other hand, argued again and again that "true musical art" was a function of a "northern" racial superiority that encompassed both countries.

Even so, the idea that there might be such an identifiable discourse, an idea around which such diverse actors as Parry and Mann could gather, is hard to shake. The notion that there is such a thing as Germanness in music underpins this book and any other like it—in particular, Applegate and Potter's seminal *Music and German National Identity*.[60] Another word for this notion would be a *Sonderweg*, a "special path" for German music. The essence of historians' rejection of the *Sonderweg* thesis more broadly is that it is next to impossible to demonstrate empirically.[61] At best, figures as disparate as Parry and Mann walked along a common *Sonderweg*, making it temporarily visible to posterity. I do not think, however, that this is where a critical analysis has to stop. What if, we might ask, the network made the concept instead of the concept the network? What I would like to propose here, using Parry as an example, is how one might employ a different view of networks as drivers of intellectual history in order to understand musical "Germanness" more fully.

There is help at hand from actor-network theory (ANT), a repertoire of approaches that emerged first in science and technology studies and is now enjoying currency in music history. In ANT, networks are not, to borrow Benjamin Piekut's description, "like a railroad system or gas pipeline."[62] The network of Germanness in music is not flat. Neither Parry nor Mann was a passive node in it. They were mediators, acting within the constraints of a seemingly endless tangle of contingencies (Parry's liberal scientific racism and spatial positioning of the "north" in music, Mann's suspicion in the *Reflections* about democracy and dislike of liberal critics). Some of these resolve contrapuntally into commonalities (e.g., their belief that great music was marked by process). Each of these contingencies and commonalities was itself the product of further entanglements. The price of admitting such complexity is parting with all-purpose generalizations such as "Germanness" in music. Just as for Bruno Latour and his followers there is no such thing as "the social," there is really no single fixed German national identity—in music or anywhere else.[63] Thus Parry and Mann can agree that serious music contributes to national strength while at the same time standing at opposite ends of a "conservative-liberal" political continuum.

Telling Parry's story in the mode of actor-network theory might also make more sense of the relationship between the English Musical Renaissance and Germany by disrupting the scale commonly used to view it. To the dismay of musicological critics such as Alain Frogley, Hughes and Stradling claimed that the renaissance, and especially the establishment of its flagship institution, the RCM, was best explained as a product of British anxiety about German economic and political hegemony. Frogley found this explanation unsatisfactory because it denied sufficient importance to the music that RCM composers such as Vaughan Williams actually wrote.[64] An ANT-inflected approach encompasses both Stradling and Hughes's thesis about Germany and Frogley's critique, but does not decide which one is primary. Instead of featuring either as a conspiratorial locale (Hughes and Stradling's "Goodly

House") or the birthplace of great composers such as Vaughan Williams, the RCM becomes—in terms an ANT scholar might use—an "obligatory point of passage" through which students, teachers, performers, donors, politicians, royal patrons, evolutionary theorists, modern technology (including musical instruments), musical editions, texts about Germany, evolution, white or "northern" supremacy, and actual Germans or Germanophiles passed. Thus the RCM, Hubert Parry at its helm, was at once the product of a nearly endless series of networks and the origin of countless others. These networks featured all of the qualities John Law identifies as constitutive of the ANT approach: semiotic relationality (different actors define one another), heterogeneity (different kinds of actors), materiality (actors can be people, ideas, and objects), process (networks are always changing), and precariousness (networks can "break" in circumstances such as war).[65]

Positioning Parry as one actor in a series of networks can also draw attention to wider concerns than the bilateral relationship between the English Musical Renaissance and Germany. The clue is in ANT's accordance of agency to nonhuman actors. The actual building in which Parry worked for most of his career was not situated accidentally. The RCM occupied (and occupies) a key location in the ensemble of institutions that run along Exhibition Road in South Kensington. In Parry's era these included the Royal Albert Hall, the RCM, the Royal College of Science (later Imperial College), and the South Kensington, later Victoria and Albert, Museum (which included science and natural history divisions). The area was planned in the wake of the Great Exhibition of 1851 and bore for many years the name "Albertopolis" in honor of the Exhibition's patron Prince Albert. The Exhibition and Albertopolis were prime physical representations of Britain's links with its empire. Objects from the empire featured heavily at the Exhibition and later in the museums, arranged in such as way as to make, among other things, contemporary theories of evolution, and the ideologies of white supremacy they underpinned, visible to as many as possible. Around the museums, planners placed educational institutions such as the RCM and the Royal College of Science. In these, young Britons (and the occasional foreigner) learned the practical skills and theoretical knowledge that they would need as educated protagonists of national and imperial improvement.[66]

Parry's music history—forged of whiteness, Germanness, liberalism, and many other elements—started its journey here and traveled to the formal empire and the rest of the English-speaking world, including the United States. There his doctrines of the superiority of "northern" music were studied and understood. In Richard Taruskin's entry on nationalism in the *New Grove Dictionary of Music and Musicians*, the transfer of Germanocentric narratives to imperial contexts earns the name "colonialist nationalism." His example is the American composer Amy Beach, who distinguished around 1900 between "we of the north" and such composers as Dvořák.⁶⁷ A few decades after Beach, the organist and music historian Warren Dwight Allen—who disagreed sharply with Parry about the natural superiority of "northern" music—noted the influence of Parry's *Evolution of the Art of Music* on American musical education, including the booming field of "music appreciation." In 1939, Allen wrote in a comprehensive survey of music histories that Parry's was "the only history of music still in general demand and widespread use."⁶⁸ Allen's observation suggests that in the 1930s, when Germanocentric (and less overtly racial) ideas came to North America (and of course also Britain) with the Nazi-era emigration they would have found a receptive audience and mixed with what was already there to create a new consensus about what constituted serious art music. The "German" view of music that until recently seemed normative and universal to Anglo-Americans might in fact rest on foundations provided by such British and American intellectual formations as liberalism, scientific racism, white settlement, and empire. These inform Taruskin's "colonialist nationalism." And they were spread throughout the English-speaking world via the reception of Parry's writings. They align musical progress along a north/south–white/black axis. A key tenet of his music history, after all, is the belief that the amount of control a composer has over their "instincts," and thus their ability to access great "northern" art, depends on their origin along this spectrum. Our sense of musical Germanness, could, in other words, rest on white supremacist foundations. This aspect of Parry's work may have been more influential than he ever dreamt.

This chapter has argued that Parry's music history, once widely influential in the English-speaking world, is a document of a liberal but racist vision of "northern" music. His vision elided national distinctions between "northern" countries such as Germany and Britain and brought both together under the umbrella of "northernness." I have suggested that Parry's history is best situated as a node in an asymmetrical network of competing imperatives: scientific progress, artistic profundity, imperial ambition, and crude "scientific" racism. A product of this network, Parry's history commits the classic sin of colonialist Eurocentrism: it brutally and casually robs vast swathes of the world's people, many then subjects of the empire at whose heart Parry worked, of their human musical agency. It does so in the name of a canon of "great works" by mostly German composers. Taruskin, responding recently to the arrival of ANT in musicology, objected that ANT-style explanations can provide human actors—such as, one presumes, Parry—with "alibis." He wants actors "to take responsibility."⁶⁹ Parry, and not his networks, should be held responsible for the view of music history that he preached. I do not believe that the account I offer here absolves Parry of his racism; in any case, it is not my role as historian to offer such absolution. Simply calling his racism by its name and moving on, however, is not a productive enough act if we are serious about understanding how Parry's views might still inform our own practices as historians, teachers, and musicians. The networks emerging from Parry's writings need to be made visible, as does our enrolment in them. If the aim is to "decolonize" musicology, then experience of musicology's "denazification" at the hands such scholars as Pamela Potter and Michael Kater—joined more recently by the controversy around the wartime activities of Hans Heinrich Eggebrecht—might be instructive.[70] To be sure, naming matters. But Tamara Levitz, in a review of Potter's seminal study of Nazi-era musicology, called for studies "that do fuller justice to the complexities of the period" and, crucially, for scholars to attempt more "sympathetic understanding" of those tangled up in its horrors.[71] I take such "understanding" to mean difficult work of interpretation and self-recognition, not platitudinous absolution along the lines of "Parry was a man of his time." For of course he was. But the horrors of British imperialism and the racism that went with it—not comparable to the Holocaust, but horrors all the same—will not go away. A more capacious view is necessary—one that takes in, and seeks to understand, the continuing entanglement of such beloved figures as Parry with ideas of white supremacy that haunt us now more than ever.

Thomas Irvine is associate professor in music at the University of Southampton, UK. His recent research explores the intellectual history of music and musical practices in transnational and global frames. In 2015–16 he was a Mid-Career Fellow of the British Academy. His book *Listening to China: Sound and the Sino-Western Encounter, 1770–1839* is published by University of Chicago Press.

Notes

Earlier versions of this chapter were presented at the annual meeting of the American Musicological Society in Vancouver in November 2016, at the University of Southampton Hartley Residency in Music in December 2016, and as part of Southampton's "Great War, Unknown War" lecture series in December 2017. I am grateful to my audiences at these events for their useful critique, in particular Richard Taruskin, Mark Everist, and Neil Gregor, and to Ruth Eldredge and Phyllis Weliver for commenting on later drafts. Wiebke Thormählen, now my collaborator in further Parry projects, has been an invaluable interlocutor. David Owen Norris first introduced me to Parry and his music, for which I cannot thank him enough. He of course bears no responsibility for the direction my work on Parry has taken since. All translations are mine.

1. Hubert Parry, "1914," in *College Addresses: Delivered to the Pupils of the Royal College of Music*, ed. H. C. Colles (London, 1920), 226.
2. Ibid., 224.
3. Ibid., 227.

4. Stefan Collini, *Public Moralists: Political Thought and Intellectual Life in Britain, 1850–1930* (Oxford, 1991).
5. Jeremy Dibble, *C. Hubert H. Parry: His Life and Music* (Oxford, 1998).
6. Meirion Hughes and R. A. Stradling, *The English Musical Renaissance, 1840–1940: Constructing a National Music*, 2nd ed. (Manchester, 2001). Anger about the book among many scholars of British music is summed up in the first half of Alain Frogley, "Rewriting the Renaissance: History, Imperialism, and British Music since 1840," *Music and Letters* 84, no. 2 (2003): 241–57.
7. One of their chapters is entitled "Being Beastly to the Hun."
8. G. Bernard Shaw, "Sir Edward Elgar," *Music and Letters* 1, no. 1 (1920): 10–11.
9. John Bridcut, *The Prince and the Composer: A Film about Hubert Parry by HRH The Prince of Wales* (London, 2011).
10. Information in this and the following paragraphs is drawn from Dibble, *C. Hubert H. Parry*, 3–177.
11. On Grove, see Hughes and Stradling, *English Musical Renaissance*, 23–51.
12. Ibid., 26.
13. Quoted in Charles Graves, *The Life and Letters of Sir George Grove, CB* (London, 1903), 205.
14. For further discussion, see Thomas Irvine, "'Behold That Twilight Realm as in a Glass, the Future': Charles Hubert Parrys Prometheus Unbound, eine musikalische Moderne für England?," in *Der Entfesselte Prometheus: Der Antike Mythos in der Musik um 1900*, ed. Laurenz Lütteken (Kassel, 2015), 37–52.
15. See David Wright, "The South Kensington Music Schools and the Development of the British Conservatoire in the Late Nineteenth Century," *Journal of the Royal Musical Association* 130, no. 2 (2005): 236–82; and Hughes and Stradling, *English Musical Renaissance*, 27–31.
16. "Lectures in the history of music given at the RCM 2nd course," MS 4306 f. 16v. Royal College of Music archive.
17. For a recent attempt, see Duncan Bell, *Reordering the World: Essays on Liberalism and Empire* (Princeton, 2016), esp. chap. 3, "What Is Liberalism?"
18. Hubert Parry, diary entry [?] December 1873, in Dibble, *C. Hubert H. Parry*, 108.
19. Ibid., 109.
20. Dibble, *C. Hubert H. Parry*, Ibid.
21. See Colin Holmes, "Goldwin Smith (1823–1910)," *Patterns of Prejudice* 6, no. 5 (1972): 25–30; and Bell, *Reordering the World*, 36–37.
22. Dibble, *C. Hubert H. Parry*, 112.
23. Ibid., 419–20 and passim.
24. Ursula Vaughan Williams, *RVW: A Biography of Ralph Vaughan Williams* (Oxford, 1993), 32.
25. Hubert Parry, *The Evolution of the Art of Music* (London, 1905), 6.
26. Ibid., 74.
27. For a recent introduction to Herder's musical thought, see Philip V. Bohlman, "Johann Gottfried Herder and the Global Moment of World-Music History," in *The Cambridge Companion to the History of World Music*, ed. Philip V. Bohlman (Cambridge, 2013), 255–76.
28. Bennett Zon, "C. Hubert H. Parry, *The Evolution of the Art of Music* (1893/96)," *Victorian Review* 35, no. 1 (2009): 68–72. See also Bennett Zon, *Evolution and Victorian*

Musical Culture (Cambridge, 2017), 130–39; and *Representing Non-Western Music in Nineteenth-Century Britain* (Rochester, 2007), 110–12, 146–50.
29. Bell, *Reordering the World*, 243.
30. Hubert Parry, *Style in Musical Art* (London, 1911), 9.
31. Ibid., 17.
32. Parry, *Evolution of the Art of Music*, 22–46. See also the discussion in Zon, *Representing Non-Western Music*, 111–12 and passim.
33. Parry, *Evolution of the Art of Music*, 46.
34. All of the quotations in this paragraph are from Hubert Parry, "[Samuel Coleridge-Taylor]: A Tribute from Sir Hubert Parry," *Musical Times* 53, no. 836 (1912): 638.
35. Hubert Parry, *The Music of the Seventeenth Century*, vol. 3 of *The Oxford History of Music* (Oxford, 1902), 99.
36. Hubert Parry, *Johann Sebastian Bach: The Story of the Development of a Great Personality* (New York, 1909), 92. See also the chapter "The Beginning of German Music" in Parry's *The Music of the Seventeenth Century* (Oxford: Oxford University Press, 1902), 409–456.
37. Carl Dahlhaus, *Nineteenth-Century Music*, trans. J. Bradford Robinson (Berkeley, 1992); Nicholas Mathew and Benjamin Walton, eds., *The Invention of Beethoven and Rossini: Historiography, Analysis, Criticism* (New York, 2013).
38. Simon McVeigh, *Concert Life in London from Mozart to Haydn* (Cambridge, 1993).
39. Parry, *Evolution of the Art of Music*, 292.
40. Ibid. He follows a similar line of argument in his discussions of the music of George Frederic Handel (an example would be *The Evolution of the Art of Music*, 126–157). Handel's gift, Parry argues, was to bring a German sensibility and Italian training before an English audience, who brought forth from him a particularly English version of "northern" music.
41. Sarah Collins productively complicates the notion of musical cosmopolitanism. See Collins, "What Is Cosmopolitan? Busoni and Other Germans," *Musical Quarterly* 99, no. 2 (2016): 201–29.
42. Dibble, *C. Hubert H. Parry*, 467–68.
43. Ibid.
44. Duncan Marlor, *Fatal Fortnight: Arthur Ponsonby and the Fight for British Neutrality in 1914* (London, 2014).
45. Dibble, *C. Hubert H. Parry*, 482, 487 and passim.
46. Ibid., 478–81.
47. Marlor, *Fatal Fortnight*, 180–81.
48. Dibble, *C. Hubert H. Parry*, 483–85.
49. Thomas Mann, *Betrachtungen eines Unpolitischen*, ed. Hermann Kurzke (Frankfurt, 2013).
50. Hans Rudolf Vaget, "National and Universal: Thomas Mann and the Paradox of 'German' Music," in *Music and German National Identity*, ed. Celia Applegate and Pamela Potter (Chicago, 2002), 159.
51. Ibid.
52. Mann, *Betrachtungen*, 264.
53. Ibid.
54. Parry, "The College in Peace and War," in *College Addresses*, 223.
55. Ibid.
56. Ibid., 239.

57. Ibid., 242.
58. Ibid., 226.
59. All quotes in this paragraph are from ibid., 260–63.
60. Celia Applegate and Pamela Potter, eds., *Music and German National Identity* (Chicago, 2002).
61. See the discussion in the introduction to this volume.
62. Benjamin Piekut, "Actor-Networks in Music History: Clarifications and Critiques," *Twentieth-Century Music* 11, no. 2 (2014): 192.
63. Bruno Latour, *Reassembling the Social: An Introduction to Actor-Network-Theory* (Oxford, 2007).
64. Frogley, "Rewriting the Renaissance," 246–47.
65. John Law, "Actor-Network Theory and Material Semiotics," in *The New Blackwell Companion to Social Theory*, 3rd ed., ed. Bryan S. Turner (Oxford, 2008), 141–58.
66. Hermione Hobhouse, *The Crystal Palace and the Great Exhibition: Science, Art and Productive Industry: The History of the Royal Commission for the Exhibition of 1851* (London, 2002). For a similar suggestion about the generation of musical knowledge in the British Empire, see James Q. Davies, "Instruments of Empire," in *Sound Knowledge: Music and Science in London, 1789–1851*, ed. Ellen Lockhart and James Q. Davies (Chicago, 2016), 145–74.
67. Grove Music Online, s.v. "Nationalism," by Richard Taruskin, retrieved 12 April 2018 from http://www.oxfordmusiconline.com/view/10.1093/gmo/9781561592630.001.0001/omo-9781561592630-e-0000050846. This use of the word "north" as racial shorthand differs from its appearance as an aesthetic category, for instance in the essays collected in the forthcoming volume *Music and Ideas of North* edited by Rachel Cowgill and Derek B. Scott (Abingdon, 2018), which I have been unable to consult.
68. Warren Dwight Allen, *Philosophies of Music History: A Study of General Histories of Music 1600–1960*, 2nd edition with a new preface (London, 1964), 113–16.
69. Richard Taruskin, "Agents and Causes and Ends, Oh My," *Journal of Musicology* 31, no. 2 (2014): 292.
70. Pamela Potter, *Most German of the Arts: Musicology and Society from the Weimar Republic to the End of Hitler's Reich* (New Haven, 1998); and Michael H. Kater, *Composers of the Nazi Era: Eight Portraits* (Oxford and New York, 2000). On Eggebrecht, see Anne C. Shreffler, Boris von Haken, and Christopher Browning, "Musicology, Biography, and National Socialism: The Case of Hans Heinrich Eggebrecht," *German Studies Review* 35, no. 2 (2012): 289–318.
71. Tamara Levitz, review of *Most German of the Arts: Musicology and Society from the Weimar Republic to the End of Hitler's Reich*, by Pamela Potter, *Journal of the American Musicological Society* 55, no. 1 (2002): 186–87. I discuss the issues around "normalizing" Nazi-era histories in Thomas Irvine, "Normality and Emplotment: Walter Leigh's 'Midsummer Night's Dream' in the Third Reich and Britain," *Music and Letters* 94, no. 2 (2013): 321–23.

Bibliography

Allen, Warren Dwight. *Philosophies of Music History: A Study of General Histories of Music 1600–1960*. 2nd edition with a new preface. London: Constable, 1964.

Applegate, Celia, and Pamela Potter, eds. *Music and German National Identity*. Chicago: University of Chicago Press, 2002.
Bell, Duncan. *Reordering the World: Essays on Liberalism and Empire*. Princeton, NJ: Princeton University Press, 2016.
Bohlman, Philip V. "Johann Gottfried Herder and the Global Moment of World-Music History." In *The Cambridge Companion to the History of World Music*, edited by Philip V. Bohlman, 255–76. Cambridge: Cambridge University Press, 2013.
Bridcut, John. *The Prince and the Composer: A Film about Hubert Parry by HRH The Prince of Wales*. London: A Crux Production/BBC Four Television, 2011.
Collini, Stefan. *Public Moralists: Political Thought and Intellectual Life in Britain, 1850–1930*. Oxford: Clarendon Press, 1991.
Collins, Sarah. "What Is Cosmopolitan? Busoni and Other Germans." *Musical Quarterly* 99, no. 2 (2016): 201–29.
Cowgill, Rachel and Derek B. Scott, eds. *Music and Ideas of North* (Abingdon: Routledge, 2018).
Dahlhaus, Carl. *Nineteenth-Century Music*. Translated by J. Bradford Robinson. Berkeley: University of California Press, 1992.
Dangerfield, George. *The Strange Death of Liberal England*. St Albans: Grenada, 1970.
Davies, James Q. "Instruments of Empire." In *Sound Knowledge: Music and Science in London, 1789–1851*, edited by Ellen Lockhart and James Q. Davies, 145–74. Chicago: University of Chicago Press, 2016.
Dibble, Jeremy. *C. Hubert H. Parry: His Life and Music*. Oxford: Clarendon Press, 1998.
Frogley, Alain. "Rewriting the Renaissance: History, Imperialism, and British Music since 1840." *Music and Letters* 84, no. 2 (2003): 241–57.
Graves, Charles. *The Life and Letters of Sir George Grove, CB*. London: Macmillan, 1903.
Hobhouse, Hermione. *The Crystal Palace and the Great Exhibition: Science, Art and Productive Industry: The History of the Royal Commission for the Exhibition of 1851*. London: A&C Black, 2002.
Holmes, Colin. "Goldwin Smith (1823–1910)." *Patterns of Prejudice* 6, no. 5 (1972): 25–30.
Irvine, Thomas. "Normality and Emplotment: Walter Leigh's 'Midsummer Night's Dream' in the Third Reich and Britain." *Music and Letters* 94, no. 2 (2013): 295–323.
———. "'Behold That Twilight Realm as in a Glass, the Future': Charles Hubert Parrys Prometheus Unbound, eine musikalische Moderne für England?" In *Der Entfesselte Prometheus: Der Antike Mythos in Der Musik Um 1900*, edited by Laurenz Lütteken, 37–52. Kassel: Bärenreiter, 2015.
Kater, Michael H. *Composers of the Nazi Era: Eight Portraits*. Oxford and New York: Oxford University Press, 2000.
Latour, Bruno. *Reassembling the Social: An Introduction to Actor-Network-Theory*. Oxford: Oxford University Press, 2007.

Law, John. "Actor-Network Theory and Material Semiotics." In *The New Blackwell Companion to Social Theory*, 3rd ed., edited by Bryan S. Turner, 141–58. Oxford: Blackwell, 2008.

Levitz, Tamara. Review of *Most German of the Arts: Musicology and Society from the Weimar Republic to the End of Hitler's Reich*, by Pamela Potter. *Journal of the American Musicological Society* 55, no. 1 (2002): 176–87.

Mann, Thomas. *Betrachtungen eines Unpolitischen*. Edited by Hermann Kurzke. Frankfurt: S. Fischer, 2013.

Marlor, Duncan. *Fatal Fortnight: Arthur Ponsonby and the Fight for British Neutrality in 1914*. London: Frontline Books, 2014.

Mathew, Nicholas, and Benjamin Walton, eds. *The Invention of Beethoven and Rossini: Historiography, Analysis, Criticism*. New York: Cambridge University Press, 2013.

McVeigh, Simon. *Concert Life in London from Mozart to Haydn*. Cambridge: Cambridge University Press, 1993.

Parry, Hubert. *The Music of the Seventeenth Century*. Vol. 3 of *The Oxford History of Music*. Oxford: Clarendon Press, 1902.

———. *The Evolution of the Art of Music*. London: Keegan, Paul, Trench & Trübner, 1905.

———. *Johann Sebastian Bach: The Story of the Development of a Great Personality*. New York: G. P. Putnam's Sons, 1909.

———. *The Music of the Seventeenth Century*. Oxford: Oxford University Press, 1902.

———. *Style in Musical Art*. London: Macmillan, 1911.

———. "[Samuel Coleridge-Taylor]: A Tribute from Sir Hubert Parry." *Musical Times* 53, no. 836 (1912): 638.

———. *College Addresses Delivered to Pupils of the Royal College of Music by Sir C. Hubert H. Parry* edited by H. C. Colles. London: Macmillan, 1920.

Piekut, Benjamin. "Actor-Networks in Music History: Clarifications and Critiques." *Twentieth-Century Music* 11, no. 2 (2014): 191–215.

Potter, Pamela. *Most German of the Arts: Musicology and Society from the Weimar Republic to the End of Hitler's Reich*. New Haven, CT: Yale University Press, 1998.

Shaw, G. Bernard. "Sir Edward Elgar." *Music and Letters* 1, no. 1 (1920): 7–11.

Shreffler, Anne C., Boris von Haken, and Christopher Browning. "Musicology, Biography, and National Socialism: The Case of Hans Heinrich Eggebrecht." *German Studies Review* 35, no. 2 (2012): 289–318.

Taruskin, Richard. "Agents and Causes and Ends, Oh My." *Journal of Musicology* 31, no. 2 (2014): 272–93.

Vaget, Hans Rudolf. "National and Universal: Thomas Mann and the Paradox of 'German' Music." In *Music and German National Identity*, edited by Celia Applegate and Pamela Potter, 155–77. Chicago: University of Chicago Press, 2002.

Vaughan Williams, Ursula. *RVW: A Biography of Ralph Vaughan Williams*. Oxford: Oxford University Press, 1993.

Wright, David. "The South Kensington Music Schools and the Development of the British Conservatoire in the Late Nineteenth Century." *Journal of the Royal Musical Association* 130, no. 2 (2005): 236–82.

Zon, Bennett. *Representing Non-Western Music in Nineteenth-Century Britain.* Rochester: University of Rochester Press, 2007.

———. "C. Hubert H. Parry, *The Evolution of the Art of Music* (1893/96)." *Victorian Review* 35, no. 1 (2009): 68–72.

———. *Evolution and Victorian Musical Culture.* Cambridge: Cambridge University Press, 2017.

———. "From Great Man to Fittest Survivor: Reputation, Recapitulation and Survival in Victorian Concepts of Wagner's Genius." *Musicae Scientiae* 13, no. 2 (2009): 415–45.

PART IV

Fantasies, Reminiscences, Dreams, Nightmares

CHAPTER 9

Between Musicology and Mythology at the *Stunde Null*
Austria's 950th "Birthday" and the 50th Anniversary of Bruckner's Death

LAP-KWAN KAM

Writers delight in rhyme, and in the title above, musicology rhymes nicely with mythology. But a question arises immediately: shouldn't the *logos* of musicology dispel the *mythos* surrounding music? *Entzauberung der Welt* (disenchantment of the world)—that is what Max Weber, though not without ambivalence, takes the development of modern science to mean. From the beginning, however, Nazi musicologists have been accused of "myth-making."[1] For many were those who should have been servants of *logos* but instead became masters of *mythos*, doctoring the history of German music in the service of Nazism. This chapter attempts, on the one hand, to extend the inquiry to the so-called *Stunde Null* (zero hour) in Austria once the Germans were gone—for beginnings often set the tone for the things to come—and, on the other hand, to adopt William McNeill's argument that the most truth historians can ever achieve "might best be called mythistory."[2] This rhetorical tactic aims not to dismiss Weber's call for the separation of fact and value in our research, but, by interrogating claims of scientific objectivity, to alert musicologists to the suppressed dimension of ethics in our profession since its beginning in the age of positivism.[3]

In the Beginning: 1885 and 1945

In the 1885 inaugural essay of the first specialized musicological journal, and of the discipline in general, Guido Adler proclaimed the twin objectives of the science of music with the rhyming couplet "Erforschung des Wahren und Förderung des Schönen" ("exploration of the True and cultivation of the Beautiful").[4] Here the position of primacy given to the True corresponds to Adler's priority of searching for "highest laws." According to the methodological divide of Wilhelm Windelband, this falls more on the "nomothetic" side of natural sciences than the "idiographic" side of the humanities.[5] "The art historian will operate the same methods as the natural scientist: primarily the inductive method," Adler makes clear; "the emphasis here lies in the analogy between the methodologies of the science of art and the science of nature."[6] In that same year, Leopold von Ranke summed up his maxim of modern historiography with this conviction: "I turned away completely from fiction and resolved to avoid any invention and imagination in my work and to keep strictly to the facts."[7] Yet not long after the nonagenarian Ranke and the thirty-year-old Adler declared their positions, a rethinking of positivistic scholarship was already emerging; an iconoclastic 1907 study by Francis MacDonald Cornford even called Thucydides—the father of "scientific history"—a "mythistorian," not unlike his predecessor Herodotus.[8] Cornford argued that even the most scientific representation of the past should be recognized as a kind of mythic narrative. But the neologism "mythistory" was perhaps too provocative for the early twentieth century and remained in a *Dornröschenschlaf*.

By the 1950s, however, the ideas of myth and mythology, literally "story" and "the telling of stories," had been taken up pervasively—most notably in the structural anthropology of Claude Lévi-Strauss, the semiotic cultural theory of Roland Barthes, and the literary criticism of Northrop Frye.[9] Later, historians reoriented their disciplines in response to the cultural and linguistic turns; they called this response the "new cultural history."[10] In his influential 1979 essay "The Revival of Narrative," Lawrence Stone rediscovered "understanding based on observation, experience, judgment and intuition" as a historical methodology.[11] The year 1985 saw McNeill reintroducing the notion of "mythistory" in his inaugural address as president of the American Historical Association.[12] Contending with "the limits of scientific history" for failing to "give meaning or intelligibility to the record of the past," McNeill aspires instead to a history that is "understandable and credible," but also "useful" as "a font of practical wisdom upon which people may draw when making decisions and taking action."[13] At the same time, he is prudent enough to concede that "the result might best be called mythistory perhaps, ... for the same words that constitute truth for some are, and always will be, myth for others," yet he believes that "ever-evolving mythistories will indeed become truer and more adequate to public life ... so that men and women will know how to act more wisely than is possible for us today."[14] As J. M. Roberts concludes in a review of McNeill's address, "from that follows the historian's public responsibility."[15]

Music-making and mythmaking provide enough materials with which to reflect on the "public responsibility" of musicologists. This is the dimension absent in Adler's inception of musicology. It was a birth defect of the discipline that manifested its symptoms in the fateful years during and after the Hitler era. In this chapter, the focus will be on the cluster of myths at the *Stunde Null* in postwar Austria: Austria as the 950-year-old "Holy Land of Music" sustained in 1946 by martyr saints such as the native Anton Bruckner, whose fiftieth death anniversary also fell in that year. Both the *tabula rasa* of the past and the identification of music-historical martyrs were crucial components of musical Austria's postwar reinvention of itself. But the most foundational myth of all was clearly the Moscow Declaration of 1943 that proclaimed Austria to have been Nazi Germany's first victim. This chapter will show that many Austrian musicologists after 1945 were propagators of these "self-flattering" mythistories, "vivid, simplified portraits of their admirable virtues and undeserved sufferings," as McNeill says.[16] Though less brutal and bloody than those Nazi mythmakers, they nevertheless hindered or at least delayed Austria's proper understanding of itself and others.

The First Concert in a New Austria

If one musical event could epitomize the bewilderments of the *Stunde Null* in Austria, it would be the very first official (but not yet public) concert of the Vienna Philharmonic Orchestra (VPO) on 27 April 1945.[17] For it was on this day that Austria's *Anschluss* with Hitler's Germany, in place since 1938, was declared null and void and a provisional government formed with the task of rebuilding an independent republic. But the orchestra and its repertoire did not quite match the occasion. Just a few weeks earlier, the same orchestra had given its last public concert—ending with Richard Wagner's *Tannhäuser* overture—in Nazi Austria.[18] Recent research has revealed that some 20 percent of the VPO's members had covertly joined the Nazi Party even before the *Anschluss* in 1938. Soon after 1938 the orchestra declared itself *Judenrein* (cleansed of Jews) and became a vessel of cultural propaganda *par excellence* for the Third Reich. By its centenary in 1942, almost half of its musicians were party members.[19]

The concert program began with Schubert (the "Unfinished" Symphony) and Beethoven (*Leonore* Overture no. 3). It was rounded off, however, with Tchaikovsky (Symphony no. 5) instead of a work from the copious Austro-German repertoire. This requires closer scrutiny. Above all, the program's Russian accent apparently was a gesture in the direction of the Soviet occupying authorities (French, American, and British troops came days later).[20] Without sanction from the Red Army, neither the cultural event nor the political proclamations of the day could have taken place at all.

On the other hand, the choice of Tchaikovsky also signaled an attempted break with Nazi cultural politics. Indeed, in the early years of the war, Tchaikovsky was generally performed in Vienna almost as often as Bruckner. From 1 September 1939 until 15 July 1941—the day Russian music was banned by the Reich Music Chamber in the wake of the German invasion of the Soviet Union (Operation Barbarossa)[21]—the VPO played works by the two composers fourteen times each; after the embargo until this first postwar concert in 1945, Tchaikovsky was performed only once and Bruckner thirty times.[22] From this perspective, then, the rehabilitation of Tchaikovsky in April 1945 should have been as gratifying to the Russians as to the Austrians.[23]

Nevertheless, a certain Josef Schöner, an Austrian diplomat dismissed by the Nazis in 1939 and reinstated in 1945, wrote in his diary after attending the concert, "besides the two [Schubert and Beethoven], Tchaikovsky appears un-European in spite of all his Western allures. ... Admirable, magnificent, but alien, never quite comprehensible for us, just like Russia!"[24] This comment needs to be understood in a local context. Even Beethoven—now a non-Austrian—was alien enough for Schöner, he continues. Only Schubert and Bruckner were truly Austrian: "[Schubert's] themes touch on the mystical essence of the soul and always seize me deeper than the combative towering blocks of Beethoven. [Schubert] possesses the direct 'divine ancestry' in music, as does after him only Bruckner."[25] These convictions were hardly unaffected by political reality. They reflected general resentment among Austrians towards both the German domination (as most Austrians now wished to see it) that had just ended and the Russian occupation that had just begun, with no end in sight.

Just as bewildering that day was that both the political and the musical acts of renewal were led by, of all people, two personages who had not resisted the *Anschluss*: the veteran socialist politician Karl Renner was among the endorsers of the union in 1938,[26] and the conductor Clemens Krauss, director of the Vienna State Opera since 1929, had "betrayed" his native Austria to pursue a career in Hitler's Germany in 1934, just months after Nazi agents assassinated Austria's chancellor Engelbert Dollfuss.[27] No wonder Schöner remarks that Krauss was greeted at the concert with audibly less applause than the orchestra and even with some hisses, since many in the audience still remembered his scandalous departure from Vienna.[28] This *Stunde Null* concert did indicate a certain break with the past. But even more, it signaled new entanglements, symbolic of things to come in Austria for decades.

New/Renewed Mythmaking, 1946

The Moscow Declaration of 1943 made the myth of the *Stunde Null* possible for Austria, for it recognized Austria as Nazi Germany's first victim. This myth formation worked in a manner not dissimilar to the later West German *Aufarbeitung der Vergangenheit* ("working through the past"), famously criticized by Theodor W. Adorno: "its intention is to close the books on the past and ... even remove it from memory" without "serious working upon the past." The irony, Adorno argues, is that "the attitude that everything should be forgotten and forgiven, which would be proper for those who suffered injustice, is practiced by those party supporters who committed the injustice."[29] This, as we shall see, was the case when it came to reframing Austria's music history after 1945. Those doing the reframing were often scholars who had told a starkly different story in the years of the *Ostmark* (the "Eastern March," Austria's official designation during the union with Nazi Germany).

The myth of the *Stunde Null* served to disconnect Austria from its past with Hitler's Germany. The other side of the coin is that additional myths emerged to reconnect it with its own long past. Not surprisingly, some historians doubted whether the so-called Ostarrîchi Document of 996, in which the German name of Austria, *Österreich* (Eastern Realm), was first recorded, could be seen as a birth certificate firm enough to justify commemorations of a 950th anniversary in 1946.[30] Politicians including the federal president and chancellor also worried that the attention to the "Eastern Realm" would evoke the Nazi designation "Eastern March."[31] Nevertheless, the festivities, which lasted seven weeks, did succeed in constructing the myth of Austrians as people of culture, as peacemakers and mediators between East and West, and, above all, as victims and not compatriots of the Germans.

Musically, a cluster of myths was also constructed during the commemoration year; the fiftieth anniversary of Bruckner's death added a contemporary accent. The order of the day was to demarcate the national and cultural identities of Austria from those of Germany—a reversal of the rhetoric leading to the *Anschluss* in 1938.[32] This program of mythmaking could be divided into three interrelated myths of transformation: first, from the politically diminished Austria into a cultural giant with a thousand-year history of adeptness; second, from "Germany, a Land of Music" into "Austria, the Holy Land of Music"; and third, from a heroic narrative to a hagiographical one: Austria as victim and even martyr, represented by saints such as Bruckner.

The first myth, that of the rump state as cultural giant with a millennium of cultural memory, was taken up by Erich Schenk, a doyen of postwar Austrian musicology with a dubious Nazi past. In the first year of the *Anschluss*, Schenk, a protégé of Hitler's chief ideologue Alfred Rosenberg but not a party member, was called to Vienna from the modest and remote Rostock University as successor to the Nazi Robert Lach. Within a year, Schenk was made chair of the musicological institute, and in 1944, just before the end of the war, he was appointed a member of the Austrian Academy of Sciences. Schenk was able to keep all these positions after 1945—bona fide membership of the Nazi Party was the sole criterion in the Austrian denazification process—and even took up the presidency of Vienna University in the academic year 1957–58.[33] Schenk's notorious *MGG* entry on himself in 1963, which covered up his wartime complicity and claimed allegiance to Adler and his legacy, reads like a study in mythmaking.[34]

Schenk organized the musical program of the 950-year commemoration in 1946 and wrote a booklet, *950 Years of Music in Austria*, which came out just in time for the occasion.[35] In its haste to disavow the Nazi ideology of ethnic purity, the booklet's very first sentence comes across like self-denazification: "the music of Austria is the result of a intermingling process of European cultural values."[36] Strikingly absent is any mention of the Nazi past; Schenk only touches on Austria's "painful experience of this century" without calling the devil by its name.[37]

The newly established semiprofessional journal *Österreichische Musikzeitschrift* (Austrian Music Journal) also devoted a double issue, in October/November 1946, to the theme "950 years of Austria." Most contributors to the issue offer the same rhetoric of suffering and sublimity.[38] The first, Peter Lafite, the journal's founder and editor, contrasts a currently "poor country" with the "immeasurable riches" of its 950-year history.[39] Another, Hans Sittner, then acting principal of the Vienna Musikhochschule, summarizes the essence ("myth") of Austrianness as "the love of the divine, of the native nature, of life itself; a love wide and manifold as the Austrian people who—geographically and historically conditioned—through the ever give and take from all sides, has obtained its cultural profile, which differs significantly from that of other German-speaking tribes."[40]

The other two myths come from musicologists to the left of Schenk on the political spectrum. Perhaps this should come as no surprise; communists, socialists, and conservatives alike had learned solidarity through suffering together under Nazi rule.[41] This particular kind of solidarity often comes across as hagiological, as if only divine intervention could reconcile the deep hostilities between the Social Democrats and the two traditionalist camps of the *Christsozialen* and *Deutschnationalen* that long predated the Nazi years and culminated in the civil war of 1934.[42] Whereas Schiller and Beethoven sing of the reunion through the *Götterfunken* of joy ("*deine Zauber binden wieder / was die Mode streng geteilt*"), here only suffering and martyrdom could possibly transcend age-old domestic political conflicts.

The second myth is of Austria as *das Heilige Land der Tonkunst* (the holy land of music). It was advocated by Wilhelm Fischer, whom Adler designated his successor at the University of Vienna, but who eventually lost out to the anti-Semite and Nazi Robert Lach.[43] Fischer's attempted canonization of Austria via its music obviously aimed at surpassing the slogan of "*Deutschland, das Land der Musik*" (Germany, the land of music), made famous through the notorious 1938 tourism poster by Lothar Heinemann.[44] In the title essay of the second issue of *Österreichische Musikzeitschrift* in 1946, Fischer claimed that Austria was the holy land of music and justified this not with the immortal works of Haydn, Mozart, Beethoven, and Schubert, but also through the composers' personal union with the "melodic sensibilities of the Austrian peoples, both German and non-German alike." The emphasis here on the "people" instead of the "heroes" is remarkable. On the victimhood of Austria in World War II, Fischer writes of "the most shameful crime ever committed against humanity around the world, [which] has drowned those sweet hopes [of Austrian music's brighter future] in a sea of blood and tears." Invoking sainthood, he states further that "the tree of art will again grow to the sky and bloom and bear splendid fruits, peaking in the spheres of immortality and broadly rooted in the soil of Austria, the holy land of music."[45]

Another contributor to the "950 years of Austria" debate was Georg Knepler, who had just returned from a decade of exile in London. Knepler—like Fischer, of Jewish ancestry—served as the cultural secretary of the Austrian Communist Party from 1946 until 1949. He then left his homeland once more to pursue his political convictions and professional career in the new East Germany.[46] Reviewing the same 950 years of Austrian music history as Erich Schenk had done, Knepler warns that "we don't want to forget that Austrian history was not as well-stocked with heroes as the French."[47] This should be read to differentiate Austria from the heroic narrative of Germany as in the Beethovenian motto of *per aspera ad astra* (through hardships to the stars). It echoes well Schöner's distaste for "the combative towering blocks of Beethoven" mentioned above.[48] Struggling, Knepler seems to suggest, is German. But suffering is Austrian.

The trajectory from victimhood to sainthood leads to the third myth: Austria as martyr saint incarnated in the figure of Anton Bruckner. He fits well into this narrative, thanks to his swift transformation from Nazi icon to mystical, pious, and ingenious Austrian. During the Nazi era, musicologists alleged that Jewish musicians such as Ferdinand Loewe and the brothers Franz and Joseph Schalk in Bruckner's circle had distorted his originality. Then, after 1945, Austrian revisionists blamed the Nazis for abusing Bruckner's "Germanness," not least in the "original" versions published in the Bruckner Collected Works series from 1930 to 1944 under the general editorship of Robert Haas, who despite having worked as Adler's assistant at the University of Vienna had joined the Nazi Party covertly in 1933.[49] Ironically, Adolf Hitler personally identified from time to time with the success of Bruckner, his compatriot from rural Upper Austria; now, after Hitler's demise, Bruckner was taken to stand for post-Nazi Austria.[50] This issue remained a matter of debate into the 1990s, especially between Austrian scholars and foreign ones. Understandably, Austrians were keen on downplaying their entanglement in Nazi ideology by arguing for Bruckner's compositional independence from Wagner. They argued that Brucker's Wagnerism was just a career tactic.[51]

Back in 1946, Bruckner was recuperated as one of the "Austrian geniuses" by Max Auer, founder and, since 1929, first president of the International Bruckner Society. Auer argues that Bruckner embodied "the highest expression of the Austrian quintessence as human and artist."[52] He also quotes the prominent Bruckner scholar Ernst Kurth's declaration that Bruckner was "the greatest musical power of the world history since Bach."[53] Auer wrote an obituary for Kurth in 1946, referring approvingly to Kurth's description of Bruckner's work as an "expiatory sacrifice" and Kurth's claim that "the world will then be mature enough for Bruckner, by the time when it needs to flee to him."[54] With such religious and mystical vocabularies as "sin offering" and "the world ... flee[ing] to him," Auer replaces a Beethovenian narrative of heroic struggling with a Christology of salvation through suffering.

A month later, Auer published another article, programmatically entitled "Tragedy and Triumph of Anton Bruckner." The triumph it signifies is not of a hero, but a martyr. First Auer sets Bruckner's biography in a tragic tone, as "a thorny life-path."[55] His assessment resonates with Schenk's portrayal of Bruckner having suffered "rather humiliating conditions" and "severe mental tumults" in his early career and been "prosecuted with the stupid fanaticism of a notorious clique system" in the later Vienna years.[56] Then Auer outdoes Schenk by exalting Bruckner's "thorny life-path" as the *Via Crucis* (the way of the cross). This allusion to Jesus's crucifixion, death and resurrection emphasizes the martyrdom of Bruckner, "whose suffering should eventually bring about the salvation of mankind."[57] The mythmaking was complete.

Commemorating Bruckner for Austria

The fiftieth anniversary of Bruckner's death was a key event within the "950 years of Austria" commemorations, and the so-called Vienna version of his Symphony no. 1 was performed at a special matinée in a lecture theater at the University of Vienna on 11 October 1946.[58] The unusual concert venue was chosen because Bruckner had taught from 1875 to 1896, mostly without remuneration, at the university, from which he received an honorary doctorate in 1891.[59] Officials of church and state were present at the 1946 ceremony, along with delegates from the Soviet Union and the Western allies—ironically, both as liberators of Austria from Germany's seven-year occupation and as representatives of an ongoing occupation. Indeed, it was another nine years before they left, after the Austrian State Treaty was signed in 1955. Under the circumstances, when Viktor Matejka, the municipal councilor responsible for culture, spoke in the opening address about "the holy obligation of Vienna to make good posthumously what malignance and ignorance had once sinned against the Master," it was not too far-fetched to hear a double entendre for both Bruckner and Austria.⁶⁰ This was again mythmaking through martyrization and hagiography.

The concert was performed by the Vienna Symphony Orchestra (VSO), which had been re-established in September 1945 after a shutdown of eight months. The denazification of the VSO had been even less effective than that of the VPO, for it had a much higher percentage of Nazi Party members among its musicians.⁶¹ The conductor of the concert was the enigmatic figure Hans Swarowsky. Banned from conducting in Nazi Germany after 1936—he was the illegitimate son of the Jewish lawyer and banker Josef Kranz and the actress Leopoldina Swarowsky—he went to work in neutral Switzerland.⁶² Both he and Clemens Krauss, however, were close to Richard Strauss—together they assisted him in the writing of the opera *Capriccio*—and Krauss was able to bring Swarowsky back to Germany as an opera dramaturge and as music editor for the Propaganda Ministry in 1940.⁶³ In 1944 Swarowsky became chief conductor of the Cracow Philharmonic Orchestra in occupied Poland, an appointment cut short by the end of the war.⁶⁴ Whatever his entanglements in the musical politics of Nazi Germany, Swarowsky was one of the few half-Jewish musicians who managed to survive and even work under the Nazis.

The version of Bruckner's Symphony no. 1 chosen for this occasion should be taken to symbolize a new Austrian identity. In 1891, Bruckner had dedicated this symphony—composed a quarter century earlier but newly revised—to the University of Vienna as a token of gratitude for the honorary doctorate conferred on him. In 1893 it was published by Doblinger with the assistance of Cyrill Hynais, a former student of Bruckner.⁶⁵ In 1935, it was re-edited as the "Vienna" version of 1890–91 by Robert Haas in the *Bruckner Complete Works*. It was accompanied in the second half of the same volume by the "Linz" version of 1865.⁶⁶ Haas intended the publication of the original Linz version to replace the "impure" Vienna version. Indeed, his edition series preferred to publish original versions cleansed of later and "foreign" (i.e., Jewish) "contaminations."⁶⁷ The reviewer of a "monthly journal for the spiritual renewal of German music" wrote that the first symphony "release[d] itself with elemental force in the swelling vitality of an extremely robust nature," and he wished that "in the ingeniously powerful Linz version [it] could conquer the deserved place in German musical life."⁶⁸ Indeed, months before its publication, the Linz version was given its first performance, at the Fourth Bruckner Festival of the International Bruckner Society in Aachen in September 1934. The conductor was Peter Raabe, successor to Richard Strauss as president of the *Reichsmusikkammer* from 1935 until his suicide shortly before the end of the war.⁶⁹

The 1946 performance of the Vienna version, consequently, could be interpreted as an act of denazification, since both Haas, the editor, and Raabe, the conductor of the premiere of the Linz version, were committed Nazis. On a deeper level, Bruckner's formal revisions in the Vienna version might also suggest, metaphorically, Austria's regaining of self-possession.[70] Ironically, the score that was used for this performance was Haas's of 1935—a revised edition of the Vienna version did not appear until 1980.[71] Further confusion was caused by questions about the political integrity of the conductor, Swarowsky; though much less prominent than Raabe, he had also worked for the Nazis, as mentioned above.[72] All in all, one could say that the whole performance as symbol of denazification and liberation was also a kind of mythmaking, albeit a confused one.

But amnesia was not so easily achieved. In the postwar years, the Linz version, whether in the 1935 Haas edition or the new one by Leopold Nowak of 1953 (Nowak replaced the disgraced Haas at both the National Library and the *Bruckner Complete Edition*), was still widely preferred, and not only in Germany—exceeding the hope of the *Zeitschrift für Musik* reviewer in 1936.[73] The Vienna version in Günter Brosche's new edition of 1980 gained currency only slowly through performances and recordings such as those by Günther Wand, Gennadi Rozhdestvensky, Riccardo Chailly, Michael Gielen, and, more recently, Claudio Abbado.[74] To make the story yet more complex, recent research has shown that neither edition of the Linz version is the "original" of 1865 or 1866 as claimed by Haas and Nowak. After leaving Linz for Vienna in late 1868, Bruckner had already undertaken some modifications of the symphony, in 1877 and 1884, though not as wide-ranging as the major revision in 1890–91.[75]

That being the case, even if most of the audience at that concert on 4 September 1934 in Aachen could neither have known nor accepted Nelson Goodman's radical thesis that performances with a single note's difference are not instances of the same work,[76] what they heard that evening, starting from the very first bar, was not exactly what the audience had heard in Linz in 1868, but a version already reflecting later revisions in Vienna.[77] But even if audiences today might not recognize differences between the editions in detail, and regardless of one's preference for youthful spontaneity or mature sophistication, the notorious Wagnerian third theme with the *Tannhäuser* figuration is unmistakable in all versions.[78] So to "de-Wagnerize" Bruckner, as advocated by some Austrian scholars, is a convoluted and complex maneuver.[79] And when that fortissimo passage was blasted out at the October 1946 concert, some among the audience should have recalled the sound world of the last concert of the Nazi era, in early April 1945—the one performed by the VPO that ended with Wagner's *Tannhäuser* Overture.[80] For all the attempts made by various parties to distance themselves from Nazi elements in this concert and in the events of which it was a part, a perceptive listener like Schöner might well have nonetheless been haunted by mythologies of all kinds.

History and Music History at the *Stunde Null*

Such confusion would hardly be surprising. The intersection of music, politics, and national identity has been a more perplexing issue in German-speaking Austria than in Germany itself.[81] The new republic born after World War I inherited an imperial heritage in which political or cultural nationalism was more the exception than the rule, but it was left with a predominantly German population whose national aspirations—originally the new 1918 republic called itself "German Austria" and declared itself part of a (greater) German Republic—proved traumatic.[82] By contrast, the founders of the Second Republic after World War II preferred a new *Staatsidee* (idea of state). At a rally of his own Austrian People's Party celebrating "950 years of Austria" on 27 October 1946, Leopold Figl, the first federal chancellor, asserted that "all people of our country are today aware of the fact that it represents something entirely their own: not the second German state in Europe and not a subspecies of the German, but an Austrian people."[83] Indeed, a certain degree of historical amnesia was a precondition for the genesis of the People's Party. Although founded in 1945, it inherited many members of the conservative camps that grew out of both the Christian Social movement of the populist anti-Semite and German nationalist Karl Lueger and the later Austrofascism of Dollfuss and Kurt Schuschnigg.[84]

This political *modus vivendi*, based on the suppression of Austria's German identity and amnesia of its entanglement with Nazism, became a long-lasting intellectual problem for postwar scholars in Austria. This could be illustrated by the two editions of the widely received reference work *Music History of Austria*.[85] The first edition was published in two volumes (in 1977 and 1979) under the aegis of the newly founded Österreichische Gesellschaft für Musikwissenschaft (Austrian Society for Musicology).[86] The book project was a product of the "1000 Years of Austria" commemoration in 1976.[87] In the two volumes, comprising almost one thousand pages, the editors devote only a subsection of two pages to the music history of the *Ostmark* under the Nazis. Within this limited space, the calamities are much played down. The author does disclose that musicians of a "politically or racially questionable nature had to reckon with debarment," but without mentioning any further persecution or consequences for individual liberty or indeed life; instead of expressing sympathy for human suffering, the primary concern falls on music making: "understandably the quality of performances in the wake of such constraints could not be guaranteed. Yet enough eminent artists remained in the country to demonstrate to the world the now politically propagated function of Vienna as the 'city of music.'"[88] In lieu of any attempt at *Vergangenheitsbewältigung*, there are only selective facts and mundane concerns. The show must go on; after all, "enough eminent artists remained in the country."[89]

On 8 May 1985, forty years after Nazi Germany's capitulation, Richard von Weizsäcker, president of West Germany, exhorted his compatriots to admit that "there was no *Stunde Null*" and to "face up as well as we can to the truth."[90] Around the same time, Kurt Waldheim, the conservative candidate for the Austrian presidency, published an autobiography in which he intentionally concealed his service in the Wehrmacht.[91] In spite (or because?) of this, Austrians voted Waldheim into office in 1986. But in the wake of the "Waldheim Affair," the commemorations of fifty years after the *Anschluss* in 1988, and last but not least the upsurge of the right-wing populist Freedom Party, whose charismatic and controversial leader Jörg Haider went as far as to praise the "orderly employment policies of the Third Reich" in 1991, the Austrian government finally admitted responsibility for the misdeeds during the Nazi era. In 1993, Chancellor Franz Vranitzky paid his first official visit to Israel to seek forgiveness and reconciliation, followed by President Thomas Klestil a year later.[92] Musicology still had not caught up. In the "second, revised and greatly expanded edition," now in three volumes, of *Musikgeschichte Österreichs* in 1995 the subsection "Music of the Eastern March" is still about two pages long. Nevertheless, it is now situated in the more explicit context of the chapter "From the First to the Second Republic"—and cold-blooded comments such as the one about "enough eminent artists remain[ing] in the country" were deleted.[93]

Mythistory and Musicology

As late as the very last years of the twentieth century, research on the *Anschluss* years was still rejected in some quarters of Austria as "patricidal."[94] This reaction in turn confirms the psychological and mythical dimensions of historiography. People, even scholars, prefer what McNeill classifies as "self-flattering" versions of mythistories of their own past.[95] In the case of Austria, political scientist Anton Pelinka and historian Gerhard Botz suggest that the myth of the Moscow Declaration functions as a national *Lebenslüge* (life-lie), a notion borrowed from Henrik Ibsen's 1884 play *The Wild Duck*.[96] In the final act of the play, Dr. Relling admits to having used a life-lie as therapy, "invented to keep up a spark of life" in one of the protagonists. Later comes the famous quote from the doctor: "deprive the average person of his life-lie, and you deprive him of his happiness at the same stroke."[97] The Moscow Declaration of 1943 is a good example of mythistory. Its "victim myth" was the "life-lie" that several generations of Austrians used to suppress their pasts and support their futures.

As the examples in this chapter have shown, several interrelated mythistories served as musical life-lies for the Austrians of 1946: that there was a *Stunde Null* at which Austria could break free from the past but which at the same time marked a return to a thousand-year history of music; that Austria was a holy land of music that embraced the cultures of different ethnicities; and finally, that this holy land was served by martyr saints such as Bruckner, whose suffering stood for Austria's fate at the hands of Nazi Germany. But such "self-flattering" version of mythistories had a price. It has taken a long time for Austrian musicologists, Guido Adler's heirs, to investigate how and why their predecessors such as Schenk had been "willing executioners" of Nazism, or how and why traditional, popular, and minority cultures had been underrepresented in the music historiography.[98]

McNeill does not discuss historians acting as "willing executioners," but he is aware that "mythical, self-flattering versions of the past may push a people toward suicidal behavior, as Hitler's last days may remind us."[99] Such cases of taking value as fact, intentionally or not, led Weber to claim that scientific research should be free of value judgment.[100] Nonetheless, McNeill advocates a kind of "mythistory" that seeks broader meaning over the kind of scientific history that produces compartmentalized knowledge. "Unalterable and eternal Truth," he concedes, "remains like the Kingdom of Heaven, an eschatological hope. Mythistory is what we actually have," even if he does retain faith in the self-correcting mechanism of the "free marketplace of ideas."[101] Admittedly, the many instances of musicological mythmaking reviewed here belong to the self-flattering type that fulfills the popular demand for "simplified portraits of ... admirable virtues and undeserved sufferings."[102] Yet McNeill's appeal to the "moral duty of the historical profession" and a "more rigorous and reflective epistemology" is all the more valid for musicology.[103]

In 1987, shortly before the still unforeseeable fall of the Iron Curtain, scholars from eastern and western Europe concerned themselves with the "political responsibility of intellectuals" in two meetings at the Institut für Wissenschaften vom Menschen (Institute for Human Sciences) in Vienna.[104] Yet there was no "contemplating" of this subject in Joseph Kerman's influential "challenges to musicology" of 1985.[105] Only in the 1990s did a younger generation of musicologists start to reflect on such "extra-musical" issues.[106] In his inaugural conception of musicology a century ago, Adler did acknowledge the "troubled condition" of arts in his time, but regarded possible contributions to its improvement by musicology only as a side-effect of the "absolute," pure, "end-in-itself," endeavors of this nascent discipline.[107] He seems to have assumed that if musicology concentrated solely its scientific and artistic vocations ("exploration of the true and cultivation of the beautiful") it would not need to bother itself with professional ethical dilemmas and conflicts.[108] But as the examples of musicology's entanglements with "self-flattering" mythology in postwar Austria convey, it is evil rather than good that can happen inadvertently, or in Hannah Arendt's dictum, banally, through all kinds of human frailties—political naiveté, career opportunism, gutless neutrality, or confused loyalty —so much so that we musicologists should no longer (if ever we could) neglect to complement our "exploration of the true" and "cultivation of the beautiful" with a conscious and judicious "pursuit of the good."

Lap-Kwan Kam studied at the Musikhochschule and the University of Vienna and teaches at National Chiao Tung University, Taiwan. His recent research is on comparative music historiographies of Taiwan, Austria, and Canada; Mahler and Viennese modernism; and sound and music in film.

Notes

Heartfelt thanks to Thomas Irvine, Neil Gregor, and the anonymous reviewers for their valuable comments and suggestions. This research is partly supported by the Taiwan National Science Council (project no. 100-2918-I-009-001).

1. Michael Meyer, "The Nazi Musicologist as Myth Maker in the Third Reich," *Journal of Contemporary History* 10, no. 4 (1975): 649–65.
2. William H. McNeill, "Mythistory, or Truth, Myth, History, and Historians," *American Historical Review* 91, no. 1 (1986): 8.
3. Guido Adler, "Umfang, Methode und Ziel der Musikwissenschaft," *Vierteljahrsschrift für Musikwissenschaft* 1, no.1 (1885): 5–20. See also Erica Mugglestone, "Guido Adler's 'The Scope, Method, and Aim of Musicology' (1885): An English Translation with an Historico-Analytical Commentary," *Yearbook for Traditional Music* 13 (1981): 1–21; and the abridged translation by Martin Cooper in *Music in European Thought, 1851–1912*, ed. Bojan Bujić (Cambridge, 1988), 348–58.
4. Adler, "Umfang, Methode und Ziel," 20. Unless otherwise noted, all translations are mine.
5. See Kevin C. Karnes, *Music, Criticism, and the Challenge of History: Shaping Modern Musical Thought in Late Nineteenth-Century Vienna* (New York, 2008), 9–10, 63–64: and Bojan Bujić, "Musicology and Intellectual History: A Backward Glance to the Year 1885," *Proceedings of the Royal Musical Association* 111, no. 1 (1984): 139–54.
6. "... wird sich der Kunsthistoriker der gleichen Methode bedienen wie der Naturforscher: vorzugsweise der inductiven Methode ... das Schwergewicht der Betrachtung liegt in der Analogie der kunstwissenschaftlichen Methode mit der naturwissenschaftlichen Methode." Adler, "Umfang, Methode und Ziel," 15; Mugglestone, "Adler's 'The Scope, Method, and Aim,'" 3, 16 (translation modified).
7. Leopold von Ranke, "Autobiographical Dictation (November 1885)," in *The Secret of World History: Selected Writings on the Art and Science of History*, ed. Roger Wines (New York, 1981), 37.
8. Francis MacDonald Cornford, *Thucydides Mythistoricus* (London, 1907).

9. See Claude Lévi-Strauss, "The Structural Study of Myth," *Journal of American Folklore* 68 no. 270 (1955): 428–44; Roland Barthes, *Mythologies* (Paris, 1957); and Northrop Frye, *Anatomy of Criticism: Four Essays* (Princeton, 1957).
10. See, for example, Lynn Hunt, ed. *The New Cultural History: Essays* (Berkeley, 1989); and Peter Burke, ed. *New Perspectives on Historical Writing* (Cambridge, 1991).
11. Lawrence Stone, "The Revival of Narrative: Reflections on a New Old History," *Past and Present* 85 (November 1979): 19.
12. McNeill, "Mythistory," 1–10. See also Joseph Mali, *Mythistory: The Making of a Modern Historiography* (Chicago, 2003).
13. McNeill, "Mythistory," 2.
14. Ibid., 8–9.
15. John Morris Roberts, review of *Mythistory and Other Essays*, by William H. McNeill, *Journal of Modern History* 60, no. 4 (1988): 732.
16. McNeill, "Mythistory," 6, 10.
17. "Concert in the Konzerthaus," program, Wiener Philharmoniker, retrieved 18 August 2018 from http://www.wienerphilharmoniker.at/concerts/concert-detail/event-id/8697/. See also Walter Pass, "Musikleben seit 1945," in *Musikgeschichte Österreichs*, ed. Rudolf Flotzinger and Gernot Gruber (Graz, 1979), 2:483.
18. This concert was held on 2 April 1945. See "Philharmonische Akademie," program, Wiener Philharmoniker, retrieved 18 August 2018 from http://www.wienerphilharmoniker.at/konzerte/konzertdetail/event-id/8415/.
19. See the 2013 reports of the research team Oliver Rathkolb, Bernadette Mayrhofer, and Fritz Trümpi, "Wiener Philharmoniker—Geschichtlicher Überblick zur NS-Zeit," on the Wiener Philharmoniker website. See also Fritz Trümpi, *Politisierte Orchester: Die Wiener Philharmoniker und das Berliner Philharmonische Orchester im Nationalsozialismus* (Vienna, 2011).
20. On 21 April 1945, the Red Army had been treated to an exclusive performance at the same venue. See "Konzert für russische Soldaten," Wiener Konzerthaus, retrieved 18 August 2018 from https://konzerthaus.at/konzert/eventid/14156 (program and performer unspecified).
21. Amtliche Mitteilungen der Reichsmusikkammer, quoted in Alan E. Steinweis, *Art, Ideology, and Economics in Nazi Germany: The Reich Chambers of Music, Theater, and the Visual Arts* (Chapel Hill, 1993), 116.
22. Statistics calculated by the author using VPO's "Archivdatenbank," an online database of all concerts since its establishment in 1842 (https://www.wienerphilharmoniker.at/konzerte/archive).
23. Thanks to Neil Gregor for bringing up this aspect.
24. Josef Schöner, *Wiener Tagebuch 1944/1945*, ed. Eva-Marie Csáky, Franz Matscher, and Gerald Stourzh (Vienna, 1992), 192 ["Neben den beiden wirkt Tschaikowsky trotz seines westlichen Parfüms doch uneuropäisch ... Bewundernswert, großartig, aber fremd, uns nie ganz faßbar, wie eben Rußland!"].
25. Ibid. ["... seine Themen rühren an mystische Urgründe der Seele und packen mich stets tiefer als die kämpferisch getürmten Blöcke eines Beethoven ... Er besitzt die unmittelbare 'Gotteskindschaft' in der Musik, wie nach ihm nur noch Bruckner"].
26. Renner is called "der Mann mit den zwei Gesichtern" (the man with the two faces) in Oliver Rathkolb, *Die paradoxe Republik: Österreich 1945 bis 2005* (Vienna, 2005), 113–18.

27. See Michael H. Kater, *The Twisted Muse: Musicians and Their Music in the Third Reich* (New York, 1997), 46–55.
28. Schöner, *Wiener Tagebuch*, 191.
29. Theodor W. Adorno, "The Meaning of Working through the Past," in *Critical Models: Interventions and Catchwords*, trans. Henry W. Pickford (New York, 2005), 89.
30. Stefan Spevak, *Das Jubiläum '950 Jahre Österreich': Eine Aktion zur Schaffung eines österreichischen Staats- und Kulturbewußtseins im Jahre 1946* (Vienna, 2003), 43–46. An earlier birth year for Austria was later set at the beginning of Babenberg rule in 976; consequently, two nationwide millennium commemorations were held in 1976 and 1996.
31. Ibid., 58–60.
32. See Robert Lach's two essays with the same title, "Das Österreichertum in der Musik" (The Austrianness in music), published in 1929 and 1938. See also Lap-Kwan Kam, "The Musicologist as Historian and Patriot: Imagining National Identity with the Musical Past in Modern Austria," *Guandu Music Journal* 11 (2009): 197.
33. See Anna Maria Pammer, "Musikgeschichte im 'Dritten Reich': Am Beispiel des Musikwissenschaftlers Erich Schenk" (MPhil thesis, University of Vienna, 2013); and Matthias Pape, "Erich Schenk – ein österreichischer Musikwissenschaftler in Salzburg, Rostock und Wien: Musikgeschichtsschreibung zwischen großdeutscher und kleinösterreichischer Staatsidee," *Musikforschung* 53 (2000): 413–31.
34. Erich Schenk, "Schenk, Erich," in *Die Musik in Geschichte und Gegenwart* [MGG], vol. 11, ed. Friedrich Blume (Kassel, 1963), columns 1664–66. See also Yukiko Sakabe, "Erich Schenk und der Fall Adler-Bibliothek," in *Musik-Wissenschaft an ihren Grenzen: Manfred Angerer zum 50. Geburtstag*, ed. Dominik Schweiger, Michael Staudinger, and Nikolaus Urbanek (Frankfurt, 2004), 383–92.
35. Spevak, *Das Jubiläum*, 52–54, 142–52, 262–63.
36. Erich Schenk, *950 Jahre Musik in Österreich* (Vienna, 1946), 3.
37. Ibid., 4. See also Kam, "Musicologist as Historian and Patriot," 197–98.
38. Peter Lafite et al., "950 Jahre Österreich: Minnesang/Renaissance/Barock/Klassik und Romantik/Zeitgenössische Musik/Der österreichische Musikdialekt," *Österreichische Musikzeitschrift* (hereafter ÖMz) 1, no. 10–11 (1946): 325–64.
39. Ibid., 325.
40. Ibid., 364.
41. Heidemarie Uhl, "From Discourse to Representation: 'Austrian Memory' in Public Space," in *Narrating the Nation: Representations in History, Media and the Arts*, ed. Stefan Berger, Linas Eriksonas, and Andrew Mycock (New York, 2008), 212.
42. For a survey of the political landscape of Austria in the twentieth century, see Ernst Hanisch, *Der lange Schatten des Staates: Österreichische Gesellschaftsgeschichte im 20. Jahrhundert* (Vienna, 1994), 117–53.
43. Pammer, "Musikgeschichte," 33–34.
44. Lothar Heinemann, "Deutschland, das Land der Musik," Reichsbahnzentrale für den Deutschen Reiseverkehr, 1938. See Pascal Huynh, "'… dunkler die Geigen …': Das 'Dritte Reich' und die Musik," trans. Uta Goridis, in *Das "Dritte Reich" und die Musik*, ed. Stiftung Schloss Neuhardenberg and Cité de la musique, Paris (Berlin, 2006), 9–19.

45. Wilhelm Fischer, "Von der Eigenart der österreichischen Tonkunst," ÖMz 1, no. 2 (1946): 46–47.
46. Gerhard Oberkofler and Manfred Mugrauer, *Georg Knepler: Musiker und marxistischer Denker aus Wien* (Innsbruck, 2014), 121–94.
47. Georg Knepler, "950 Jahre Österreich: wichtigstes Kapitel unserer Musikgeschichte," *Die Woche*, 13 and 20 October 1946, 4.
48. Schöner, *Wiener Tagebuch*, 192.
49. See Morten Solvik, "The International Bruckner Society and the NSDAP: A Case Study of Robert Haas and the Critical Edition," *Musical Quarterly* 82, no. 2 (1998): 362–82; and Benjamin Korstvedt, "Defining the 'Problem': The Development of Postwar Attitudes toward Bruckner Versions," *Journal of Musicological Research* 32, no. 1 (2013): 1–27.
50. See Christa Brüstle, *Anton Bruckner und die Nachwelt: Zur Rezeptionsgeschichte des Komponisten in der ersten Hälfte des 20. Jahrhunderts* (Stuttgart, 1998), 57–72.
51. See Bryan Gilliam, "The Annexation of Anton Bruckner: Nazi Revisionism and the Politics of Appropriation," *Musical Quarterly* 78, no. 3 (1994): 584–604; and the subsequent debate between Gilliam and Manfred Wagner, with further contributions by Leon Botstein and Korstvedt, all in *Musical Quarterly* 80, no. 1 (1996): 1–11, 118–160. See also Neil Gregor's chapter in this volume.
52. Max Auer, "Der Genius austriacus bei den Salzburger Festspielen," ÖMz 1, no. 7 (1946): 236 ["höchste Ausdruck österreichischen Wesens als Mensch und Künstler"].
53. Ibid. ["größte musikalische Macht der Weltgeschichte seit Bach"].
54. Max Auer, "In memoriam Dr. Ernst Kurth," ÖMz 1, no. 9 (1946): 315 ["Sühneopfer … die Welt wird für Bruckner dann reif sein, wenn sie zu ihm flüchten muß"].
55. Max Auer, "Tragik und Sieg Anton Bruckners," ÖMz 1, no. 9 (1946): 289 ["einen dornenreichen Lebensgang"].
56. Schenk, *950 Jahre Musik in Österreich*, 98 ["unter recht demütigenden Bedingungen," "unter schwersten seelischen Erschütterungen"], 99 ["verfolgte ihn … mit dem stupiden Fanatismus eines notorischen Cliquentums"].
57. Auer, "Tragik und Sieg," 289 ["ja einen Kreuzweg, dessen Qual sich schließlich zum Heil für die Menschheit auswirken sollte"].
58. Viktor Matejka, ed., *Wiener Bruckner-Fest zum 50. Todestag des Meisters veranstaltet von der Stadt Wien … 10.–27. Oktober 1946* (Vienna, 1946).
59. Hans-Joachim Hinrichsen, ed. *Bruckner-Handbuch* (Stuttgart, 2010), xiii–xxiii. It should be noted that the Universities of Cambridge and Philadelphia rejected Bruckner's approach regarding an honorary degree in 1882 and 1885, respectively.
60. Spevak, *Das Jubiläum*, 145.
61. Manfred Permoser, *Die Wiener Symphoniker im NS-Staat* (Frankfurt, 2000).
62. See *Oesterreichisches Musiklexikon Online*, s.v. "Swarowsky, Hans," by Erika Hitzler, retrieved 18 August 2018 from https://www.musiklexikon.ac.at/ml/musik_S/Swarowsky_Hans.xml; and Manfred Huss, "Hans Swarowsky und die Lehre von der Interpretation in der zweiten Wiener Schule," in *Die Lehre von der musikalischen Aufführung in der Wiener Schule: Verhandlungen des Internationalen Colloquiums Wien 1995*, ed. Markus Grassl and Reinhard Kapp (Vienna, 2002), 377.
63. See Hans Joachim Moser, "Von der Tätigkeit der Reichsstelle für Musikbearbeitungen," in *Jahrbuch der deutschen Musik*, ed. Hellmuth von Hase

(Leipzig, 1943), 78; and Fred K. Prieberg, *Handbuch Deutsche Musiker 1933–1945*, 2nd ed. (Auprès de Zombry, 2009), 7613–14.

64. See Bálint András Varga, "Hans Swarowsky: 1899–1975," in *From Boulanger to Stockhausen: Interviews and a Memoir* (Rochester, 2013), 99–106.
65. Anton Bruckner, *Erste Symphonie (c-Moll) für grosses Orchester*, ed. Cyrill Hynais (Vienna, 1893), plate no. D.1868.
66. Bruckner, *I. Symphonie c-Moll (Wiener und Linzer Fassung): Partituren und Entwürfe mit Bericht*, ed. Robert Haas, vol. 1, *Anton Bruckner: Sämtliche Werke* (Vienna, 1935). See also Brüstle, *Anton Bruckner*, 142–48.
67. Benjamin Korstvedt, "'Return to the Pure Sources': The Ideology and Text-Critical Legacy of the First Bruckner *Gesamtausgabe*," in *Bruckner Studies*, ed. Paul Hawkshaw and Timothy Jackson (Cambridge, 1997), 91–109.
68. Horst Büttner, "Die Linzer Fassung von Bruckners Erster Sinfonie," *Zeitschrift für Musik: Monatsschrift für eine geistige Erneuerung der deutschen Musik* 103, no. 4 (1936): 471 ["in ihr die quellende Lebenskraft einer urgesunden Natur mit elementarer Gewalt sich entlädt"], 473 ["daß sich die Erste in ihrer kraftgenialischen Linzer Fassung den gebührenden Platz im deutschen Musikleben erobert"].
69. Nina Okrassa, *Peter Raabe: Dirigent, Musikschriftsteller und Präsident der Reichsmusikkammer (1872–1945)* (Vienna, 2004), 181.
70. Julian Horton, "Psychobiography and Analysis," in *Bruckner's Symphonies: Analysis, Reception and Cultural Politics* (Cambridge, 2004), 240–55.
71. Bruckner, *I. Symphonie c-Moll. Wiener Fassung 1890/91*, ed. Günther Brosche, 2nd rev. ed., vol. I/2, *Anton Bruckner: Sämtliche Werke* (Vienna, 1980).
72. Moser, "Reichsstelle für Musikbearbeitungen," 78; Prieberg, *Handbuch*, 7613–14.
73. Büttner, "Die Linzer Fassung," 473.
74. See the Bruckner discography compiled by John F. Berky: "Discography," abruckner.com, retrieved 18 August 2018 from https://www.abruckner.com/discography/symphonyno1incmino/.
75. Thomas Röder, "Die Erste Symphonie als 'Linzer' Werk: Eine vorläufige Bilanz," in *Bruckner-Tagung Wien 1999: Bericht*, ed. Elisabeth Maier, Andrea Harrandt, and Erich Wolfgang Partsch (Vienna, 2000), 47–57.
76. Nelson Goodman, *Languages of Art: An Approach to a Theory of Symbols* (Indianapolis, 1968), 186.
77. Edited by Thomas Röder and premiered by Cornelius Meister with the ORF Radio-Symphonieorchester Wien at the Salzburg Festival in August 2014. See Röder, "Zur Neuausgabe der ersten Symphonie von Anton Bruckner."
78. Figure C in the editions of Haas (1935) and Nowak (1953), Figure F in Brosche (1980); in the latter version, the trombones are reinforced by the trumpets. See also Brüstle, *Anton Bruckner*, 148.
79. See Manfred Wagner, "Response to Bryan Gilliam regarding Bruckner and National Socialism," *Musical Quarterly* 80 no. 1 (1996): 123.
80. See n. 18 above.
81. See Celia Applegate and Pamela Potter, eds., *Music and German National Identity* (Chicago, 2002). There, the discussion about Austria is mainly subsumed under Germany; Austria is in focus only in the last few pages (302–4).
82. For an overview that traces the quandary back to the failed 1848 revolution and the constitutional era of the 1860s, see David Brodbeck, *Defining* Deutschtum: *Political*

Ideology, German Identity, and Music-Critical Discourse in Liberal Vienna (New York, 2014), 1–22.
83. Quoted in Spevak, *Das Jubiläum*, 184 ["Die gesamte Bevölkerung unseres Landes ist sich heute der Tatsache bewußt, daß sie etwas durchaus Eigenes darstellt, nicht den zweiten deutschen Staat in Europa und auch keine Abart des deutschen Volkes, sondern ein österreichisches Volk"].
84. See Anton Pelinka, "Die Österreichische Volkspartei (ÖVP)," in *Christlich-demokratische und konservative Parteien in Westeuropa*, vol. 1, *Bundesrepublik Deutschland, Österreich*, ed. Hans-Joachim Veen (Paderborn, 1983), 195–265.
85. See Lap-Kwan Kam, "Writing Music History in Austria and Taiwan: Some Preliminary Observations," *Humanitas Taiwanica* 61 (November 2004): 110–16.
86. Rudolf Flotzinger and Gernot Gruber, eds., *Musikgeschichte Österreichs*, 2 vols. (Graz, 1977, 1979).
87. Flotzinger and Gruber, "Einleitung," in ibid., 1:27. Note that there was another millennium commemoration in 1996 (see n. 30 above).
88. Friedrich C. Heller, "In der Ostmark," in ibid., 2:414 ["bei politischer oder 'rassischer' Bedenklichkeit hatten sie mit Berufsverbot zu rechnen. Solche Zwänge konnten begreiflicherweise die Qualität des Dargebotenen nicht garantieren. Doch waren genug bedeutende Künstler im Land verblieben, um der Welt die nunmehr politisch propagierte Funktion Wiens als 'Musikstadt' vorzuführen."]
89. Ibid.
90. "Gedenkveranstaltung im Plenarsaal des Deutschen Bundestages zum 40. Jahrestag des Endes des Zweiten Weltkrieges in Europa," retrieved 18 August 2018 from http://www.bundespraesident.de/SharedDocs/Reden/DE/Richard-von-Weizsaecker/Reden/1985/05/19850508_Rede.html.
91. Kurt Waldheim, *Im Glaspalast der Weltpolitik* (Düsseldorf, 1985).
92. Gerhard Botz and Gerald Sprengnagel, eds., *Kontroversen um Österreichs Zeitgeschichte: verdrängte Vergangenheit, Österreich-Identität, Waldheim und die Historiker* (Frankfurt: Campus, 1994).
93. Friedrich C. Heller, "Musik der 'Ostmark'," in Flotzinger and Gruber, eds., *Musikgeschichte Österreichs*, 2nd ed., 3:185–87.
94. Michael Staudinger, "Ein 'vatermörderisches' Projekt? Zur Geschichte der Wiener Musikwissenschaft 1920–1960," in *Musik-Wissenschaft an ihren Grenzen: Manfred Angerer zum 50. Geburtstag*, ed. Dominik Schweiger, Michael Staudinger, and Nikolaus Urbanek (Frankfurt, 2004), 393–406.
95. McNeill, "Mythistory," 5–7.
96. Gerhard Botz, "'Infelix Austria': Lebenslüge und nationale Identität in Österreich heute," *Das Jüdische Echo: Zeitschrift für Kultur und Politik* 29, no. 1 (1990): 116–20; see also Anton Pelinka, "Von der Funktionalität von Tabus: zu den 'Lebenslügen' der Zweiten Republik," in *Inventur 45/55: Österreich im ersten Jahrzehnt der Zweiten Republik*, ed. Wolfgang Kos and Georg Rigele (Vienna, 1996), 23–32.
97. Henrik Ibsen, *The Wild Duck*, in *Eight Plays* (New York, 1982), 329 (translation modified).
98. Recent efforts include Cornelia Szabó-Knotik, "Mythos Musik in Österreich: Die zweite Republik," in *Memoria Austriae I. Menschen, Mythen, Zeiten*, ed. Emil Brix, Ernst Bruckmüller, and Hannes Stekl (Vienna, 2004), 243–70; and Michael Staudinger, "'Finstere Dämonen': Zur Geschichte der Musikwissenschaft an der

Universität Wien in den Jahren 1938–1945," in *Musik in Wien 1938–1945: Symposion 2004*, ed. Carmen Ottner (Vienna, 2006), 239–55. The phrase "willing executioners" is borrowed from Daniel Jonah Goldhagen, *Hitler's Willing Executioners: Ordinary Germans and the Holocaust* (New York, 1996).
99. McNeill, "Mythistory," 6.
100. Max Weber, *The Methodology of the Social Sciences*, ed. and trans. Edward A. Shils and Henry A. Finch (Glencoe, IL, 1949).
101. McNeill, "Mythistory," 10, 4.
102. Ibid., 6.
103. Ibid., 7, 8.
104. Ian MacLean, Alan Montefiore, and Peter Winch, eds., *The Political Responsibility of Intellectuals* (Cambridge, 1990).
105. Joseph Kerman, *Contemplating Music: Challenges to Musicology* (Cambridge, MA, 1985).
106. For example, Philip V. Bohlman, "Musicology as a Political Act," *Journal of Musicology* 11, no. 4 (1993): 411–36; Ralph P. Locke, "Musicology and/as Social Concern: Imagining the Relevant Musicologist," in *Rethinking Music*, ed. Nicholas Cook and Mark Everist (Oxford, 1999), 499–550; and Kay Kaufman Shelemay, "The Impact and Ethics of Musical Scholarship," in ibid., 531–44. This awareness was partially influenced by the uptake in English-language reception of Adorno's critical theory, see Rose Rosengard Subotnik, "Adorno and the New Musicology," in *Adorno: A Critical Reader*, ed. Nigel Gibson and Andrew Rubin (Oxford, 2000), 234–54.
107. Adler, "Umfang, Methode und Ziel," 18-19 ["Die Wissenschaft wird dann *neben* der Verfolgung ihrer absoluten Bestrebungen, denen zu Folge sie sich als Selbstzweck betrachtet ... bei der Zerfahrenheit der modernen Kunstzustände und dem offenbaren Schwanken der künstlerischen Productionsthätigkeit *auch* zur Hebung der actuellen Kunstzustände beitragen"] (italics added). The original emphasis is somehow lost in the translation by breaking down Adler's long sentence into two (Mugglestone, 17) or three (Cooper, 352).
108. Adler, "Umfang, Methode und Ziel," 19 [" Vor Allem aber muß die Wissenschaft ... in richtiger Würdigung ihrer nächstliegenden Aufgaben sich selbst beschränken und so zur Meisterschaft gelangen"]; 20 ["... die Wirkung, welche hohe Güter in sich birgt: Erforschung des Wahren und Förderung des Schönen."]. The allusion to the three transcendentals of the Good, the True, and the Beautiful is missed in the translations of Mugglestone (18) and especially Cooper (353).

Bibliography

Adler, Guido. "Umfang, Methode und Ziel der Musikwissenschaft." *Vierteljahrsschrift für Musikwissenschaft* 1, no. 1 (1885): 5–20.

Adorno, Theodor W. "The Meaning of Working through the Past." In *Critical Models: Interventions and Catchwords*, translated by Henry W. Pickford, 89–103. New York: Columbia University Press, 2005.

Applegate, Celia, and Pamela Potter, eds. *Music and German National Identity*. Chicago: University of Chicago Press, 2002.

Auer, Max. "Der Genius austriacus bei den Salzburger Festspielen." *Österreichische Musikzeitschrift* 1, no. 7 (1946): 235–36.

———. "In memoriam Dr. Ernst Kurth." *Österreichische Musikzeitschrift* 1, no. 9 (1946): 315.

———. "Tragik und Sieg Anton Bruckners." *Österreichische Musikzeitschrift* 1, no. 9 (1946): 289–91.

Barthes, Roland. *Mythologies*. Paris: Éditions du Seuil, 1957.

Bohlman, Philip V. "Musicology as a Political Act." *Journal of Musicology* 11, no. 4 (1993): 411–36.

Botstein, Leon. "Music and Ideology: Thoughts on Bruckner." *Musical Quarterly* 80, no. 1 (1996): 1–11.

Botz, Gerhard. "'Infelix Austria': Lebenslüge und nationale Identität in Österreich heute." *Das Jüdische Echo: Zeitschrift für Kultur und Politik* 29, no. 1 (1990): 116–20.

———, and Gerald Sprengnagel, eds. *Kontroversen um Österreichs Zeitgeschichte: verdrängte Vergangenheit, Österreich-Identität, Waldheim und die Historiker*. Frankfurt: Campus, 1994.

Brodbeck, David. *Defining Deutschtum: Political Ideology, German Identity, and Music-Critical Discourse in Liberal Vienna*. New York: Oxford University Press, 2014.

Bruckner, Anton. *Erste Symphonie (c-Moll) für grosses Orchester*, edited by Cyrill Hynais. Vienna: Doblinger, 1893, plate no. D.1868.

———. *I. Symphonie c-Moll (Wiener und Linzer Fassung): Partituren und Entwürfe mit Bericht*, edited by Robert Haas. Vol. 1, Anton Bruckner: Sämtliche Werke. Vienna: Musikwissenschaftlicher Verlag der Internationalen Bruckner-Gesellschaft, 1935.

———. *I. Symphonie c-Moll. Wiener Fassung 1890/91*, 2nd rev. ed., edited by Günther Brosche. Vol. I/2, Anton Bruckner: Sämtliche Werke. Vienna: Musikwissenschaftlicher Verlag der Internationalen Bruckner-Gesellschaft, 1980.

Brüstle, Christa. *Anton Bruckner und die Nachwelt: Zur Rezeptionsgeschichte des Komponisten in der ersten Hälfte des 20. Jahrhunderts*. Stuttgart: J. B. Metzler, 1998.

Bujić, Bojan. "Musicology and Intellectual History: A Backward Glance to the Year 1885." *Proceedings of the Royal Musical Association* 111, no. 1 (1984): 139–54.

———, ed. *Music in European Thought, 1851–1912*. Cambridge: Cambridge University Press, 1988.

Burke, Peter, ed. *New Perspectives on Historical Writing*. Cambridge: Polity, 1991.

Büttner, Horst. "Die Linzer Fassung von Bruckners Erster Sinfonie." *Zeitschrift für Musik: Monatsschrift für eine geistige Erneuerung der deutschen Musik* 103, no. 4 (1936): 471–73.

Cornford, Francis MacDonald. *Thucydides Mythistoricus*. London: Edward Arnold, 1907.

Fischer, Wilhelm. "Von der Eigenart der österreichischen Tonkunst." *Österreichische Musikzeitschrift* 1, no. 2 (1946): 45–47.
Flotzinger, Rudolf, and Gernot Gruber, eds. *Musikgeschichte Österreichs*. 2 vols. Graz: Styria, 1977, 1979.
———. *Musikgeschichte Österreichs*. 2nd rev. ed., 3 vols. Vienna: Böhlau, 1995.
Frye, Northrop. *Anatomy of Criticism: Four Essays*. Princeton: Princeton University Press, 1957.
Gilliam, Bryan. "The Annexation of Anton Bruckner: Nazi Revisionism and the Politics of Appropriation." *Musical Quarterly* 78, no. 3 (1994): 584–604.
———. "Bruckner's Annexation Revisited: A Response to Manfred Wagner." *Musical Quarterly* 80 no. 1 (1996): 124–31.
Goldhagen, Daniel Jonah. *Hitler's Willing Executioners: Ordinary Germans and the Holocaust* New York: Knopf, 1996.
Goodman, Nelson. *Languages of Art: An Approach to a Theory of Symbols*. Indianapolis: Bobbs-Merrill, 1968.
Hanisch, Ernst. *Der lange Schatten des Staates: Österreichische Gesellschaftsgeschichte im 20. Jahrhundert*. Vienna: Ueberreuter, 1994.
Heller, Friedrich C. "In der Ostmark." In *Musikgeschichte Österreichs*, edited by Rudolf Flotzinger and Gernot Gruber, 2:414–15. Graz: Styria, 1979.
———. "Musik der 'Ostmark.'" In *Musikgeschichte Österreichs*, edited by Rudolf Flotzinger and Gernot Gruber, 2nd ed., 3:185–87. Vienna: Böhlau, 1995.
Hinrichsen, Hans-Joachim, ed. *Bruckner-Handbuch*. Stuttgart: J. B. Metzler, 2010.
Horton, Julian. *Bruckner's Symphonies: Analysis, Reception and Cultural Politics*. Cambridge: Cambridge University Press, 2004.
Hunt, Lynn, ed. *The New Cultural History*. Berkeley: University of California Press, 1989.
Huss, Manfred. "Hans Swarowsky und die Lehre von der Interpretation in der zweiten Wiener Schule." In *Die Lehre von der musikalischen Aufführung in der Wiener Schule: Verhandlungen des Internationalen Colloquiums Wien 1995*, edited by Markus Grassl and Reinhard Kapp, 377–84. Vienna: Böhlau, 2002.
Huynh, Pascal. "'… dunkler die Geigen …': Das 'Dritte Reich' und die Musik," translated by Uta Goridis. In *Das "Dritte Reich" und die Musik*, edited by Stiftung Schloss Neuhardenberg and Cité de la musique Paris, 9–19. Berlin: Nicolai, 2006.
Ibsen, Henrik. *Eight Plays*. Translated by Eva Le Gallienne. New York: Modern Library, 1982.
Kam, Lap-Kwan. "Writing Music History in Austria and Taiwan: Some Preliminary Observations." *Humanitas Taiwanica* 61 (November 2004): 103–38.
———. "The Musicologist as Historian and Patriot: Imagining National Identity with the Musical Past in Modern Austria." *Guandu Music Journal* 11 (2009): 191–206.
Karnes, Kevin C. *Music, Criticism, and the Challenge of History: Shaping Modern Musical Thought in Late Nineteenth-Century Vienna*. New York: Oxford University Press, 2008.

Kater, Michael H. *The Twisted Muse: Musicians and Their Music in the Third Reich.* New York: Oxford University Press, 1997.

Kerman, Joseph. *Contemplating Music: Challenges to Musicology.* Cambridge, MA: Harvard University Press, 1985.

Knepler, Georg. "950 Jahre Österreich: Wichtigstes Kapitel unserer Musikgeschichte." *Die Woche* 2, no. 42 (1946): 3–4.

Korstvedt, Benjamin M. "Anton Bruckner in the Third Reich and After: An Essay on Ideology and Bruckner Reception." *Musical Quarterly* 80, no. 1 (1996): 132–60.

———. "'Return to the Pure Sources': The Ideology and Text-Critical Legacy of the First Bruckner *Gesamtausgabe.*" In *Bruckner Studies,* edited by Paul Hawkshaw and Timothy Jackson, 91–109. Cambridge: Cambridge University Press, 1997.

———. "Defining the 'Problem': The Development of Postwar Attitudes toward Bruckner Versions." *Journal of Musicological Research* 32, no. 1 (2013): 1–27.

Lach, Robert. "Das Österreichertum in der Musik." *Volkswohl: Wissenschaftliche Monatsschrift* 20, no. 12 (1929): 447–52.

———. "Das Österreichertum in der Musik." *Allgemeine Musikzeitung* 65, no. 36 (1938): 529–31.

Lafite, Peter, Bernhard Paumgartner, Leopold Nowak, Wilhelm Fischer, Roland Tenschert, Andreas Ließ, and Hans Sittner. "950 Jahre Österreich: Minnesang/Renaissance/Barock/Klassik und Romantik/Zeitgenössische Musik/Der österreichische Musikdialekt." *Österreichische Musikzeitschrift* 1, no. 10–11 (1946): 325–64.

Lévi-Strauss, Claude. "The Structural Study of Myth." *Journal of American Folklore* 68, no. 270 (1955): 428–44.

Locke, Ralph P. "Musicology and/as Social Concern: Imagining the Relevant Musicologist." In *Rethinking Music,* edited by Nicholas Cook and Mark Everist, 499–550. Oxford: Oxford University Press, 1999.

MacLean, Ian, Alan Montefiore, and Peter Winch, eds., *The Political Responsibility of Intellectuals.* Cambridge: Cambridge University Press, 1990.

Mali, Joseph. *Mythistory: The Making of a Modern Historiography.* Chicago: University of Chicago Press, 2003.

Matejka, Viktor, ed. *Wiener Bruckner-Fest zum 50. Todestag des Meisters veranstaltet von der Stadt Wien ... 10.—27. Oktober 1946.* Vienna: Amt für Kultur und Volksbildung, 1946.

McNeill, William H. "Mythistory, or Truth, Myth, History, and Historians." *American Historical Review* 91, no. 1 (1986): 1–10.

Meyer, Michael. "The Nazi Musicologist as Myth Maker in the Third Reich." *Journal of Contemporary History* 10, no. 4 (1975): 649–65.

Moser, Hans Joachim. "Von der Tätigkeit der Reichsstelle für Musikbearbeitungen." In *Jahrbuch der deutschen Musik,* edited by Hellmuth von Hase, 78–82. Leipzig: Breitkopf & Härtel, 1943.

Mugglestone, Erica. "Guido Adler's 'The Scope, Method, and Aim of Musicology' (1885): An English Translation with an Historico-Analytical Commentary." *Yearbook for Traditional Music* 13 (1981): 1–21.

Oberkofler, Gerhard, and Manfred Mugrauer. *Georg Knepler: Musiker und marxistischer Denker aus Wien.* Innsbruck: Studienverlag, 2014.

Okrassa, Nina. *Peter Raabe: Dirigent, Musikschriftsteller und Präsident der Reichsmusikkammer (1872–1945).* Vienna: Böhlau, 2004.

Pammer, Anna Maria. "Musikgeschichte im 'Dritten Reich': Am Beispiel des Musikwissenschaftlers Erich Schenk." MPhil thesis, University of Vienna, 2013.

Pape, Matthias. "Erich Schenk – ein österreichischer Musikwissenschaftler in Salzburg, Rostock und Wien: Musikgeschichtsschreibung zwischen großdeutscher und kleinösterreichischer Staatsidee." *Die Musikforschung* 53 (2000): 413–31.

Pass, Walter. "Musikleben seit 1945." In *Musikgeschichte Österreichs*, edited by Rudolf Flotzinger and Gernot Gruber, 2:481–532. Graz: Styria, 1979.

Pelinka, Anton. "Die Österreichische Volkspartei (ÖVP)." In *Christlich-demokratische und konservative Parteien in Westeuropa.* Vol. 1, *Bundesrepublik Deutschland, Österreich*, edited by Hans-Joachim Veen, 195–265. Paderborn: Schöningh, 1983.

———. "Von der Funktionalität von Tabus: zu den 'Lebenslügen' der Zweiten Republik." In *Inventur 45/55: Österreich im ersten Jahrzehnt der Zweiten Republik*, edited by Wolfgang Kos and Georg Rigele, 23–32. Vienna: Sonderzahl, 1996.

Permoser, Manfred. *Die Wiener Symphoniker im NS-Staat.* Frankfurt: Peter Lang, 2000.

Prieberg, Fred K. *Handbuch Deutsche Musiker 1933–1945.* 2nd ed. Auprès de Zombry: self-published, 2009.

Ranke, Leopold von. "Autobiographical Dictation (November 1885)." In *The Secret of World History: Selected Writings on the Art and Science of History*, edited and translated by Roger Wines, 33–52. New York: Fordham University Press, 1981.

Rathkolb, Oliver. *Die paradoxe Republik: Österreich 1945 bis 2005.* Vienna: Zsolnay, 2005.

———. Bernadette Mayrhofer, and Fritz Trümpi. "Wiener Philharmoniker—Geschichtlicher Überblick zur NS-Zeit." Wiener Philharmoniker. Retrieved 18 August 2018 from http://www.wienerphilharmoniker.at/orchester/geschichte/nationalsozialismus.

Roberts, John Morris. Review of *Mythistory and Other Essays*, by William H. McNeill. *Journal of Modern History* 60, no. 4 (1988): 731–32.

Röder, Thomas. "Die Erste Symphonie als 'Linzer' Werk: Eine vorläufige Bilanz." In *Bruckner-Tagung Wien 1999: Bericht*, edited by Elisabeth Maier, Andrea Harrandt, and Erich Wolfgang Partsch, 47–57. Vienna: Musikwissenschaftlicher Verlag, 2000.

———. "Zur Neuausgabe der ersten Symphonie von Anton Bruckner." (2014). Retrieved 18 August 2018 from http://www.alkor-edition.com/fileadmin/Domain/User/Alkor/Alkor-PDFs/Pressemappe_web.pdf.

Sakabe, Yukiko. "Erich Schenk und der Fall Adler-Bibliothek." In *Musik-Wissenschaft an ihren Grenzen: Manfred Angerer zum 50. Geburtstag*, edited by Dominik Schweiger, Michael Staudinger, and Nikolaus Urbanek, 383–92. Frankfurt: Peter Lang, 2004.

Schenk, Erich. *950 Jahre Musik in Österreich*. Vienna: Bellaria-Verlag, 1946.

———. "Schenk, Erich." In *Die Musik in Geschichte und Gegenwart*, edited by Friedrich Blume, vol. 11, columns 1664–66. Kassel: Bärenreiter, 1963.

Schöner, Josef. *Wiener Tagebuch 1944/1945*. Edited by Eva-Marie Csáky, Franz Matscher, and Gerald Stourzh. Vienna: Böhlau, 1992.

Shelemay, Kay Kaufman. "The Impact and Ethics of Musical Scholarship." In *Rethinking Music*, edited by Nicholas Cook and Mark Everist, 531–44. Oxford: Oxford University Press, 1999.

Solvik, Morten. "The International Bruckner Society and the NSDAP: A Case Study of Robert Haas and the Critical Edition." *Musical Quarterly* 82, no. 2 (1998): 362–82.

Spevak, Stefan. *Das Jubiläum '950 Jahre Österreich': Eine Aktion zur Schaffung eines österreichischen Staats- und Kulturbewußtseins im Jahre 1946*. Vienna: Oldenbourg, 2003.

Staudinger, Michael. "Ein 'vatermörderisches' Projekt? Zur Geschichte der Wiener Musikwissenschaft 1920–1960." In *Musik-Wissenschaft an ihren Grenzen: Manfred Angerer zum 50. Geburtstag*, edited by Dominik Schweiger, Michael Staudinger, and Nikolaus Urbanek, 393–406. Frankfurt: Peter Lang, 2004.

———. "'Finstere Dämonen': Zur Geschichte der Musikwissenschaft an der Universität Wien in den Jahren 1938–1945." In *Musik in Wien 1938–1945: Symposion 2004*, edited by Carmen Ottner, 239–55. Vienna: Doblinger, 2006.

Steinweis, Alan E. *Art, Ideology, and Economics in Nazi Germany: The Reich Chambers of Music, Theater, and the Visual Arts*. Chapel Hill: University of North Carolina Press, 1993.

Stone, Lawrence. "The Revival of Narrative: Reflections on a New Old History." *Past and Present* 85 (November 1979): 3–24.

Subotnik, Rose Rosengard. "Adorno and the New Musicology." In *Adorno: A Critical Reader*, edited by Nigel Gibson and Andrew Rubin, 234–54. Oxford: Blackwell, 2000.

Szabó-Knotik, Cornelia. "Mythos Musik in Österreich. Die zweite Republik." In *Memoria Austria I. Menschen, Mythen, Zeiten*, edited by Emil Brix, Ernst Bruckmüller, and Hannes Stekl, 243–70. Vienna: Verlag für Geschichte und Politik, 2004.

Trümpi, Fritz. *Politisierte Orchester: Die Wiener Philharmoniker und das Berliner Philharmonische Orchester im Nationalsozialismus*. Vienna: Böhlau, 2011.

Uhl, Heidemarie. "From Discourse to Representation: 'Austrian Memory' in Public Space." In *Narrating the Nation: Representations in History, Media and the Arts*, edited by Stefan Berger, Linas Eriksonas, and Andrew Mycock, 207–21. New York: Berghahn Books, 2008.

Varga, Bálint András. *From Boulanger to Stockhausen: Interviews and a Memoir*. Rochester: University of Rochester Press, 2013.

Wagner, Manfred. "Response to Bryan Gilliam regarding Bruckner and National Socialism." *Musical Quarterly* 80, no. 1 (1996): 118–23.

Waldheim, Kurt. *Im Glaspalast der Weltpolitik*. Düsseldorf: Econ, 1985.

Weber, Max. *The Methodology of the Social Sciences*. Edited and translated by Edward A. Shils and Henry A. Finch. Glencoe, IL: The Free Press, 1949.

Weizsäcker, Richard von. "Gedenkveranstaltung im Plenarsaal des Deutschen Bundestages zum 40. Jahrestag des Endes des Zweiten Weltkrieges in Europa." Der Bundespräsidialamt. 8 May 1985. Retrieved 18 August 2018 from http://www.bundespraesident.de/SharedDocs/Reden/DE/Richard-von-Weizsaecker/Reden/1985/05/19850508_Rede.html.

CHAPTER 10

Hearing the Nazi Past in the German Democratic Republic
Antifascist Fantasies, Acoustic Realities, and Haunted Memories in Georg Katzer's Aide –Mémoire (1983)

MARTHA SPRIGGE

The German Democratic Republic (GDR) was fanatically bureaucratic. From monitoring and maintaining records about its citizens through the Ministerium für Staatssicherheit (Ministry for State Security, or Stasi) to controlling the contents of and access to national archives, the ruling Sozialistische Einheitspartei Deutschlands (Socialist Unity Party, or SED) established a series of documentary practices that both scrutinized and policed cultural and social life in the East German state. While scholarship on East German music has benefited exponentially from the vast array of archival resources that have become accessible since the country's dissolution in 1990, issues surrounding the treatment of sound as a material object have yet to be examined carefully. This chapter considers the status of the sound archive in the GDR, focusing on materials from the Third Reich that became part of the commemorative repertoires of the East German state. What were these musical documents? How did they circulate, and what histories did they reveal in their transition from material to audible phenomena? How did documentary aesthetics become a crucial means of challenging the foundational narratives of the East German state?

Music was integral to East German commemorative practice throughout the state's forty-year existence. East Germany was officially an "antifascist" state, where narratives of the German past, and particularly the Third Reich, were tightly controlled.[1] World War II was not ignored, but fashioned into a history of Soviet salvation. The war's end represented communist victory over fascism, rather than a total defeat that left the nation in ruins and its citizens responsible for the rise of the Nazi Party. Soviet soldiers, antifascist resistance fighters, and communist martyrs were widely celebrated, commemorated in stone, and honored through regular pilgrimages and commemorative events. In her landmark study of East German literature, Julia Hell regards these narratives of socialist heroes as dually foundational: they not only were upheld by the SED as a means of legitimizing state power, but also offered a narrative framework for inscriptions of postfascist subjectivity in East German texts.[2] In the field of music, *Kampflieder* (songs of struggle)—with their easily singable melodies, rousing choruses, and connections to prewar customs of communal working-class singing—provided a soundtrack to commemorative rituals and a musical foundation for the antifascist state. This repertoire further circulated through recordings and song anthologies, providing East Germans with material links to their nation's communist heritage for use in everyday life.

Ideologies of antifascism continued to hold sway throughout the GDR's forty-year existence. In 1982, Georg Katzer was one of two composers commissioned by the Verband der Komponisten und Musikwissenschaftler der DDR (East German Association of Composers and Musicologists of the GDR, or VKM) to write a piece for an East German radio program marking the fiftieth anniversary of the Nazi *Machtergreifung* (seizure of power). At the premiere on East German Radio in January 1983, he presented a work of *musique concrète* titled *Aide –Mémoire*. But rather than a sonic counterpart to this official historical narrative, Katzer offered a fragmentary collage in which Nazi speeches clash with folk songs, jingoistic marching songs are cut alongside masterpieces of the Austro-Germanic canon, and the sounds of the Third Reich are presented in their original form, with no markers or explanation. Katzer thus used the framework of a state commemorative event to voice his own reading of German history.

On the surface, *Aide –Mémoire* reflects the gulf between the closely monitored propagandistic "socialist realism" of the immediate postwar years and the disillusionment of "real existing socialism" in the late 1970s and 1980s. In her recent monograph on the reception of nineteenth-century music in the GDR, Elaine Kelly charts an increasing penchant toward melancholy in late socialist works, including *Aide –Mémoire* as an example.[3] In this chapter I explore the underlying parallels between antifascist commemorative practices at the beginning and end of East Germany's forty-year existence. I take a medium-specific approach to the aesthetic and affective shifts underlying these two concepts of realism, foregrounding continuities across East German commemorative repertoires at the level of musical process and sonic material. The two types of sound document represented in East German song anthologies and Katzer's *Aide –Mémoire*, printed and recorded, both encapsulate similar tensions between music as a material object and its sonic realization that opened up a space for presenting alternative accounts of the Third Reich within the framework of official commemorative events.[4] More broadly, Katzer's turn to *musique concrète* raises questions about the role of sound within a documentary history and archival practice that has traditionally focused on texts and scores.[5] Sound sources require another layer of mediation to transition from the archive into performative or performance (con)texts. This layer created a conceptual slippage that Katzer used as both a compositional tool and a means of navigating the politically charged system of musical commissions in the GDR.

Antifascist Histories

The GDR's founding myth of antifascism cast Germany's Nazi past in binary terms. According to this paradigm, fascism was a direct result of capitalism, and fascism and communism were mutually exclusive. Since the Soviet Red Army "rescued" East Germany at the end of World War II and communists who had been subject to Nazi persecution now ran the country, fascism had simply ceased to exist in the East and was festering in capitalist countries in the West.[6] Many East German citizens adopted, or at least displayed little outward resistance to, antifascism because it offered what historian Bill Niven describes as "a psychological deal of exchange."[7] If East Germans accepted the Soviets as their saviors and committed to communist ideologies, they could avoid confronting or accepting any personal or collective responsibility for the Third Reich.

A bustling commemorative calendar further bolstered this highly selective narrative of World War II.[8] Antifascist rituals celebrated political (i.e., communist) victims of the Holocaust, while other persecuted groups in the Third Reich, such as Jews, Roma, and homosexuals, were almost entirely ignored in official discourse. Fritz Cremer's memorial at Buchenwald concentration camp is just one example of the SED's consecration of East German hierarchies of victimhood in overbearing monuments.[9] Erected in 1961, the statue celebrates political prisoners of Buchenwald, who had "self-liberated" the camp at the end of World War II.[10] The SED's fanatic commitment to new antifascist memorials and accompanying commemorative rituals betrayed an underlying anxiety about East Germany's identity, particularly given the competition for German national legitimacy coming from the Federal Republic. East Germany had few sites of specifically communist legacy to demonstrate connections to a long-standing cultural and political heritage, which made these new monuments especially significant.[11]

Pocket scores and anthologies of *Kampflieder* were material objects with integral links to German communism in the Weimar Republic that offered a means of circulating antifascist narratives in the present. At early meetings of the East German Politburo and the Academy of the Arts, Prime Minister Otto Grotewohl urged composers to use these prewar *Kampflieder* as their models for new music.[12] A section of the Akademie der Künste (Academy of the Arts, or AdK) was dedicated to collecting workers' songs from around the world. Jewish communist Inge Lammel—who had survived the Holocaust by escaping on the last *Kindertransport* (children's transport) to London on 1 September 1939 (the same day Germany invaded Poland)—led the Arbeiterlied Archiv (Workers' Song Archive, or ALA), which engaged in ethnographic fieldwork, archival projects, and published accessible anthologies.[13] The ALA's landmark ten-volume publication *Das Lied im Kampf geboren* (The song born of struggle), published between 1957 and 1962, collected the songs used to support the German proletariat from the 1848 revolutions onwards—a struggle that was seen to have been ultimately resolved with the founding of the GDR.[14] While *Kampflieder* were used as the sonic backbone of state commemorative events, anthologies were a way to establish the German communist party's legitimacy in the GDR and part of a larger effort to promote the history of German communism in the newfound state.[15]

Songbooks for East German children and young adults included many songs intended to serve as emblems of antifascist resistance.[16] Most of these pieces, however, have more complicated histories than the selective meaning ascribed to them in the GDR. The first song in the volume of the ALA's publication project dedicated to concentration camp songs demonstrates the inherent polysemy of this repertoire, particularly when performed in commemorative context. Rudi Goguel wrote "Die Moorsoldaten"/"Das Moorsoldatenlied" (The Peat-Bog Soldiers' Song), while he was a political prisoner at Börgemoor concentration camp in 1933. It became a global emblem of resistance during the Spanish Civil War and World War II, popularized through Hanns Eisler's arrangement (published in 1935) and Ernst Busch's recording from the Spanish Civil War (made in 1936).[17] The song also circulated in songbooks at concentration camps established later in the Third Reich, particularly Sachsenhausen, opened in 1936. Sachsenhausen had a strong presence of German political prisoners, but many other categories of victim, including homosexuals, "asocials," and Jews, were also incarcerated at this concentration camp.[18] Thus, even before the start of World War II, "Die Moorsoldaten" was circulating in contexts that juxtaposed different groups of Nazi-persecuted subjects, though it took on added symbolic value for communists and political prisoners in this period. Guido Fackler notes that "Die Moorsoldaten" was one of the most popular songs in many concentration camps, "symbolizing for the inmates both protest and determined endurance."[19] The fact that it was repeatedly prohibited from performance—even though SS guards often forced prisoners to sing iconic works from their own repertoire as a form of humiliation—further enhances this song's representational power as a symbol of protest.[20]

In East Germany, Goguel and Eisler's arrangements of "Die Moorsoldaten" were published as the first song in the seventh volume of *Das Lied im Kampf geboren*, titled *Lieder aus den faschistischen Konzentrationslagern* (Songs from fascist concentration camps, see Figures 10.1 and 10.2).[21] In the introductory

Figures 10.1 and 10.2. Hanns Eisler and Rudi Goguel, "Die Moorsoldaten," in *Das Lied im Kampf geboren*, vol. 7: *Lieder aus den faschistischen Konzentrationslagern. Das Lied im Kampf geboren*, ed. Inge Lammel and Gunter Hofmeyer, 14–15, 18 (Leipzig: VEB Friedrich Hofmeister, 1962). Eisler's version is Figure 10.2.

blurb for this volume of the anthology, "Die Moorsoldaten" is hailed as a rallying cry of solidarity for antifascists imprisoned in Nazi camps, drawing attention to the song's history of protest within the camp system.[22] Eisler's arrangement—with its more upbeat tempo, rhythmic adjustments that add some swing to the chorus, and a few new leaps in the melodic line—was the preferred version for anthologies and performances released in the GDR. Goguel did not like Eisler's altered melody, because he felt it eliminated the meaning of his original: "the three steady tones with which the song begins should characterize the bleakness of the moor and the difficult situation under which the Moor-soldiers had to live."[23] Despite Goguel's complaints, suffering remains palpable both musically and textually throughout the strophic verses. The choruses of political singer Busch's popular 1936 recording, made while he was fighting in the Spanish Civil War, seem to convey perseverance rather than mobilization. Eisler's own biography further speaks to the multiple subjects of discrimination under the Nazis: he penned his arrangement of "Die Moorsoldaten" while living in exile, having fled the Third Reich not just for being communist, but for being Jewish as well.

While music was co-opted as part of the East German commemorative agenda, works like "Die Moorsoldaten" cannot entirely cover up the overlooked aspects of the Nazi past. No amount of historiographical wordplay can erase historical facts: these songs display traces of their shared Jewish and communist heritage because they were created and circulated in spaces of Nazi persecution and extermination. Moreover, in the context of East German commemorative festivals, works originally written in concentration camps were often *re*-performed at these same sites. From 1961 onwards, primary school education in the GDR included a visit to a concentration camp, where the SED had erected memorials to antifascist prisoners.[24] "Die Moorsoldaten" is just one example of a work that was accepted as a sonic marker of German socialism in the early postwar years, even though its history is significantly more complicated. But the larger issue might be that this oversight was possible at all. East Germany's first leaders, themselves antifascists, were so committed to reframing the Nazi past as a struggle between fascism and communism that the plurality of these pieces was overlooked. While anthologies were framed around celebrations of antifascism and the working class, their contents are clearly more complex. Beneath the printed circulation of these song anthologies lie more complex aural histories of the German past.

Audio Histories

Antifascist rhetoric had a unique hold on many East German citizens. According to David Bathrick, the legacy of antifascism was one of the key distinctions between the GDR and other Soviet satellites, which had made much more progress in the area of cultural freedom by the late 1980s with the advent of *perestroika*. Because the political leaders of the GDR emphasized their persecution during the Third Reich, there was a barrier of guilt that prevented many citizens who had remained compliant during the Third Reich from staging a resistance against those who had been actual victims of the Third Reich's policies.[25] These narratives had a particularly powerful influence on the generation born shortly before the outbreak of war, which historian Mary Fulbrook calls "the 1929ers," or the *Aufbau* (Reconstruction) generation, who reached adulthood in the early postwar years.[26] This was the group that benefited most from the legacies of antifascism, and the experiences of their parents and elders provided them with unspoken reminders of this fact. When asked in the early years of German reunification why East Germans did not revolt sooner and more vocally, author Christa Wolf (1929–2011) described how her generation "felt a strong reluctance to organize resistance against people who had been in concentration camps during the Nazi period."[27] Even the folk singer Wolf Biermann (b. 1936), one of the most outspokenly critical citizens of the GDR, who was ultimately expelled for defaming his country, declared—at the very concert that prompted his expulsion—that East Germany had "fortunately" rid itself of Nazis.[28]

Aide –Mémoire, a work by another member of the *Aufbau* generation, Georg Katzer, demonstrates a musical confrontation with these issues. Katzer was born in 1935 in Bystrzyca Kłodzka—a small medieval town near the Polish-Czech border. His early childhood overlapped with Hitler's announcement that he had annexed these regions in a series of invasions that ultimately triggered World War II in 1939. Though Katzer was not old enough to participate in the war directly, *Aide –Mémoire's* subtitle, "Seven nightmares from the thousand-year night," gives a sense of the trauma this period left on his psyche. Katzer describes the work as follows:

> I was obsessed for a long time by the idea of composing a piece on this subject, but I could not find a way to make the impossible possible. In the end I found that the only way I could grasp this period of German history was as a terrible dream. Therefore: no chronicle of events, no attempt at explanation—but a monstrous collage of phrases, slogans, march music, mass cries, all cut from original sound documents of the Nazi period and put together to form seven nightmares, between which the sleeper can find no rest; asleep, beset by terrible dreams, but at the same time afraid to wake up and find these dreams are truth.[29]

Katzer fixates on traumatic rupture between his continual "obsession" with creating a musical work on "this subject" and the impossibility of his obsessive task. Indeed, the precise parameters of "this subject" remain unspecified, perhaps indicating the confusing overlaps between his early memories of the

Third Reich, World War II, and a growing awareness of the Holocaust in the early postwar years, all of which are represented within the soundscape of *Aide –Mémoire*. Drawing on the techniques of *musique concrète*, Katzer created a collage that confronted these overlapping pasts in documents. In a 1988 interview, he described how he understood collage as a technique through which heterogeneous materials could clash, or bounce around as if by accident, always at risk of falling apart.[30] His emphasis on the potential for collage to fail—to become undone, to wear out, to be incomprehensible—hints at why he found this technique particularly appropriate for use in *Aide –Mémoire*. He takes a very literal, even physical approach to *musique concrète*, noting that for all his electronic equipment, "the first instrument was the scissors."

Aide –Mémoire was premiered for the fiftieth anniversary of Hitler's appointment on 30 January 1933 as Reich chancellor. The fact that this occasion became a commemorative event speaks to the power of antifascist discourse over national history in the GDR: antifascism held such weight that Hitler's seizure of power in 1933 could be reframed as an opportunity to celebrate the country's communist heritage. It was an opportunity to "warn" a new generation of the dangers of fascism and to celebrate the "antifascist victory" over the Third Reich anew. To mark this anniversary, the VKM commissioned Katzer and his colleague Friedrich Schenker to prepare radio works that would address the theme of fascism, intended for realization at the end of January 1983 on Radio-DDR II, the radio channel dedicated to cultural programming.[31] Katzer had previously voiced his unease about writing works on commission, and his first response to the radio programmer when asked to introduce *Aide –Mémoire* was to stress his artistic autonomy from the commemorative occasion. He described the work's premiere as part of this anniversary to be "more of an accident," because he had been planning to compose such a work, in this style, for a long time.[32] These anxieties about maintaining aesthetic independence go further back. In 1972, Katzer remarked that he "preferred to compose without a commission," because the money involved had led to bad experiences where he could not "preserve his autonomy from the piece or society."[33]

Yet the commission system underlying East German art had definite advantages, and without it, Katzer's music would not have received a significant audience in the GDR.[34] Katzer ultimately knew this. In the same interview from 1972, he lauded the radio as one of the few places in the GDR that supported new music, which was particularly important for a composer well versed in, and enthusiastic about, avant-garde techniques.[35] Premiering *Aide –Mémoire* on the radio as part of an official commemorative event thus presented Katzer with challenges and opportunities. While he faced intense critique during the radio interview, he nevertheless could use it as the opportunity to publically challenge official narratives of the past. Furthermore, without the financial and technological support of East German Radio, the work might have remained unrealized; until the establishment of an official electroacoustic studio in 1986, radio studios were the one of the few places in the GDR where composers could create electroacoustic music.[36]

In previous analyses of *Aide –Mémoire*, Sabine Feisst, Rudolf Frisius, and Elaine Kelly have excavated many of Katzer's raw materials, deciphering the symbolic saturation of the work as a whole.[37] Each author notes how Katzer organizes his materials into seven loosely chronological nightmares (see Table 10.1). Katzer assembles the work from four types of sound: Nazi speeches, pre-recorded music, electronic sounds, and original compositions. Despite his comment that the work is not a chronicle, its nightmares are in roughly chronological order. Sources from Nazi radio broadcasts dominate the work, triggering connections to World War II. As Ansgar Diller describes in his study of radio politics in the Third Reich, among the mass media available for Nazi mobilization, the radio "let itself with the most ease be incorporated by the Nazis for their goals."[38] Capitalizing on symbolically charged, historically loaded sound materials, Katzer uses speeches from the Nazi period that mark specific historical events to delineate each nightmare, such as Hitler's announcement of the invasion of Poland (September 1939) at the start of nightmare three and Goebbels's declaration of "total war" (18 February 1943) as the basis of nightmare seven. His musical excerpts are also from repertoires that had taken on special significance during the Nazi period in daily radio broadcasts.[39] The first three nightmares, for example, juxtapose light music genres such as folk songs (the four-part a cappella harmonization of *Der Lindenbaum*, the popular *Badenweilermarsch*, and samples of *Schlagermusik*), which constituted a central component of radio programming in the Third Reich.[40] Channels that focused on light entertainment appealed to the sensibilities and tastes of the *Volksgemeinschaft* and served as a foil for disseminating political messages in less overbearing ways.[41] Later nightmares call on works that were used to convey certain messages from the front. The third movement of Beethoven's Ninth, for example, was broadcast to mark the funerals of Nazi officers.[42] Katzer inverts this piece's Nazi associations: he uses it midway through the nightmare representing the Holocaust to mourn those Jews who died in concentration camps. The symbolic power of Liszt's *Les Préludes* is similarly evoked and revoked. The piece prefaced coverage from the warfront in the Third Reich and is heard over the final collage of destruction in *Aide – Mémoire*.[43] To those alive during the wartime years, the compositional palette of *Aide –Mémoire* is filled with sounds that are immediately recognizable, even if they have been banned from the German airwaves—both East and West—since the end of the war.[44]

Analyzing the work for the East German journal *Musik und Gesellschaft* (Music and Society) in 1983, the musicologist Stefan Amzoll remarked that

Table 10.1. Nightmares of *Aide –Mémoire* (1983).

Nightmare	Time Period / Topic / Recognizable Voices	Musical Sources
Prologue	Prewar	Schubert, arr. Friedrich Silcher (1848) *Der Lindenbaum*
I (0:56)	*Machtergreifung* (1933): • Adolf Hitler	Tango *Schlagermusik*: Robert Stolz and Robert Gilbert's "Nur bei uns, nur bei uns gibt's Gemütlichkeit" (from soundtrack to *Hochzeit am Wolfgangsee* [Wedding at Wolfgangsee], 1933) Aria from Richard Strauss's *Arabella* (premiered June 1933) *Badenweiler March*
II (2:57)	Invasion of Poland (1939): • Adolf Hitler	*Badenweiler March*
III (4:39)	Nazi propaganda	Children's songs
IV (6:28)	The Holocaust (1940–45)	Unidentified Jewish folk melody Katzer, *Miserere* Beethoven's Ninth Symphony (third movement)
V (8:35)	Resistance movements (1933–44): • Roland Freisler (president of the Nazi People's Court) • Erich Weinert (president of the National Committee for a Free Germany, NKFD)	Rudi Goguel, "Die Moorsoldaten" (1933)
VI (10:14)	Early War (1939–42)	Nazi songs: "Siehst du im Osten das Morgenrot?" (1931) Tango (same piece as Nightmare II) Soldier's songs against: the Soviet Union ("Nach Ostland geht unser Ritt"); France ("Nach Frankreich hinein"); and England ("Denn wir fahren gegen Engelland").
VII (12:09)	Total War (1943–45): • Josef Goebbels	Franz Liszt, *Les Préludes*
Epilogue (13:28)	Postwar • Thomas Mann	Song sung by the Soviet Army

Source: Compiled from information provided in the notes to Katzer's "*Aide –Mémoire*," track 2 of *CMCD: Six Classic Concrete, Electroacoustic and Electronic Works: 1970–1990*. I also consulted previous analyses of this work by Sabine Feisst, Rudolf Frisius, and Elaine Kelly in compiling this table (citations below).

Introduction (8:35)	Part One (9:00)	Part Two (9:24)
Text: "Haben Sie das Geld?" (Do you have the money?)	Text [Roland Freisler]: Nazi People's Court. Prosecution following the failed attempt to assassinate Hitler, 20 July 1944.	Text [Erich Weinert]: Excerpt from the Manifesto of the *Nationalkomitee "Freies Deutschland"* (NKFD), 20 July 1943.
Sounds: Slow, group footsteps; laser shots; dogs barking		
	Sounds: Court dramatization	
Music (8:45): "Die Moorsoldaten" (opening)		Music (9:24): "Die Moorsoldaten" (chorus)

Figure 10.3. Outline of the fifth nightmare of Katzer's *Aide –Mémoire* (resistance movements).

while "the fields of association" in this piece "are broad," the close presentation of so many different sound materials in such a "confined space" enhances its traumatic effect.[45] Along similar lines, Feisst considers the piece a work of "traumatic realism," drawing attention to its jarring and unredemptive montage of sonic materials.[46] Yet Amzoll's emphasis on the traumatic associations of *Aide –Mémoire* indicates that presenting this piece in a table or other decoded format (including Table 10.1) sanitizes the listening experience. For when *Aide –Mémoire* was premiered, listeners encountered the piece not only without a listening guide, but through the same medium that was so central to Nazi propaganda: the radio. In other words, the trauma inherent in Katzer's soundscape was heightened by the acousmatic circumstances of its premiere.

A closer examination of the fifth nightmare (see Figure 10.3) demonstrates the potential of acousmatic sound for unsettling narratives of the past within the East German context. Katzer manipulates three main pre-recorded sound sources: (1) the voice of Roland Freisler, president of the Nazi "People's Court" that tried anyone who attacked the Nazi Party; (2) a speech delivered by Erich Weinert, a member of the German Communist Party during the Weimar Republic, who had spent the wartime years in exile in Moscow, where he was a founding member of the Nationalkomitee "Freies Deutschland" (National Committee for a Free Germany, or NKFD); and (3) Goguel's (rather than Eisler's) "Die Moorsoldaten." Figure 10.3 shows how these materials intersect over the course of the ninety-second nightmare.

"Die Moorsoldaten" is heard twice, both times entering at a barely audible level, so that the listener only gradually becomes aware of the sound. The opening line is used at the end of the introduction, and then the chorus accompanies the second part of the nightmare, just as quietly. Notably, there is no music in the central section (labeled Part One in Figure 10.3), which presents bourgeois rather than proletariat resistance fighters. Its source materials are recordings from the Nazi People's Court session, held in August 1944, where eight aristocratic army officers and members of the German resistance were prosecuted for their failed attempt to assassinate Hitler.[47] The sounds that dominate are aggressively delivered lines from Freisler, who was notorious for the way he screamed at defendants in violent outbursts. The extreme dynamic imbalance between Freisler and the brief, muted interjections from the defendant reflects the sonic environment of the trial itself, which was filmed for use in the documentary *Verräter vor dem Volksgericht* (Traitors before the People's Court).[48] The amplifications of Freisler's voice fit within the larger sonic representation of Nazi voices as dehumanized, which runs throughout Katzer's work as a whole.

"Die Moorsoldaten" returns when the focus shifts to communist resistance in Part Two, though the humming hardly pierces through the soundscape. It is only at the very end of the nightmare that the melody is comfortably, if briefly, audible. Part Two represents the heroes more common in East German history books: communists who spent the war living in exile in Moscow, such as Wilhelm Pieck, Walter Ulbricht, and Weinert. These were the politicians who, backed by the USSR, returned to lead what became East Germany after the war.[49] Katzer takes excerpts from Weinert reading the manifesto signed by members of the NKFD, founded by exiles in Moscow on 20 July 1943.[50] This is the German communist legacy that enabled the SED to present their nation as a "victim" of fascism. Weinert's speech is the only voice that Amzoll mentions by name in his review of *Aide –Mémoire* for *Musik und Gesellschaft*, in which he (slightly inaccurately) encourages the listener to notice that Weinert is one of the "only human voices" in the entire work.[51] In this section, Katzer streamlines and reorders the text of the NKFD manifesto, taking a short section from the middle, and using only the lines that emphasize Germany's moral reprehensibility and damaged international reputation (see Table 10.2).

Katzer is sampling a speech that had been delivered by a member of the communist resistance and a celebrated antifascist in the GDR. But he has selected a passage of the text that does not draw attention to these factors, and instead focuses on attributing blame for the Third Reich to Hitler alone. While this might represent a "psychological deal of exchange" similar to the one that lent widespread support to the antifascist myth in the GDR, the text does not operate using conventional antifascist rhetoric. Katzer's chosen lines position Weinert within a model of German historiography that seeks to cordon off the Third Reich from the nation's "healthier" national identity and traditions. This is the type of selective self-fashioning that Thomas Mann critiqued in his lecture on "Germany and the Germans" at the Library of Congress on 29 May 1945.[52] In the context of Katzer's *Aide –Mémoire*, this passage draws attention to the various overlapping methods of selective forgetting that took place in

Table 10.2. Excerpts from the *Manifesto of the National Committee for a Free Germany* used in *Aide –Mémoire*.

Original Excerpt from the *Manifest des Nationalkomitees "Freies Deutschland"* (July 1943)*	Reordered Excerpt used in Katzer's *Aide— Mémoire*, Nightmare Five (Resistance Movements)
(1) Er [Hitler] hat ganz Europa zum Feind des deutschen Volkes gemacht und dessen Ehre besudelt. (2) So ist er verantwortlich für den Haß, der Deutschland heute umgibt. (3) Kein äußerer Feind hat uns Deutsche jemals so tief ins Unglück gestürzt wie Hitler. (4) Die Tatsachen beweisen: Der Krieg ist verloren. (5) Deutschland kann ihn nur noch hinschleppen um den Preis unermeßlicher Opfer und Entbehrungen. (6) Die Weiterführung des aussichtslosen Krieges würde das Ende der Nation bedeuten. (7) Aber Deutschland darf nicht sterben!	(3) Kein äußerer Feind hat uns Deutsche jemals so tief ins Unglück gestürzt wie Hitler. (1) Er hat ganz Europa zum Feind des deutschen Volkes gemacht und dessen Ehre besudelt. (2) So ist er verantwortlich für den Haß, der Deutschland heute umgibt. (7) Aber Deutschland darf nicht sterben!
(1) [Hitler] has made the whole of Europe an enemy of the German people and has besmirched its honor. (2) So it is he who is responsible for the hatred which surrounds Germany today. (3) No external enemy has ever thrown the German people so deeply into disaster as Hitler. (4) The facts prove: the war is lost. (5) Germany can only drag it out at the price of uncountable of victims and immeasurable deprivation. (6) The continuation of this lost war would mean the end of the Nation. (7) But Germany must not die!	(3) No external enemy has ever thrown the German people so deeply into disaster as Hitler. (1) He has made the whole of Europe an enemy of the German people and has besmirched its honor. (2) So it is he who is responsible for the hatred which surrounds Germany today. (7) But Germany must not die.

* "Manifest des Nationalkomitees 'Freies Deutschland' an die Wehrmacht und an das deutsche Volk," in Walter Ulbricht, *Zur Geschichte der Neuesten Zeit: Die Niederlage Hitlerdeutschlands und die Schaffung der antifaschistisch-demokratischen Ordnung*, 2nd ed. (Berlin, 1955), 365–71.

both East and West Germany during the postwar period, while simultaneously undercutting these attempts to detach from the Third Reich through the jarring juxtaposition of different sonic sources. Slowly hummed in the background, the chorus of "Die Moorsoldaten" enhances the gravitas of Weinert's declaration, transforming the speech into a moment of melodrama. Two central symbols of the antifascist resistance myth in East German historiography thus deliver a mournful lament on the fate of postwar Germany. By using melodrama as his manner of delivery, this moment of *Aide –Mémoire* resonates with other works in the antifascist tradition, such as Eisler's *Deutsche Sinfonie* (*German Symphony*, written between 1935–1957 and premiered 1959). After initial critiques in the 1950s, this work became an archetype for antifascist works in the 1960s, adopted by composers such as Günter Kochan in *Die Asche von Birkenau* (*The Ashes of Birkenau* 1965).[53]

Katzer thus evokes a specifically East German tradition of antifascist works, but does not use the conventions of melodrama to narrative ends. The close of the fifth nightmare is one of the quietest passages in the entire work, particularly when placed immediately after Freisler's screeching. It is a far cry from the depiction of valiant and bombastic communist heroes represented in antifascist discourse. Most disturbingly, however, this moment of reflection is cut short. A final excerpt from the People's Court concludes the nightmare: Freisler declaiming "Anyone you know to have knowledge of a plan to assassinate the Führer is an outlawed man." Katzer, who has already challenged the SED's heroic narratives of resistance, now collapses his own aesthetic dichotomy between the "humanized" sounds of resistance and the dehumanized manipulations he reserves for Nazi speeches. Nothing in *Aide –Mémoire* provides comfort—even this lament goes practically unheard. These are the nightmares from which Katzer, by his own admission, "can find no rest."

Authentic Histories

While Katzer's use of recognizable Nazi speeches throughout *Aide –Mémoire* recalls the "phonocentrism" of the Nazi Party, it exposed a contradiction at the heart of the antifascist narrative.[54] East German antifascist discourse downplayed Hitler's charisma and presented Nazi rule as the result of capitalist economic systems. Antifascists, by contrast, were depicted as martyrs moulded from common men.[55] The composer's decision to develop a work that used Nazi voices was thus itself an affront to this narrative in both message and material. Collapsing the voices of antifascists, bourgeois resistance figures, Nazi leaders, the sounds of *Kampflieder*, nineteenth-century music, and many other sources into the same musical work exposed the fallacies of antifascism on multiple levels. Not only were the actual sonic traces of this period out of sync with the public narratives that had been forged about World War II in the GDR, but for those who had been alive during this period, many of these sounds were a far more accurate presentation of their wartime experience than that given in any East German history book. By drawing on raw sound materials, Katzer consistently exposes and exploits the affective power and overwhelming reach of radio broadcasts in the Third Reich.

Two members of the four-person studio audience found this overlap particularly reprehensible at the work's premiere. In a heated discussion about his compositional choices led by the program's host Klaus Richter, with Amzoll, his colleague Friedrich Schenker, and Wolfram Seidner (a doctor at East Berlin's *Charité* hospital who specialized in speech therapy) as discussants, Katzer was asked to defend his compositional choices. Seidner, the strongest critic, declared the entire piece a "plot failure" that did not give listeners an accurate picture of the Third Reich. Adopting a model of realism that more in keeping with conventions of socialist dramaturgy, Seidner declared *Aide –Mémoire* confounding on a narrative level, which led him to question the work's historical accuracy.[56] Richter similarly suggested that Katzer had used materials that were too cryptic for their lack of historical context, which was particularly problematic for those who had not lived through the Third Reich and could not understand the "signals" conveyed by the sounds of Katzer's work.[57] He found Katzer's lack of historical placement particularly reprehensible in the fifth nightmare for its juxtaposition of Freisler and Weinert. Both Richter and Seidner reprimanded Katzer for (re-)exposing listeners to the hysterical tones of Freisler's voice and giving no clear indication that Weinert was an antifascist, particularly when his voice was heard in close succession with Freisler's. Without this information, they argued, listeners not already familiar with the historical context (and even some that were) were denied an accurate depiction of the Third Reich.[58]

Katzer countered with another definition of realism, relying on the veracity of his audio documents and his attempt to realistically depict the affective force of the Nazi soundscape. Pointing to the subtitle of his work—*Seven Nightmares from the Thousand Year Night*—he defended what Seidner had called his "plot failure" as deliberate: *Aide –Mémoire* was supposed to be a "relatively short sequence of nightmares," in which the aggression and "hysterical yelling" that characterized life in the Third Reich were clear, but the "plot" remained necessarily obscured.[59] Even the title, *Aide –Mémoire* does not imply a plot but a fragment intended to trigger recollections, and this holds for both the diplomatic and generic sense of the term. Instead of a socialist-realist heroic trajectory of struggle and salvation, Katzer forged a psychologically probing representation of the Third Reich through a collage of sonic debris. Amzoll picked up on Katzer's aesthetic stance in his article following the premiere, describing how *Aide –Mémoire* realistically presented the "mammoth bestiality of the time" through a collage of extreme breaks and cracks.[60] At the premiere itself, he defended Katzer by positioning him within a musical tradition of "contending with antifascism," and providing the audience with a broader artistic context for understanding *Aide –Mémoire*.[61] Amzoll cited examples from a long line of musicians who developed antifascist pieces: beginning with "the Exiles"—citing composers renowned and respected in East German music culture: Ernst Hermann Meyer, Eisler, and Paul Dessau, who had continued this tradition of creating antifascist works in the GDR. He also emphasized the connection to a more popular discourse of antifascism, referencing Busch's political songs, who had been the subject of a television documentary, *Busch singt*, just a year prior (1981–82). Using the latest advances in compositional technique (i.e., *musique concrète*) Katzer represented a new phase in this important tradition.[62]

Acousmatic Histories

In her study of East German instrumental music from the 1970s onwards, Nina Noeske notes how East German composers increasingly adopted documentary aesthetics in their compositional styles.[63] In the late socialist period, documentary modes of musical expression often provided a means for composers in the Eastern bloc to express emotional reactions to events that were frequently framed as heroic or celebratory at official commemorative events in East Germany.[64] Historical documents allowed composers to participate in official commemorative culture, but also provided a way for them to reclaim and reshape narratives of the past that had been so warped by socialist historiography. As references to the sounds of Katzer's own youth, the original sounds of *Aide –Mémoire* had not just documentary value, but an overpowering ability to conjure up memories of both personal and collective pasts. By presenting this work as an official commission, this private lament on his country's past simultaneously serves as a public intervention in his country's present. *Aide –Mémoire* sonically disputes East Germany's official narratives of the Third Reich at a commemorative event designed to bolster that same view of history.

Yet musical documents have always been integral to antifascist commemoration in the GDR. As I have demonstrated, they were just as crucial to the earliest attempts to establish a distinctly East German national antifascist identity through songbooks and material traces of Weimar communism in the 1950s as they were to Katzer's efforts to unravel these fallacies of antifascism in the 1980s. Positioning Katzer's piece within a forty-year history of antifascist commemorative practice rather than against it exposes the gap that emerged from the earliest uses of "real" musical documents in selective interpretations of the German past in the early GDR and Katzer's reappropriation of the concept of "realism" in the twilight years of the East German state. Katzer's stance toward his source materials not only challenges East Germany's foundational myths, it positions the composer within broader discussions about the work's genre: *musique concrète*.

At its core, *musique concrète* is both archival and documentary. In his "search for a concrete music" in the late 1940s, electroacoustic pioneer Pierre Schaeffer cataloged what he called "sonic fragments," taking sounds and categorizing them by their abstract acoustic qualities rather than their contextual function.[65] Taken in these terms, *Aide –Mémoire* becomes an archive within an archive, where radio broadcasts from German history are refracted through Katzer's electronic manipulations.[66] There is, however, a key difference between the two composers: for Schaeffer, the aim of *musique concrète* is to build pieces from abstracted sounds. Taking a sound out of context draws attention to its inherent qualities and ideally detaches a sound from their original sources. But as Brian Kane notes in his recent study of acousmatic sound, works in this vein often achieve their fullest effects through dissociation: either through a belated discovery of what the source is, or in recognizing a sound and then tracing its distortion.[67]

It is this cycle of recognition that saturates *Aide –Mémoire*, particularly because Katzer exploits situations of sonic similarity to create re-readings of German history. This provided a means to challenge the state through sound. But crucially, it stems from, and is fundamentally connected to, the gap between musical material and sonic phenomena that characterized the earliest uses of commemorative music in the GDR. From the printed archives of the workers' song book to the raw acoustic documents of Katzer's *musique concrète*, this shifting notion of what a musical document was and could be not only offers a more complicated narrative of East German commemorative practices, but connects these modes of confronting the past with much broader trends in sonic expression throughout the postwar period.

Martha Sprigge is assistant professor of musicology at the University of California, Santa Barbara. Her current research examines musical expressions of mourning and loss in twentieth-century Germany. She has published various articles and is currently writing a book about commemorative culture in the German Democratic Republic.

Notes

1. The landmark account of the role of antifascism within East German discourse is Antonia Grunenberg's *Antifaschismus – ein deutscher Mythos* (Reinbek, 1993). Jeffrey

Herf's work on public memory of the Holocaust in postwar Germany places this ideology in comparative context with West Germany. See Herf, *Divided Memory: The Nazi Past in the Two Germanys* (Cambridge, MA, 1997).
2. Julia Hell, *Post-Fascist Fantasies: Psychoanalysis, History, and the Literature of East Germany* (Durham, NC, 1997), 2.
3. Elaine Kelly, *Composing the Canon in the German Democratic Republic: Narratives of Nineteenth-Century Music* (New York, 2014), 137–42.
4. This argument aligns with David Bathrick's assertion that East German intellectuals challenged the SED from "within the mastercode" of East German discourse. Bathrick, *The Powers of Speech: The Politics of Culture in the GDR* (Lincoln, 1995), 2.
5. In this regard, my chapter contributes to a recent body of musicological literature that focuses on materials of transmission. For recent literature that focuses on tape, see Andrea Bohlman and Peter McMurray, eds., "Tape," special issue, *Twentieth-Century Music* 14, no. 1 (2017). For scholarship that focuses on tape and transmission in the Eastern bloc during the latter decades of the Cold War, see Andrea Bohlman, "Solidarity, Song, and the Sound Document," *Journal of Musicology* 33, no. 2 (2016): 232–69; and Martin Daughtry, "'Sonic Samizdat': Situating Unofficial Recording in the Post-Stalinist Soviet Union," *Poetics Today* 30, no. 1 (2009): 27–65.
6. Herf, *Divided Memory*, 163–67.
7. Bill Niven, "The GDR and Memory of the Bombing of Dresden," in *Germans as Victims: Remembering the Past in Contemporary Germany*, ed. Bill Niven (New York, 2006), 114.
8. Sigrid Meuschel and Barbara Könczöl, "The Sacralization of Politics in the GDR," *Telos* 136 (2006): 26–58.
9. On official memory at Buchenwald, see Sarah Farmer, "Symbols That Face Two Ways: Commemorating the Victims of Nazism and Stalinism at Buchenwald and Sachsenhausen," *Representations* 49 (1995): 97–119; and Claudia Koonz, "Germany's Buchenwald: Whose Shrine? Whose Memory?," in *The Art of Memory: Holocaust Memorials in History*, ed. James Young (New York, 1994), 111–19.
10. Other concentration camps had been liberated by Allied armies as they moved closer to the German capital.
11. Eric Weitz notes that German communism was forged on the streets of the Weimar Republic rather than around specific monuments. See Weitz, *Creating German Communism: From Popular Protests to Socialist State* (Princeton, 1997), 233.
12. David Tompkins, "Sound and Socialist Identity: Negotiating the Musical Soundscape in the Stalinist GDR," in *Germany in the Loud Twentieth Century*, ed. Florence Feiereisen and Alexandra Merley Hill (New York, 2011), 112.
13. Inge Lammel, *Jüdische Lebenswege: Ein kulturhistorische Streifzug durch Pankow und Niederschönhausen* (Berlin, 2007).
14. Inge Lammel, ed., *Das Lied im Kampf geboren*, 10 vols. (Leipzig, 1957–62).
15. Inge Lammel, *Arbeitermusikkultur in Deutschland, 1844–1945: Bilder und Dokumente* (Leipzig, 1984). For further analysis of the role of folk music in the GDR, see Philip V. Bohlman, "600 Jahre DDR-Musikgeschichte am Beispiel deutsche Volkslieder demokratischen Charakters," in *Musikwissenschaft und Kalter Krieg: Das Beispiel DDR*, ed. Nina Noeske and Matthias Tischer (Cologne, 2010), 79–87.
16. For further discussions of the content and ideology of East German songbooks, see Bohlman, "600 Jahre DDR-Musikgeschichte," 79–87; and Joy Calico, "'We Are

Changing the World!' *New German Folk Songs* for the Free German Youth (1950)," in *Musical Childhoods and the Cultures of Youth*, ed. Susan Boynton and Roe-Min Kok (Middletown, CT, 2006), 190–204.
17. Gisela Probst-Effah, "Das Moorsoldatenlied," *Jahrbuch für Volksliedforschung* 40 (1995): 75–83.
18. Shirli Gilbert, *Music in the Holocaust: Confronting Life in the Nazi Ghettos and Camps* (Oxford, 2005), 105, 111–12.
19. Guido Fackler, "Music in Concentration Camps 1933–1945," trans. Peter Logan, *Music and Politics* 1, no. 1 (2007): 4.
20. Ibid.
21. Hanns Eisler and Rudi Goguel, "Die Moorsoldaten," in *Das Lied im Kampf geboren*, vol. 7 *Lieder aus den faschistischen Konzentrationslagern*, ed. Inge Lammel and Günter Hofmeyer (Leipzig, 1962), 14–15, 18.
22. Ibid., 16.
23. Rudi Goguel, quoted in Probst-Effah, "Das Moorsoldatenlied," 78.
24. Thomas C. Fox, *Stated Memory: East Germany and the Holocaust* (Rochester, 1991), 41.
25. Bathrick, *Powers of Speech*, 10–13.
26. Mary Fulbrook, *Dissonant Lives: Generations and Violence through the German Dictatorships* (New York, 2011), 330.
27. Christa Wolf, *Im Dialog* (Frankfurt, 1990), 136.
28. The concert was recorded and released as Wolf Biermann, *Das geht sein' sozialistischen Gang*, CBS Records International, 1977. While Biermann is famous for his ironic tone and political critique, subsequent interviews suggest that he genuinely believed in the connection between communism and antifascism promoted by the SED. See Wolf Biermann, Jack Zipes, and Thomas Hoernigk. "Two Interviews with Wolf Biermann," *New German Critique* 10 (1977): 13–27.
29. Georg Katzer, notes to "Aide –Mémoire: Seven Nightmares from the Thousand Year Night…," track 2 on *CMCD: Six Classic Concrete, Electroacoustic and Electronic works: 1970–1990*, ReR Records, 2005.
30. Georg Katzer and Stefan Amzoll, "Kompositionsverfahren im 20. Jahrhundert," in *Komponieren zur Zeit: Gespräche mit Komponisten der DDR*, ed. Mathias Hansen (Leipzig, 1988), 132.
31. Details of the commemorative commission can be found in the archive of the Verband der Komponisten und Musikwissenschaftler der DDR (VKM), now housed at the Archive of the Akademie der Künste (AdK) in Berlin, in file VKM 835 – Auftragswerke/Rundfunk.
32. The program was broadcast on 18 January 1983 and is now available as a recording in the Deutsche Rundfunkarchiv (German Radio Archive, or DRA) in Babelsberg, Potsdam. "Radio DDR – Musikklub: 'Aide –Mémoire' von Georg Katzer und 'Schaffott-Front' von Friedrich Schenker.", StMG 3061, Collection: Tonträger DRA Babelsberg. References from the premiere are drawn from this archival recording, with quotes cited by time stamp.
33. From a 1972 interview, now part of the archive of the Akademie der Künste der DDR (East German Academy of the Arts, AdK–O) at the AdK in Berlin. AdK der DDR (Sektion Musik): "Korrespondenz mit Meisterschülern der Sektion zur Vorbereitung der Publikation 'Die Lehrer und ihre Schüler'." AdK–O 2748, 81–2.

34. Christian Schmidt serves as a useful comparison. A composer who was not a member of the AdK, Schmidt felt artistically isolated and his works were rarely premiered in the GDR. See Kelly, *Composing the Canon*, 155.
35. AdK-O 2748, 82.
36. Tatjana Böhme-Mehner, "The Big Beginning at the End: The Formation of a Fully-Fledged Generation of Composers of Electroacoustic Music in the Last Years of the GDR," *Contemporary Music Review* 30, no. 1 (2011): 119.
37. Sabine Feisst, "Represence of Jewishness in German Music Commemorating the Holocaust since the 1980s: Three Case Studies," in *Dislocated Memories: Jews, Music, and Postwar German Culture*, ed. Tina Frühauf and Lily E. Hirsch (New York, 2014), 222–42; Rudolf Frisius, "Stimmen der Medien," in *Stimme. Stimmen—(Kon)texte. Stimme—Sprache—Klang. Stimmen der Kulturen. Stimme und Medien. Stimme in (Inter)Aktion*, ed. Institut für Neue Musik und Musikerziehung in Darmstadt (Mainz, 2003), 110–36; Kelly, *Composing the Canon*, 139–42; and Elaine Kelly, "Reflective Nostalgia and Diasporic Memory: Composing East Germany after 1989," in *Remembering and Rethinking the GDR: Multiple Perspectives and Plural Authenticities*, ed. Anna Saunders and Debbie Pinfold (New York, 2013), 116–30.
38. Ansgar Diller, *Rundfunkpolitik im Dritten Reich* (Munich, 1980), 9–10. For an in-depth English language study of radio in the Third Reich, particularly the gap between the Nazi image of the radio compared to the realities of dissemination, see: Brian Currid, *A National Acoustics: Music and Mass Publicity in Weimar and Nazi Germany* (Minneapolis, 2006).
39. Carolyn Birdsall stresses the auditory dimensions of Nazi propaganda in her work on Nazi acoustics. She also demonstrates how this audiocentricity shapes memories of the Third Reich for Germans in the postwar period. See Birdsall, *Nazi Soundscapes: Sound, Technology and Urban Space in Germany, 1933–1945* (Amsterdam, 2012); and Birdsall, "Earwitnessing: Sound Memories of the Nazi Period," in *Sound Souvenirs: Audio Technologies, Memory and Cultural Practices*, ed. Karin Bijsterveld and José van Dijck (Amsterdam, 2009), 169–81.
40. David Bathrick, "Making a National Family with the Radio: The Nazi Wunschkonzert," *Modernism/Modernity* 4, no. 1 (1997): 116; Currid, *A National Acoustics*, 21–29.
41. Rita von der Grün, "Funktionen und Formen von Musiksendungen im Rundfunk," in *Musik und Musikpolitik im faschistischen Deutschland*, ed. Hanns Werner Heister and Jochem Wolf (Frankfurt, 1984), 101.
42. Volker Ackermann, *Nationale Totenfeiern in Deutschland: Von Wilhelm I. bis Franz Josef Strauss. Eine Studie zur politischen Semiotik* (Stuttgart, 1990), 265.
43. Frank Trommler, "Conducting Music, Conducting War: Nazi Germany as an Acoustic Experience," in *Sound Matters: Essays on the Acoustics of Modern German Culture*, ed. Nora Alter and Lutz Koepnick (New York, 2004), 68–69.
44. Ibid., 69.
45. Stefan Amzoll, "Neue Musik gegen den Faschismus," *Musik und Gesellschaft* 33, no. 4 (1983): 247.
46. Feisst, "Represence of Jewishness," 238.
47. Eight participants in the failed coup were tried at the Volksgerichtshof on 7 and 8 August 1944. Other conspirators—including Claus von Stauffenberg—had been shot the night of the coup itself. On the trial of the plotters from the failed coup of 20

July 1944, see Peter Hoffmann, "Claus von Stauffenberg and the Military Ethos," in *Leadership and Responsibility in the Second World War*, ed. Brian P. Farrell (Montreal and Kingston, 2004), 167–81.
48. Excerpts from this documentary are available through the Steven Spielberg Film and Video Archive of the United States Holocaust Memorial Museum, Story RG-60. 4633, Film ID 2842. The original recording is housed at the Bundesarchiv in Berlin: Archive Number 3179/BSP 15712 R1+2.
49. See Herf, *Divided Memory*, 3–39.
50. Members of the NKFD began broadcasting speeches on Moscow radio in 1942, hoping to appeal to Wehrmacht soldiers and German prisoners of war to revolt against the Nazis and reclaim Germany from within. The manifesto of the NKFD became an official statement of these principles. Herf, *Divided Memory*, 22.
51. Amzoll, "Neue Musik," 248.
52. Thomas Mann, "Germany and the Germans," in *Thomas Mann's Addresses, Delivered at the Library of Congress, 1942–1949* (Washington, DC, 1963), 47–66.
53. On the *Deutsche Sinfonie* as a paradigmatic antifascist work, see Thomas Phleps, *Hanns Eislers "Deutsche Sinfonie": Ein Beitrag zur Ästhetik des Widerstands* (Kassel, 1988).
54. Cornelia Epping-Jäger, "Hitler's Voice: The Loudspeaker under National Socialism," *Intermediality: History and Theory of the Arts, Literature and Technologies* 17 (2011): 84.
55. Konrad Jarausch, "The Failure of East German Antifascism: Some Ironies of History as Politics," *German Studies Review* 14, no. 1 (1991): 89.
56. DRA: StMG 3061 (8:06– 8:28).
57. DRA: StMG 3061 (8:56–9:30).
58. DRA: StMG 3061 (12:53–13:03).
59. DRA: StMG 3061 (10:50–12:04).
60. Amzoll, "Neue Musik," 247.
61. According to Feisst, Amzoll played a significant role in ensuring *Aide –Mémoire* was premiered as well. Feisst, "Represence of Jewishness," 229.
62. DRA Archiv: StMG 3061 (14:40–17:04). These are the same arguments Amzoll reiterates in his essay "Neue Musik," 246–48.
63. Nina Noeske, *Musikalische Dekonstruktion: neue Instrumentalmusik in der DDR* (Cologne, 2007), 401.
64. For examples from the Soviet Union, see Margarita Mazo, "The Present and Unpredictable Past: Music and Musical Life of St. Petersburg and Moscow since the 1960s," *International Journal of Musicology* Vol. 5 (1996): 371–400.
65. Pierre Schaeffer, *In Search of a Concrete Music*, trans. Christine North and John Dack (Berkeley, 2012), 13–14.
66. This practice extends beyond the East German context. In a recent article, I position Katzer within a larger postwar German history of using recordings from the Third Reich to formulate responses to the Nazi past. See Martha Sprigge, "Tape Work and Memory Work in Postwar Germany," *Twentieth–Century Music* 14, no. 1 (2017): 49–63.
67. Brian Kane, *Sound Unseen: Acousmatic Sound in Theory and in Practice* (New York, 2014). His theoretical outline of acousmatic sound comes through most clearly in chapter 5, "Kafka and the Ontology of Acousmatic Sound," 134–61.

Bibliography

Recordings

Biermann, Wolf. *Das geht sein' sozialistischen Gang.* CBS Records International, 1977.
Katzer, Georg. "Aide –Mémoire." On *CMCD: Six Classic Concrete, Electroacoustic and Electronic Works: 1970–1990.* ReR Records, 2005.

Printed Sources

Ackermann, Volker. *Nationale Totenfeiern in Deutschland: Von Wilhelm I. bis Franz Josef Strauss. Eine Studie zur politischen Semiotik.* Stuttgart: Klett-Cotta, 1990.
Amzoll, Stefan. "Neue Musik gegen den Faschismus." *Musik und Gesellschaft* 33, no. 4 (1983): 246–48.
Bathrick, David. *The Powers of Speech: The Politics of Culture in the GDR.* Lincoln: University of Nebraska Press, 1995.
———. "Making a National Family with the Radio: The Nazi *Wunschkonzert.*" *Modernism/Modernity* 4, no. 1 (1997): 115–27.
Birdsall, Carolyn. *Nazi Soundscapes: Sound, Technology and Urban Space in Germany, 1933–1945.* Amsterdam: Amsterdam University Press, 2012.
———. "Earwitnessing: Sound Memories of the Nazi Period." In *Sound Souvenirs: Audio Technologies, Memory and Cultural Practices,* edited by Karin Bijsterveld and José van Dijck, 169–81. Amsterdam: Amsterdam University Press, 2009.
Biermann, Wolf, Jack Zipes, and Thomas Hoernigk. "Two Interviews with Wolf Biermann." *New German Critique* 10 (1977): 13–27.
Böhme-Mehner, Tatjana. "The Big Beginning at the End: The Formation of a Fully-Fledged Generation of Composers of Electroacoustic Music in the Last Years of the GDR." *Contemporary Music Review* 30, no. 1 (2011): 119–23.
Bohlman, Andrea. "Solidarity, Song, and the Sound Document." *Journal of Musicology* 33, no. 2 (2016): 232–69.
Bohlman, Andrea, and Peter McMurray, eds. "Tape." Special issue, *Twentieth-Century Music* 14, no. 1 (2017).
Bohlman, Philip V. "600 Jahre DDR-Musikgeschichte am Beispiel deutsche Volkslieder demokratischen Charakters." In *Musikwissenschaft und Kalter Krieg: Das Beispiel DDR,* edited by Nina Noeske and Matthias Tischer, 79–87. Cologne: Böhlau, 2010.
Calico, Joy. "'We Are Changing the World!' New German Folk Songs for the Free German Youth (1950)." In *Musical Childhoods and the Cultures of Youth,* edited by Susan Boynton and Roe-Min Kok, 190–204. Middletown, CT: Wesleyan University Press, 2006.
Currid, Brian. *A National Acoustics: Music and Mass Publicity in Weimar and Nazi Germany.* Minneapolis: University of Minnesota Press, 2006.

Daughtry, Martin. "'Sonic Samizdat': Situating Unofficial Recording in the Post-Stalinist Soviet Union." *Poetics Today* 30, no. 1 (2009): 27–65.
Diller, Ansgar. *Rundfunkpolitik im Dritten Reich*. Munich: Deutscher Taschenbuch Verlag, 1980.
Epping-Jäger, Cornelia. "Hitler's Voice: The Loudspeaker under National Socialism." *Intermediality: History and Theory of the Arts, Literature and Technologies* 17 (2011): 83–104.
Fackler, Guido. "Music in Concentration Camps 1933–1945." Translated by Peter Logan. *Music and Politics* 1, no. 1 (2007). Retrieved 8 April 2016 from http://dx.doi.org/10.3998/mp.9460447.0001.102.
Farmer, Sarah. "Symbols That Face Two Ways: Commemorating the Victims of Nazism and Stalinism at Buchenwald and Sachsenhausen." *Representations* 49 (1995): 97–119.
Feisst, Sabine. "Represence of Jewishness in German Music Commemorating the Holocaust since the 1980s: Three Case Studies." In *Dislocated Memories: Jews, Music, and Postwar German Culture*, edited by Tina Frühauf and Lily E. Hirsch, 222–42. New York: Oxford University Press, 2014.
Fox, Thomas C. *Stated Memory: East Germany and the Holocaust*. Rochester: Camden House, 1991.
Frisius, Rudolf. "Stimmen der Medien." In *Stimme. Stimmen—(Kon)texte. Stimme—Sprache—Klang. Stimmen der Kulturen. Stimme und Medien. Stimme in (Inter) Aktion*, edited by Institut für Neue Musik und Musikerziehung in Darmstadt, 110–36. Mainz: Schott, 2003.
Fulbrook, Mary. *Dissonant Lives: Generations and Violence through the German Dictatorships*. New York: Oxford University Press, 2011.
Gilbert, Shirli. *Music in the Holocaust: Confronting Life in the Nazi Ghettos and Camps*. Oxford: Clarendon, 2005.
Grün, Rita von der. "Funktionen und Formen von Musiksendungen im Rundfunk." In *Musik und Musikpolitik im faschistischen Deutschland*, edited by Hanns Werner Heister and Jochem Wolf, 98–106. Frankfurt: Fischer Taschenbuch, 1984.
Grunenberg, Antonia. *Antifaschismus – ein deutscher Mythos*. Reinbek: Rowohlt, 1993.
Hell, Julia. *Post-Fascist Fantasies: Psychoanalysis, History, and the Literature of East Germany*. Durham, NC: Duke University Press, 1997.
Herf, Jeffrey. *Divided Memory: The Nazi Past in the Two Germanys*. Cambridge, MA: Harvard University Press, 1997.
Hoffmann, Peter. "Claus von Stauffenberg and the Military Ethos." In *Leadership and Responsibility in the Second World War*, edited by Brian P. Farrell, 167–81. Montreal and Kingston: McGill-Queen's University Press, 2004.
Jarausch, Konrad. "The Failure of East German Antifascism: Some Ironies of History as Politics." *German Studies Review* 14, no. 1 (1991): 85–102.

Kane, Brian. *Sound Unseen: Acousmatic Sound in Theory and in Practice*. New York: Oxford University Press, 2014.

Katzer, Georg, and Stefan Amzoll. "Kompositionsverfahren im 20. Jahrhundert." In *Komponieren zur Zeit: Gespräche mit Komponisten der DDR*, edited by Mathias Hansen, 109–41. Leipzig: VEB Deutscher Verlag für Musik, 1988.

Kelly, Elaine. "Reflective Nostalgia and Diasporic Memory: Composing East Germany after 1989." In *Remembering and Rethinking the GDR: Multiple Perspectives and Plural Authenticities*, edited by Anna Saunders and Debbie Pinfold, 116–30. New York: Palgrave Macmillan, 2013.

———. *Composing the Canon in the German Democratic Republic: Narratives of Nineteenth-Century Music*. New York: Oxford University Press, 2014.

Koonz, Claudia. "Germany's Buchenwald: Whose Shrine? Whose Memory?" In *The Art of Memory: Holocaust Memorials in History*, edited by James Young, 111–19. New York: Prestel, 1994.

Lammel, Inge, ed. *Das Lied im Kampf geboren*. 10 vols. Leipzig: Hofmeister, 1957–62.

———. *Arbeitermusikkultur in Deutschland, 1844–1945: Bilder und Dokumente*. Leipzig: Deutscher Verlag für Musik, 1984.

———. *Jüdische Lebenswege: Ein kulturhistorische Streifzug durch Pankow und Niederschönhausen*. Berlin: Hentrich & Hentrich, 2007.

Lammel, Inge, and Günter Hofmeyer, eds. *Das Lied im Kampf geboren*. Vol. 7. *Lieder aus den faschistischen Konzentrationslagern*. Leipzig: VEB Friedrich Hofmeister, 1962.

Mann, Thomas. "Germany and the Germans." In *Thomas Mann's Addresses, Delivered at the Library of Congress, 1942–1949*, 47–66. Washington, DC: Library of Congress, 1963.

Meuschel, Sigrid, and Barbara Könczöl. "The Sacralization of Politics in the GDR." *Telos* 136 (2006): 26–58.

Mazo, Margarita. "The Present and Unpredictable Past: Music and Musical Life of St. Petersburg and Moscow since the 1960s." *International Journal of Musicology* 5 (1996): 371–400.

"Manifest des Nationalkomitees 'Freies Deutschland' an die Wehrmacht und an das deutsche Volk." In *Zur Geschichte der Neuesten Zeit: Die Niederlage Hitlerdeutschlands und die Schaffung der antifaschistisch-demokratischen Ordnung*, by Walter Ulbricht. 2nd edition, 365–371. Berlin: Dietz, 1955.

Niven, Bill. "The GDR and Memory of the Bombing of Dresden." In *Germans as Victims: Remembering the Past in Contemporary Germany*, edited by Bill Niven, 109–29. New York: Palgrave Macmillan, 2006.

Noeske, Nina. *Musikalische Dekonstruktion: neue Instrumentalmusik in der DDR*. Cologne: Böhlau, 2007.

Phleps, Thomas. *Hanns Eislers "Deutsche Sinfonie": Ein Beitrag zur Ästhetik des Widerstands*. Kassel: Bärenreiter, 1988.

Probst-Effah, Gisela. "Das Moorsoldatenlied." *Jahrbuch für Volksliedforschung* 40 (1995): 75–83.

Schaeffer, Pierre. *In Search of a Concrete Music*. Translated by Christine North and John Dack. Berkeley: University of California Press, 2012.
Sprigge, Martha. "Tape Work and Memory Work in Postwar Germany." *Twentieth-Century Music* 14, no. 1 (2017): 49–63.
Tompkins, David. "Sound and Socialist Identity: Negotiating the Musical Soundscape in the Stalinist GDR." In *Germany in the Loud Twentieth Century*, edited by Florence Feiereisen and Alexandra Merley Hill, 111–23. New York: Oxford University Press, 2011.
Trommler, Frank. "Conducting Music, Conducting War: Nazi Germany as an Acoustic Experience." In *Sound Matters: Essays on the Acoustics of Modern German Culture*, edited by Nora Alter and Lutz Koepnick, 68–69. New York: Berghahn, 2004.
Weitz, Eric. *Creating German Communism: From Popular Protests to Socialist State*. Princeton, NJ: Princeton University Press, 1997.
Wolf, Christa. *Im Dialog*. Frankfurt: Luchterhand, 1990.

CHAPTER 11

Sprockets + Autobahn
Kraftwerk Parodies, German Electronic Music, and Retro Dreams in Amerika

SEAN NYE

We have a special type of black humour. We always wear black. It has to do with truth and certain aspects of the truth. Funny and serious at the same time. Revolutionary and funny.
—Ralf Hütter

That is one of the greatest things that Jerry Seinfeld ever said about my stuff. And that is, you managed to break all rules of American parody. You parodied something that nobody knew—in both Dieter and in Austin Powers.
—Mike Myers

Ask the average music fan from the United States or the United Kingdom who has come of age after the 1960s—and who has an interest in German music—what his or her primary associations of Germanness and music are, and the answer will not necessarily include any discussion of great classical composers from prior to World War II. Indeed, it might include not a verbal answer at all, but a range of parodic bodily gestures invoking a machine. The technopop band that is the primary reference for this parodic response is Kraftwerk—the so-called "Beach Boys from Düsseldorf."[1] In fact, these machine gestures now have a long history; thus, the responses will likely also refer to various techno flowerings and industrial variations that have developed in the wake of Kraftwerk.

Such gestural responses, made by countless British and Americans, and many other nationalities, since the 1970s, are often not only parodies of musical Germanness, but, as we shall see, imitations of *already established* American and British parodies of Kraftwerk. These technopop parodies have proven highly influential for the receptions of music and German identity across various channels and oceans. In the spirit of this transatlantic humor and parodic exchange, I trace here the ways in which Kraftwerk—and Kraftwerk imitations—have spread through Anglo-American popular culture since the

1970s. I explore how Kraftwerk was instrumental in creating an *electronic turn* in international conceptions of German musical identity, set within the larger traditions of German electronic music: Krautrock, *Neue Deutsche Welle*, electronic body music (EBM), goth-industrial, techno (from trance to minimal), and more. Kraftwerk's own careful reception of British and American culture will in turn be explored, as well as the various stages of their bodily comportments and poses.

Kraftwerk's relationship to parody is itself complex and multivalent. I thus first situate Kraftwerk's own engagement with parody, especially as it relates to Germanness. Here, I argue that Kraftwerk's performative modes established technopop as a specific form of musical parody of industrial culture and its media signposts. Supposedly personal and human, identity in Kraftwerk's various modes and albums during the 1970s and 1980s, especially *The Man-Machine* (1978), takes on the model of identity as a machine. As industrial performance, Kraftwerk's success distinctively marks the popularization of cyborg humor in electronic music.[2] To put it in a poetic way, involving more subtle bodily gestures, this parody of machines invites one to see the winking technopop eye behind the unblinking robot eye.

What was implicit in Kraftwerk's performance was then explicitly, and sometimes excessively, developed by musicians, filmmakers, writers, and comedians in national and international contexts. Technopop music and parody became industries themselves. Accordingly, in the second and third sections of this chapter, I trace the two most advanced and influential modes of technopop humor in its transatlantic context. Beginning in 1987 and immediately following Kraftwerk's *Electric Cafe* (1986), which embraced the term "technopop,"[3] an intriguing character named Dieter was introduced on Canadian television by the comedian Mike Myers. Dieter later became a comic icon in American pop culture, between 1989 and 1993, as host of a recurring comedy sketch known as "Sprockets." This sketch was featured on the longest-running and most influential comedy and variety series in American TV history: *Saturday Night Live (SNL)*. Thanks to its popularity with American audiences in the 1990s, "Sprockets" was arguably even more successful than Kraftwerk in introducing technopop postures in the United States. In this context, the significance of encountering the parody *without* its historical referent will be addressed, specifically for American receptions of musical Germanness after the electronic turn.

Finally, I will explore the reception of both Kraftwerk and "Sprockets" in the Coen brothers' 1998 film *The Big Lebowski*. This film features the (fictional) technopop band Autobahn in conflict with the great icon of Californian hippie-rock identity, Jeff "The Dude" Lebowski. Often cited as the first cult film of the digital age, *The Big Lebowski* has been as significant to American film as *SNL* is to American TV.[4] In it, the Coen brothers offer a critical take on understandings of Germans as Kraftwerk machines. By drawing attention to parody and the construction of identity as a historical process, this metaparody calls on American culture to address post-1989 cultural and political reality. In doing so, the film takes a retro turn in exploring American dreams of Germans. This move is appropriate since Kraftwerk offers a special case of a retro-pop band in its own engagement with past futures. In fact, retro becomes the parallel song beside machine parody and its various material presents.

Exploring this history will help to address a number of questions regarding the cultural work that parodies of Kraftwerk do. Is Kraftwerk already performing a parody of itself, and of Germanness? If so, what do British or American parodies of Kraftwerk accomplish? Who is playing the joke on whom? And fundamentally, how does this machine humor function? To be sure, the best comedy does not give its jokes away easily, but invites one in. It also does not apologize for its style of performance. In this spirit, I will contend that Kraftwerk demonstrates *the industrial art of deadpan humor*. Indeed, Kraftwerk's wit works so well precisely because it rubs against Anglo-American stereotypes that Germans are humorless.

Tanz-Musik: Kraftwerk's Poses, 1970–87

The unique history of Kraftwerk in representing German identity in Anglo-American pop culture took a number of twists and turns. The Düsseldorf-based band was founded in 1968 as Organisation. Their first album, *Tone Float* (1970), was released not in West Germany, but in the United Kingdom, a foretaste of the group's international connections and receptions.[5] Ralf Hütter and Florian Schneider, the two primary members, changed the band's name to Kraftwerk that same year. Their experimental productions in this period became linked to other West German bands, lumped by the British press under the long-contested name of "Krautrock."[6] Under various configurations, Kraftwerk released three albums in this instrumental "Krautrock" phase: *Kraftwerk* (1970), *Kraftwerk 2* (1972), and *Ralf & Florian* (1973).

A decisive shift occurred, however, with the release of their fourth album, *Autobahn* (1974). The title track became a revolutionary blueprint for technopop, as well as an exploration of German-engineered identity.[7] While the original clocked in at 22:42, a shortened radio-friendly version marked the song as electronic pop. It was this version that hit the airwaves and climbed the charts in the United States in early 1975.[8] In April of that year, Kraftwerk toured the United States for the first time, leading to a momentous German-American "first contact" with the music journalist Lester Bangs in Detroit. Bangs's interview with Hütter and Schneider resulted in his influential article "Kraftwerkfeature: Or, How I Learned to Stop Worrying and Love the

Balm," which was published in the UK under the sensational title "Kraftwerk: The Final Solution to the Music Problem?"[9] In its awful analogy between the Holocaust, Germanness, and efficiency, this title pointed to the nascent punk satire of taste and morals as well the 1970s examinations of, to borrow Susan Sontag's term, "fascinating fascism."[10] The conversation with Bangs, a study in intercultural communication, reveals Kraftwerk working out their own presentation of music, technology, and Germanness abroad.

Following this tour, Kraftwerk entered a phase marked by an extraordinary level of productivity and innovation. With the addition of Wolfgang Flür and Karl Bartos to complete the classic four-member configuration of the band, Kraftwerk released four concept albums in the new "technopop" style: *Radio-Activity* (1975), *Trans-Europe Express* (1977), *The Man-Machine* (1978), and *Computer World* (1981). These albums featured strategically placed English- and German-language releases, which resulted in sustained reception by the international music press and by club culture. Another American tour, and world tour, followed in 1981, and as the band's production activities wound down, their final album in their "classic" period, *Electric Cafe* (1986), later retitled *Techno Pop*, was released.

Central to their constructions of German identity during this period were Kraftwerk's representations of the body, dance, and technology. Some key developments followed the longhaired Krautrock years, which had signified countercultural resistance to what was regarded as reserved "mainstream" West German society. A notable shift can be found in their third album, *Ralf & Florian*. Having linked up with the artist Emil Schult, who offered important input on music, image, and design, Hütter and Schneider refined their techniques of visual presentation. On the cover, they suddenly appear like sound engineers, or just plain scientists, rather than rock heroes. *Ralf & Florian* also explores German identity, but through the British artists Gilbert & George. In fact, Kraftwerk's initial explorations in German posture might have been inspired by Gilbert & George's presentation of British uprightness through their art of "living sculptures." As Tim Barr explains, Gilbert & George's "appearance was that of two very straight, square, quintessentially English, civil servants. This image was in direct contrast to the radicalism of their artistic strategies."[11] In other words, classic English and German reserve becomes a binational pop art.[12] On the cover of *Ralf & Florian*, Florian has already fully taken on this persona, while Ralf is on his way. Kraftwerk also invites the listener to imagine the cyborg kinetics of electronic dance music, featured on such tracks as "Tanzmusik" and the proto-techno "Kristallo."

A year later, on *Autobahn*, Kraftwerk refined this image by turning from the stiff British Gilbert & George to the relaxed sunshine of the Beach Boys. The title track's engagement with Californian and West German car culture was encapsulated in the mistranslation of the Beach Boys' "Fun fun fun" (a teenage joyride in a Ford Thunderbird) to *"Fahr'n Fahr'n Fahr'n"* (an experiential trip in a Volkswagen or Mercedes-Benz). Cultural (mis)translations of language, music, and dance become here an important foundation for cyborg humor. Indeed, Kraftwerk's translations of figures such as Gilbert & George and the Beach Boys proceed through both distance and proximity. Kraftwerk's distinctively German speech-song on the title track engages in a cultural translation of both *Schlager* and surf rock. The English lyrics on their later albums made literal this process of translation, moving between techno-German and accented English.

"Autobahn" was itself an export word—a German trope needing no translation. It reflected the twin status of German music and engineering as traditional exports. Kraftwerk's *Autobahn* would thus twist the usual associations of German music from the classical to the electronic tradition. The accessibility of "Autobahn" car culture to Anglo-American ears further elicits the question of the links between identity, tourism, and stereotypes. Paul Alessandrini, a French rock critic who worked with Kraftwerk, notes, "They have always made use of stereotypes, it's like they say, 'We came from a country which evokes a certain type of imagery, a lot of clichés, so let's play this game, let's transform ourselves into these stereotypes.'"[13] This view reflects Kraftwerk's exploration of the Beach Boys' extraordinary success in representing California—so much so that the band and the Golden State can hardly be separated. As Hütter explained to Bangs in 1975, "We are not aiming so much for the music; it's the psychological structure of someone like the Beach Boys."[14]

Kraftwerk's interpretation of postwar musical history and technology at this time is also significant. In discussion with Bangs, Hütter expresses the view that (West) Germany had no cultural identity between the late 1940s and early 1960s beyond Anglo-American pop and dreadful *Schlager*. He reverses traditional assumptions regarding Germany as primarily a cultural and musical nation. Germany in this era is the Germany of the *Wirtschaftswunder*, involving prosaic and "nonmusical" bourgeois life. This mundanity is the primordial surrounding for technopop. The historical picture is thus reversed: following 1945, (West) German political and economic modernization comes early, whereas culture and music arrive late. The prosaic industrialism of the *Wirtschaftswunder* becomes the historical impetus for the post-1960s exploration of various industrial pasts and signposts of identity.

The supposed destruction of German culture by the Nazis makes matters even more complicated. Kraftwerk had to carefully access and reassess prewar art and music. Here postwar culture gains an *anxious* industrial foundation. This anxiety regarding West German postwar cultural expression and music became especially apparent in British satire during the 1970s. After all, "Krautrock" was primarily a British coinage. Unlike the export word "Autobahn," the import word "Krautrock" is both a marker of international success and fandom and a reminder of the particularity, not the universality, of German music.[15] Krautrock satire was rife in the UK of the 1970s. As David Stubbs points out, this was in the tradition of British satire: "Goose-stepping, combs pressed under noses and straplines filled with *Achtungs!*, Panzer and Luftwaffe references were all part of the merriment."[16] This satire included article titles such as "Can: They Have Ways of Making You Listen…" and the aforementioned "Kraftwerk: The Final Solution to the Music Problem?"[17] While praising the music, the tendency in both the United Kingdom and the United States to reduce machine music and technopop identity to send-ups of Germans thus became a repeated challenge during the Krautrock era and after.

Kraftwerk's poses took on various modes following *Autobahn* and the band's intense international reception. By 1975, the group presented itself in the unified image of a four-piece pop band. As Diedrich Diederichsen argues, the three primary inspirations for Kraftwerk's presentations came from camp (as stylized performance exceeding an explicit message), the image of the pop artist (which, importantly, is transferable across media), and the discovery of a sense of "Germanness."[18] These multiple modes included the Weimar-meets-*film-noir* suits featured on the album cover of *Trans-Europe Express* (1977) and in the music video for the title track. These images were augmented by Kraftwerk's classic engagement with Düsseldorf fashion and club culture in "Showroom Dummies," another track from the album. Following the amusing (mis)translation "We are standing here, exposing ourselves," the "Showroom Dummies" break through the glass and conclude: "We go into a club, and there we start to dance." Indeed, in 1977, the same year as the release of Giorgio Moroder and Donna Summer's Eurodisco epic "I Feel Love," Kraftwerk's music takes on a pose informed by club culture. And here, just as industrial deadpan humor rubs against the stereotype of humorless Germans, Kraftwerk offers a surprising presentation of a German disco dance.

From the identity established in the proclamation "We are Showroom Dummies," Kraftwerk moved to a more direct statement of machine identity: "We Are the Robots," on *The Man-Machine* (1978). Wolfgang Flür explains, "In the many reviews and articles that appeared in the international music press … we were often described as puppet-like, cold and robotic. This gave us the idea to build on our theme of being window dummies."[19] The 1978 music video to "The Robots" accordingly takes the form of a cyborg *Technotanz*. The album represents Kraftwerk's most iconic pop mode—that of a red-uniformed organization with actual robots on stage. This heightened form of technopop parody can be compared to previous, playful responses to 1970s Krautrock discourse. Kraftwerk's cyborg image is here a late example of Julian Cope's "Five Classic Images of Krautrock," a delineation of excessive performances of Krautrock-Germanness, which partly responded to Anglo-American satire.[20] Cope's selection includes the Teutonic covers of Amon Düül II's *Live in London* (1973), depicting a steel-helmeted monster invading the British capital, and *Made in Germany* (1975), featuring the tracks "Mr. Kraut's Jinx" and "La Krautoma." Such depictions of technology and invasion were later represented in David Bowie's 1977 homage to Kraftwerk as rocket fantasy, "V-2 Schneider."

Yet, in *The Man-Machine*, the identity markers of satirical Krautrock excess are at once more subtle and abstract; the red, white, and black cover represents both central Europe and eastern Europe, a generalized exotic European Other. The geographic locus could be Communist Russia, the German Empire, Weimar Germany, or Nazi Germany. As Teutonic moment, *The Man-Machine* challenges easy interpretation by turning east and wearing red shirts. From Gilbert & George and the Beach Boys, we now have a mix of *Metropolis* and El Lissitzky, Russian revolution and German revolution/reaction.

One might have expected this eastern and central European imagery to be alienating in the world of Anglo-American pop. *The Man-Machine*, however, proved a massive hit in the United Kingdom. It set off a wave of synthpop, emulated by stars like Gary Numan, with "The Model" subsequently climbing to the top of the British charts in 1982. If Kraftwerk had once imitated Gilbert & George, British synthpop now imitated Kraftwerk. But by flirting with Teutonic imagery, Kraftwerk also fell into a trap. Despite the Russian references, *The Man-Machine* gave the world a chance to fixate on their exotic cyborg Germanness, which dominated their subsequent reception and in turn their own comportment. Kraftwerk has reinforced these associations to this day; on tour, the band is always introduced as the *"Mensch-Maschine."* Indeed, with an album that begins with "The Robots," includes the single "The Model," and ends with "The Man-Machine," Kraftwerk had saturated its exploration of cyborg humor and technopop parody as bodily performance.

Minimalist and digital refinements followed on *Computer World*, inspired by global networks and a focus that moved even further east, to Japan, with the reception of Yellow Magic Orchestra and computer game culture, along with the office worker performances of "Pocket Calculator." At the same time, Kraftwerk explored anxieties regarding technopolitical surveillance invoked by the terrorism and political drama of the *"deutsche Herbst"* of the late 1970s. The band's image became a kind of simulacrum. The album cover depicted their digital countenances on a computer screen, while all other album images were of the robot dummies.

Starting in the 1980s, Kraftwerk donned all black while on tour, and their album *Electric Cafe* (1986) added a computer-modeled 3-D touch to their evolving techno style. By this time, intense international interest had moved the band's reception beyond the Krautrock moment of the mid 1970s. In the United States, club culture and hip-hop became the loci for Kraftwerk's music, which also inaugurated a key electronic turn in links between African American and German musical styles. Kraftwerk was sampled on Afrika Bambaataa and the Soulsonic Force's "Planet Rock" (1982), and techno and electro artists, such as Los Angeles–based Egyptian Lover and Detroit-based Cybotron, were heavily influenced by the band. Derrick May thus described Detroit techno as follows: "It's like George Clinton and Kraftwerk are stuck in an elevator with only a sequencer to keep them company."[21] These developments established Kraftwerk firmly in American club culture in the 1980s, an engagement paralleled by the postpunk, industrial, and synthpop reception in Britain.

Indeed, Kraftwerk's final album from this period, *Electric Cafe*, aka *Techno Pop*, is primarily a response to the new ubiquity of electronic dance music as *technopop*. If it is a concept album, then it is the meta-concept of technopop itself. Industrial and computer music are revealed to be the new universal, moving German pop beyond regional particularity. Kraftwerk reflects their British emulators here on such synthpop-inspired tracks as "The Telephone Call." Originally forging a new German musical identity, Kraftwerk was now incorporated into British synthpop, African American electro and techno, and a nascent global club culture. A new transnational pop unity beckoned. And yet, on the music video for "The Telephone Call," released in 1987, we see Kraftwerk in a style that points to what will follow. In a black-and-white retro video, the band appears in black turtlenecks: expressionism meets MTV. Aside from the leather gloves, the outfits look like the model for Dieter, a comic character who would reemphasize Kraftwerk's Germanness. Dieter arrived on the American stage in 1989 to spread technopop across the United States—and beyond the cultures of musical fandom. Through Dieter and his (fictional) show, *Sprockets*, Kraftwerk's music would echo across the Atlantic as the sounds of German pop. These echoes gave rise to a delightful comedy of errors—a musical, linguistic, and cultural (mis)translation.

"Sprockets": Dieter in New York, 1989–93

Following its debut in 1989, the "Sprockets" series became the definitive North American portrayal of Germans and technopop in the post-Krautrock era. The *SNL* sketch featured Dieter, a German art- and culture-obsessed dandy, along with a monkey sidekick named Klaus. While primarily known through "Sprockets," the Dieter character had a significant prehistory. Myers had originally developed Dieter in the mid 1980s for his comedy routine at punk shows in Toronto. The character made his television debut in 1987 on the Canadian TV series *It's Only Rock & Roll*. In the introductory sketch, Dieter is a member of an "electropop" band, and in a mock interview in the style of *This Is Spiñal Tap*, he clarifies who his musical influences are: "Well, Kraftwerk, of course. ... Captain Beefheart."

This Kraftwerk reference aside, Myers has emphasized that the singer and performance artist Klaus Nomi first inspired the creation of the character.[22] In fact, the idea for Dieter came from watching *Saturday Night Live* itself. When Myers was a teenager growing up in Toronto, he saw on 15 December 1979 David Bowie's *SNL* performance with two impressive backup singers. Myers explains: "One of them was Klaus Nomi and I went, what the ..., that's fantastic! That is the weirdest thing I've ever seen in my life. And so, I had never seen German TV, but I thought, *I bet it's like that.*"[23] Dieter's eccentric performances and his queer sexuality certainly demonstrate Nomi's influence. Nomi wore black on *SNL*, just as Dieter would later on "Sprockets." However, when Myers developed the sketch, it became clear that by then the design and music were explicitly influenced by Kraftwerk. The result was a meeting between Kraftwerk and Nomi as German musical parody.

Following Myers's move to New York to join *SNL*, Dieter was introduced on 15 April 1989, now transformed into the host of the West German talk show *Sprockets*. The dominance of Kraftwerk in setting up this new Germanic

Figure 11.1. Dieter is introduced in the "Sprockets" title sequence (screenshot by the author).

aesthetic is clear and striking. Americans viewing *SNL* between 1989 and 1993 would have been introduced to Kraftwerk's music through a sped-up version of "Electric Cafe." This track was played during the title sequence and at the end of each show during the iconic "Sprockets dance"—a *Technotanz* performance in the style of Kraftwerk's "The Robots"—and following Dieter's famous declaration, "Now is the time on *Sprockets* when we dance!" This moment was central to the spreading of German machine parodies throughout the United States. The set design also clearly imitates the constructivist cover of *The Man-Machine*, while Dieter's black turtleneck attire is comparable to the band's performance style in "The Telephone Call." Thus, *The Man-Machine* and *Electric Cafe*, as well as *Computer World*, became the primary stylistic reference points for Kraftwerk parodies on "Sprockets" and in the future. The malleable pop image was fixed. Earlier performance styles during the Krautrock years, *Autobahn*, *Radio-Activity*, and *Trans-Europe Express* were largely forgotten in this new mix.

To be sure, the majority of Americans encountering "Sprockets" would have had little to no knowledge of this earlier history, let alone of the later

Figure 11.2. Technopop Germanness on display. Dieter meets Karl-Heinz (Kyle MacLachlan) to discuss "Germany's Most Disturbing Home Videos" (screenshot by the author).

Figure 11.3. The Sprockets Dance—with full set viewable in the style of *The Man-Machine* (screenshot by the author).

development of Kraftwerk. Yet the parody works on its own; viewers would take away a vague sense that Germans and techno were linked, along with one other musical tradition: atonal and experimental film music. This was the other primary musical element of "Sprockets," reflecting Dieter's expressionist obsessions. This music functions as a soundtrack to the retro art films introduced by various guests and on two sketches entirely devoted to film parody: "Dieter in Space" and "Dieter's Dream." The latter is a humorous mix of expressionism and surrealism. Its "dream" interpretation plays with Freudian psychoanalysis as the primary representation of exotic German identity involving deep subjectivity and sexual/psychic perversion. In sum, Dieter's primary musical associations are technopop and avant-garde film music—no references to the Baroque or Romantic traditions, or other popular music such as jazz or rock, are used in establishing this presentation of musical Germanness.

Aside from these film parodies, "Sprockets" featured two types of sketches. First, the skits consist of interviews that parodied talk shows. Dieter interviews either fellow German artists, in which case the Germanness is ramped up, or American entertainers. When Americans appear, a comedic culture clash ensues. Dieter's idolization of art and obsessive analysis stumble upon

American entertainment. This can be summed up in Dieter's introduction of Jimmy Stewart: Hollywood film star, icon of wholesome White Anglo-Saxon Protestantism, and later in life, writer of sentimental poems. Dieter states:

> Tonight our guest is one of America's foremost poets of anarchy and rebellion. An obsessed outcast, whose dark visions drag us to the edge. His book, *Jimmy Stewart and His Poems*, is filled with biting images that assault the senses, unmasking both reader and poet alike in a macabre dance of despair. ... He has also appeared in films. ... Please welcome, Jimmy Schtewart!

The sketch, however, does not just offer a cliché of American entertainment versus German art. Jimmy Stewart (Dana Carvey) reveals himself to be a kind of William S. Burroughs figure involved in drugs, prostitution, and murder, though still writing sentimental poems like "My Kitten, My Pal." The (mis)translation of American and German culture is brought home by Stewart's inability even to pronounce Dieter's name: "I'd be honored, Dodder." "Dieter!" "Dooder." "Dieter!" "Yeah...."

The second type of sketch on "Sprockets" featured parodies of American TV through, again, comedy as German (mis)translation. These skits, and their American sources, included "Germany's Most Disturbing Home Videos" (*America's Funniest Home Videos*), "Love Werks" (*The Dating Game*), "Das Ist Jeopärdy" (*Jeopardy*), and, most importantly for music, "Dieter's Dance Party" (MTV's *Spring Break*). Of particular interest here is the presentation of Kraftwerk and technopop in the context of German unification. It was fortuitous that little more than a month after the Jimmy Stewart sketch, the Berlin Wall came down. "Sprockets" was thus a key American comedic representation of Germanness at a time of rapid political change, including the death of the GDR and the birth of the Berlin Republic, not to mention the developing culture of rave and techno, reflected in Kraftwerk's compilation *The Mix* (1991).

The fall of the Wall was captured as a transatlantic musical moment in diverse ways. In popular memory, the event was represented more by rock music than classical music; above all, the mood was scored in the Scorpions' 1990 power ballad "Wind of Change." There was also, immediately after the fall, the *Konzert für Berlin* at the Deutschlandhalle on 12 November 1989, which included appearances by Melissa Etheridge and Joe Cocker. A number of Anglo-American concerts at the Berlin Wall followed, such as Crosby, Stills, and Nash on 21 November 1989 and Pink Floyd on 21 July 1990. Most notorious was David Hasselhoff's 1989 New Year's Eve performance of "Looking for Freedom," a single that had topped the German charts for eight weeks that summer.[24]

But before most of these examples came "Sprockets." On 18 November 1989, just days after the inner German borders opened, the sketch featured a satirical report that offers considerable surprises. Dieter's report is subdued despite the political jubilation. As always, he focuses on art and film:

> It has been a very busy week here in Berlin: Jürgen von Keitel's exhibit "Scabs on Canvas" opened at the Schüsselkeller; the Gertrude Brauff troupe previewed their performance in wax at the Theater of Unhappiness ... and the Berlin Wall was dismantled. For the masses the Wall's collapse represents freedom and opportunity. But for me, it is a chance to meet the most brilliant countercultural filmmaker in the East, Gregor Voss!

The meeting with Voss does not go as planned, however; Voss (Woody Harrelson) is overly enthusiastic about the opportunities to consume and travel in the West and no longer cares about art. In a certain sense, Dieter represents a clichéd West German child of the *Wirtschaftswunder*. He naively assumes artistic revolution in Voss's enthusiasm: "I see genius. By seemingly embracing the clichés of the West, he is underscoring its excruciating banality!" In this sketch, *SNL* was certainly bold to present such a parody of German unification just several days following the fall of the Wall.

A retro sci-fi parody, "Dieter in Space," followed a month later, and then, the most musical skit of the series arrived on 17 March 1990: "Dieter's Dance Party" (DDP). This sketch represents German technopop and dancing at its most striking. Like Dieter's original debut on Canadian TV, a clash of musical influences is put on display. However, German taste remains particular. For the average American viewer, DDP would appear as a delightfully strange translation of the current universal: Anglo-American pop culture. As a dance party, DDP clearly references MTV's *Spring Break*, but it flips the college beach party and Florida sunshine into a technopop party that meets goth-industrial club—with German dancers clad in black and inspired by Kraftwerk. Dieter announces, "It is Spring Break here in Germany, so we have a very special show; this week, *Sprockets* Presents: Dieter's Dance Party!" DDP proves to be a Teutonic amalgam of dance and variety shows—a photographic negative of *Spring Break*, along with other Anglo-American music variety programs: *Top of the Pops*, *Soul Train*, *Club MTV*, and others.

At DDP, Kraftwerk's "Electric Cafe" is first played for an extended period, followed by technopop parodies such as "Weird Nun" by Schreibmaschine. Dieter then presents the Euro-Music Charts, a clear reference to *Top of the Pops*. After Schreibmaschine takes the number 2 slot, Dieter announces, "And number 1 for the fifth week in a row, 'Escapade' by Janet Jackson." Myers and his writers emphasize here the European whiteness of Kraftwerk and DDP through the musical love for Jackson, who already had considerable transatlantic pop success by this time. A parody of teenage acne advertisements follows—"Clearasil: Macht das pimplen kaputt!"—which works as a reminder of more standard and US-inspired German youth culture, such as is found on the TV channel RTL and in the pop magazine *BRAVO*. After this comedic ad, the show returns to DDP for a visit by a French dancer and former rent boy named Étienne (Rob Lowe). A parody of dance fads follows, including Étienne's "trout" dance performed to a techno track in the developing style of the new "rave society."

With such a sketch in 1990, "Sprockets" clearly parodies electronic dance music. Though the last "Sprockets" episode was broadcast in 1993, the series continues to resonate in the current fascination with, and export success of, German techno. Myers departed *SNL* in 1995, but Dieter remained iconic and crucial to the legacy of the show. For example, in 2015, *Rolling Stone* selected Dieter as the seventh-greatest character in the forty-year history of *SNL*.[25] Dieter made one more appearance, in 1997, when Myers—who had in the meantime become a comic superstar—hosted *SNL* to promote *Austin Powers: International Man of Mystery*. In fact, following the box office success of the first two Austin Powers films, it became increasingly likely that Dieter and "Sprockets" would enter mainstream American culture on a new level. The production of a feature film was planned for the year 2000. With a script that included references from Hasselhoff to Wim Wenders, not to mention a sample of Kraftwerk's "Autobahn," the film might have definitively planted German technopop and art film as household objects in American pop.[26] The production was canceled, however, as a result of a series of disputes regarding its artistic direction. Dieter and "Sprockets" would stay at the level of niche and hipster fame. Despite this setback, another feature film, *The Big Lebowski*, would echo the "Sprockets" tradition through references to technopop and "Autobahn." Moreover, it would offer new variations on the transatlantic comedy of (mis) translation and firmly plant Kraftwerk parodies in a new pop generation.

Autobahn: Nihilists in Los Angeles, 1998

The Big Lebowski has an exceedingly complex plot line, as well as an enigmatic logic of cultural and historical reference. As an American form of industrial deadpan humor involving pop play and the signposts of identity, the Coen brothers' cult film has a comedic voice as original as that of Kraftwerk. Its parodic tone is also distinct from Myers's British-influenced performance style. Indeed, the Coen brothers' take on film, mythology, and American culture is transferred to explore a quite different pop setting: Los Angeles in the 1990s. Compared to *SNL*'s location in New York, Germany is now even more distant. The strangeness of Kraftwerk's technopop takes on new dimensions in this context. The film reveals itself to be a true comedy of errors in the form of missed messages and mistranslations, including between technopop and American rock.

A postmodern take on the classic film noir *The Big Sleep* (1946), *The Big Lebowski* tells the tale of Jeff "The Dude" Lebowski, an iconic Californian dude and leftover from the 1960s political and cultural revolutions. The Dude's life consists of listening to music, hanging out, smoking pot, drinking White Russians, and bowling with his best buddies, Walter Sobchak, a Jewish-American Vietnam veteran, and Donny (see Figure 11.7). However, the Dude suddenly becomes embroiled in a mystery of intrigue, kidnapping, and mistaken identities, which sets him on a trip through the labyrinth of Los Angeles in his Ford Torino (which becomes progressively battered during this journey). He needs to rescue Bunny, the trophy wife of an ostensibly rich and successful millionaire named Jeff "The Big" Lebowski. Apparently, she has been kidnapped and is being held for ransom, though the Big Lebowski's feminist-artist daughter, Maude, does not believe this to be the case.

During this mission, the Dude becomes concerned with what would appear to be his true enemy, and the kidnappers of Bunny: a group of German "nihilists" who have somehow ended up in Los Angeles. Indeed, this conflict with a bizarre German adversary has much to say about German technopop and its sedimentation in American culture. The musical links are made evident when the Dude, in a key scene, declares to Maude that the kidnapping of Bunny is a "complicated case" involving a "lot of strands to keep in [his] head." At this moment, he holds an additional *strand* in his hand: an LP entitled *Nagelbett*. Apparently, this record was produced by the German nihilists and their head, Uli Kunkel. Maude had brought *Nagelbett* to the Dude's attention while explaining Uli's complex history: "He's a musician, used to have a group, Autobahn. Look in my LPs; they released one album in the late seventies. Their music is sort of … ugh … technopop." The Dude's subsequent dig through vinyl history to locate Autobahn mirrors the film's logic of cultural sampling and mistranslations.

With Autobahn, we have driven full circle from Kraftwerk's translation of the Beach Boys in 1974 to the Coen brothers' L.A. meta-parody of Kraftwerk in 1998. In this late-1990s comic mix, the Coen brothers borrow from "Sprockets" and Dieter in exploring the electronic turn in German musical representations. In fact, Dieter was the original name for the head nihilist in the unrevised version of the film script.[27] This reference to Dieter is, moreover, historically accurate, since *The Big Lebowski* takes place around the time of the Gulf War, which was when "Sprockets" was appearing regularly on *SNL*. However, in contrast to Dieter's camp mix of technopop, TV, and art film, the Coen brothers comment on Hollywood film's depictions of identity through a mix of genres: film noir, the western, and comedy, among others. In other words, just as "Sprockets" makes German mistranslations of American TV, the Coens translate these classic film genres into a bizarre 1990s context with constant parodic references to identity. The Nazis of *film noir* become the technopop nihilists of *neo-noir*.

However, this update is not clear to the film's protagonists. The ambiguity is retained in the Autobahn cover. It is evidently in the style of Kraftwerk's *Man-Machine*, but the elements from the Russian Revolution and Weimar Germany are largely missing; the Teutonic imagery has been ramped up. *Nagelbett* has a sadomasochist and industrial flair, with the rows of nails in a formation like Nuremberg storm troopers (or perhaps, in the Dude's mind, a dystopian bowling alley). Here, the Coen brothers mix various genres of electronic music into a typical Anglo-American fantasy of what "German" technopop might be: a 1990s American update to 1970s British Krautrock satire. To be sure, the "Autobahn" name, the *Man-Machine* cover, and Maude's dismissive definition of the style as "technopop" link the music to Kraftwerk. Yet at the same time, *Nagelbett* and the black leather outfits of the nihilists place them closer to the EBM and goth-industrial tradition of bands like Deutsch Amerikanische Freundschaft. By the time of *The Big Lebowski*'s release in 1998, this tradition

Figure 11.4. The Dude discovers Autobahn's *Nagelbett* album (screenshot by the author).

had also been maximalized and commercialized in Rammstein's metal performances of über-Teutonic kitsch.

Even after Maude's explanation, however, the Dude remains ignorant of the strange musical practices of the Germans. He never expresses an interest in listening to the album. This is especially surprising given that the Dude's identity is defined by music. His favorite band is Creedence Clearwater Revival (CCR), and he mentions having worked in the music business.[28] Perhaps as an old Californian rocker he simply has no interest in technopop. He is also, by this time, understandably focused on his own safety. Earlier, the nihilists had threatened the Dude with nothing less than castration. "The Big" Lebowski had falsely informed the Germans that the Dude had the ransom money. Aiming to obtain it, they break into the Dude's home while he is taking a bath and listening to *Song of the Whale: Ultimate Relaxation*. With a small ferret used as tickling torture (an animal sidekick equivalent to Dieter's monkey, Klaus), they threaten to cut off the Dude's "johnson," warning him with their classic line "We believe in nothing!" Thereafter, the Dude suffers from, in short, *Autobahn anxiety*. His fears are comically invoked while he drives his Torino and listens to CCR; suddenly, he becomes so worried by a Volkswagen Beetle following him that he crashes his car.

This conflict between the Californian icon Dude and the Kraftwerk-imitating nihilists develops into one of the great comedic encounters in Hollywood cinema. With the Dude in peril, his friend Walter, the Vietnam

Figures 11.5 and 11.6. The Dude, discussing the "complicated case" while holding Autobahn's technopop album (screenshots by the author).

veteran, takes it upon himself to save the day. However, Walter often makes matters worse through ill-conceived schemes, although ultimately he defeats the Germans. This conflict also becomes personal for him; a Polish Catholic who has converted to Judaism, Walter has multiple reasons to both fear and hate the Germans. Yet he cannot *identify* who these strange technopop Germans are. In the *neo-noir* context, he goes through a list of accusations: "nihilists," "Nazis," "cowards," "crybabies," and "anti-Semites." Initially, he views nihilism as such an existential threat that he makes the following extraordinary comment: "Nihilists!? Fuck me. I mean, say what you want about the tenets of National Socialism, Dude, at least it's an ethos."

By the end of the conflict, however, the nihilists reveal themselves to be just as confused about this "complicated case" as the Dude is. Persisting in believing that he has the ransom money, the Autobahn Germans finish off the Dude's Ford Torino, setting fire to it in the bowling alley parking lot. This sets up the final battle scene of the film. With a boombox playing their technopop hit, "*Wie Glauben*" [sic], the nihilists attempt to threaten the Dude. Their comic status as an enemy, however, has already been established. The little boombox and their black leather outfits make no impression on Walter. By this time, his opinion of the nihilists has flipped. When Donny asks if the technopop Germans are Nazis, Walter responds, "No Donny, these men are nihilists. There's nothing to be afraid of," and he later adds, "These men are cowards." Finally, when the nihilists complain about not receiving any money,

Figure 11.7. Desert Storm in Los Angeles. (Right to left) The Dude, Walter Sobchak, and Donny in the parking lot (screenshot by the author).

Figure 11.8. Desert Storm in Los Angeles. Autobahn in the parking lot—Uli Kunkel in the center (screenshot by the author).

Walter calls them crybabies and prepares to attack them. As the technopop plays, he throws a bowling ball into the chest of one nihilist and bites off Uli's ear. He finishes Uli off by punching him in the face and yelling, "Anti-Semite!" In this final accusation, he attempts to give world-historical meaning to a parking lot brawl in the 1990s that has no meaning.

The question here remains: Is there any logic to the presence of these technopop Germans in 1990s Los Angeles? In terms of musical and film history, there is. The musical logic is clear in the automotive links between Kraftwerk, the Beach Boys, Autobahn, and the Dude's Torino. In terms of film, the Coens engage new Hollywood conceptions of German-coded villains in the context of action and science fiction films. Indeed, by the 1990s, Nazis had been comically invoked as an entertaining retro enemy. This trend was summed up in the nostalgic adventure film *Indiana Jones and the Last Crusade* (1989); when Jones encounters Nazis yet again, he remarks with sly wit, "Nazis! I hate these guys." In the 1980s, science fiction films had also transformed the German villain into a Man-Machine Other, as strange Teutonic invaders. *Blade Runner* (1982) presents a *future noir* Los Angeles infiltrated by cyborg "replicants," most strongly represented by the leader, Roy (Rutger Hauer). This L.A. cyberpunk dystopia was followed by Arnold Schwarzenegger as the Austro-Teutonic Terminator in 1984 and 1991.

In their references to nihilism, the Coen brothers' Autobahn also recalls the West German terrorist gang in the blockbuster action film *Die Hard* (1988). This L.A.-based group, now with international recruits, appears to carry on

Figure 11.9. Eurofashion terrorists invade Los Angeles in Die Hard (1988) (screenshot by the author).

the revolutionary legacy of the Red Army Faction; yet in the end, like the Autobahn nihilists, the Germans in Die Hard only want money. Musically, their Germanness is stereotypically represented by a "pop" classic, the "Ode to Joy" movement from Beethoven's Ninth Symphony. In this context, director John McTiernan offers some striking remarks on the entertainment value of German villains for Hollywood cinema:

> German terrorists are neutral. They weren't Middle Eastern terrorists. They weren't connected with anything that made any sense or was sensitive. I know that was part of what we were concerned with. Let's not gratuitously step on people's toes. Let's not get involved in politics, because it's supposed to be entertainment, not politics.[29]

These comments address a film released in 1988, a year prior to German unification and many years prior to the post-9/11 War on Terror. According to McTiernan, the German as enemy is already viewed as a benign subject of history. Indeed, the German terrorists in Die Hard, sporting Eurofashion style, might as easily have terrorized to a technopop soundtrack.[30]

The Big Lebowski reveals a similar cultural logic to the extent that the entertaining fight is with retro Germans, yet the actual political context is that of the Gulf War. The Coen brothers use Kraftwerk and the traditions of German electronic music to firmly place German identity in a post-1960s—specifically, a 1990s—pop cultural context. They emphasize this entirely American perception of Germanness through a technopop simulacrum produced by Carter Burwell (no actual Kraftwerk musical samples are used). In this sense, the nihilists are even further removed from Kraftwerk musically and culturally than "Sprockets," which at least samples "Electric Cafe." This comedy of (mis)translation is driven home by the fact that two of the actors portraying the nihilists are not even German.[31] The deliberately stylized "German" accents, in both *Die Hard* and *The Big Lebowski*, reflect Hollywood's comic portrayals of otherness and retro samplings that are supposed to have no political or historical consequences. In the final parking lot brawl, the technopop nihilists reveal themselves to be neither Nazis nor cyborgs. Rather, they are quite confused, comical, and *all-too-human* adversaries. They try to pose a threat, but end up only as posers.

To be sure, how American (and European) audiences respond to Autobahn depends on how much they know about Kraftwerk and Dieter. In turn, how Americans respond to Dieter depends on how much they know of Kraftwerk. The ways in which "Sprockets" and Autobahn have affected Anglo-American perceptions of Kraftwerk itself, as parodies encountered before the source, are the flipside of these questions of reception. Indeed, this later history, after crossing the Atlantic, has carried us far afield from Kraftwerk's specific cultural and musical engagements in both Europe and the United States during the 1970s and 1980s. And yet, this comedy of errors and round dance of parody between Kraftwerk, "Sprockets," and *The Big Lebowski* reveals an extraordinary web of artistic and political references related to post-1960s pop culture. The references offer themselves as messages in bottles to be collected on various shores. Together, they offer a new road map of the electronic dreams, electronic industries, and electronic turns in German music.

Sean Nye is assistant professor of practice (musicology) at the University of Southern California. His articles, translations, and reviews have appeared in edited collections and academic journals, including *Journal of Popular Music Studies, Cultural Critique*, and *New Literary History*.

Notes

Epigraphs: (1) Ralf Hütter, interview by Andrew Darlington, *The Hot Press*, 6 August 1981, quoted in Tim Barr, *Kraftwerk: From Düsseldorf to the Future (with Love)* (London, 1998), 137; (2) Mike Myers, interview by Marc Maron, 28 July 2014, in *WTF with Marc Maron*, podcast, ep. 518, http://www.wtfpod.com/podcast/episodes/episode_518_-_mike_myers.

1. This nickname was invented in the American press following the release of *Autobahn*. See Pascal Bussy, *Kraftwerk: Man, Machine and Music*, 2nd ed. (London, 2001), 57–58.
2. In 1976, Hütter referred to Kraftwerk's comedic mode as "electronic humour." Kraftwerk, interview by Paul Alessandrini, *Rock & Folk*, November 1976, retrieved 26 February 2018 from http://www.thing.de/delektro/www-eng/kw11-76.html.

3. Technopop was a 1980s genre designation that marked the global links of electronic music and dance pop. It remains today most closely associated with Kraftwerk and Yellow Magic Orchestra.
4. For studies of *SNL*'s role in television history, see Nick Marx, Matt Sienkiewicz, and Ron Becker, eds., *Saturday Night Live and American TV* (Bloomington, 2013). For analysis of *The Big Lebowski* and its cult status, see Bill Green et al., *I'm a Lebowski, You're a Lebowski: Life,* The Big Lebowski, *and What Have You* (New York, 2007); and Edward P. Comentale and Aaron Jaffe, eds., *The Year's Work in Lebowski Studies* (Bloomington, 2009).
5. Ingeborg Schober states that in 1970 practically no one in West Germany had access to *Tone Float*. See her interview in the documentary film *Kraftwerk and the Electronic Revolution* (New Malden, UK: Sexy Intellectual, 2008), DVD.
6. The secondary literature on Kraftwerk and Krautrock is extensive. My study here relies on the following works: Sean Albiez and David Pattie, eds., *Kraftwerk: Music Non-Stop* (London, 2011); Tim Barr, *Kraftwerk: From Düsseldorf to the Future (with Love)* (London, 1998); David Buckley, *Kraftwerk: Publikation* (London, 2012); Bussy, *Kraftwerk: Man, Machine and Music*; Julian Cope, *Krautrocksampler: One Head's Guide to the Great Kosmische Musik – 1968 Onwards*, 2nd ed. (Calne, 1996); Wolfgang Flür, *Kraftwerk: I Was a Robot*, trans. Janet Porteous (London, 2000); and David Stubbs, *Future Days: Krautrock and the Building of Modern Germany* (London, 2014).
7. See Melanie Schiller, "'Fun Fun Fun on the Autobahn': Kraftwerk Challenging Germanness," *Popular Music and Society* 37, no. 5 (2014): 618–37.
8. Bussy, *Kraftwerk: Man, Machine and Music*, 59.
9. Lester Bangs, "Kraftwerkfeature: or, How I Learned to Stop Worrying and Love the Balm," *Creem*, September 1975, reprinted as "Kraftwerk: The Final Solution to the Music Problem?," *New Music Express*, 6 September 1975. Page references are to the reprinted article ("Kraftwerkfeature [1975]") in Lester Bangs, *Psychotic Reactions and Carburetor Dung*, ed. Greil Marcus (New York, 2003), 154–60.
10. Susan Sontag, "Fascinating Fascism," *New York Review of Books*, 6 February 1975: 23–30.
11. Barr, *Kraftwerk: From Düsseldorf*, 71.
12. Ibid.
13. Bussy, *Kraftwerk: Man, Machine and Music*, 57.
14. Bangs, "Kraftwerkfeature," 158.
15. See the debate on the term "Krautrock" in Stubbs, *Future Days*, 3–9.
16. Ibid., 43.
17. Ibid.
18. See Diederichsen's interview in *Kraftwerk and the Electronic Revolution*.
19. Flür, *Kraftwerk: I Was a Robot*, 99.
20. See the back cover of Cope, *Krautrocksampler*.
21. Liner notes to *Techno! The New Dance Sound of Detroit!*, 10 Records DIXCD 75, 1988, compact disc.
22. For an introduction to Nomi, see *The Nomi Song*, directed by Andrew Horn (2004; New York: Palm Pictures, 2005), DVD. Myers has indicated that Dieter was also inspired by a waiter he knew in Toronto. "The Rivoli Toronto," clubZone.com, n.d., retrieved 26 February 2018 from http://clubzone.com/places/the-rivoli-toronto/.
23. Myers interview, *WTF with Marc Maron*.

24. Emma Hartley, "David Hasselhoff's Role in the Fall of the Berlin Wall," *Guardian*, 19 March 2013.
25. Rob Sheffield, "40 Best 'Saturday Night Live' Characters of All Time," *Rolling Stone*, 16 February 2015.
26. See the first draft at Mike Myers, Jack Handy, and Michael McCullers, "Sprockets," screenplay, 1999, retrieved 26 February 2018 from http://www.dailyscript.com/scripts/Unprocessed/Sprockets.txt. See also Bradford Evans, "*Dieter*: The Surprisingly Funny Mike Myers Movie That Never Was," *Vulture*, 9 October 2013.
27. See "The Big Lebowski," n.d., retrieved 26 February 2018 from http://web.mit.edu/putz/Public/big_lebowski.txt. According to assistant editor Alex Belth, the name was changed to Uli during the final stage of preproduction. Belth, *The Dudes Abide: The Coen Brothers and the Making of* The Big Lebowski (self-pub, 2014), Kindle single. Autobahn's nihilism also echoes Dieter's ennui. For example, Dieter praises a film entitled *Here Child, Finish Your Nothing*, while Autobahn's trademark line is "We believe in nothing."
28. He was a roadie for Metallica, whom he describes as "a bunch of assholes." For an analysis of roots rock and music, see Diane Pecknold, "Holding Out Hope for the Creedence: Music and the Search for the Real Thing in *The Big Lebowski*," in Comentale and Jaffe, *Lebowski Studies*, 276–94.
29. Audio commentary, *Die Hard*, directed by John McTiernan (1988; Beverly Hills: Twentieth Century Fox Home Entertainment, 2013), DVD.
30. On the German terrorists and Eurofashion, see Jackson De Govia's audio commentary in ibid.
31. One nihilist is played by Flea, a member of the L.A. band Red Hot Chili Peppers.

Bibliography

Albiez, Sean, and David Pattie, eds. *Kraftwerk: Music Non-Stop*. London: Continuum, 2011.
Bangs, Lester. "Kraftwerkfeature (1975)." In *Psychotic Reactions and Carburetor Dung*. Edited by Greil Marcus, 154–60. New York: Anchor, 2003.
Barr, Tim. *Kraftwerk: From Düsseldorf to the Future (with Love)*. London: Ebury, 1998.
Belth, Alex. *The Dudes Abide: The Coen Brothers and the Making of* The Big Lebowski. Self-published, Amazon Digital Services, 2014. Kindle single.
Buckley, David. *Kraftwerk: Publikation*. London: Omnibus, 2012.
Bussy, Pascal. *Kraftwerk: Man, Machine and Music*. 2nd ed. London: SAF, 2001.
Cope, Julian. *Krautrocksampler: One Head's Guide to the Great Kosmische Musik—1968 Onwards*. 2nd ed. Calne: Head Heritage, 1996.
Evans, Bradford. "*Dieter*: The Surprisingly Funny Mike Myers Movie That Never Was." *Splitsider*, 9 October 2013. Retrieved 26 February 2018 from http://splitsider.com/2013/10/dieter-the-mike-myers-franchise-that-never-was/.
Flür, Wolfgang. *Kraftwerk: I Was a Robot*. Translated by Janet Porteous. London: Sanctuary, 2000.

Green, Bill, Ben Peskoe, Will Russell, and Scott Shuffitt. *I'm a Lebowski, You're a Lebowski: Life, The Big Lebowski, and What Have You*. New York: Bloomsbury, 2007.

Comentale, Edward P., and Aaron Jaffe, eds. *The Year's Work in Lebowski Studies*. Bloomington: Indiana University Press, 2009.

Hartley, Emma. "David Hasselhoff's Role in the Fall of the Berlin Wall." *Guardian*, 19 March 2013. Retrieved 26 February 2018 from http://www.theguardian.com/commentisfree/2013/mar/19/david-hasselhoff-berlin-wall-fall/.

Marx, Nick, Matt Sienkiewicz, and Ron Becker, eds. *Saturday Night Live and American TV*. Bloomington: Indiana University Press, 2013.

Pecknold, Diane. "Holding Out Hope for the Creedence: Music and the Search for the Real Thing in *The Big Lebowski*." In *The Year's Work in Lebowski Studies*, edited by Edward P. Comentale and Aaron Jaffe, 276–94. Bloomington: Indiana University Press, 2009.

Schiller, Melanie. "'Fun Fun Fun on the Autobahn': Kraftwerk Challenging Germanness." *Popular Music and Society* 37, no. 5 (2014): 618–37.

Sheffield, Rob. "40 Best 'Saturday Night Live' Characters of All Time." *Rolling Stone*, 16 February 2015. Retrieved 26 February 2018 from http://www.rollingstone.com/tv/lists/40-best-saturday-night-live-characters-of-all-time-20150216/7-dieter-20150216/.

Sontag, Susan, "Fascinating Fascism," *The New York Review of Books*, February 6, 1975: 23–30.

Stubbs, David. *Future Days: Krautrock and the Building of Modern Germany*. London: Faber & Faber, 2014.

INDEX

9/11, 17, 291

Aachen, 129, 229–30
Abbado, Claudio 230
Abbate, Carolyn, 171, 178
Abelsdorf, Ruth, 127
Abendroth, Walter, 114
acculturation, 18, 130, 136
Actor-Network Theory (ANT), 208
Adenauer, Konrad, 56
Adler, Guido, 221–2, 226–7, 233
Adorno, Theodor, 224–25
Aesthetics, documentary, 247, 262
affect, 3, 5–8, 55, 73–5, 85–90, 248, 261
Afrika Bambaataa and the Soulsonic Force, 279
Aida, 161
Akademie der Künste (GDR), 249
Akiba Junichirō, 180
Akimoto Rofū, 170, 180–4
Albers, Hans, 56
  Grosse Freiheit Nr. 7, 56
  Auf der Reeperbahn nachts um halb eins, 56
Allen, Warren Dwight, 210
Alessandrini, Paul   276
American Historical Association. 222
American Historical Review, 20
Amon Düül II, 278
  Live in London (1973), 278
  Made in Germany (1975), 278
Amzoll, Stefan, 255, 257–58, 261–62
Anderson, Benedict, 1, 34
Anesaki Chōfū, 170, 176–79, 183
anthropology, 3, 222
Antifascism, 15, 248–49, 252–54, 260–62
Anti-Semitism, 123, 129, 132–34, 175, 199
Appadurai, Arjun, 34
Applegate, Celia, 1–4, 12, 34, 73, 169, 208

Arbeiterliedarchiv (Workers' Song Archive) (ALA), 250
Arendt, Hannah, 234
Aschaffenburg, 130, 133, 135
Attfield, Nicholas, 98
audiences, 7–8, 19, 33–41, 43–7, 55, 58, 60–1, 63, 73–4, 77, 86–7, 104, 110, 113, 127–8, 131, 136, 148, 157, 169, 179, 183–85, 203, 206, 224, 230, 254, 261–62, 273, 292
Auer, Max, 101–2, 105–6, 228
Augsburg, 130
Austria , 14–15, 97, 100, 105–7, 109, 112, 179, 221–34
  Academy of Sciences 225
  Anschluss with Germany (1938), 223–25, 232,
  Austrian State Treaty (1955), 228
  Austrian Freedom Party (FPÖ), 232
  Austrian People's Party (ÖVP), 231
Authoritarianism, 12, 62, 156

Bab, Julius, 125
Bach, Johann Sebastian, 13, 108, 194, 201–2, 204, 228
  Ich hatte viel Bekümmernis BWV21, 202
Badenweiler March, 225
Bad Kissingen, 130
Bamberg, 130, 133–35
Bangs, Lester, 274–76
Barr, Tim, 275
Barthes, Roland, 222
Bartos, Karl, 275
Bathrick, David, 252
Baumann, Kurt, 124
Baumeister, 157
Bavaria, 127–36
Bavarian Jewish Community (*Bayerisches Israelitisches Kultusgemeinde*), 129

Bavarian Radio Symphony Orchestra, 110, 114
Bavarian State Opera, 7, 9, 11, 156–57
Bayernhymne, Die, 159
Beach, Amy, 209–10
Beach Boys, the, 272, 275–76, 278, 286, 290
Beatlemania, 54, 59
Beatles, the, 54, 57, 59, 61
Bekker, Paul, 36–8, 40–1, 43
  Die Weltgeltung der deutschen Musik, 37
Beethoven, Ludwig van, 13, 19, 37–8, 44, 100, 108, 158–9, 169, 194, 201, 203, 223–24, 226–28, 255, 291
  Fidelio, 160
  Leonore Overture No 3, 223
  Ninth Symphony, 158, 291
  Die Weihe des Hauses, 159
Bell, Duncan, 201
Berberich, Ludwig, 103, 105–7
Berghain, 7, 73–89
  Lab.Oratory, 76–9, 84–8
  Kubus, 76–7
  Panorama Bar, 76, 85–6
Berlin, 7–8, 11, 16, 44, 55, 73–5, 77–82, 87–90
  Berlin Wall, 153, 283–84
  Deutsche Oper, 149
  East, 77, 261
  Friedrichshain, 77
  Kreuzberg, 77
  OstGut (club), 75, 77, 84
  O2 World, 77
  Philharmonie, 158
  Prenzlauer Berg, 77
  West, 149, 158
Berliner Morgenpost, 44
Berry, Chuck, 56
Best, Pete, 59
Biermann, Wolf, 253
Bildung, 6, 38, 55, 125
Bildungsbürgertum, 39, 125. *See also* bourgeoisie, middle class, *Bürgertum*
Bismarck, Otto von, 174
Bizet, Georges, 179
  Carmen, 179
Black Madonna, The (DJ). *See* Stamper, Marea

black market, 147
Blade Runner (1982), 290
Blake, William, 195, 204
Böhm, Karl, 161
Boer War, 195
Bonn, 129
Borders, 16–18, 172, 283
border thinking, 18–19
Bornemann, Fritz, 149
Botz, Gerhard, 232
bourgeoisie, 11, 205. *See also* middle class, *Bildungsbürgertum*, *Bürgertum*
Bowie, David, 278, 280
Brahms, Johannes, 13, 194, 196–97, 201, 203–4
Brenner, Michael, 130, 135
Brexit, 17
Bridcut, John, 196
Brillig, Hildegard, 127
British Beat, 54
British Broadcasting Company (BBC), 195–96
Broadwood, Walter Stewart, 197
Brosche, Günter, 230
Bruckner, Anton, 5, 10, 97–115, 221, 223–25, 227–230, 233
  D minor Mass, 105–6
  E minor Mass, 103–4, 106–7
  F minor Mass, 103, 105–6, 110
  Symphony No.1, 228–30
  Symphony No. 3, 115
  Symphony No. 4, 108
  Symphony No. 5, 99, 101–2, 110
  Symphony No. 6, 103
  Symphony No. 7, 99, 110
  Symphony No. 8, 103, 109–10, 112
  Symphony No.9, 99, 103, 109–10
  Te Deum, 101–2, 105
  50th anniversary of death, 223, 225, 228
Bruckner Association for the Cultivation of Spiritual Music, 104
Buchbinder, Rose, 113
Buchenwald, 249
Buddhism, 176
Burghaslach, 133
Bürgertum, 39. *See also* middle class, bourgeoisie, *Bildungsbürgertum*

Burroughs, William S., 283
Burwell, Carter, 291
Busch, Ernst, 250, 252, 262
Busoni, Feruccio, 37–8
Butterworth, George, 204
Bystrzyca Kłodzka, 253

Cahn-Speyer, Rudolf, 35
California, 172, 273, 275–76, 286, 288
Cambridge, University of, 20
canon (of musical works), 2, 5, 14–15, 43, 73, 11, 114, 123, 127, 161, 210, 248
Cape Town, University of, 19
Capitalism, 55, 60, 63, 74, 249
Carvey, Dana, 283
Celibidache, Sergiu, 115
Chailly, Riccardo, 230
chanson (French), 61
Charles, Prince of Wales, 196
Chicago, 85, 87
China, 17, 170, 172–73, 181, 183–84, 201
  Heian Period, 183–4
Chinese-Japanese War (1894–5), 173
Christian Social Union (CSU). *See* Christlich-Soziale Union
Christlich-Soziale Union, 10, 146
Clinton, George, 279
Cocker, Joe, 283
Coen Brothers, the 273, 285–87, 290–91
  The Big Lebowski (1998), 16, 273, 285–88, 291–92
Cold War, The, 14
Coleridge-Taylor, Samuel, 14, 202
  Hiawatha, 202
Collini, Stefan, 195
Cologne, 129, 149
  Neues Theater, 149
Colonialism, 11, 13, 15, 19, 170, 209–11
Communism, 11, 60, 247–50, 252, 258, 262, 278
Communist Manifesto, 11
Communist Party of Austria (KPÖ), 227
Communist Party of Germany (KPD), 257
Community, 1, 5–8, 33–4, 36–7, 39, 44–7, 55, 63, 74, 77, 88–9, 100, 103, 112, 123–34, 136, 158, 160, 175, 184
Concentration Camps, 249–50, 252–53, 255

concert hall, 5–8, 33–47, 101, 103, 105–6, 136, 174
Conder, Josiah, 174
Conrad, Sebastian, 12, 16–18
Conservative Party (UK), 195
Consumerism, 55, 57, 60, 62
Cope, Julian, 277–78
Copland, Aaron, 45, 161
Cornell University, 199
Cornford, Francis MacDonald, 222
Cosmopolitanism, 17, 55, 203
Crakow Philharmonic Orchestra, 229
Creedence Clearwater Revival, 288
Cremer, Fritz, 249
Crosby, Stills and Nash, 283
cultural history of music, 3, 5, 12, 18
culture transfer, 13, 18
Czechoslovakia, 253

Dahlhaus, Carl, 202
Dallas, 158
Dannreuther, Walter, 197
Danube, the, 13, 97
DDR. *See* German Democratic Republic
Decsey, Ernst, 101–2
Della Casa, Lisa, 161
Denk, Peter, 58
Dessau, Paul, 262
Deutsch Amerikanische Freundschaft, 287
Deutsche Herbst, 278
Dibble, Jeremy 195, 199
Die Hard (1988), 16, 290–92
Die Moorsoldaten/Das Moorsoldatenlied, 250
Die Musik, 98
Diederichsen, Dietrich, 277
Diefendorf, Jeffrey, 147–48, 150
Dieter's Dance Party, 283–85
Diller, Ansgar, 255
Disco, 277
Disraeli, Benjamin, 199
Doblinger Verlag, 229
Dollfuss, Engelbert, 224, 231
Donegan, Lonnie, 57
Dortmund, 129
Dresden, 44
Dude, the, 273, 286–90
  his Johnson, 288

Duisburg, 129
Düsseldorf, 153, 160, 272, 274, 277
Dvořák, Antonín, 14, 202, 210

Eckert, Franz, 173
Eckhorn, Peter, 58
Economic Miracle (*Wirtschaftswunder*), 57, 59, 276, 284
Edam, 133
Edo. *See* Tokyo
Edward, Prince of Wales (later Edward VII), 198
Eggebrecht, Hans Heinrich, 211
Egk, Werner, 10, 161
Ehlers, Paul, 100–1
Eisler, Hanns, 250, 252, 257, 260, 262
   Deutsche Sinfonie, 260
electronic dance music (EDM), 5, 73–5, 77–80, 83–6, 88–9, 273, 275, 279, 285
Elgar, Edward, 195–96, 198, 203
El Lissitzky, 278
Enigma Variations, 196
Engels, Friedrich, 11
England, 47, 55, 57, 63, 206
English Musical Renaissance, 195, 208–09
Enlightenment, 6, 124–25, 132, 134
Epp, Franz Ritter von, 104–05
Erck, Erich, 129–30, 134
Essen, 129
Esser, Hermann, 105
Etheridge, Melissa, 283
Ethnomusicology, 3, 75
Eton College, 197
Eurocentrism, 16, 20, 210
Euroterrorist, 16
Everist, Mark, 18
Evolution, 54, 99, 169, 196, 200–01, 203, 209–10
Exhibition, Great. *See* Great Exhibition
Exile, 11, 60, 227, 252, 257–58, 262
Exis (existentialists), 61–2

Fackler, Guido, 250
Färber-Strasser, Emma, 131
Fantasies, 14–15, 18, 74, 183
Fascher, Horst, 62
Fauser, Annagret, 18

Federal Republic of Germany, 9, 55, 148, 158, 232, 260, 249, 274, 276
Feisst, Sabine, 255
fetish gear, 73, 80
fetish culture, fetishism, 73, 75–7, 79–84, 88-90
Fiehler, Karl, 100, 104
Figl, Leopold, 231
Fight for Right, 195, 204–05
First World War. *See* World War I
Fischer, Wilhelm, 226–27
Fischer-Dieskau, Dietrich, 161
folk music, 2, 127, 133, 135, 175, 200
Flür, Wolfgang, 275, 277
France, 36, 47, 80, 171
Franco-Prussian War (1870–1), 173
Franconia, 129, 131, 133
Frank, Hans, 105
Frankfurt (am Main), 6–8, 40–1, 44, 129, 148, 158
   Opera house, 40, 149
   Auschwitz Trials, 158
Frankfurter Zeitung, 36
Freeden, Herbert, 126
Freidenreich, Harriet Pass, 132
Freisler, Roland, 257–58, 260–01
Freund, Hilde, 133
FRG. *See* Federal Republic of Germany
Frisius, Rudolf, 255
Fritsch-Vivié, Gabriele, 127
Frogley, Alain, 208
Frye, Northrop, 222
Fürth, 129–30
Fulbrook, Mary, 253

Galliano, Luciana, 173
Garmisch-Partenkirchen, 9
Geertz, Clifford, 47
Geissler, F.A., 44
Genji Monogatari (The Tale of Genji), 184
German Democratic Republic (GDR), 15, 247–50, 252–55, 258, 261–63, 283
   Politburo, 249
Germanness, 1, 4, 7–8, 11, 13, 15–17, 35, 41–3, 47, 55, 63, 73–4, 89, 107, 127, 132, 171, 196, 207–09, 227, 272–75, 277–79, 282–83, 291

Germany
  Economic Miracle (*Wirtschaftswunder*),
    57, 59, 276, 284
  Federalist traditions in, 98
  Imperial (1871–1918), 14, 99, 134, 136
  Nationalism in, 8–10, 12, 36–7, 39, 55,
    63, 113, 128, 134, 209
  Anschluss with Austria (1938), 223–5,
    232
  Reunification of, 253, 283–84, 291
  West (1949–1990). *See* Federal Republic
    of Germany
  East (1949–1990). *See* German
    Democratic Republic
  Unification (1871), 123, 135
Gesamtkunstwerk, 75
Geyer, Michael, 33
Gielen, Michael, 230
Gilbert & George, 275–76, 278
Gilliam, Bryan, 98
Globalization, 2, 16, 74
global turn, 11–12, 16
Glocalization, 74
Gloucester Cathedral, 198
Gluck, Carol, 170, 175
Gluck, Christoph Willibald, 179
  Orfeo e Euridice, 179
Goebbels, Joseph, 98, 128, 255
Goethe, Johann Wolfgang von, 179–80
  Faust, 180
Goguel, Rudi, 250, 252, 257
Goodman, Nelson, 230
Goppel, Alfons, 159
Gotthilf, Alfred, 133
Gotthilf, Heiny Michael, 133
Gotthilf, Herthe, 133
Gounod, Charles, 179
  Faust, 179
Grand Tour, the, 90
Gräflinger, Anton, 113
Great Britain, 11, 17, 54, 57, 59, 62,
  194, 196, 200, 204, 206–07, 209–10,
  279
Great Exhibition (1851), 13, 198, 209
Gregor, Neil, 147
Grotewohl, Otto, 249
Grove, George, 197–98

Dictionary of Music and Musicians,
  197–98, 209
Gulf War (1990), 288, 291
Gurney, Ivor, 204

Haas, Robert, 227, 229–30
Hagen, 153
Haider, Jörg, 232
Hamburg, 2, 7–8, 54–63, 145, 148, 153
  Kaiserkeller, 57–8, 60–1
  Lido Ballroom, 57
  Opera house, 145, 148
  Reeperbahn, 55–9
  St Pauli, 54–60
  Star Club, 54, 58–9
Handel, George Frideric, 13
  Julius Caesar, 161
Hanslick, Eduard, 40
Harrelson, Woody, 284
Hartmann, Georg, 157
Hartmann, Karl Amadeus, 10, 111, 158, 161
Hartmann, Rudolf, 155, 157
Harvard University, 19–20
Hasselhoff, David, 283, 285
Hauer, Rutger, 290
Hausegger, Siegmund von, 99–100, 103,
  105, 112
Hayashi Hisamori, 173
Haydn, Joseph, 13, 107, 194, 227
Haley, Bill, 56
Hegel, Johann Georg Wilhelm Friedrich, 19
Heike Monogatari (The Tale of the Heike),
  184
Heimat (concept of), 9, 97, 107, 151, 181
Heinemann, Lothar, 226
Hell, Julia, 247
Herbert, Maude, 197
Herder, Johann Gottfried, 201–02
Herodotus, 222
Hindenburg, Paul von, 104
Hinkel, Hans, 128–29
hip-hop, 278
Hirsch, Lily, 126
Hirsch, Paul, 41
Historicism, 200
Hitler, Adolf, 59, 61, 100, 104, 110, 124,
  222–25, 227, 233, 253–55, 258, 260

Holl, Karl, 46
Hollywood, 283, 286, 288, 290–92
Holocaust, the, 14, 16, 211, 249, 254–55, 275
Houston Symphony Orchestra, 133
Hughes, Meirion, 195–96, 208
Hürlimann, Ernst, 159
Hütter, Ralf, 272, 274–76
Hynais, Cyrill, 229

Ibsen, Henrik, 232
  The Wild Duck, 232
identity, 1–4, 8–10, 16–18, 33–4, 39, 41, 46, 54–5, 73, 75, 79–80, 84, 88, 90, 99, 104, 111, 123, 127–28, 132, 146, 148, 151–2, 158–9, 196, 205, 208, 229, 231, 249, 258, 262, 272–79, 282, 285–88, 291
Ikuta Chōkō, 176
Imperialism. *See* colonialism
Inbal, Eliahu, 115
India, 17, 201
Indiana Jones and the Last Crusade (1989), 290
Indorockers, 57
International Bruckner Festival, 100, 103
International Bruckner Society (IBG), 98, 228–29
Iraq, 17
Ireland (Home Rule for), 195, 199
Ishikura Kosaburo, 178–79
Israel, 232
It's Only Rock & Roll, 279
Itō Hirobumi, 174

Jackson, Janet, 284
Japan, 11–13, 17, 169–185
  Young Germany movement, 178
Jazz, 12, 44–5, 56–7, 61, 282
Jensen, Marius, 172
Jewishness, 123, 127–29, 132, 135
Jews, 10–11, 123–26, 128–31, 134, 136, 223, 249–50, 255
  German, 11, 123–26, 128–30, 134, 136
Joachim, Joseph, 196–97
Jüdischer Frauenbund, 132
Judt, Tony, 147

Kabasta, Oswald, 99, 111–13, 115
Kaiserslautern, 160
Kampfbund für deutsche Kultur, 100
Kampflieder (Songs of Struggle), 248–50, 260
Kane, Brian, 263
Kaplan, Marion, 126
Karajan, Herbert von, 158, 161
Kastner, Rudolf, 44
Kater, Michael, 211
Katzer, Georg, 15, 248–49, 253–55, 257–58, 260–63
  Aide –Mémoire, 15, 248, 253–55, 257–58, 260–63
Kärnten, 106
Keio University, 178–80
Kelly, Elaine, 248, 255
Kemp, Gibson, 58, 63
Kennedy, John F., 158–59
Kerman, Joseph, 233
Kiel, 160
Kingsize Taylor & the Dominoes, 58
Kirchherr, Astrid, 61–3
Kitzingen, 130
Kleinbauer, Franz, 130
Knepler, Georg, 227
Kochan, Günter, 260
  Die Asche von Birkenau, 260
Kokoro no Hana, 180
Koeber, Raphael von, 179
Kommunistische Partei Deutschlands (KPD), 257
Koschmider, Bruno, 57
Koshar, Rudy, 148
Kraftwerk, 272–88, 290–92
  Autobahn (1974), 274–77, 281
  Computer World (1981), 275, 278, 281
  Electric Cafe (1986), 273, 275, 278–79, 281
  Kraftwerk (1970), 274
  Kraftwerk 2 (1972), 274
  Radio-Activity (1975), 275, 281
  Ralf & Florian (1973), 274–75
  Tone Float (1970), 274
  Trans-Europe Express (1977), 275, 277, 281
  The Man-Machine (1978) 275, 277–78, 281, 287

Kranz, Josef, 229
Krauss, Clemens, 224, 229
Krautrock, 273–79, 281, 287
Krefeld, 129
Kristallnacht (Reichspogromnacht), 129
Krontjong, 57
Kulturbund deutscher Juden (Cultural Association of German Jews), 10–11, 123–37
Kufstein, 112
Kurth, Ernst, 228

Lach, Robert, 225–26
Lachner, Johann (Hans Mollier), 145–46, 153
Lafite, Peter, 226
Lamm, Heinrich, 130
Lammel, Inge, 249
Landau, Anneliese, 124, 127, 131
Lang, Oskar, 114
Last Night of the Proms, 195
Latour, Bruno, 208
Law, John, 209
Law for the Restoration of the Professional Civil Services (*Gesetz zur Wiederherstellung des Berufsbeamtentums*), 124, 129, 131
Lehemann, Suse, 133
Lennon, Cynthia Powell, 59
Lennon, John, 57, 59, 61
Léon, Victor, 102
Leppert, Richard, 39, 41
Lessing, Gotthold Ephraim, 124–25
  Nathan der Weise 124–25
Lévi-Strauss, Claude, 222
Levitz, Tamara, 211
Liberalism, 13, 55, 196, 198–99, 210
Lindenbaum, der, 255
Liszt, Franz, 36, 255
  Heldenklage, 36
  Les Préludes, 255
Liverbirds, the, 59, 61
Liverpool, 57–59, 61–3
Los Angeles, 279, 285–86, 290
Loewe, Ferdinand, 99, 101, 115, 227
London, 13, 195–97, 202, 206, 227
  Albertopolis, 209

Crystal Palace, 197
Hyde Park, 197
National Training School for Music, 198
Royal Albert Hall, 195, 205, 209
Royal College of Music (RCM), 13, 194–200, 202, 204, 206, 208–09
Royal College of Science, 13, 198, 209
St. Paul's Cathedral, 195
South Kensington, 13–14, 198, 204, 209
Victoria and Albert Museum, 13, 209
Wagner Society, 197
Louis, Rudolf, 101, 113
Lowe, Rob, 285
Ludwig, Christa, 161
Lueger, Karl, 231

MacmIllan, Harold, 58
Madonna (pop star), 79
Mahler, Gustav, 9, 44
Malkin, Jeanette R., 124
Mann, Thomas,
  Betrachtungen eines Unpolitischen (*Reflections of an Unpolitical Man*), 205, 207–08
Mantegazza, Paolo, 183
Manyōshū, 182
Martin, Bernd, 174
Marx, Hilde, 133
Marx, Karl, 11
Mason, Timothy W., 99
Matejka, Viktor, 228
May, Derrick, 279
Mayer, Otto, 106–107
McGlory, Mary, 59
McNeill, William, 222–24
McSpadden, J. Walker, 183–84
McTiernan, John, 291
Meiji Restoration, 12, 170–72, 178, 182–85
Memel, 133
Memmingen, 130
Mennerich, Adolf, 103
Mexico, 172
Meyer, Ernst Hermann, 262
middle class 5, 39–40, 42, 44, 57, 58, 125–126, 130, 151, 176.
  See also bourgeois, *Bürgertum*, *Bildungsbürgertum*

Mignolo, Walter, 18
Minagawa Masaki, 183
Ministry of Public Enlightenment and Propaganda (*Ministerium für Volksaufklärung und Propaganda*), 128–29, 229
Missouri, University of, 19
Mori Ōgai, 173, 179,
Moroder, Giorgio, 277
Moscow 257, 258
  Moscow Declaration (1943), 223–24, 232
Moyn, Samuel, 20
Mozart, Wolfgang Amadeus 13, 107–08, 170, 194, 203, 227
  Don Giovanni, 20, 161
Munich
  Akademie der Tonkunst, 131
  As 'Bruckner City', 99
  Bombing of, 152
  Freunde des Nationaltheaters, 152, 155–158
  Hebrew Theater, 133
  Jewish Chamber Orchestra (Jüdisches Kammerorchester München), 130
  Kulturbund Orchestra, 131
  Odeon concert hall, 103, 105
  Main Synagogue, 129, 132
  Marionette Theatre of Jewish Artists, 130
  Michaels-Hofkirche, 105–06
  and National Socialism, 99–103, 111, 150–51
  Theatinerkirche, 104
  Residenztheater (Cuvilliés-Theater), 150
  Tonhalle, 101, 103, 105–06
Munich Philharmonic Orchestra, 99–100, 104–05, 108, 110–12, 115
Müller, Sven Oliver, 54
Münchner Neueste Nachrichten, 100–01, 104, 108
Music and Letters, 196
Musica Viva, 111, 158,
musicking, 5–9, 16–20, 39, 54, 74
Musicology, xi, xii, 2–3, 19–20, 109, 210–211, 221, 225, 232–34
Musique Concrète, 248, 254, 262–63
Musik in Geschichte und Gegenwart (MGG), 225

Musik und Gesellschaft, 255
Myers, Mike, 273, 279–280, 284–285
  Austin Powers: International Man of Mystery, 285
Myth (Mythmaking, Mythologizing, Mythistory), 84, 99, 147, 155, 158, 170, 175, 184–85, 221–223, 224–228, 229–230, 232–234, 285
  Founding myth of GDR history, 249, 258, 260, 263

Nakagawa Seibei, 173
Nagai Kafū, 173
Narratives, 5, 13, 16, 19, 74, 98–101, 147, 156, 162, 209, 222, 260, 262–263
  Of Austrian history, 225–227
  Of German history, 2–3, 9, 15, 247–248, 253–254, 257, 261
  Of German-Jewish history, 126, 128
Nationalkomitee Freies Deutschland, 257, 259,
Nationalism, German. See Germany, nationalism
Natsume Sōseki, 173
National Socialism, 9–10, 15, 19, 113, 124–26, 151, 289
Nazi Germany,
  Nazi Seizure of Power, 99, 108, 248, 254
  persecution of Jews, 10, 123, 127–128, 132, 136, 252
  persecution of homosexuals, 249–250
  persecution of Roma, 249–250
  resistance to, 15, 247, 250, 258, 260,
  Reichsmusikkammer (Reich Chamber of Music), 229
  Volksgerichtshof (People's Court), 256–258, 260
Neo-Romanticism, 124
Neue Deutsche Welle, 273
New Musicology, 1
Nietzsche, Friedrich, 170–71, 174, 176, 178, 179, 194
  Also sprach Zarathustra, 170
  The Birth of Tragedy, 170, 176
nightmares, 4, 14, 253, 260, 261
Niven, Bill, 249
Noeske, Nina, 262
Nomi, Klaus, 280

Nowak, Leopold, 230
Nürnberger-Fürther Isrealitisches Gemeindeblatt, 129
Nuremberg, 130–31, 133, 287
  Nazi Party Rallies, 100

Oberammergau Passion Play, 104
Ofer, Dalia, 132
Okkotsu Saburō, 179
Orff, Carl, 10
  Trionfo, 161
Österreichische Gesellschaft für Musikwissenschaft, 231
Österreichische Musikzeitschrift, 226
Ott, Alfons, 110
Oxford University, 13, 19, 194, 197, 199–201
  Dramatic Society, 203

Painter, Karen, 99
Palestine, 127, 135
Pander, Oscar von, 108–09
Panofsky, Walter, 159
Paolozzi, Eduardo, 61
Paris, 45–6, 77–8, 80, 88–9
Parker, Roger, 171, 178
Parry, C. Hubert H., 11–14, 194–220
  The Acharnians, 203–04
  Blest Pair of Sirens, 195
  College Addresses, 196, 206
  Evolution of the Art of Music, 200–01, 210
  "I was Glad," 195
  "Jerusalem," 195, 205
  Prometheus Unbound, 198
  Songs of Farewell, 204
  Symphony no. 5, 196
Perry, Matthew C., 172
Parry, Thomas Gambier, 199
Perestroika, 253
Peters, Paulhans, 157
Pfitzner, Hans 37–9
  Das Dunkle Reich, 109
Pieck, Wilhelm, 258
Piekut, Benjamin, 208
Pierson, Henry Hugo, 197
Pink Floyd, 283
Pohl, Ferdinand 197

Poland, 229, 250, 255
Ponsonby, Arthur, 203–04
Popular (pop) music, 2, 5, 63, 74, 282
Postcolonialism, 3, 18
Potter, Pamela, 1–4, 12, 73, 135, 169, 208, 211
Presley, Elvis, 56
Preußner, Eberhard, 46
Prussia, 16, 149, 173, 194–95, 205–06, 207
Purcell, Henry, 195

Raabe, Peter, 229–30
race, 20, 35, 44, 175, 196, 201–02
racism, 88, 196, 199, 208, 210–11
Radio Luxembourg, 56
Rammstein, 288
Ranke, Leopold von, 222
Recklinghausen, 129
reconstruction, post-war 9, 146–49, 152, 155–57, 162, 253
Red Army, the, 223, 249
Red Army Faction, 291
Regensburg, 100, 102, 130, 133, 135
  Minoritenkirche, 101
  Walhalla Monument, 97
Reger, Max, 204
Rehding, Alexander, 44
Reichsmusikkammer (National Socialist Reich Music Chamber). *See* Nazi Germany – Reichsmusikkammer
Renner, Karl, 224
Richter, Klaus, 261
Rieger, Fritz, 115
Riphahn, Wilhelm, 149
Roberts, J.M., 222
rock and roll, 5–7, 54–8, 61–3
rockers, 57, 60
Roman Catholicism, 104, 109–113
Romanticism, 124
Rosenberg, Alfred, 225
Rosenfeld, Gavriel, 150
Rostock
  University of, 225
Rovit, Rebecca, 125
Royal College of Music. *See* London – Royal College of Music
Royal Caribbean Steel Band, 57

Rory Storm & the Hurricanes, 58
Rozhdestevensky, Gennadi, 230
Rudolf, Lloyd, 43
Rudolf, Susanne, 43
Russia, 36, 45–6, 79, 169, 171, 173–74, 223–224, 278, 287
Russian Revolution, the (1917), 278, 287
Rypinski, Else, 133

Sachsenhausen, 250
Sakurai Motosuke, 182
Salzburg, 107
Samurai, 169
    Tokugawa clan, 172
Sartori, Andrew, 20
Saturday Night Live (SNL), 16–7, 273, 279–285
"Sprockets," 279–285
Schaeffer, Pierre, 263
Schalk, Franz, 103, 227
Schalk, Joseph, 227
Scharnagl, Karl, 112
Scharoun, Hans, 158
Schemm, Hans, 130
Schenk, Erich, 225–228, 233
Schenker, Friedrich, 254
Schlamme-Sprinz, Marie, 133
Schmid, Josef, 103
Schmidt-Grohe, Johanna, 157
Schneider, Florian, 274–275, 278
Schoenberg, Arnold, 19, 45–46
Schöner, Josef, 224
Schopenhauer, Arthur, 97, 103, 108–09, 170, 176, 178, 179
    The World As Will and Representation / Die Welt als Wille und Vorstellung, 176
Schubert, Franz, 13, 44, 100, 224, 227, 256, 108, 194, 201, 203
    'Unfinished' Symphony, 223
Schult, Emil, 275
Schumann, Clara, 195
Schumann, Robert, 12, 194, 203
Schuschnigg, Kurt, 231
Schwarzenegger, Arnold, 290
Schwebsch, Erich, 102
Second World War. *See* World War II
Seidner, Wolfram, 261

Seikanshōin, 180
Sewell, Anna, 183
    Black Beauty, 183
Shaw, George Bernard, 195–96, 207
Siegfried, Detlef, 63
Singer, Adolf, 105–6
Singer, Kurt, 124–126, 129
Sittner, Hans, 226
Sheridan, Tony, 57
skiffle, 57
Small, Christopher, 33, 39, 54
Smith, Goldwin, 199
Snax Club, 7–8, 73–96
Social Darwinism, 201
Sontag, Susan, 275
Sozialdemokratische Partei Deutschlands (SPD), 146
Sozialistische Einheitspartei Deutschlands (SED), 14–5, 247–49, 252, 258, 260
Social Democratic Party of Germany. *See* Sozialdemokratische Partei Deutschlands
Socialist Unity Party. *See* Sozialistische Einheitspartei Deutschlands (SED)
Sonderweg (Special Path) thesis, 12, 19, 208
sound studies, 2
Soviet Union, the, 224, 228, 256
Space, 4–9, 11, 14, 36, 47, 55, 58, 62, 76, 83–4, 87, 89, 97–98, 103, 106–07, 111, 128, 151, 231, 252
Spanish Civil War, 250, 252
Spencer, Herbert, 201
Spitta, Philipp, 197
spornosexual, 82
Stalingrad, Battle of, 109
Stamper, Marea (The Black Madonna), 75, 84–89
"Star-Spangled Banner, The," 159
Steffi (DJ), 84
Steiermark, 106
Stern, Irma, 131
Stewart, James "Jimmy," 283
Stone, Lawrence, 222
Storck, Karl, 33, 35
Stradling, Robert, 195–96, 209
Strauss, Franz Joseph, 10

Strauss, Richard, 9–10, 146, 156
  Arabella, 256
  Die Frau ohne Schatten, 160, 161, 229
  Ein Heldenleben, 194
  Metamorphosen, 152
Stravinsky, Igor, 45–6
Stubbs, David
Stuckenschmidt, Heinz Heinz, 34, 41–3
Stuttgart, 197
  State Theater, 148, 153
suffragettes, 199
Sullivan, Arthur, 198
Summer, Donna, 277
Sumo, Tama (DJ), 84
Süddeutsche Zeitung, 10, 145, 153, 155, 157, 159
Sutcliffe, Stu, 59, 61
Swarowsky, Hans, 229–30
Swarowsky, Leopoldina, 229
Swift, Jonathan, 183
synthpop, paneuropean, 74, 86, 278–79
Syria, 17
Szapor, Judith, 134

Taiyō, 176
Takayama Chogyū, 176, 179
Takenaka Toyu, 171, 177–78
Takeuchi Fumiko, 176
Taruskin, Richard, 209–10
Taylor, Charles, 4
Tchaikovsky, Peter Ilyich, 223–24
  Symphony No.5, 223
technopop music (techno), 16, 74, 76–84, 86, 88–89, 272–92
techno-tourism, 74, 78
television, 16, 58, 262, 273, 279
  BBC Four, 196
  MTV, 279, 283–284
Teufele, Michael, 77
The Big Sleep (1946), 286
Thielemann, Christian, 115
Third Reich. *See* Nazi Germany
This is Spiñal Tap, 280
Thormann, Norbert, 77
Three Choirs Festival, 198
Thucydides, 222
Tokyo, 169, 171–72, 176, 183

Tokyo Imperial University, 178
Tokyo School of Music, 179
Toronto, 279–80
transculturation, 18
Trump, Donald, 17
Tsubouchi Shōyō, 173
Turino, Thomas, 4
Tyrol, 200–01

Ueda Bin, 173
Ulbricht, Walter, 258–59
United Kingdom, 272, 274, 277–78
United States of America, 17, 54–55, 85, 133, 159, 169, 172, 199, 209–210, 272–74, 277–79, 281, 292
  Civil War, 172

Vaget, Hans Rudolf, 205
Vaughan Williams, Ralph, 195, 199, 208–209
Verband der Komponisten und Musikwissenschaftler der DDR (VKM), 248, 254
Vienna, 103, 145, 149, 153, 221–46
  Institute of Human Sciences, 233
  Musikhochschule, 226
  University of Vienna, 225–29
  Vienna Philharmonic Orchestra (VPO), 223
  Vienna State Opera, 160, 224
  Vienna Symphony Orchestra (VSO), 229
Vincent, Gene, 60
Volksgemeinschaft, 47, 107, 128, 255
Vollmer, Jürgen, 60–1
Voorman, Klaus, 61
Vranitsky, Franz, 232

Wagner, Adolf, 105
Wagner, Manfred, 114
Wagner, Richard, 9–13, 19, 75, 98, 101, 104, 151, 156, 169–185, 194, 196–97, 201, 207, 227
  Das Rheingold, 176
  Das Judenthum in der Musik, 123, 199
  Der fliegende Holländer, 176
  Die Meistersinger von Nürnberg, 159–61
  Lohengrin, 174, 176, 179–80, 185

Prelude and Liebestod (Tristan und Isolde), 115
Rienzi, 103
Tannhäuser, 223
Tristan und Isolde, 115, 146, 171
Waguneru Monogatari (Wagner Stories), 184–85
Waldheim, Kurt, 232
Walter, Bruno, 9
War on Terror, the, 291
Weber, Gerhard, 149
Weber, Max, 221
Weimar Republic, the, 12, 35, 37–8, 40, 43, 249, 257
Weinert, Erich, 257–58, 260–61
Weiss, Alma, 131
Weissleder, Manfred, 58
Weizsäcker, Richard von, 232
Wenders, Wim, 285
West Germany. *See* Germany, West (1949–1990)
Western civilization, 17–8
Westphal, Kurt, 35
whiteness, 202–03, 209, 284
white supremacism, 196
Willenkovich, Max von, 103
Williams, Allan, 57

Windelband, Wilhelm, 221
Wismeyer, Ludwig, 156
World War I, 6–10, 33–35, 40, 43–44, 99, 114, 124, 195, 231
World War II, 10, 14, 100, 147–8, 151, 158, 171, 227, 231, 247, 249–50, 253, 255, 261, 272
Wolf, Christa, 253
Wolf, Reinhard, 61
Wunderlich, Fritz, 161
Wuppertal, 129
Würzburg, 130–31, 133135

Yale University, 19
Yodelling, 200–01
Yoshida Toyokichi, 179
Younghusband, Francis, 205

Zeitschrift für Musik, 106, 230
Zentner, Wilhelm, 100–02, 106, 109–10
Ziegler, Hannelore, 133
Ziegler, Manfred Kurt, 133
Ziegler, Joseph, 132
Ziegler, Sonja 131, 132–133
Zillig, Winfried, 159
Zionism, 134
Zon, Bennet, 201